Renato Beluche

Renato Beluche. From a portrait by Francisco Capuleta.
Courtesy Museo Naval de Venezuela, Mamo

Renato Beluche

Smuggler, Privateer

and Patriot

1780–1860

JANE LUCAS DE GRUMMOND

Louisiana State University Press
Baton Rouge and London

Copyright © 1983 by Louisiana State University Press
All rights reserved
Manufactured in the United States of America

Designer: Albert Crochet
Typeface: Linotron Primer
Typesetter: G&S Typesetters, Inc.
Printer: Thomson-Shore, Inc.
Binder: John H. Dekker & Sons

LIBRARY OF CONGRESS CATALOGING IN PUBLICATION DATA

De Grummond, Jane Lucas, 1905–
    Renato Beluche, smuggler, privateer, and patriot, 1780–1860.

  Bibliography: p.
  Includes index.
    1. Beluche, Renato, 1780 or 81–1860.
2. Venezuela—History—War of Independence, 1810–
1823.   3. South America—History—Wars of Independence, 1806–1830.   4. Caribbean Area—History.
5. Privateering—Caribbean Area.   6. Shipmasters—
Caribbean Area—Biography.   7. New Orleans (La.)—
Biography.   8. Venezuela—Biography.   I. Title.
F2235.5.B45D4   1983   980'.02'0924 [B]   82-14969
ISBN 0-8071-2459-1

For Joy, Beth, Ron, and Miki

Contents

Acknowledgments   xiii

On the Trail of Renato Beluche   1

1 Renato Beluche, Senior   11
2 Impact of the French Revolution   26
3 Shipmaster Renato Beluche   38
4 Privateer for France and the United States   53
5 Privateer for Cartagena   67
6 Patterson and the Baratarians   79
7 The British Invade Louisiana   92
8 Sitting Ducks   106
9 Cartagena, 1815   130
10 The Aux Cayes Expedition   140
11 The *General Arismendi*   151
12 Prizes and Prize Money   157
13 The King Versus René Beluche   171
14 Beluche and Bolívar to 1822   185
15 The Battle of Lake Maracaibo   202
16 Puerto Cabello and the *Contesta*   218

17 The Sea of Matrimony and Other Seas   226

18 Bolívar's Tragedy, Beluche's Melodrama   239

19 With Venezuela's Immortals   259

Bibliography   281

Index   291

Illustrations

Renato Beluche   *Frontispiece*

The author and her escort on Taboga, 1954   75

On the site of Renato Beluche's home on Taboga   75

Site of Beluche's home on Taboga   76

The author with Beluche descendants, Panamá, 1954   76

The author with Beluche descendants, Caracas, 1955   77

Renato Beluche   77

The Beluche family plot, Rancho Grande Cemetery,
  Puerto Cabello   78

Maps

Beluche's Gulf of Mexico and Caribbean Theater   8

New Orleans, 1780   18

Smugglers' Paradise   40

Cartagena   68

Venezuela's Confederation of Independent Provinces, 1810   72

Theater of British Invasion of Louisiana and the Gulf Coast   82

British Advances, December 23, 1814, to January 8, 1815   94

Last Round in the Battle of New Orleans, January 8, 1815   124

The Aux Cayes Expedition, March 31 to July 17, 1816   146

Bolívar's Colombia   186

Penetration of New Granada, 1819, and Carabobo, 1821   188

Battle of Lake Maracaibo   204

Puerto Cabello, 1823   220

Route of Beluche's Voyage from Puerto Cabello to Guayaquil   250

Acknowledgments

For their patient help through the years, I wish to thank the following staff members of the LSU library: Evangeline M. Lynch and Denise Claire Landry, Louisiana Room; M. Stone Miller, Gisela J. Lozada, and Merna W. Whitley, Department of Archives and Manuscripts; and Jimmie H. Hoover, Government Documents.

I am also deeply grateful to the following: Alice Daly Forsyth, Archivist, St. Louis Cathedral, New Orleans; Linda Faucheux, Historic New Orleans Collection; John R. Kemp, Curator of the Department of Manuscripts and Archives, and Ghislane Pleasanton, Associate Curator of Manuscripts, Louisiana State Museum; Rose Lambert, Librarian, Louisiana State Museum Library; Wayne Everard, New Orleans Public Library; R. Neal Nichols, who deciphered and translated French manuscripts for me and translated the Spanish reports of mutiny on the corvette *Urica*; Clifford P. Duplechin, who prepared the maps; Guy Boyd Lucas, who was the first to read and improve my manuscript; and Patricia O'Brien Smylie, who edited the manuscript before I submitted it to the LSU Press.

Renato Beluche

On the Trail of Renato Beluche

I first encountered Renato Beluche in the fall of 1943 when, as a graduate student at Louisiana State University, I was deciphering the manuscript diary of John G. A. Williamson, the first diplomatic representative of the United States to the Republic of Venezuela. In describing a revolution that he witnessed in Caracas in 1835, Williamson told how Beluche had assembled a navy for the rebels. Not long afterward, I discovered that Beluche was an associate of Jean Laffite and his brothers, and helped Andrew Jackson win the Battle of New Orleans.

A year or so later, Enrique Planchart, director of the Biblioteca Nacional in Caracas, sent me an article about Beluche's career as a commodore in the Colombian navy, written by Isidro Beluche of Panamá. In 1947, I flew to Panamá to find Isidro Beluche, who was a descendant of Renato Beluche, then to Caracas to meet Enrique Planchart and Vicente Lecuna, dean of Venezuelan historians. This was my first visit to the areas where Beluche had operated as a privateer and patriot.

In December, 1947, I married Ernest Augustus De Grummond, but I continued to teach at LSU and to do research in its library. In its Louisiana Room, its archives, and its repository of government documents I found many items about Beluche's legitimate voyages and his voyages as a privateer for France and for the United States.

I learned that Beluche was born in New Orleans—Mary M. Impastato, secretary and archivist of St. Louis Cathedral in New Orleans, discovered his birth record in the Register for 1780. From the time he was three years old until he was eight, Beluche lived on a plantation south of the city, later known as Chalmette Plantation, and, as a young man, he fought in the Battle of New Orleans, the last round of which was fought at Chalmette on January 8, 1815.

My husband and I visited the Chalmette battlefield and made several trips exploring Barataria, the area across the Mississippi River from New Orleans, extending as far west as Bayou Lafourche and south to the Gulf of Mexico. One Saturday, we went to Pointe a la Hache to visit Dr. Henry Leonard Ballowe, who told us that Beluche had buried treasure in Barataria and had returned to get it after he became an admiral in the Venezuelan navy. But Dr. Ballowe never did say exactly where in all that area Beluche had buried his treasure.

In 1954, the summer after Ernest died, I made a second visit to Panamá. Isidro Beluche, his young daughter Semíramis, and their cousin Benito Suárez met me at the airport. Later in the day, I met Isidro's three sons, one of whom was named Renato. Isidro said, "There has always been a Renato Beluche in our family."

That night, Doctora Lidia Sogandares held a reception in her home, where I met many Beluche cousins. Among them was Señor Laffargue, who lived on the island of Taboga and was called "el cacique de Taboga." As Lidia and Isidro chanced to be the center of a little group, someone remarked how much alike these two cousins looked. Lidia said that frequently new acquaintances mistook them for twins because each had the same strong nose—the nose of Renato Beluche. Their grandmother told me that Beluche had been a strong man with very broad shoulders, commanding in appearance, even though he was short.

The next day, Señor Laffargue, Benito, Isidro, and Semíramis took me to Taboga, twelve miles across the bay from the Pacific entrance to the Panama Canal. There were no automobiles, wagons, or bicycles on Taboga, so we walked. Almost immediately we began to climb, for Taboga is a volcanic peak. We stopped first at the little church of San Pedro, where Beluche's son Blas was baptized.

After leaving the church, we climbed farther up the slope to the site where Renato Beluche and Candelaria Esquivel had lived in 1831. Only the foundation pillars of the house remained. Next we walked to the cemetery, where Isidro showed me the grave of Beluche's son. The inscription on the stone read:

Blas Beluche
Nació 3 de Febrero de 1832
Murió 10 de Junio de 1893

Late in the afternoon we returned to the city of Panamá, and that night the Beluches held a banquet. Pablo Enrique Beluche sat beside me and talked, but I was drowsy and slightly bewildered from the day spent in the sun and in the atmosphere of a bygone age, and I heard very little of what he said. Part of his conversation did return to me later: "I know you are going to Caracas to find Beluches," he said. "Do you know there are supposed to be Beluches in Florida also?"

Heading for Caracas the next day on the plane, I was almost asleep when a brisk voice asked, "Who are you?"

I looked up, saw the purser, and told him that I was a history teacher. He said he would return for a lesson; when he did, I told him about the man I was investigating—Renato Beluche.

"Renato Beluche!" he exclaimed. "He is my brother. What do you want with him?"

When I asked where his brother got that name, he said, "My grandfather was named Renato Beluche. There has always been a Renato Beluche in my family."

The purser was F. C. Scala, and he lived in Miami. He said there were many Beluches in Florida.

Harry Kendall, whom I had known as a graduate student at LSU, was working for the United States Information Service in Caracas. He arranged for me to speak about Renato Beluche one evening in the Casa de Escritores in Caracas, and he published notices saying that I would like to meet descendants of Beluche there.

Twenty or more of them came, and one of them, José Antonio Olavarría y Braun, was a descendant of Beluche's daughter María Reneta. José Antonio commented on the names Renato and Reneta. "In one form or another," he said, "there had always been a Renato Beluche in our family."

That was the third time in ten days I had heard the refrain "always a Renato Beluche"—in Panamá, in Florida, and in Venezuela.

At the airport the next day I had a telephone call from Rafael Pineda. He said, "My paper has just had a telegram from a Renato Beluche in Puerto Cabello. He wants to help you. What shall I tell him?"

"Tell him to write me and give me his address, and that I will be back in the spring."

My next leave was during the 1955 spring semester, and I spent the month of February in Philadelphia. At the Historical Society of Pennsylvania I found a letter in the Dreer Collection that Beluche had written to Henry H. Williams of Philadelphia, asking him to send a mainmast to Puerto Cabello for the corvette *Urica*. I also found James Evans Hele's letters to his mother, written between February 13, 1825, and March 4, 1827, while Hele was serving as a junior officer under Commodore Beluche.

I returned to Venezuela in April, as I had promised. Again Harry Kendall and Rafael Pineda helped me find Beluche descendants. There were at least twenty-two descendants in the third generation, and in the fourth and fifth generations there are now more than a hundred. There is a tradition in the family that during the Wars for Independence, Bolívar entrusted the Acta de Independencia to Beluche for safekeeping. The Acta was discovered in 1907 in Valencia, where many Beluches live today.

Oscar Ruíz Beluche, a medical student at the University of Caracas, took me to his home in Valencia. From there, Oscar, his parents, and I went by bus to Puerto Cabello. After walking along the wharf and studying the harbor, we went to the cemetery. The caretaker had been instructed by Dr. Salvador Carvallo Arevelo, a descendant of Beluche's daughter Ana Colombia, to watch for us and take us through it.

An ironwork fence surrounded the Beluche plot, but what first caught our attention was the exquisite marble shaft bearing this inscription: "A la memoria de María Mezelle Beaudri de Beluche. Falleció a la edad de 49 años el 13 de Setiembre de 1840."

While Oscar and I tried to make out the lines of poetry on the shaft signed "R. B.," his mother exclaimed, "Here is the tomb of my grandfather!"

We looked at the inscription on the marker:

<blockquote>
Coronel Diego Beluche
Febrero de 1863
35 años
</blockquote>

Then we saw four more markers. The one for Renato Beluche said:

<blockquote>
General Renato Beluche
Octubre 4 de 1860
79 años
</blockquote>

On returning to Caracas, I searched a few days more in the Archivo Nacional, the Biblioteca Nacional, and the library of the Academia de la Historia. The results were meager. Then I flew over the Andes to Bogotá.

Enrique Ortega Ricaurte, director of the Archivo Nacional of Colombia, listened to my story of Beluche. He showed me Beluche's service record for the years 1812 to 1830, and his secretary typed a copy for me. Members of Dr. Ortega's staff brought us boxes of uncatalogued documents. We went through them and found many letters written by Beluche, but we did not find the log of Beluche's voyage in the frigate *Colombia* from La Guaira, down the Atlantic coast of South America, and around Cape Horn to Guayaquil. Beluche had been very proud when Bolívar chose him to head "the squadron destined for the Pacific."

I returned to LSU for the 1955 summer session and found that some volumes of naval history by Francisco Alejandro Vargas, a retired army lieutenant, had been sent to me from Caracas by Dr. Eduardo Machado Rivero. A chapter in one of the volumes was about Beluche.

After summer school I flew to Caracas, and Stephanie Bunzl drove me to Los Teques to meet Lieutenant Vargas. I am indebted to him for an insight into the character of José Padilla, who was admiral of the Colombian navy after the death of Luis Brion—but he had the title of general, not admiral, as Beluche had later.

The next day I flew to Lima but found no documents about Beluche in the National Library of Peru. At the Archivo Historico del Ministerio de Hacienda, I met Dr. Antolín Bedoya Villa Corta, who for years had been cataloguing materials in the Palacio de Justicia. He did not remember having seen the name Beluche, but we made a search—an unsuccessful one.

From Lima I flew to Guayaquil, where my hotel faced the Rio Guayas. I walked several blocks down the river front to the Municipal Library; but again, as in Lima, I was doomed to disappointment. Fire had destroyed the library in the 1890s, but I went each day to search the shelves.

One morning, on the very top shelf, I found a bound volume of the small newspaper *El Colombiano de Guayas*, for the year 1830. I took my treasure to a table and opened it. Worms had eaten all the printed part, leaving only the margins.

Beluche's service record says that he left Guayaquil for the Departments of the North. How? Did he sail, or go overland? I flew to Quito to see if I could pick up his trail there. Again, as in Lima, I searched in the National Archives and National Library.

On my last afternoon in Quito, I had an appointment with Father Aurelio Espinosa Pólit at the Jesuit Instituto Superior de Humanidades Clasicas. I waited only a few minutes in the reception hall before Father Espinosa appeared. I told him about Beluche and that I had found nothing about him in Lima or Guayaquil. He said, "I have the only complete file of *El Colombiano de Guayas* in existence. There should be something about him there."

Father Espinosa sent for the 1830 volume, and we scanned it together. He spied the notice first, in Number 27, dated Thursday, February 4, 1830. It said: "On this date we have received official communication from the Señor Comandante Jeneral de la Escuadra de Colombia en el Pacifico, Jeneral Renato Beluche, dated yesterday at the Puná, in which he announces his safe arrival in the Frigate of War *Colombia* after a voyage of one hundred and sixty-one days from Puerto Cabello."

We found several articles in May issues describing a mutiny on the *Urica*, the other vessel in Beluche's squadron. "Let me begin copying right away," I said, "because I am leaving tomorrow."

Father Espinosa said, "My secretary will go through these papers carefully and type every bit that has anything to do with Beluche, and I will mail the notes to you. Come, let me show you the library."

"How can I ever repay you for all that you are doing for me?" I asked.

"Please don't try," he answered. "When I was in the United States, I was so well treated that I resolved to do whatever I could for any of its citizens who might come my way."

The next morning I left for a three-day stop in Bogotá, then flew on to Port-au-Prince. Dr. Mesadieux F. Bazelais and Madame Max Larencule, at the National Archives of Haiti, said they would make a thorough search of marriage records (one of Beluche's wives was born in Port-au-Prince) and of whatever vital statistics they had. Then I walked to the National Library. It was one room, not as large as the classroom at LSU where I taught freshman history.

Colonel Pierre Haspil, the commandant at Aux Cayes, where I spent the weekend, took me to see the monument that marked the spot where Bolívar landed in 1815, when Beluche brought him to Aux Cayes on his privateer *La Popa*. I looked over the wide, calm harbor where Beluche and the president of Haiti helped assemble a squadron of seven little vessels on which Bolívar and his expeditionary force sailed in March, 1816, to conquer half a continent.

During the first two months of my 1962 spring semester leave, I went through newspaper files in the LSU library for Beluche's period. Many times these papers quoted items from Kingston, Spanishtown, and Port-of-Spain papers. So I went to Jamaica that semester and to Trinidad after summer school, and found excellent information about the period of privateering and Spanish America's wars for independence.

My last flight to Venezuela was in July, 1963, to observe the exhumation of Beluche's remains from the Rancho Grande Cemetery in Puerto Cabello, and to take part in the inhumation ceremony at the Panteón Nacional in Caracas.

In 1976 I retired from teaching, and, after researching in various parts of the Louisiana State Museum in New Orleans and in the Historic New Orleans Collection of the Kemper and Lelia Williams Foundation, I began to write Beluche's biography.

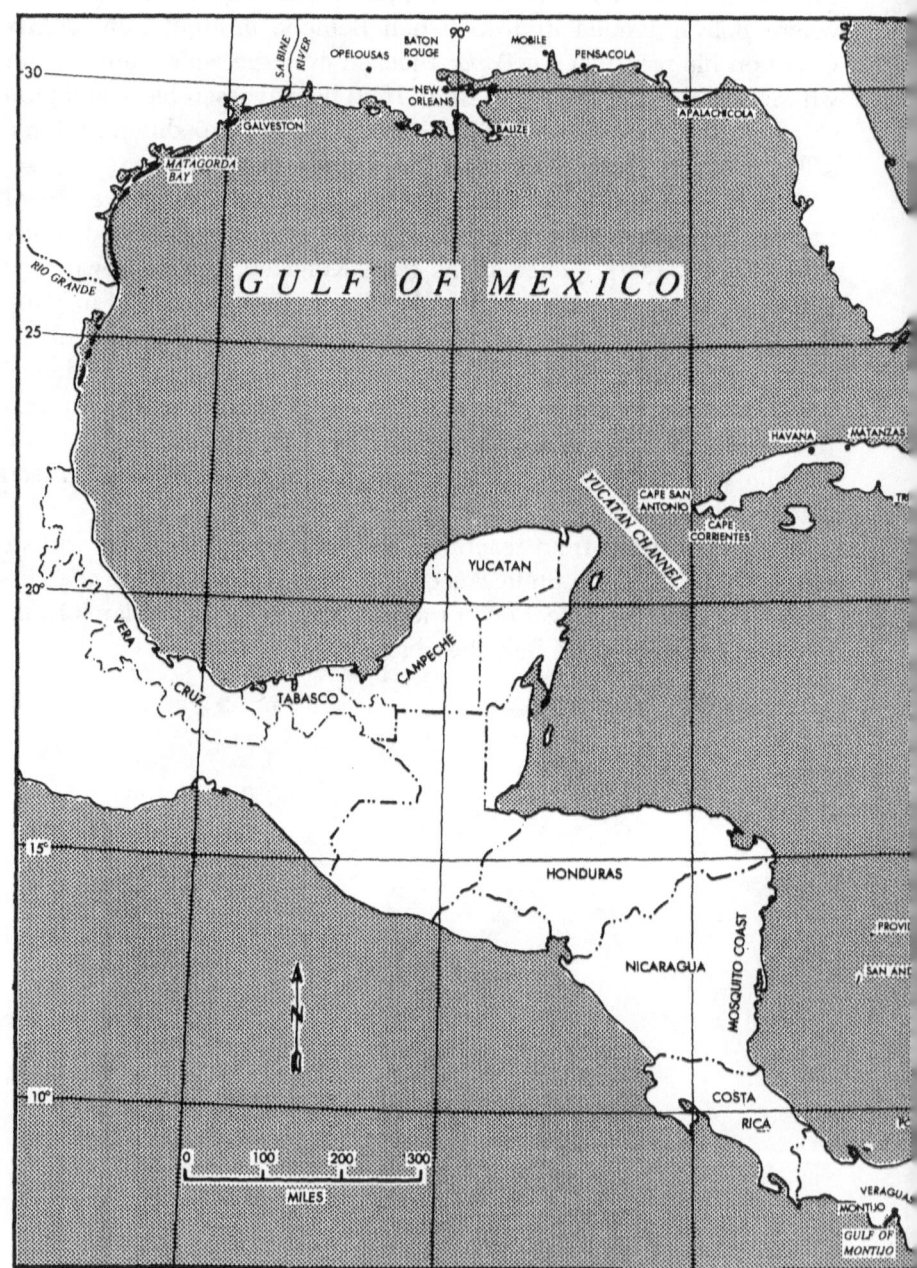

Beluche's Gulf of Mexico and Caribbean Theater

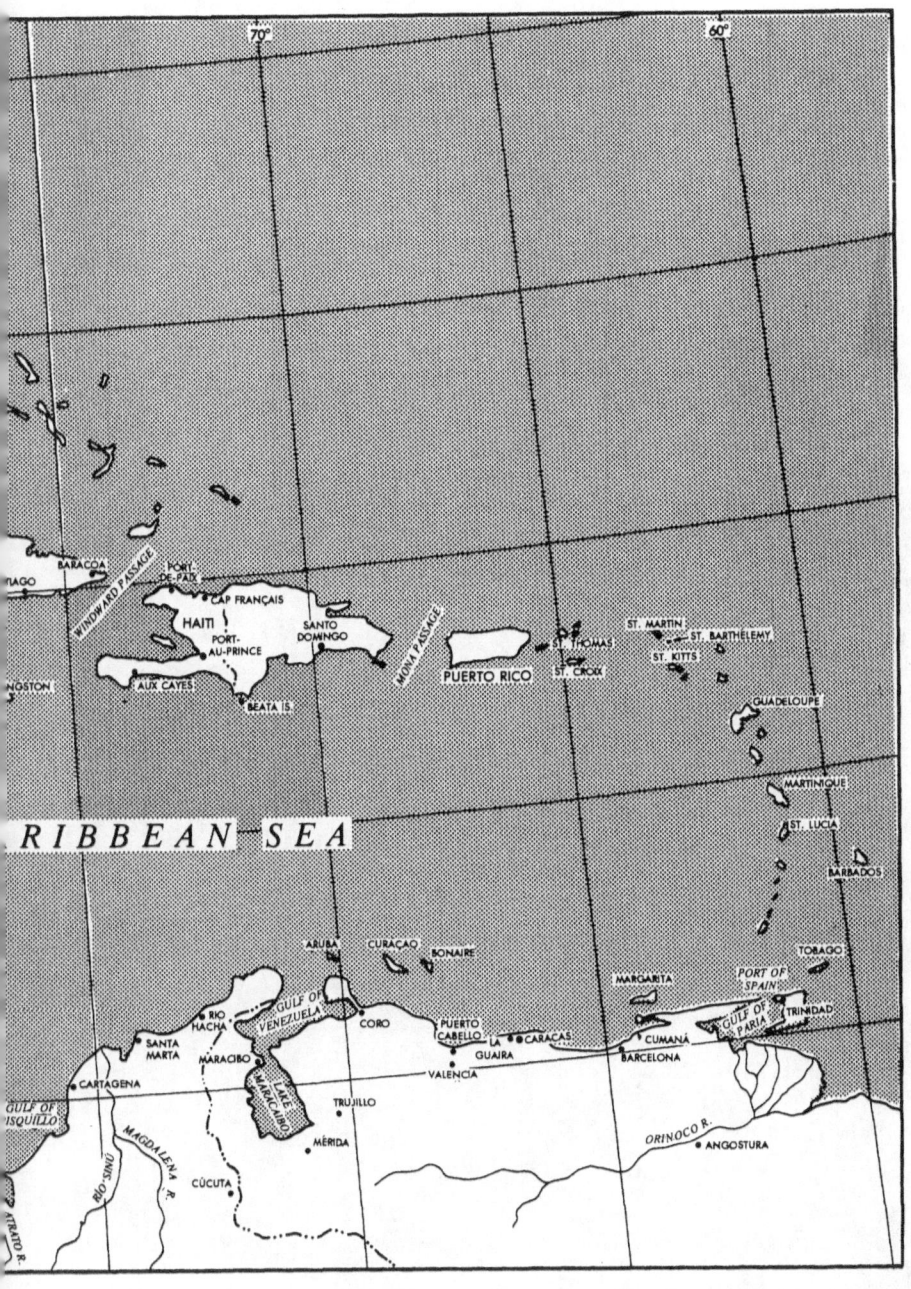

CHAPTER 1

Renato Beluche, Senior

The second world war of the eighteenth century began in Europe in 1740 and quickly spread to wherever France, England, and Spain had colonies. During this war (known in America as King George's War), English privateers and warships destroyed or captured 2,185 French vessels, including half of the ships that France had in the Caribbean.[1] The four years from 1744 to 1748 were leaner than usual in New Orleans; only a few supply ships from France and her islands in the Caribbean had been able to enter the Mississippi because of the English blockade at its mouth and along the Gulf Coast. The war halted in 1748, but for only six years.

By the 1750s, the population of the whole Louisiana territory numbered only 5,000 whites. More than half of these were in the New Orleans area, and the rest were strung along the Mississippi to the Illinois country like isolated beads on a string. French Canada could boast of only 65,000 whites. By contrast, the thirteen English colonies between the Atlantic coast and the Appalachian Mountains suffered from a population explosion. They had 1,500,000 whites. Anglo-Saxons spilled over the mountains into the valleys claimed by France.

In 1754, a band of Virginians was building a fort in western Pennsylvania where the Allegheny and the Monongahela rivers join to form the Ohio River. Canadians drove the Virginians away, completed the fort, and named it Fort Duquesne for the governor of Canada. The governor of Virginia sent troops to drive the Canadians away, and the war for empire—the French and Indian War—began. England's objective was to strip France of its overseas possessions.

In 1758 the English took Fort Duquesne, renamed it Fort Pitt, and

1. John G. Clark, *New Orleans, 1718–1812: An Economic History* (Baton Rouge, 1970), 85.

then moved into the Ohio Valley. The next year they took Quebec, and by 1762 they had captured all the French colonies in the Caribbean except Saint Domingue (Haiti). That same year, the English occupied Spanish Havana and completed the isolation of New Orleans. France did not have the ships or the manpower to break the British blockade of the Gulf Coast or to defend Louisiana, which extended from the crest of the Appalachians, at the western boundaries of the thirteen English colonies, to the Rocky Mountains.

France knew it would have to surrender the Ohio and Tennessee valleys when the war ended, but it wanted a friendly ally in control of Louisiana west of the Mississippi and on the Isle of Orleans east of the Mississippi. By the Treaty of Fontainebleau, signed November 3, 1762, France ceded all of Louisiana west of the Mississippi and the Isle of Orleans to Spain. The city of New Orleans dominates this isle, which is bounded by the Mississippi River, Bayou Manchac, the Amite River, Lake Pontchartrain, Lake Maurepas, Lake Borgne, and the Gulf Coast.

Statesmen had already converged on Paris to use the victories and defeats of their countries as pawns in the international game of writing treaties. France had the fewest pawns. On February 10, 1763, French diplomats signed a humiliating treaty that stripped France of its power in India and North America. France had to give England all of Canada except two little fishing islands in the Gulf of St. Lawrence, all of Louisiana east of the Mississippi except the Isle of Orleans, and the right to navigate the Mississippi.

In order to get Havana back, Spain gave Florida to England. Florida's panhandle at that time extended west to the Mississippi, so England now had control of the Mississippi north of Bayou Manchac and control of the Gulf Coast from the Isle of Orleans to the Atlantic.

England did return some islands in the Caribbean to France. They were St. Martin, St. Barthélemy or St. Barts, Guadeloupe, and Martinique and its dependencies. Merchants and shipowners from these islands, and also those of Saint Domingue, Spanish Cuba, and New Orleans, resumed their shuttle trade with each other and with France; and more entrepreneurs came from France. One such entrepreneur was Renato Beluche, another was Marcus Laffite.

"Le Sieur René Beluche, master wigmaker . . . and a native of the city of Tours, Saint Etiene [sic] Parish, son of Sieur Charles Beluche, townsman of the aforesaid place, and of Anne Huberte," came to New Orleans sometime after 1763. Beluche entered into a marriage contract with Rosa Laporte on January 22, 1768. He was thirty years old and Rosa about fifteen. Her name in the marriage contract is given as Dominique Rose, and in her baptismal record it is Rosalie, but the form of her name in later records is Rosa.[2]

Rosa's parents were present and acted for her when the marriage contract was signed before the royal notary in New Orleans. Also present were friends of both parties. On the side of the intended husband were Jacques Aulier, "likewise a master wigmaker in this city"; Ignace de Lorio, bookkeeper of a frigate; and Luis Ranson, a businessman. These witnesses indicate that Beluche had other interests besides wigmaking. Representing the intended wife were her father, Jean Baptiste Laporte; her mother, Dominique Joly; her uncle, Joseph Laporte; Saint Florian Coutet, a ship's captain; and Jean Monget, whose occupation is not legible on the contract.

In the presence of both parties, "the aforesaid intended spouses do promise to celebrate their nuptials in the Holy Apostolic Roman Catholic Church . . . in consequence of which marriage the aforesaid spouses will be one and the same with regard to each and all of their goods, be they movable or immovable, received or earned, that they may produce or receive during the course of their future marriage; to the contrary, neither will be held to the debts acquired or made by the other prior to their future marriage, such debts acquired before their marriage will be paid by him or her who may have caused them and without recourse to the property of the other."

The property of the intended wife consisted of a bed with mattress and bedclothes, one low armoire, six stuffed chairs, one rocking chair, one pair of "composite" candlesticks, one silver service, and two walnut tables, "all of which furniture has been appraised by the said friends at the sum of one thousand pounds, which sum will enter into the community to have and hold."

The aforesaid intended spouses bestowed on one another "for mu-

2. Marriage contract of Beluche and Rosalia Laporte, in Succession of Renato Beluche, 1788, Spanish Document No. 1951, Box 52, pp. 134–38, Louisiana State Museum Archives, New Orleans. When Frère Maximin baptized Rosa on June 7, 1753, he did not record her birthdate. Act 43, Baptismal Book III (1753–59), p. 4, St. Louis Cathedral Archives, New Orleans.

tual endowment and profit, the sum of five hundred pounds which the survivor shall take and remove from the community property either in cash or in goods according to the inventory which will be made at such time, at his or her choice and option; and the survivor shall rightfully enjoy it as if it were his or her own legally acquired property."

Beluche also endowed his intended wife with a dowry of five hundred pounds, "of which dowry the aforesaid intended wife shall enjoy the usufruct under bond, for the assurance of which the said intended husband does bind, charge and mortgage all of his property both present and future."

Rosa, her parents, her uncle Joseph, Captain Coutet, Monget, Beluche, Aulier, de Lorio, and Ranson all signed the contract in the presence of the notary Jean Garric and two witnesses who were residents of New Orleans. One of these, François Goudeau, was either the son-in-law or the grandson of the Widow Marin, who owned an inn on Dumaine Street.[3]

There is no reason to believe that the "intended spouses" were not married in St. Louis Parish Church. The page on which marriages were recorded for December, 1767, and January, 1768, was partially burned in the 1788 fire, but the marriage of Renato and Rosa may have been Act 105.[4]

Rose Emilie, their first child, was born on October 16, 1768. She was two weeks old when rebels in New Orleans expelled the first governor that Spain sent to Louisiana. Governor Antonio de Ulloa, with a small retinue of officers and troops in a single vessel, the frigate *Volante*, anchored in front of the city on March 5, 1766, a wet, cold day. Chilled and rain-soaked, Ulloa and his officers and soldiers stepped ashore and entered the Place d'Armes, where acting governor Philippe Aubry had drawn up his troops to receive the Spaniards.[5]

Ulloa did not proclaim that Louisiana now belonged to Spain; he did not order the French flag lowered and the Spanish flag run up in its

---

3. Beluche marriage contract, in Succession of Renato Beluche, 134–36.
4. Marriage Book B (1764–74), p. 64, St. Louis Cathedral Archives; letter of Alice D. Forsyth, Archivist, St. Louis Cathedral, New Orleans, September 7, 1977, in author's possession.
5. Baptismal Book VI (1767–71), p. 34, St. Louis Cathedral Archives; John Preston Moore, *Revolt in Louisiana: The Spanish Occupation 1766–1770* (Baton Rouge, 1976), 1–2.

place. When the French troops saw that Ulloa had only ninety men, most of whom were old veterans incapable of real combat, they refused to serve under him. Aubry actually ruled for Ulloa, but he was unable to control the growing rebellion. Nearly a thousand armed men and settlers from surrounding parishes demonstrated in the streets while the Superior Council ordered Ulloa to leave. He and his family boarded the French frigate *César* (the *Volante* needed repairs) and sailed to Havana on the first day of November.[6]

When the rebels took possession of Ulloa's "ship of state," they were guilty of an act of piracy. More than nine months passed before the next governor arrived, and meanwhile the "pirates" in New Orleans were uneasy. They did not know whether they had won or lost, but on August 15, 1769, they found out.

On that day, General Alejandro O'Reilly arrived with the most imposing naval spectacle ever seen on the river. He came with a fleet of four warships and three thousand of the best-trained soldiers to be found in Cuba—one soldier for every inhabitant in New Orleans. Cannon boomed from one of the ships as troops debarked and marched to the Place d'Armes, where they lined up on three sides of the square. The French troops under Aubry were already lined up on the side nearest the cathedral.

As O'Reilly came ashore, every vessel fired a salute, and so did the Spanish artillery and infantry in the square. Then, amid the roll of drums and blare of trumpets, General Alejandro O'Reilly entered the square, attended by men in brilliant uniforms bearing silver maces as emblems of power. All this was planned to demonstrate the uselessness of any opposition to Spanish rule.

General O'Reilly promptly arrested the ten ringleaders of the rebellion, proclaimed a full pardon for all the other rebels, and called a meeting at which the inhabitants took the oath of allegiance to the Spanish government. No one was forced to take the oath, but if anyone refused, he was given time to arrange his affairs and then leave the colony.

The ten prisoners were tried and found guilty, and five were condemned to be hanged. They were executed the next day. Of the re-

---

6. Moore, *Revolt in Louisiana*, 150–63.

maining five, one was sentenced to prison for life, two were sentenced for ten years, and two for six years. They were shipped to Havana and jailed there; but soon after, at the request of the French ambassador, the king of Spain pardoned them.[7]

O'Reilly replaced the French Superior Council with the Spanish Cabildo and organized militia companies throughout Louisiana. Renato ("Big René"—a nickname that indicates he had attained some importance) Beluche was one of the twenty-five "Drummers and Fifers" in the First Militia Company of New Orleans. At that time he lived in a house at No. 10 Royal Street.[8]

General O'Reilly did not like the way English merchant vessels of every description hogged the waterfront, and he did not like the way English merchants dominated the economic life of New Orleans or their rampant illegal smuggling of goods into Louisiana from Pensacola via the lakes, the Amite, and Bayou Manchac, and from boats that descended the Mississippi from the colonies of the Northeast. The English flag flew over forts and trading posts from Pensacola to Natchez.

There was no way that O'Reilly could take away the right of Englishmen to navigate the Mississippi, but he could and did expel English merchants who lived in New Orleans. Moreover, he decreed that all trade carried on in the colony must be with Spain or Havana, and that all cargo must be carried in Spanish ships. This decree meant no food from Yankees; no wine, liqueurs, or sugar from the French West Indies; and no sale to them of Louisiana lumber products, rice, and hides.

Luis de Unzaga had come to Louisiana with O'Reilly to be governor after O'Reilly sailed away in March, 1770. Governor Unzaga was a gentle old man who soon won the good will of the colonists. He knew that Spain could not feed Louisiana, so he discreetly closed his eyes to infractions of Spain's commercial regulations. Flour continued to come to Louisiana from Philadelphia, grain and other items from the Ohio Valley.

Renato Beluche's affairs prospered during these years. His wigmaking business may have been a front for smuggling slaves and other

7. *Ibid.*, 185–215.
8. Jacqueline K. Voorhies (trans. and comp.), *Some Late Eighteenth-Century Louisianians: Census Records of the Colony, 1758–1796* (Lafayette, La., 1973), 381.

contraband from the French West Indies, since New Orleans demanded French as well as English goods; and as Spain's trade restrictions relaxed, the French replaced the English as the dominant element in the economy of New Orleans. The LaFitte and Pedesclaux merchants of Bordeaux introduced goods to Louisiana, routing their vessels via St. Domingue.[9] Beluche in New Orleans and Marcus Laffite in Port-au-Prince may have been agents of LaFitte (anglicized spelling of Laffite) and Pedesclaux.

Marcus Laffite was born at Pontarlier, France, in 1744. In 1765 he married Maria Zora Nadrimal. They moved to Port-au-Prince in Saint Domingue with their infant daughter and Maria Zora's mother about the same time that Renato Beluche settled in New Orleans. Two daughters and five sons were born to Marcus and Nora in Port-au-Prince. The two youngest sons were Jean and Pierre; the oldest was Alexandre Frédéric, later known as Dominique You.[10]

Alexandre Frédéric was about seven years old when he stowed away on a ship in Port-au-Prince harbor. It was some distance from Saint Domingue when sailors discovered him, and the captain accepted him as a cabin boy. One explanation for his nickname is that he refused to tell his name, but the sailors knew he was from Saint Domingue. When they wanted him to do something they would yell, "Domingue, vous!" or "Dominique, You!"

Renato Beluche and Marcus Laffite were related through the Laporte family. Another bond that they had in common was their growing families. Beluche's second child, Marie Eulalie, was baptized on April 21, 1771 (her birthdate is not given in the baptismal record).[11] Beluche's first son, Jacques René, was born on December 28, 1773. Marie Renée, the fourth child of Renato and Rosa, was born on September 10, 1777. She was not baptized until June 21, 1778.[12]

One month later, on July 30, Beluche bought a lot on Dumaine Street. This property was part of a larger lot on the corner of Dumaine and Royale streets closest to the church square, originally granted to

9. Clark, *New Orleans: An Economic History*, 222–23.
10. Stanley Clisby Arthur, *Jean Laffite, Gentleman Rover* (New Orleans, 1952), 282–83.
11. Baptismal Book VI, p. 108.
12. Baptismal Book VII (1772–76), p. 43, and Act 133, Baptismal Book 1 (1777–86), p. 23, both in St. Louis Cathedral Archives.

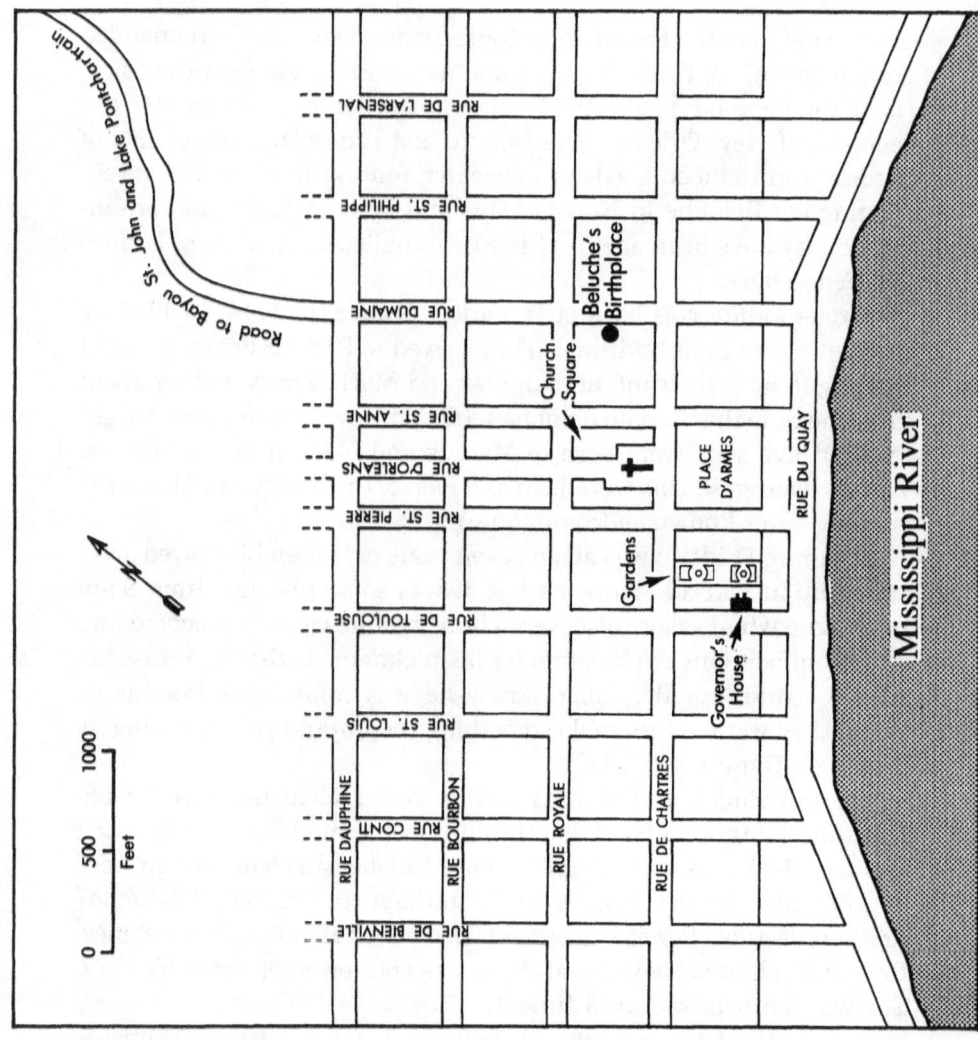

New Orleans, 1780

Jean Pascal, a sailing master from Provence who came to New Orleans in 1722.[13] Dumaine was a good street for a sailor or smuggler, or for a merchant in collusion with sailors and smugglers. It ran into the por-

13. Samuel Wilson, Jr., "'Madame John's Legacy' Rooted in Early City History," New Orleans *Times-Picayune*, April 4, 1953.

tage path only four blocks from the river; that is, a sailor, smuggler, or merchant on Dumaine Street had both a front door and a back door into New Orleans. He was only a few yards from the Dumaine Street dock on the Mississippi, and about five miles (via the portage and Bayou St. John) from Lake Pontchartrain.

Pascal was one of the casualties in the 1729 war against the Natchez Indians, and his widow Elizabeth and daughter Marie inherited the property on the corner of Dumaine and Royale. Elizabeth soon found herself another sailor, François Marin, and married him.[14] They built a tavern on the Dumaine Street side of her property, perhaps because of the longer frontage there. The tavern was set back several feet from the street. Maps of New Orleans in 1731 and 1732 show the tavern flanked by two small buildings flush with Dumaine. The building on the corner was also flush with Royal Street.

Marin died sometime during the 1740s, and his widow did not remarry. Her daughter Marie Pascal married François Goudeau. Because Marie died before her mother, Marie's son François became the widow Marin's heir.[15] In 1776 the widow Marin sold the building on the corner of Royal and Dumaine to Juan Bautista Laporte, Renato Beluche's father-in-law. She died the next year, and her grandson sold the rest of the property to Santiago Lamelle, who sold it in 1778 to Beluche.

The property, in the Act of Sale, is described as a piece of land with an old house and kitchen on it. The lot had four sides, but it was not a true rectangle. Its dimensions were 108 (French) feet on Dumaine, 73 feet bordering on the property of Juan B. Laporte; 107 feet in the rear; and 76 feet on the side toward the river. Beluche paid Lamelle 950 pesos fuertes (hard money), and the deal was closed on July 30, 1778.[16]

Beluche's fifth child was born in the Dumaine Street house on December 15, 1780. Father Pedro Vélez baptized him on January 7, 1781, with the name of his father, and recorded the first part of the name as "Ray." The next letter is not clear, but it may be n, and the ending is

---

14. *Ibid.*
15. This information is from the "History of Madame John's Legacy" that hangs on the wall of the first room one enters in the building that today stands on the lot that Beluche, Senior, bought from the Widow Marin.
16. Act No. 9 (1778), pp. 361–63, in Notarial Archives, Civil Courts Building, New Orleans.

"ado." "Renato" sounded to Father Vélez, a Spaniard, like "Raynado." The important fact is that this second son was named for his father.[17]

Meanwhile, Louisiana had been taking part in the American Revolution. Bernardo de Gálvez, the young governor of Louisiana who had succeeded the aged Unzaga, was ready to drive the British from Florida when he learned that Spain had declared war against Great Britain in May, 1779.

Before the English could launch a surprise attack on New Orleans, Gálvez and his troops marched eighty miles up the east bank of the Mississippi to the English fort at Manchac, captured it, and moved fifteen more miles up the Mississippi to the fort at Baton Rouge. The British surrendered Baton Rouge on September 21, 1779, and agreed to pull out of Natchez also. Gálvez had to take two more bases, Mobile and Pensacola, to regain all of Florida for Spain. With ships and troops from Havana to supplement his Louisiana forces, Gálvez took Mobile on March 14, 1780, and Pensacola the following year on May 10.

The war ended when Lord Cornwallis surrendered to General Washington at Yorktown on October 9, 1781. By the Treaty of Paris, signed on September 3, 1783, His Britannic Majesty acknowledged the United States "to be free, sovereign and independent States," with boundaries that ran from Nova Scotia through the Great Lakes and the Lake of the Woods, "thence on a due west course to the river Mississippi," down the Mississippi to Spanish Florida, then east to the Atlantic Ocean. The new nation had no Gulf Coast because the peace settlement also returned all of Florida to Spain. Spain thus controlled the whole coast from Yucatán to the Atlantic.

On September 3, 1783, the day the Treaty of Paris was signed, Renato Beluche sold the property on Dumaine Street that he had bought five years earlier for 950 pesos fuertes to Lieutenant Manuel de Lanzos, who paid Beluche 3,500 pesos for it. Beluche moved his family to a plantation that he owned one and a half leagues below New Orleans. it had a frontage on the river of 8½ arpents and was located between the plantations of Antonio Ramis and Madame Bienvenu. On March 29, 1784, Beluche bought the Ramis plantation "2 leagues down the river"

---

17. Act 449, Baptismal Book 1, p. 115.

from New Orleans, which had a frontage of 12½ arpents and a depth of 40 arpents. Included in the sale were various buildings (warehouses, cabins for slaves), sixteen slaves, seventeen big and little cows, eighteen big and little sheep, five pigs, and all the proper and necessary tools for said habitat.[18]

The selling price for the Ramis plantation was 18,000 pesos. Beluche paid 2,000 pesos down, and promised to pay 2,500 pesos within the year and 4,500 pesos each following year until the total amount was paid; that is, the last payment would be due on March 29, 1788. As security, Ramis accepted a mortgage on the plantation that Beluche already owned and on six of his slaves.[19]

Beluche now had a total of 840 arpents or 714 acres, with a frontage of 21 arpents or four-fifths of a mile on the Mississippi, where he had his own private landings. His children must have played on the levee and explored every bayou in the area during the next five years. At the time that Renato, Senior, bought the Ramis plantation, his son Renato was three years old. Thirty-two years later, Renato, the son, and Dominique You became famous in the battle fought on this plantation, which was then owned by Ignace Martin Lino de Chalmette.

A third son was born to the senior Beluche and Rosa on September 11, 1786. Fray Antonio de Sedella, better known as Père Antoine, baptized him with the name Francisco Basilio on December 25, 1786.[20]

Renato Beluche, Senior, was a good family man and, in a way, a good businessman. At least, he outmaneuvered his creditors when they instituted action against him for the collection of debts he owed them. On September 10, 1784, Juan Bautista Macarty sold Beluche several mill parts for which Beluche promised to pay 969 pesos, but he did not keep his promise. On June 6, 1785, Macarty petitioned the Court of

---

18. Act No. 7 (1783), pp. 484–85, Act No. 2 (1784), pp. 235–37, both in New Orleans Notarial Archives. "The river planters usually designated the size of their holdings as so many 'arpents front.' An 'arpent' was a tract of one arpent upon the river bank extending backwards so as to include a total area of forty arpents. The area of an arpent is about .85 of an English acre. A plantation of twenty arpents front would thus have an area of 800 arpents, or 680 acres, slightly more than a square mile." William O. Scroggs, "Rural Life in the Lower Mississippi Valley About 1803," *Proceedings of the Mississippi Valley Historical Association*, VIII (1914–15), 271. A linear arpent is 192.5 feet.

19. Act No. 2 (1784), pp. 235–37, New Orleans Notarial Archives.

20. Act 82, Baptismal Book 2 (1786–96), p. 80, St. Louis Cathedral Archives.

Alcaldes to order Beluche to acknowledge the debt and deliver his deposition to the plaintiff so that Macarty could enforce his rights.[21] On June 14 Alcalde Nicholas Forstall ruled: "Let the defendant acknowledge, swear, and declare to the contents, as requested; entrust the taking of his deposition to the Escribano, and done, deliver it to the Plaintiff."

Escribano (Clerk of Court) Fernando Rodríguez inquired that day in various parts of New Orleans for Renato Beluche and was told by many persons that he made his home in the country. Then Macarty requested "a Writ of Citation, to be entrusted to any competent person for delivery"; and the alcalde ordered that Renato Beluche be instructed to appear in the escribano's office to be informed of a certain decree.

Before the day ended, Deputy Sheriff Nicholas Fromentin appeared before the escribano and reported that he had notified Renato Beluche of the foregoing writ, having gone to his plantation. The next day, June 16, the escribano received Beluche's oath that the contents of the bill were correct and true.

Macarty then prayed the court to order a writ of execution against any and all of the defendant's property, sufficient to satisfy the debt, its one-tenth (for the sheriff), and costs. The alcalde received this petition, examined the records, and on July 4 ordered: "Issue a Writ of Execution in favor of Juan Bautista Macarty against Renato Beluche."

Deputy Sheriff Fromentin reported to the escribano on August 5 that he had requested Beluche to pay Macarty immediately, "and as he did not pay, the Deputy Sheriff seized his plantation situated two leagues from this city." Macarty's next move was to pray the court to order the plantation cried for sale, which was set for October 15.

On that day the escribano "looked everywhere in the City for Renato Beluche," but since he could not find Beluche, the sale proceeded without him. The escribano, "standing in the door of his Public Office, by the voice of the Town Crier, called the sale of Renato Beluche's plantation." Although many persons were present, no bids were offered.

Two months passed with no action; then on December 14, Macarty petitioned the court to order a taxation of the costs of the case up to

---

21. The account of Macarty's efforts to collect 969 pesos from Beluche is from Laura L. Porteous, "Index of Spanish Judicial Records of Louisiana," with marginal notes by Walter Prichard, *Louisiana Historical Quarterly*, XXIX (1946), 527–31.

that time. The alcalde ruled: "Let the costs be taxed and paid by Renato Beluche." Luis Lioteau, "Official Taxer for Court Costs," proceeded to issue the order, and on December 23 he declared the costs to be 15 pesos, 6 reales.

Macarty's next move was to grant power of attorney on January 10, 1786, to Public Attorney Antonio Mendez, "to act for him and in his name to represent his rights, to demand, receive and collect the sum of 969 pesos from Renato Beluche." Mendez's efforts resulted in three public calls for the sale of Beluche's plantation on September 14 and 23, and on October 2, 1786, but the sale was never consummated because no bids were made.

Meanwhile, Beluche was being hounded by other creditors who had also instituted action against him for the collection of debts amounting to 5,161 pesos. None of these debts had been paid when fire destroyed most of New Orleans on Good Friday, March 21, 1788. This "dreadful conflagration originated in the house of a zealous Catholic; who, not satisfied with worshipping God in his usual way, had a chapel, or altar erected in his house for the purpose of paying adoration, which he had illuminated with 50 or 60 wax tapers, as if his prayers could not ascend to heaven without them; these lights being left neglected at the hour of dinner, set fire to the ceiling; from there proceeded the destruction of the most regular, well-governed, small city in the western world."[22]

The fire could not be put out because "the confusion caused by the explosion of powder, which some citizens had cautiously hidden in their houses in violation of government orders, intimidated the most daring and utterly disconcerted the others." Moreover, there were "neither fire engines, buckets, hooks, nor ladders, so that every effort was in vain. The whole town was laid in ashes before eight o'clock at night, excepting the front row and two streets to the westward, which were preserved by the wind blowing strongly the whole time from the south and the south-east side."

In his report of the fire, Governor Estevan Miro said: "Had this un-

22. Index cards of Renato Beluche's succession, in Louisiana State Museum Library, New Orleans. These cards are cited instead of the succession papers themselves, which are being withheld until they can be restored. See also "Extract of a Letter from New Orleans," dated March 26, 1788, in Walter Prichard, "Supplementary Notes," to Laura A. de Rojas, "The Great Fire of 1788 in New Orleans," *Louisiana Historical Quarterly*, XX (1937), 586.

fortunate event happened in the small hours of the night, it would have caused the loss of many lives; but, thanks to God, the only casualties were some people slightly hurt, and a sick negress who was killed. . . . If I could only describe with vivid colors what my eyes have seen and my hands touched, it would seem unbelievable. Families who a few hours before had enjoyed large fortunes and more than the average comforts of life were spread all over the fields, crying and filled with consternation at the fate which had fallen upon this city, which in less than five hours had been transformed into an arid and horrible desert; a city which was the product of seventy years of labor."[23]

Miro distributed tents to the homeless and rations of rice. The inhabitants dried their tears and cleared away the debris. Then the governor took 24,000 pesos from the royal treasury and dispatched three ships to Philadelphia with this money to buy three thousand barrels of flour. He also removed all restrictions on trade with citizens of the United States. Soon supplies came down the river from the Ohio Valley or up the river from Philadelphia and other Atlantic seaboard cities, and the work of reconstruction began.

Like other homeless inhabitants, Captain de Lanzos built another house on the Dumaine Street lot where Renato Beluche, Junior, had been born in 1780. The house, a sturdy brick and cypress structure, has defied time, fire, and weather. It so fascinated George Washington Cable that he named it "Madame John's Legacy" and made it the scene for his story "Tite Poulette."[24]

Beluche, Senior, did not live long after the great fire. He died on his plantation below New Orleans and was buried in St. Louis Cemetery No. 1. The inscription on his tomb reads: "Renat Beluche, husband of Dona Rosa Laporte, Age 50 years, Died September 3, 1788."

He was survived by a pregnant widow, six children (all still considered minors), and a long list of debts. These included the debts so far

23. Report of Estevan Miro, April 1, 1788, in Survey of Federal Archives in Louisiana, *Despatches of the Spanish Governors of Louisiana, 1766–1792: Messages of Estevan Miro, 1788* (6 books; Baton Rouge, 1937–38), Book 3, Vol. XV, 16.

24. Tite Poulette was the daughter of a beautiful quadroon named Zalli and Monsieur John. When he died, the house became known as Madame John's Legacy. George W. Cable, *Old Creole Days* (New York, 1927), 213–43. Mrs. I. I. Leman bought the house in 1935 and presented it to the Louisiana State Museum in 1947. Ray Samuels, "Dwelling on Dumaine," New Orleans *Times-Picayune Sunday Magazine*, July 17, 1949, p. 23. The present address of Madame John's Legacy is 632 Dumaine Street.

mentioned, several others that were presented when his succession was opened, and the last payment of 4,500 pesos on the Ramis plantation, which had been due since March 29, 1788.

Rosa gave birth to a daughter on February 3, 1789. When Father José de Venetz baptized her on March 20, he recorded her name as Selina Blus and her parents' names as Rene Blus and Rosa Laport.[25]

Since Beluche died intestate, Rosa was appointed tutor for her children. She granted their power of attorney to her brother-in-law Vicente Fangui. Creditors immediately presented their debts for collection. Rosa filed a copy of her marriage contract with the succession, then begged the court to order a public auction of all properties left by the deceased in order to satisfy creditors of the said succession.[26]

Rosa must have retrieved her dowry and perhaps more, but she failed in her effort to retain the "eight arpents more or less" with the house where she and her family had lived ever since the Dumaine Street property was sold. When that part of the estate was auctioned, Vicente Fangui was the highest bidder, and it was awarded to him. However, when the court discovered that he had bid for the widow, who did not have any money, it held Fangui responsible and ordered him incarcerated in the public jail. Andrés Almonester y Rojas, justice of the peace, ordered a new auction, at which the "eight arpents more or less" were sold to Antonio Morales for 6,520 pesos.

Before Beluche died, he had paid Ramis 13,500 pesos of the 18,000 he had promised to pay for the twelve and a half arpents two leagues from New Orleans. The balance due on these arpents was 4,500 pesos, and they were auctioned to Etienne de Boré for 4,710 pesos.

The two parts of Beluche's plantation sold for a total of 11,230 pesos. Since the record shows that the estate was auctioned for 12,854 pesos, a couple of slaves must have been sold also. After the auction costs of 547 pesos, court costs, and debts of at least 9,661 pesos were paid, there may have been a few pesos left over for Rosa. Where she and the children lived after their home was sold is a mystery. Rosa's two brothers, Pierre and François Laporte, may have given them homes.[27]

---

25. Act No. 488, Baptismal Book 2, p. 67.
26. Rosalia Laporte Beluche Index Cards 1–3, in Louisiana State Museum Library.
27. René Beluche Index Cards 3, 5–8, in Louisiana State Museum Library.

CHAPTER 2

Impact of the French Revolution

"Liberty, Equality, Fraternity"—these were the watchwords of the French Revolution that began in 1789. Soldiers landing at Cap Français (later Cap Haïtien) on the northern coast of Saint Domingue embraced the blacks as brothers and passed out copies of the Declaration of the Rights of Man and various radical pamphlets. Some of these reached literate slaves who read them to others before authorities instructed the soldiers as to their proper conduct. The soldiers obeyed the authorities, but it was too late to keep the leaven of "Liberty, Equality, Fraternity" from fermenting.

A voodoo priest and his followers hatched a simple plot at meetings held during the early summer of 1791 in the richest sugar area, the plantations on the plains behind Cap Français. On a given night, slaves would kill their masters and burn their houses, sugar mills, and cane; then they would take Cap Français. The night chosen for the insurrection was August 22.

That night, thousands of slaves began to massacre their masters and burn their property. A vivid copper sky and a few whites who escaped warned the residents of Cap Français, and by the end of the week, when slave hordes attacked the Cap, defense works had been completed around the city. The defenses held; the slaves were thrown back. Many were captured and murdered. The rest returned to the plantations they had destroyed; and for two short years the revolution was contained in the North. Some plantation owners with sugar expertise fled to Cuba and Louisiana, but they did not leave in large numbers until events in Europe aroused the whole of Saint Domingue.

Monarchy with all its trappings was abolished in France on September 21, 1792; and the king, Louis XVI, was guillotined on January 21,

1793. The crowned heads of Europe were frightened, and even Spain, France's longtime ally, joined the coalition against the French Republic.

As foreign armies prepared to invade France on all fronts, the Committee of Public Safety appointed young, audacious officers to command the men who rushed to defend their country. A new song that warmed the blood like wine spread through the land; and to the chant of the "Marseillaise," French armies drove out the invaders and put them on the defensive. The English had taken Toulon, France's most important naval arsenal and the key to control of the Mediterranean, but a short, skinny, twenty-four-year-old artillery officer named Napoleon Bonaparte recaptured the port in December, 1793.

France had no naval units to counter Great Britain's offensive in the Caribbean. Expeditions from English Jamaica landed on Saint Domingue's two western peninsulas, where the planters welcomed them. To the east, troops from Spanish Santo Domingo crossed the frontier into French Saint Domingue.

Able mulatto leaders like Alexandre Pétion checked the English at Aux Cayes and held that enclave on the south coast. On the north coast, General Étienne Laveaux was able to stop the English advance at Port-de-Paix because privateers kept him supplied with food and war matériel.[1]

One of these privateers, a Captain La Rieux, sailed from Cap Français about the middle of December, 1793, aboard the schooner *L'Atlanta*, headed west and north along the coast of Cuba. On December 16, Captain Pedro (Pierre) Laporte, bound for New Orleans with a cargo of sugar and tafia (a cheap grade of rum) on his schooner *Ana María*, sailed from Havana and cruised along the coast until six in the evening; then he steered northwest to go around the Tortugas. At seven o'clock the next morning, he sighted *L'Atlanta* to the south and tried to run away from it, but three hours later *L'Atlanta* overtook the *Ana María* on its leeward side.[2]

---

1. Jean Baptiste Carvin and Jean Bouteille were the most famous of these privateers. Melvin H. Jackson, *Privateers in Charleston 1793–1796* (Washington, D.C., 1969), 117–18.
2. Baron de Carondelet to Don Luis de Las Casas, Janaury 6, 1794, in SFA, *Despatches of the Spanish Governors of Louisiana*, VI, Pt. 4, pp. 193–96.

Laporte ordered the Spanish flag raised. *L'Atlanta* responded with a cannon shot, and Laporte, after throwing his mail overboard, lowered his flag. La Rieux ordered Laporte to lower a launch and come to his ship. There the two captains negotiated ransom terms: 2,500 piasters payable in Philadelphia at the offices of Messieurs Dutil and Warmouth, merchants of that city. Then, as La Rieux reported: "We released the Sieur La Porte and his ship, retaining as surety Monsieur Jacques Beluche, his nephew."

Jacques René Beluche was first mate on the *Ana María*. He was twenty years old at this time, and his little brother Renato was thirteen. The two youngest Laffite boys in Port-au-Prince were about the same age. Pierre was fourteen and Jean was eleven.

Businessmen like the Laffites' father and plantation owners welcomed the English forces from Jamaica and made it possible for them to take Port-au-Prince in June, 1794. But their way of life was soon changed by a slave genius named François Dominique Toussaint. He was the grandson of an African king and earned the sobriquet "l'Ouverture."

Toussaint was in control of a central strip of Saint Domingue that stretched from the Spanish border to Gonaïves on the western coast. On February 4, 1794, the government in France decreed the emancipation of slaves. Six weeks later Toussaint heard this news. Spain had not freed her slaves; no nation except France had officially done so. Toussaint began to negotiate with General Laveaux, and in May he allied his forces with those of the French. Both men wanted a better world based on free labor.

Laveaux gave Toussaint a free rein, and by the end of July the creole leader had pushed the Spaniards back into their own part of the island. Then Toussaint concentrated on driving out the English and on making the plantations productive again. When he invited the planters to return, some did, but by this time many had escaped to Louisiana, taking along their slaves who were skilled in the production of sugar.

When the first Saint Domingue refugees arrived, caterpillars of the chenille species had already begun the destruction of Louisiana's main money crop, indigo. Owners of indigo plantations were desperate, panic-stricken after a second season of helpless inaction during which caterpillars devoured all the leaves of their indigo plants. What crop could take the place of indigo? Cotton could easily be grown, but picking seeds out of cotton was too tedious and costly. True, in 1793 Eli Whitney had invented the cotton gin, but Louisianians did not know about the gin until much later, and no one had any faith in sugar as a paying crop.

Iberville brought some canes from Guadeloupe in 1700, but they turned yellow and sour before he could plant them. Jesuits who had a sugar plantation in Saint Domingue sent some canes in 1751 to their branch establishment in New Orleans. They also sent slaves who knew how to make the canes grow and how to produce sugar. The Jesuits planted those canes in their gardens immediately above the city (where Canal Street is today). The canes grew but did not mature in a single season; however, the Jesuits persisted in planting year after year and finally naturalized the canes. Other planters obtained canes from them, and some attempted large-scale production, only to fail in making the cane juice granulate.

All of those who planted cane in the 1750s and 1760s tried to make sugar, but when they boiled the cane juice, it turned into a thick gummy mass, like guava paste or marmalade. When this gummy mass was left in a damp place, it turned into syrup. However, planters discovered that they could turn that syrup into tafia or rum that even the poorest could afford to buy. Soon Governor Jean Jacques d'Abbadie was reporting that "the immoderate use of tafia has stupefied the whole population."[3]

By 1769 most planters had given up on sugar; but one of those who continued planting was Antonio Mendez, the same public official to whom J. B. Macarty had granted power of attorney in 1786 so that he could "demand, receive and collect the sum of 969 pesos from Renato Beluche." Mendez's plantation was about ten miles below New Orleans at Terre-aux-Boeufs. There, Mendez employed Antoine Morin, a refugee from Saint Domingue, to make sugar for him.[4] Morin did make a few barrels of sugar in 1792, but for some strange reason Mendez did not commercialize his success.

---

3. D'Abbadie was governor from 1763 to 1765. William O. Scroggs, *The Story of Louisiana* (Indianapolis, 1924), 150.
4. The only source that gives Morin's first name is W. G. Taggart and E. C. Simon, *A Brief Discussion of the History of Sugar Cane* (Baton Rouge, 1956), 8.

Etienne de Boré was almost bankrupt after two seasons of indigo crop failure when he risked everything he had left on sugar. He bought sugarcane from Mendez and planted it on the plantation he still owned six miles above New Orleans. De Boré wore down the resistance of moneylenders and with borrowed money hired Morin to build sugar works similar to those in Saint Domingue. All the labor was done by slaves, and the total cost of the sugar house was $4,000. "This expense will no doubt appear very moderate for so large and important an establishment. In San Domingo it would have cost 200,000 pounds to put up an establishment of this sort."[5]

The sugar house was completed in 1795. In February of that year, de Boré planted sugarcane over most of his plantation. His slaves began cutting the cane in October. Finally the day came when the mill was to grind out juice for Morin's first attempt to make sugar from de Boré's cane. People crowded into the sugar house to be present at the success or failure of the first kettle of juice to be boiled. Would it granulate?

The crowd grew tense as de Boré watched the boiling juice for the critical moment when enough water had evaporated for the sugar to crystallize. Suddenly the sugar-maker cried, "It granulates!" and the crowd shouted, "It granulates!"[6]

De Boré made $12,000 from sugar that year. He could have made more, but he did not have enough slaves to harvest his entire crop. The next year, his neighbors planted sugarcane and built sugar houses. Morin helped those planters after he had made sugar from de Boré's crop.

As "King Sugar" in Louisiana and "King Cotton" in Mississippi and other southern states demanded more and more slaves, the revolution gained momentum in Saint Domingue. Toussaint harassed the English invaders until they were glad to leave in 1798. His next move was to crush the mulatto-dominated state in the south. He was master of all of Saint Domingue by 1800, but among the important mulatto leaders who had escaped to France was Alexandre Pétion.

The next year, Toussaint overran Spanish Santo Domingo. Then,

---

5. "Translation of General Collot's Description of de Boré's Sugar House and Comparison with the West India Cane," *Louisiana Historical Quarterly*, I (1918), 327–29.

6. Charles Etienne Arthur Gayarré, *History of Louisiana* (4 vols.; New Orleans, 1903), III, 349.

master of the whole island, he wrote a constitution for it that gave him sole power, and, although it declared the island to be a protectorate of France, there was no room in his constitution for any French official. Unfortunately for Toussaint, when he sent this constitution to France it went to a similar dictator, Napoleon Bonaparte. Although he occupied a larger stage than Toussaint, his rise to power was comparable to that of Toussaint.

Napoleon, now First Consul of the French Republic, needed the wealth that Toussaint's island and Spanish Louisiana produced. On October 1, 1800, the king of Spain agreed in a secret treaty that Louisiana would be returned to France when Napoleon gave the Spanish king's son-in-law a kingdom in Italy. One year later, on October 1, 1801, Napoleon concluded the Preliminary Peace of Amiens with England, the only nation with whom he was still at war. This gave him a brief interval of peace during which he continued restructuring France, remaking the map of Europe, and eliminating Toussaint.

Charles Victor Emmanuel Leclerc, Napoleon's brother-in-law, commanded the invasion force that was to seize important coast towns of Toussaint's island and win over his lieutenants within fifteen days; from these bases he was then to send flying columns to shatter resistance, arrest and deport Toussaint, disarm the blacks, and restore slavery.

The expedition sailed from France on November 21, 1801. Dominique You was with Leclerc's artillery.[7] Alexandre Pétion and other mulatto leaders also sailed with Leclerc. By January 29, 1802, several divisions totaling twelve thousand troops had anchored in Samaná Bay on the eastern coast of the island. Leclerc divided them into four striking forces. He sent the comte de Rochambeau with one division west along the north coast to take Fort Liberté, a second general to take Santo Domingo City, and a third to take Port-au-Prince. Leclerc kept the largest division, five thousand troops, and appeared before Le Cap (Cap Français) on February 2.

Toussaint had troops spread out all over the island but no concentration of troops at any of the four targets. In Santo Domingo City and in the south the French met little resistance. Black workers, resentful

---

7. Henry A. Castellanos, *New Orleans As It Was* (New Orleans, 1905), 87.

over forced labor and the way that Toussaint favored the whites, did not rise against the invaders. Many of the officers surrendered and joined Leclerc.

Discouraged, Toussaint negotiated with Leclerc, riding to meet him at Le Cap on May 6. Then he returned to his plantation. A few days later his chief lieutenant, Jean Jacques Dessalines, allied with Leclerc. Dessalines, the former slave of a black master, his body scarred from whip lashes, was an almost illiterate military genius who was playing for time.

In his own home on June 7, 1802, Toussaint was bound like a criminal and shipped to France. There he was starved and tormented to death in a freezing cell in the Jura Mountains. Toussaint's fatal flaw had been his inability to emancipate himself completely from the white man.

Fortune favored Leclerc during the first five months of 1802, then his luck changed. The ally upon which Dessalines was depending began to strike—yellow fever. It was already decimating Leclerc's troops when refugees arrived from Guadeloupe, saying that Napoleon had restored slavery there and that it was to be restored in all the French islands. Now the black workers, under their own local leaders, harassed the French troops, keeping their nerves on edge. Dessalines, Pétion, and other black and mulatto officers fled with their troops to the interior, where they were supported by men, women, and children. All recognized Dessalines as chief, Pétion as second in command.

As the blacks drove the French from one port city after another, white and mulatto planters with faithful slaves fled in greater numbers than before to Louisiana and Cuba. Jean and Pierre Laffite and other ship captains shuttled them to New Orleans and came back for more. Dominique You returned to France; and Renato Beluche, now twenty-one years old, was serving as a pilot's mate on the schooner *Catalina*, flagship of the Louisiana fleet patrolling the Louisiana-Florida coast.[8]

Leclerc died of yellow fever on November 2, 1802. Napoleon had sent him 34,000 veterans; more than 24,000 had died, and 8,000 men

---

8. Manuel Juan de Salcedo to Marquis de Someruelos, February 12, 1802, in Papeles de Cuba, Legajo 2355, Archivo General de Indias (transcript in Ayer Collection, Newberry Library, Chicago).

were in hospitals. Rochambeau, on whom the command fell, had only 2,000 exhausted troops to contain the black volcano.[9]

During the fall and winter of 1802–1803, Napoleon assembled two armies in Holland. One army was to reinforce Rochambeau, and the other was to occupy Louisiana, where Spanish governors still ruled. Napoleon dispatched Pierre Clement Laussat to New Orleans in January, knowing that England would soon declare war and that she would blockade Saint Domingue. Moreover, Napoleon expected that England's first objective would be to take Louisiana, and he had no way to defend that vast colony. On April 30, 1803, he sold Louisiana to the United States.

Great Britain declared war on France two weeks after the sale. During the summer and fall, a few supply ships did get through the English blockade to Rochambeau, but the blacks had him and his few remaining troops holed up in Le Cap. On November 29 they surrendered to the British and sailed away.

Dessalines and his officers met at Gonaïves on December 31 and listened while the final draft of their declaration of independence was read. The next day, New Year's Day, 1804, Dessalines proclaimed the independence of this former colony that he and his men had renamed Haiti—the name it had when Europeans first invaded the Caribbean.

In Louisiana, meanwhile, not until November 25, 1803, did Laussat receive official instructions that he was to claim the province for France, so that he could in turn transfer it to the United States.[10] The marqués de Casa Calvo had already arrived from Havana to assist feeble old Governor Juan Manuel de Salcedo. They met Laussat at the Cabildo on November 30 to effect the transfer of Louisiana from Spain to France.

The day was cold and gloomy, but many people stood in the Place d'Armes waiting for the three men to finish the business of making

---

9. C. L. R. James, *The Black Jacobins* (New York, 1938), 294. The total loss of officers, troops, sailors, employees, and whites from France, according to Jean Price-Mars, was 50,270 men. *La République d'Haïti et la République Dominicaine* (2 vols.: Port-au-Prince, 1953), I, 32. James and Price-Mars are the two main sources for the successful revolt in Saint Domingue.

10. Marietta Marie LeBreton, "A History of the Territory of Orleans, 1803–1812" (Ph.D. dissertation, Louisiana State University, 1969), 30.

them French subjects without having consulted them, and with no regard whatsoever for their feelings in this matter. Laussat, like Ulloa (1766–1768), had come with no force behind him to uphold his authority. Would the inhabitants of New Orleans accept this transfer, or would they turn against him as their predecessors had turned against Ulloa?

The crowd in the Place d'Armes knew that the formal transfer was completed when they saw Laussat, Casa Calvo, and Salcedo come out on the Cabildo balcony to watch the ceremony of lowering the Spanish flag and raising the French flag. Then Laussat explained to the people below that France had ceded Louisiana to the United States because of the war in Europe, and that very soon they would be citizens of the United States.[11]

There were no incidents. The crowd dispersed quietly, but Laussat was uneasy. He hoped that the American commissioners—William Charles Cole Claiborne, governor of the Mississippi Territory, and General James Wilkinson—would soon arrive. Claiborne and Wilkinson had known for some time that they were to accept Louisiana for the United States, but they could not do so until they had received official orders. Claiborne was at Natchez when these were delivered to him, but Wilkinson did not arrive there until December 4. Seven days later a flotilla of boats sailed down the Mississippi carrying the two commissioners, five hundred regular troops, and one hundred Mississippi volunteers. By December 17 they were camped above New Orleans. The next day Claiborne and Wilkinson rode into the city and presented their credentials to Governor Laussat; the three men then planned the transfer ceremonies. Governor Laussat rode to the camp of the two United States commissioners to return their visit on December 19.

The next day, December 20, was one of those bright balmy days that nature sometimes bestows on Louisiana in December. That morning, while the United States troops with Claiborne and Wilkinson at the head of the column marched toward the city, all the militia companies of New Orleans assembled in the Place d'Armes in front of the Cabildo. Governor Laussat (he had been governor for twenty days) reviewed

---

11. *Ibid.*, 31–36.

them from the Cabildo balcony, then they lined up in the square to Laussat's left.

It was nearly noon when cannon boomed from the forts of the city announcing that the Americans were marching down the narrow Rue de Chartres. Streets, balconies, and windows were jammed with Louisianians. They watched Claiborne and Wilkinson dismount and enter the Cabildo while their troops formed in line opposite the French militia.

Inside the Cabildo, the two American commissioners climbed the stairs to the large council room on the second floor. There Governor Laussat met them. After the three men had read and signed the necessary documents, Laussat gave Claiborne the keys to the city and led him out on the balcony to present him to the people in the Place d'Armes. Addressing the crowd in French, Laussat said: "Louisianians, such of you as choose to pass under the new domination are absolved of all allegiance to the French Republic. You are now American citizens and will soon take new oaths to your new country."

As Laussat continued speaking, a traveler in the crowd, C. C. Robin, asked himself: "How can my country cease to be mine? My country, whose name flatters my pride and awakens in me such great sentiments of love and gratitude—can my country cease to be mine? Can I break the ties which unite me to her?"[12]

Robin watched Laussat present Claiborne as the new governor of Louisiana. This young man (he was only twenty-eight years old) stepped forward and earnestly addressed the crowd—in English. "The American people," he said, "receive you as brothers and extend to you a participation in those inestimable rights which have formed the bases of their own unexampled prosperity. . . . Every exertion will be made on my part to foster your internal happiness."[13]

When Claiborne finished speaking, there was no applause—perhaps because the people did not understand English, perhaps for other reasons. In dead silence they watched the French flag descend from the mast in the middle of the Place d'Armes. At the same time the flag

---

12. C. C. Robin, *Voyages dans l'intérieur de la Louisiane, de la Florida Occidentale, et dans les isles de la Martinique et de Saint-Domingue; pendant les années 1802, 1803, 1804, 1805 et 1806* (3 vols.; Paris, 1806), II, 137–38.

13. *American State Papers. Documents, Legislative and Executive, of the Congress of the United States* (38 vols.; Washington, D.C., 1832–61), *Foreign Relations*, II, 538.

of the United States ascended. The two flags met midway. A signal gun was fired. The forts of the city responded with all their cannon as a French militiaman took the flag of France, folded it, and silently returned to his place in line.[14]

Then the spectators noticed that the United States flag had not moved. It had stuck, "as though it were ashamed to occupy the place of the flag to whom it owed its own independence." Not a murmur was heard as the Americans struggled to free it. Suddenly it shot to the top of the mast. A few Kentuckians at one corner of the square cheered, but no emotion was evident in the rest of the crowd. "Those few shouts," said Robin, "only made more doleful the silence and immobility of the new citizens of the United States."[15]

Renato Beluche, one of those new citizens, may have been in the crowd that day, as he is known to have been in New Orleans a few days later, attending the wedding of his cousin Juana María Fangui. On January 7, 1804, Juana María, daughter of Vicente Fangui and Magdalena Laporte, married Juan Felipe de Agesta, native of Havana and son of Francisco Antonio de Agesta and María Rafaela Echevarry. Renato was one of the four witnesses who signed the marriage record. The other three were Magdalena Laporte (mother of the bride and sister of Beluche's mother), Felicite Fangui (sister of the bride), and her husband Bartolome Bosch.[16]

The impact of Spanish, French, and English cultures on one another is shown in the various spellings of the names Bartolome Bosch and Felicite Fangui in church and city records. Their marriage record shows that "Bartholome Bosque native of Palma in Mallorca son of Cayetano Bosque and Cathalina Ponz, natives of Palma" on January 9, 1793, married "Felicitas Fanguy native of this Parish daughter of Vicente Fanguy a native of Montpellier in France and of Magdalena Laporte native of this Parish." Their daughter Cayetana Susana "Bosques" was born on August 7, 1796. The record of her baptism lists her parents as

---

14. Robin, *Voyages*, II, 138–39.
15. *Ibid.*, II, 139.
16. Alice Daly Forsyth (ed.), *A Collection of Marriage Records from the St. Louis Cathedral During the Spanish Regime and Early American Period, 1784–1806* (New Orleans, 1977), 156, Vol. I of Alice Daly Forsyth (ed.), *Louisiana Marriages*.

"Don Bartolome Bosques" and "Dona Felicidad Fangui."[17] In due time, the couple also had five sons.

Bartolome had built a house in 1795 on Chartres Street (at what is now No. 617–621). The United States owned the whole block opposite Bartolome's property. Claiborne's residence in this block was on the corner of Levee Street (Rue du Quay) and Toulouse Street, and his garden extended to Chartres. Bosque's children and servants could look across Chartres Street and see everything that happened in the governor's garden, and by walking to Levee Street they could find out who was entering or leaving his mansion.

Susana Bosque, Beluche's first cousin once removed, became Claiborne's third wife at a critical moment in history. Susana was almost eight years old when Claiborne's first wife Eliza and his two-year-old daughter, Cornelia Tennessee, arrived from Nashville in June, 1804. This was a bad time for anyone to come to hot, humid New Orleans. The whole city was unclean, including streets, alleys, and "courtyards of the houses, water-closets, drain pipes, stables, etc." Filth and rubbish thrown on the batture made "the principal promenades of the city odious as well as unsanitary. The stench and corruption of said filth is particularly bad in warm weather."[18]

Yellow fever hit the city soon after Eliza Claiborne and her daughter arrived. They both died of the disease on September 26, 1804, and were buried in St. Louis Cemetery No. 1.[19]

---

17. *Ibid.*, 83; Act 355, Baptismal Book 3 (1796–1802), pp. 56–57, St. Louis Cathedral Archives.

18. Claiborne's wife was Elizabeth (Eliza) W. Lewis, daughter of William Terrell Lewis, a prominent Nashville leader. Joseph T. Hatfield, *William Claiborne: Jeffersonian Centurian in the American Southwest* (Lafayette, La., 1976), 207. See also Pedro Dulcido Barran, El Sindico Procurador, to Cabildo, January 24, 1800, in Laura L. Porteous (trans.), "Sanitary Conditions in New Orleans Under the Spanish Regime, 1799–1800," *Louisiana Historical Quarterly*, XV (1932), 614.

19. New Orleans *Louisiana Gazette*, September 28, 1804. In 1811, Benjamin H. Latrobe designed the monument erected over their graves and that of Eliza's brother Micajah Lewis. An Italian sculptor, Franzoni, who had come to the United States to work on its capitol, carved the low-relief sculpture ornamenting the monument. Friends of the Cabildo, *The Cemeteries* (Gretna, La., 1974), 93–94, Vol. III of Friends of the Cabildo, *New Orleans Architecture*.

CHAPTER 3

Shipmaster Renato Beluche

"Batt^e Bosque" was one of fifty-five merchants in New Orleans who, on January 9, 1804, "respectfully" petitioned the Congress of the United States because the "Rights and Privileges of Citizens" with regard to commerce had not yet been extended to them. "For want of proper Documents to navigate with," they explained, "the Ships and Vessels of your Memorialists are now laid up, in a perishing State, unauthorised to hoist any Flag whatever: Their Capitals are unemployed; their Merchandize has no Vent. Duties are levied according to the Spanish Tarif, on all the exports of this Province, and on its Imports even from the United States. . . . We feel it is hard to be subject to these partial Regulations while other United States Ports carry on a free and untaxed Intercourse, and their Exports are subject to no Duty whatever."[1]

Congress responded favorably to this petition by passing an act of twelve sections, granting the requested "Rights and Privileges." Two sections of the act provided for "registering and recording ships and vessels" sailing to foreign ports, and "enrolling and licensing ships or vessels to be employed in the coasting trade and fisheries."[2]

By the time President Thomas Jefferson signed this act on February 24, 1804, Congress had passed several sections of "An Act erecting Louisiana into two territories, and providing for the temporary government thereof." That part of the Louisiana Purchase north of the thirty-third parallel was named the District of Louisiana. It was almost as large as all the rest of the United States. The part south of the thirty-third parallel was named the Territory of Orleans. It had most of the

---

1. "Batt^e Bosque" is the way Bosque signed the petition. Clarence Edwin Carter (comp. and ed.), *The Territorial Papers of the United States* (28 vols.; Washington, D.C., 1934–75), IX, 157–58.
2. The act is found in John Bioren, W. John Duane, and R. C. Weightman (eds.), *Laws of the United States of America from the 4th of March, 1789, to the 4th of March, 1815* (5 vols.; Philadelphia and Washington, 1815), III, 569–74.

population of the Louisiana Purchase, and Jefferson chose to keep Claiborne in Orleans as territorial governor.[3]

Section Ten of the act prohibited the importation of slaves into the Territory of Orleans "from places without the limits of the United States." Early in March, "a Paper was received in New Orleans from the Seat of Government" which stated that the Senate had passed Section Ten. Merchants and planters in New Orleans and adjacent settlements viewed this restriction as a serious blow to their interests, since they needed slaves and could easily import them from Caribbean sources. The states of the United States could still import slaves, and South Carolina was the main importer. Louisianians were convinced that Congress wanted "to make South Carolina the Sole importer for Louisiana."[4]

Planters, merchants, and others petitioned Congress to remove this discrimination against the Territory of Orleans, but the act passed with Section Ten intact, and President Jefferson signed it on March 6, 1804. Consequently, Louisianians who needed slaves and all those who made money importing slaves ignored Section Ten, and ships with slave cargoes and other contraband continued to use the smuggling routes they had used during the period of Spanish rule. Some smugglers used the bays and waterways of the Atchafalaya Basin, but the only secure harbor on the Gulf Coast between the Sabine River and the mouth of the Mississippi was Smugglers' Anchorage on the island of Grande Terre.[5]

This island and Grand Isle shield Barataria Bay from the Gulf of Mexico. François Mayronne owned Grande Terre. He also owned a large part of the riverbank land on the west side of the Mississippi a short distance above New Orleans. This property was adjacent to Dubreuil's Canal, which began about two arpents from the Mississippi and ended at a bayou that leads to Barataria Bay and Smugglers' Anchorage. Events of 1804 caused Mayronne, and the smugglers and their associates in New Orleans, to use Dubreuil's Canal, the bayou that leads to Barataria, Barataria Bay, and Smugglers' Anchorage, for illegal commerce.[6]

3. *Ibid.*, III, 603–10.
4. Claiborne to James Madison, March 10, 1804, in Dunbar Rowland (ed.), *Official Letter Books of W. C. C. Claiborne, 1801–1816* (6 vols.; Jackson, Miss., 1917), II, 25.
5. A. Lacarrière Latour, *Historical Memoir of the War in West Florida and Louisiana in 1814–1815. With an Atlas* (Philadelphia, 1816), 14.
6. Betsy Swanson, *Historic Jefferson Parish from Shore to Shore* (Gretna, La., 1975), 88–89, 149–50.

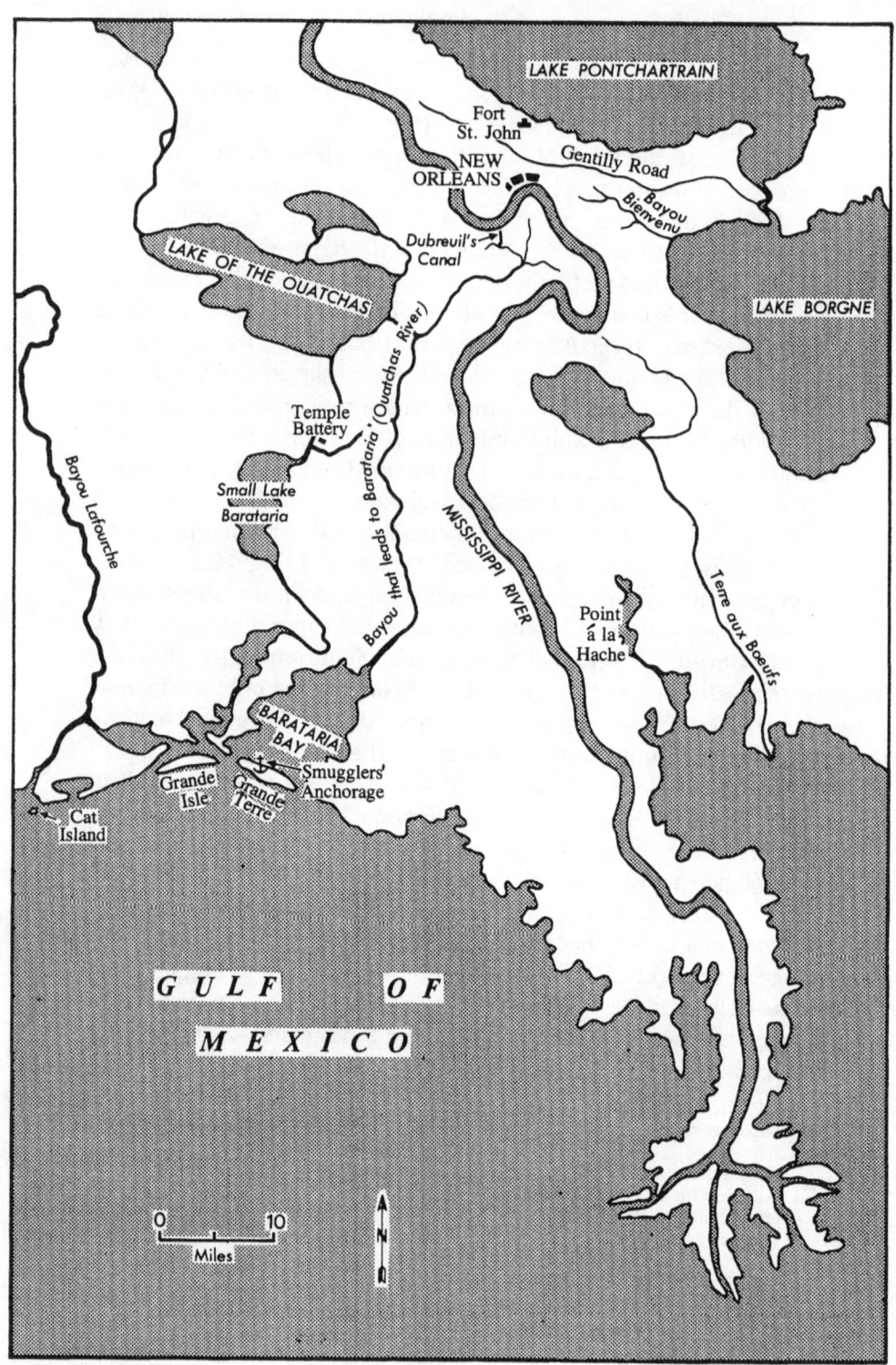

Smugglers' Paradise

An eyewitness in New Orleans reported: "The whole adjacent coast was disquieted and kept in terror by pirates; among the latter the most conspicuous were the brothers Laffite, Beluche, Dominique, Gamba and others, who were time and again seen walking about, publicly, in the streets of New Orleans which they usually paraded arm in arm." They captured English and Spanish ships on the high seas and unloaded their cargoes of slaves and manufactured goods at Smugglers' Anchorage. The eyewitness continued: "This place was visited by sugar planters, chiefly of French origin, who bought up the stolen slaves at from 150 to 200 dollars per head, when they could not have procured as good stock in the city for less than 600 or 700 dollars."[7]

In their January 9 petition to Congress, the fifty-five New Orleans merchants had not complained about their coastwise trade because it was flourishing, but, as noted above, Congress provided for ship enrollments as well as ship registers (ship enrollments registered vessels engaged in the coasting trade and fisheries; ship registers were issued only to vessels engaged in foreign trade). The first ship register at the port of New Orleans was issued on March 31, 1804.[8]

We do not know when the first ship enrollment was made, because enrollment records for the early years have disappeared. Beluche's name does not appear in the extant ship registers and crew lists until Bosque registered his schooner *Two Sisters* on February 27, 1805. The *Two Sisters* was 67' × 20'9" × 9'11", and had one deck, two masts, a square stern, and a round tuck.[9] Beluche, as master of this schooner, made four voyages for Bosque in a one-year period. On each voyage he had a crew of seven men.

Beluche cleared the *Two Sisters* from New Orleans on March 5, 1805, bound for Vera Cruz, and did not return to New Orleans until May 25. This run took almost three months. On July 2, Beluche cleared for Havana and returned on August 16. He cleared again for Havana on August 30 and returned nine weeks later, on November 1. His last voyage in the *Two Sisters*, at least so far as records show, was to Vera

7. Vincent Nolte, *Fifty Years in Both Hemispheres* (New York, 1854), 189, 207.
8. Survey of Federal Archives in Louisiana, *Ship Registers and Enrollments of New Orleans, 1804–1870* (6 vols.; Baton Rouge, 1941), I, vii, 125, 176; Survey of Federal Archives in Louisiana, *Crew Lists United States Customs Archives, Port of New Orleans, September 1803–December 1816* (5 vols.; Baton Rouge, 1938–39), I, 9, 35.
9. Place and date of construction not shown. SFA, *Ship Registers*, I, 131.

Cruz. The sailing date listed was November 15. He returned on March 10, 1806. This run to Vera Cruz took almost four months, more than a month longer than his first run there.[10] All four of these voyages could have been made in less time. Beluche had taken the *Two Sisters* to Vera Cruz and to Havana, but where else had he been?

The smugglers had an able lawyer, Edward Livingston, brother of Robert Livingston, minister of the United States in Paris, who played a major role in negotiations with France for the purchase of Louisiana. Edward Livingston came to New Orleans early in 1804, when refugees from Haiti were swelling the city's population. He married one of these refugees, the widow Louise Moreau de Lassy, née Davezac de Castera, on June 3, 1805.[11]

Three weeks after Livingston's marriage, Aaron Burr arrived in New Orleans with letters of introduction from General Wilkinson, who at this time was a ranking general in the U.S. army, Agent No. 13 in Spain's secret service, and governor of the District of Louisiana—that part of the Louisiana Purchase north of the thirty-third parallel. Wilkinson had supplied Burr with "an elegant barge, sails, colors and ten oars, with a sergeant and ten able, faithful hands." He also had written a letter to Daniel Clark saying that Burr, "that great and honorable man would communicate to him many things improper to letter, and which he would not say to any other."[12]

Every important businessman and public official in New Orleans except one fell under the spell of Aaron Burr, who told them that he would return in the fall of 1806. The one official who knew nothing of Burr's conspiracy was Governor Claiborne.[13]

When Burr arrived in New Orleans, Beluche was absent. He had sailed from New Orleans on April 18, 1806, bound for Tabasco, as master of the brig *Thomas*. For some reason, this brig had not been registered. Its six-man crew included Silvain, "a Sambo boy belonging to Etne [*i.e.*, Étienne] Debon, owner of said brig." Debon, like Bosque, was a merchant, but, unlike Bosque, he had not signed the Merchant's

10. SFA, *Crew Lists*, I, 43, 52, 123, 137, 177, 197.
11. William B. Hatcher, *Edward Livingston: Jeffersonian Republican and Jacksonian Democrat* (Baton Rouge, 1940), 106, 102.
12. Gayarré, *History of Louisiana*, IV, 80–81.
13. Henry Adams, *History of the United States of America* (9 vols.; New York, 1890–91), III, 307.

Memorial to Congress. When Beluche returned to New Orleans on July 19, Governor Claiborne was absent.

Unaware of the true situation in New Orleans, Claiborne had begun an inspection of his "counties" (parishes) on July 5. He "passed up the East side of the Mississippi," where the richest sugar plantations were located, and reported to President Jefferson that "it is not uncommon with 20 working hands to make from 10 to 14 thousand Dollars, and there are several planters whose field negroes do not exceed forty who make more than 20,000 Dollars each year. . . . On yesterday [July 10] I dined with Mr. [Jean Noël] Destrehan; he is esteemed the best sugar planter in the Territory, and is perhaps the wealthiest; his sugars bring him near thirty thousand Dollars per Annum, and his rents in the city about six thousand Dollars."[14]

On July 15 Claiborne crossed the Mississippi to "Mr. Barranger's 66 miles from New Orleans." From there, he informed the president that "the county of the Attackapas and of Opelousas which adjoins it, is the most beautiful I ever beheld; the Prairies are extensive; replenished with the richest verdure, and affording Food for numerous Stocks of Cattle. The River Teche (which communicates with the sea) passes through the two Counties: it may be navigated to a considerable distance by vessels of Fifty Tons burthen. . . . I am now not more than 10 leagues distant from the sea, and there is not a Tree to interrupt the Sea Breezes. . . . I shall proceed in a few days to the Opelousas."

It was two weeks before Claiborne left the Attakapas. He explained to Henry Dearborn, secretary of war, that "I have been greatly delayed on my Journey, by an attack of fever, and altho' it has now left me, I nevertheless am so enfeebled that I fear it will not be in my power to visit the several Counties of the Territory."[15]

Claiborne never mentioned either to Jefferson or Dearborn that he was courting a girl who lived in the Attakapas. Her parents were Martin Milony Duralde, born in Biscaya, Spain, and Marie Josephe Perrault, a native of Quebec.[16]

Fever or no fever, Claiborne had to continue his inspection. He vis-

---

14. Rowland (ed.), *Claiborne Letter Books*, III, 361–65, 369–71.
15. July 29, 1806, in *ibid.*, III, 374.
16. Stanley Clisby Arthur and George Campbell Huchet de Kerneon (comps. and eds.), *Old Families of Louisiana* (Baton Rouge, 1971), 147.

ited the Opelousas and Concordia Parish, then crossed the Mississippi River to Natchez. He was in Natchez when a messenger arrived with news that Spaniards had crossed the Sabine in considerable force on August 8 and were establishing a garrison near Bayou Pierre in the neighborhood of Natchitoches.

Claiborne recrossed the river and headed for Natchitoches. He arrived there on August 24 and on August 26 began negotiations with the Spanish commander. Two weeks or more passed. The Spaniards seemed disposed to remain quiet, and Claiborne, knowing that General Wilkinson would soon arrive to take command, left for the Attakapas. He spent a few days there and then returned to New Orleans on October 6. The next day this notice appeared in the *Louisiana Gazette*: "Married—At Attakapas, on Saturday, 27th ult., His Excellency William C. C. Claiborne, to the amiable Miss Clarice Duralde, daughter of Martin Duralde, Esq. member of the legislature of this territory."

No one seemed to pay any attention to the arrival of Claiborne and his bride, except perhaps the Bosque family; and Claiborne seemed unaware that the city was excited about something else. His letters to the secretary of war and to Wilkinson indicated that everything was tranquil in the city. In a brief letter to the president on November 5, Claiborne wrote: "I observe by the Western Papers that Colo. Burr is in the Western States, and that a public Dinner was lately given him at Nashville; I know not the views of this Gentleman, but I fear they are political and of a kind most injurious."[17]

There was no way that Claiborne could have known that Wilkinson had betrayed Burr and had written to Jefferson about "Burr's Conspiracy"—as though Burr alone was the schemer. Moreover, the world seemed good to Claiborne. He was very much in love and finally, on November 12, revealed this fact in a letter to President Jefferson. "On my visit to the U States," he wrote, "I anticipate the pleasure of introducing to your acquaintance M^{rs} C; She is a native of Louisiana, born and educated in the Prairies of Opelousas, and unites to other qualities, which to me were interesting, those of a sincere attachment to the Government of the U States, and to the American Character; This Lit-

17. Roland (ed.), *Claiborne Letter Books*, IV, 33.

tle Stranger solicits that her most affectionate wishes for your health and happiness, may accompany those of your faithful friend."[18]

Two ominous letters were written that day, November 12, not by Claiborne but to him. One was from General Andrew Jackson. He wrote from the Hermitage, warning Claiborne that "I fear treachery has become the order of the day. . . . Put your Town in a state of defense. Organize your militia, and defend your City as well against internal Enemies as external. . . . I fear you will meet with an attack from quarters you do not at present expect. Be upon the alert; keep a watchful eye upon our Genl. . . . You have enemies within your City that may try to subvert your Government and try to separate it from the Union."[19]

The second letter was from Wilkinson. It was written at Natchez, marked "Sacredly Confidential," and told Claiborne of the military force that he had sent from Natchitoches "on the 6th Inst, by Major Porter who descends with all the Artificers and one hundred men . . . to be immediately followed by Col. Couching and every other man but one Company. You are surrounded by dangers of which you dream not and the destruction of the American Union is seriously Menaced. The Storm will probably burst in New Orleans, where I shall meet it and triumph or perish."[20]

Claiborne received Wilkinson's letter on November 17 and Jackson's either that day or the next; Wilkinson himself arrived in New Orleans on November 25. For a few days he did not take any drastic action. He was waiting not only for the troops he had dispatched from Natchitoches but also for troops from Mobile, which belonged to Spain.[21]

Étienne De Bon (or Debon—records are not consistent), like other merchants in the city, was uneasy about what would happen to his shipping when the troops arrived. Would his seamen be impressed? (De Bon had recently bought the brig *Gayoso*.) Beluche returned on November 18 from a second run in the *Thomas* to Tabasco, and De Bon

---

18. Carter (comp. and ed.), *Territorial Papers*, IX, 687.
19. John Spencer Bassett (ed.), *Correspondence of Andrew Jackson* (7 vols.; Washington, 1926–35), I, 152–53.
20. Rowland (ed.), *Claiborne Letter Books*, IV, 55–56.
21. Claiborne to Wilkinson, November 17, and to James Madison, December 4, in *ibid.*, IV, 40–41, 44.

gave him command of the *Gayoso*. They assembled a crew of five free men and five slaves. Three of the slaves belonged to De Bon, and two others, Frank and Antonio, belonged to Beluche and were listed as waiting boys.[22]

Beluche sailed from New Orleans bound for Tabasco on December 3. Three days later, on December 6, Wilkinson demanded that Claiborne declare martial law, then abdicate. Claiborne refused. He would not sanction the declaration of martial law, the illegal arrest of suspected persons, nor the impressment of seamen. However, he was aware that the commanders of United States armed vessels then in port could not get enough seamen to man their vessels, so he called a meeting of merchants and principal inhabitants at the Government House on December 9 to get their help in solving this problem.

Wilkinson addressed the meeting and told his audience of the "rebellious army" descending on them. He ended by saying that Colonel Burr expected the cooperation of the British navy in transporting his expedition to Mexico, "but not until these adventurers had plundered the banks at New Orleans; seized the shipping, and helped themselves to every thing of which an army of seven thousand men could stand in need of!"[23] This last sentence "seized instantly on the whole nervous system of his audience." The persons present were principally merchants, and their banks, their ships, and the goods in their warehouses were all "menaced with the merciless requisitions of seven thousand hardy and half naked adventurers!"

At this moment someone proposed that the ships in port be detained and the crews discharged so they could serve on vessels of the United States. The merchants promptly agreed, and an embargo was laid, which they soon discovered they too had to obey. No outward-bound vessel was suffered to pass the fort on the river without written permission from the governor or the general.

In a few days some of the merchants recovered from the shock they had received on December 9. When they "complained that they had

22. The *Gayoso* was built in Philadelphia in 1787 and was registered in the name of Stephen De Bon, May 3, 1806 (SFA, *Ship Registers*, I, 51). SFA, *Crew Lists*, II, 158, 212;. Ship News Column, New Orleans *Louisiana Gazette*, November 18, 1806.
23. *A Faithful Picture of the Political Situation of New Orleans at Close of Last and Beginning of Present Year 1807* (Boston, 1808), 14.

been unfairly surprised" into agreeing to the embargo, Wilkinson reacted as though martial law had been declared. On Sunday, December 14, he made his first arbitrary arrests. The merchants knew that Wilkinson could charge each of them with being an accomplice of Burr, so Wilkinson's reign of terror continued until Burr's arrival in the Mississippi Territory "with a few common boats and about forty men unprepared for any military expedition set the public mind at ease."[24]

Beluche returned from Tabasco in the *Gayoso* on February 23, 1807.[25] A few days later, Burr was arrested and sent to Richmond, Virginia, for trial. Then, on March 2, 1807—before Beluche could sail again—Congress approved an act that prohibited the importation of slaves into any port or place within the jurisdiction of the United States, from and after the first day of January, 1808. After that date, even South Carolina could no longer legally import slaves. This act, with the embargo declared later in the year, increased the demand for smuggled slaves.

Beluche sailed in the *Gayoso* from New Orleans on March 9, 1807, again bound for Tabasco. This time only four slaves were listed with the crew, and all four belonged to De Bon. The *Gayoso* returned to New Orleans on June 17.[26]

The next ship on which Beluche sailed was the $133^{77}/_{95}$-ton schooner *Centurion*, which had been built in Saybrook, Connecticut, and was registered in New Orleans on July 31, 1806. John Michael Fortier II of New Orleans, his son John Michael III, and Archibald Gracie of New York, all three of whom were merchants, owned the *Centurion*.[27]

They and Étienne De Bon must have been part of the operation that Napoleon's banker, J. G. Ouvrard, organized between 1804 and 1806 to get Mexican silver to Napoleon. Ships from New England, New York, Philadelphia, and other ports brought European merchandise to New Orleans. Ouvrard's agent, Vincent Nolte, arrived in New Orleans on Easter Sunday, 1806, to receive these cargoes, load them on smaller vessels (with masters like Beluche, who could outwit British ships patrolling the Louisiana coast), get their cargoes to Mexican ports, and

24. *Ibid.*, 16, 19.
25. SFA, *Crew Lists*, II, 212.
26. *Ibid.*, II, 372.
27. The *Centurion* had one deck, two masts, and a square stern. Its dimensions were 80'9" x 20' x 9'7". SFA, *Ship Registers*, I, 22.

return to New Orleans with 150,000 to 200,000 Spanish dollars.[28] Larger vessels transported this hard money to France.

Beluche was not master when the *Centurion* sailed for Vera Cruz on August 3, 1807. The master was Honoré Fortier, brother of John Michael Fortier II. However, Beluche's named headed the eleven-man crew list, and for the first time he gave his birthplace and residence as New Orleans, his citizenship as "USA." Frequently on the crew lists masters did not give this information, and Beluche was one who never did when he sailed as master. The *Centurion* returned to New Orleans on November 9, 1807.[29]

Before Beluche sailed on another cruise, the flourishing shuttle trade between New Orleans and Vera Cruz, Campeche, Tabasco, and Laguna was seriously threatened when President Jefferson signed the Embargo Act on December 22, 1807. Several weeks passed before New Orleans learned of the embargo, so Beluche was able to sail from New Orleans on January 1, 1808, bound for Vera Cruz on the brig *Emilie*. The *Louisiana Gazette* on March 1, 1808, reported that the *Emilie* had entered the Balize nine days after leaving Vera Cruz—a record run. It took Beluche four days to work his way upriver from the Balize to New Orleans. When he canceled this voyage in New Orleans on March 5, the embargo was known and supposed to be in effect.[30]

The act forbade any ship to sail from United States ports to any foreign port. The embargo was deemed necessary because both Great Britain and Napoleon were in the process of annihilating the merchant marine of the United States. British orders in council by the end of 1807 declared that any neutral carrier en route to a European port would be subject to capture unless it first put in at a British port and paid a fee. Napoleon retaliated with decrees in December, 1807, that ordered any neutral ship to be confiscated when it arrived at a European port if it had previously stopped in an English port or had submitted to search at sea by a British warship.

Merchants and shippers from New England, New York, Philadelphia, Baltimore, Charleston, and New Orleans had been making huge profits from the carrying trade to and from Europe. Now they were

28. Nolte, *Fifty Years in Both Hemispheres*, 77–99.
29. SFA, *Crew Lists*, II, 499.
30. *Ibid.*, II, 552.

called upon to outwit British orders in council and Napoleon's decrees by "peaceful coercion"—that is, by staying at home.

When rumors of the embargo reached New Orleans, merchants bought up all the flour and cotton in the city, shipping the cotton to England and the flour to Caribbean ports. According to the crew lists, between January 1 and January 30, 1808, thirty-five vessels left New Orleans for foreign ports. Ten of these sailed to Europe: five to Liverpool, two to Nantes, and one each to Bordeaux, Belfast, and Greenock. Eleven ships sailed to Mexico: eight to Vera Cruz, two to Laguna, one to Campeche. Thirteen ships sailed to West Indian ports: five to Havana, three to Santiago de Cuba, two to "ports of the West Indies," and one each to Cuba, Curaçao, and Kingston. One ship sailed to "Pensacola then London."[31]

This last vessel, the *President Jefferson* of Kennebunk, Maine, which sailed on January 30, 1808, was more truthful than some of the others when it gave its destination as "Pensacola then London." Nine of the vessels that sailed to Mexico and the West Indies did not return to New Orleans to cancel their voyages, so they must have gotten papers in Spanish or English colonial ports that allowed them to sail to Europe as Spanish or English vessels.

From January 30, 1808, until February 15, 1809, only four Louisiana merchant vessels reported their departures—that is, in spite of the embargo, officials in New Orleans agreed to and registered their departures. All four sailings were in the month of May, 1808. One vessel was bound for Nassau, the other three for Havana.[32]

No more departures from New Orleans for foreign ports were recorded until February, 1809, when everyone knew that the embargo was about to be repealed. On March 1 it was replaced by the Nonintercourse Act, which permitted trade with all ports except those of France and England.

The embargo and the Nonintercourse Act resulted in an increase in smuggling, as did Napoleon's loss of Spain as an ally. In the late spring of 1808, Napoleon proclaimed his brother Joseph king of Spain. Spaniards refused to accept Joseph and set up juntas in nearly all their cities to rule in the name of Ferdinand, who was living in France. Napo-

31. *Ibid.*, II, 551–93.
32. *Ibid.*, II, 578, 581–82, 590.

leon's armies sustained Joseph in Spain, but England, who had preyed for centuries on Spain's colonies, suddenly discovered that Spain was its "natural ally."

With Spain now the enemy, French privateers in the Caribbean and the Gulf of Mexico could no longer find bases in Cuba, Santo Domingo, and Puerto Rico. Moreover, by 1809, when England captured Martinique, France had only one base left in the Caribbean—the island of Guadeloupe and its dependencies, including St. Barthélemy (St. Barts) and St. Martin.

French privateers needed a place to escape from English warships and Spanish *guardacostas*, and a place where they could dispose of the prizes they had captured. They found their way to Smugglers' Anchorage in Barataria Bay and to anchorages in bays to the west: Timbalier, Terrebone, Atchafalaya, and Vermilion.

A surveyor for the United States had reported on this coastal area to the secretary of the treasury when Spain was still an ally of France. He said that Bayou Teche was considered a branch of the "Chafalaya," and that Lafourche and other bayous, together with all the lakes in the area, gave continous water communication with New Orleans. He especially cited a portage of only four miles from Vermilion Bay to Bayou Teche: "By this portage the Spaniards conveyed immense quantities of buillion and specie from Vera Cruz and the coast of Mexico, in small gunboats running within the oyster banks, islands and shoals and thus escaped pursuit or capture. When once embarked on the Teche, an easy inland navigation conveyed the treasure to New Orleans."[33]

Smuggling complicated Governor Claiborne's problems, as did another factor—the French refugees from Haiti who had fled to Cuba. They were now considered spies in Cuba and had to leave. The mayor of New Orleans reported that by August 7, 1809, a total of 1,507 whites, 1,452 free people of color and free blacks, and 1,629 slaves had arrived, and that more were expected.[34]

Claiborne explained to the territorial secretary why he allowed the refugees to keep their slaves: "Under the Law of 1808, the slaves were reported to me by the Collector of Customs, and I was requested to

33. Luis Dumain to Albert Gallatin, July 20, 1807, in *American State Papers*, Class II, Vol. I, 840–42.
34. Rowland (ed.), *Claiborne Letter Books*, IV, 381–82.

name a person to whom they should be delivered. As to their disposition, I had alone to consult my own discretion, for neither the laws of the United States, or of the Territory had made express provision on this point:—To have confined them in Prison, would have been an inhuman act, it would moreover have been attended with an expense which I was neither authorized or prepared to incur;—to have deprived the owners of the present use of the negro's, would have been to have thrown them (the owners) as Paupers upon this Community, who are already sufficiently burthened with contributions for the poor, the sick and the aged Emigrants. These are some of the considerations which induced me to place the negro's in possession of their masters, upon their entering into bond that they shall be forthcoming on the requisition of the Governor of the Territory."[35]

The exodus of refugees from Cuba to Louisiana, the embargo, and nonintercourse all touched the life of Renato Beluche, even though we have only two clues that tell us what Beluche may have been doing from March 5, 1808, when he returned in the *Emilie* to New Orleans, until February 26, 1810, when he left New Orleans in the *Camillus*. It is apparent from the evidence that Beluche was sailing ships and perhaps transporting refugees, because sometime during 1809 he married one of these refugees, Marie Magdeleine Victoire Milleret, a native of Port-au-Prince. One wonders why they went to Campeche to get married. This voyage on the sea of matrimony must have been a rough one, because after six months Beluche abandoned Marie Magdeleine, and she found a home with her aunt, Marie Catherine Loublan, the widow Thomas, who lived on Bourbon Street.[36]

The second clue is the record of a court case at the end of 1809 concerning the schooner *Camillus*, which Beluche had bought on credit. Benedict Fabrigos testified that Beluche never had any money and that on several occasions he borrowed money from the captain, Joseph Duro, for his own private use. Beluche may have been getting married when he let Duro make a run in the *Camillus* to Havana. Duro sailed from New Orleans on June 11, 1809, returned on September 26 or 27, and presented Beluche with a padded expense account in which Duro

---

35. *Ibid.*, IV, 390–91.
36. Suit No. 3059 (Suit for Separation), February 21, 1822, in Parish Court of New Orleans Records, New Orleans Public Library.

allowed himself wages of $80 per month and rations for a crew of twelve, although he had only seven crew members. Beluche refused to pay the bill, and Duro took him to court on November 23.

Dominique Mayronne, mariner, being duly sworn on the part of the defendant, was cross-examined as follows:

> *Question*: Does the captain of a schooner or other small vessel ever receive as high wages as 80 dollars per month for his services?
> *Answer*: The usual pay for a master of a vessel is 60 dollars per month, and a dollar per day besides for his board. The captain of a schooner generally receives as much as the captain of any other vessel.
> *Question*: When the crew of a vessel are discharged, can they rightfully claim any compensation beyond that period—for instance, up to the time they are paid, or does their pay absolutely cease when they are thus discharged?
> *Answer*: When a crew are discharged, it is not customary to make them any compensation beyond that period.
> *Question*: Is it customary at Havana to allow for the board of seven seamen at the rate of four dollars per day?
> *Answer*: No, I do not think it is. I never myself allowed more at that place than a bit and a half to each sailor for his board on shore, and the same custom prevails at this place.
> *Question*: Do you believe that a captain and seven seamen could consume in 34 days passage, 194 dollars worth of stores and provisions?
> *Answer*: No, I do not think it is possible. I should be ashamed to bring such an amount to my owner, lest I should be turned out of employment.

The court reduced the amount of Duro's wages and board for crewmen and made several other deductions also. It declared that the total sum due Duro was $365.44, not $622.44. The record does not show that Beluche paid the $365.44.[37]

On February 26, 1810, with a crew of eight, Beluche sailed the *Camillus* from New Orleans to Pensacola, where he sold it and paid and dismissed his seamen. When they returned to New Orleans, they certified on May 3 that Beluche "paid our passage home to New Orleans at his own expense, and that we have been satisfied by said Master, of all demands against the said Schooner Camillus and her Officers."[38]

---

37. Survey of Federal Archives in Louisiana, *Conspicuous Cases in the United States District Court of Louisiana. Transcriptions of the Case Papers and Other Interesting Documents Pertaining to Trials and Indictments, Dating from the Establishment of the Federal Court in 1806*, (1st Ser., 7 vols.; Baton Rouge, 1939–40), Book A, Case No. 312.
38. SFA, *Crew Lists*, III, 316–17.

CHAPTER 4

Privateer for France and the United States

The British gained possession of the whole island of Guadeloupe by February 10, 1810, but not of two of its dependencies, St. Barthélemy and St. Martin. Therefore, privateers could still get letters of marque at these last two French bases in the Caribbean. This ability, plus the facts that no slaves could legally be imported into the United States and the Nonintercourse Act prohibited trade with any French or English port, caused a flurry of activity in New Orleans. If the laws of the United States were obeyed, the merchants believed, everyone in the Territory of Orleans would suffer, and there would be a depression.

Ways to bypass these laws had to be found. The territorial legislature did its part when it approved an act on March 16, 1810, directing that slaves imported into Orleans in violation of the law should be sold and the proceeds turned over to the Territory (the act was not to apply to slaves imported from Cuba in 1809 for whose appearance security had been given).[1]

Shipbuilders, merchants, mariners, and Captain General Ernouf of St. Martin did their part. *L'Intrépide*, "built by some of our good citizens under the guns of Fort St. Charles," sailed sometime in January, 1810, from New Orleans bound for St. Barthélemy. Joseph Sauvinet, a merchant, was one of the passengers. When the ship arrived at St. Barthélemy, its master, "a captain Rogers," sold her to Sauvinet. Then the other passengers became her crew, and Pierre Brugman—an alias that Beluche used many times—took command and sailed *L'Intrépide* to St. Martin.[2]

---

1. Carter (comp. and ed.), *Territorial Papers*, IX, 882.
2. Caspar F. Goodrich, "Our Navy and the West Indian Pirates," *United States Naval Institute Proceedings*, XLII (1916), 1463–64.

There Captain General Ernouf backdated "Brugman's" letter of marque to February 10. The first paragraph of this commission states:

> I do authorize Pierre Brugman, captain of the corsair *L'Intrépide* of about 70 tons burden (commissioned and equipped for war at the port of Marigot, St. Martin, by Mr. Joseph Sauvinet), by this letter of marque issued as number 15, duly registered in the Bureau of Maritime Registry of Marigot, St. Martin, to lead or send into the ports of France or its colonies all ships of enemies of the Empire, and pirates, rovers and unavowed persons that he might capture and make prisoners, unless the said captain of the said corsair *L'Intrépide* or whoever is given charge by him of the said prize, have been forced by bad weather or by enemies to put in at any Neutral port. In that case he will be required to explain the reasons for putting in, and to give full notice to those concerned, of the commission held by said Pierre Brugman or by his prize captain, and to make to the Administrative Officer of the Maritime Registry in the place of his return or of his putting in, the report required by law, and to follow those relative to maritime prizes.[3]

The officer and crew list made at Marigot showed that a total of eighty males signed on the seventy-ton *L'Intrépide*. There were twenty officers (including Brugman), eight apprentices, five helmsmen, three able seamen, seventeen sailors, twenty volunteers, five cabin boys, and two supernumeraries. The list gives the place of birth, rank, age, height, *poil* (*i.e.*, beard), and number of shares each of the eighty was to receive when prize money was divided.[4]

Brugman was thirty years old and five feet three inches tall. His *poil* was brown. His tallest officer was five feet six inches in height; the shortest, five feet one inch. Brugman's birthplace was given as Curaçao, that of the oldest officer as Naples. The other seventy-eight males were from thirteen different ports and inland towns of France.

Shares of officers ranged from the captain's eight shares to one and a half shares. Each novice was to receive three-fourths of a share; each able seaman, one and one fourth shares; each sailor, one share; one volunteer, one and one fourth shares; each of the other nineteen volunteers, three-fourths of a share; the sixteen-year-old cabin boy, three-fourths of a share; the other four cabin boys (ranging in age from fif-

---

3. Cat. 44-2, Doc. 1, Case 25, Historic New Orleans Collection, Kemper and Leila Williams Foundation, New Orleans. Translations from the French of this manuscript and following French manuscripts are by R. Neal Nichols.

4. Cat. 44-2, Doc. 2, Case 25, Historic New Orleans Collection.

teen to thirteen), a half share each; and each supernumerary, two shares.

Before Brugman had captured enough specie and other cargo to put into the Mississippi River "in distress," the *Duc de Montebello* did so. This fourteen-gun, 150-ton schooner was originally a Baltimore merchantman that was "purchased by a Captain White" and cleared for St. Barthélemy, where its name was changed to *Amiable*. Then it "put into Savanna [sic], armed, shipped part of her crew, sailed, and received the rest from on board a vessel commanded by Captain Kuhn. She assumed off the bar of Charleston the French character and name she now wears; sailed on a cruize, robs, sinks, burns, and destroys every American, Spanish and English vessel she falls in with, until, glutted with plunder, she is compelled to put into this port [New Orleans] under pretense of distress."[5]

The *Duc de Montebello* entered the Mississippi River on March 7. Its captain, Baptiste Besson, his officers, and the crew reported that day, as their letter of marque instructed them to do, that "the want of water and the great number of damages that have been caused us by the successive pursuits of various enemy ships of war . . . oblige us to put in in consequence of the damages."[6]

Lieutenant B. F. Reed was in command at the Balize. He accepted the report and allowed the *Duc de Montebello* to proceed upriver. In New Orleans its owner, Ange Michel Brouard, "did fulfil faithfully all the formalities which the Laws of Nations and the Laws of the United States required of him by presenting to the constituted authorities the papers of said vessel and furnishing them satisfactory proofs of the necessity which compelled the said vessel to put into this Port." Then Governor Claiborne issued orders to have the vessel provisioned and repaired, after which it was to leave the river.[7]

If the *Duc de Montebello* were libeled for violation of the Nonintercourse Act and for having fitted out as a privateer in ports of the United States, the commanding officer of the U.S. Naval Station in New Orleans, Commodore David Porter, would receive one-fourth of the pro-

---

5. Quoted in Goodrich, "Our Navy and the West Indian Pirates," 1463.
6. Cat. 44-2, Doc. 16, Case 25, Historic New Orleans Collection.
7. Petition of Brouard to Joshua Lewis, in Rowland (ed.), *Claiborne Letter Books*, V, 26; Claiborne to Robert Smith, March 30, 1810, in *ibid.*, V, 24–26.

ceeds from the sale of the big 150-ton schooner and its cargo. So Commodore Porter hurried downriver to the Balize with a fleet of gunboats and arrived there on March 16. By March 20 the *Duc de Montebello* had returned from New Orleans, *L'Intrépide* had entered the Mississippi, and *L'Epine* came in a few days later.[8]

Porter took care of the *Duc de Montebello* first. At 8:00 A.M. on March 20, he sent a detachment to inspect the *Duc de Montebello*. These men "stove in ten barrels of biscuits" and tried to subvert the crew. Other detachments arrived, and Captain Besson was arrested and transferred to a bombardier while Porter's men inspected the cargo and took all papers and personal possessions. The next morning, March 21, Captain Besson and thirty-eight of his men were given a pilot boat and permission to go to New Orleans on condition that they would go ashore in the city at their own expense. Aboard the pilot boat on March 23, they prepared a protest "against all the insults directed against the French flag."[9]

Meanwhile, Beluche, alias Brugman, had disappeared. He was too clever to let Porter—who had been in command of the station at New Orleans since July, 1807, and had suffered many frustrations as smugglers and their associates outwitted him in his attempts to suppress their activities—recognize him.

Lieutenant Godefroy Bouny was in command of *L'Intrépide* when Porter began action against that vessel. Bouny, his officers, and boatswain J. B. Moran wrote a letter of protest on March 27 "aboard the said corsair presently moored in the bayou of the Lighthouse of the Mississippi River." In the protest they declared that

> Commodore Porter, who sailed in a dinghy from one of the 3 United States warships moored in the river in front of the said bayou, came at 3:00 P.M. alongside the corsaire, and resting his hand on the gunwale signified that he was seizing the said vessel, and retired. Whereupon Mr. Dussac, purser, on orders from the lieutenant commanding the corsair, landed, found the commodore in the home of the Master Pilot of the Lighthouse, told him that

---

8. Porter to Paul Hamilton, March 21, 1810, quoted in Goodrich, "Our Navy and the West Indian Pirates," 1466–67. Porter's actual rank was master commandant, but he had the courtesy title of commodore as commander of the New Orleans station. The rank of commodore was not created until 1862. John Spencer Bassett, *The Life of Andrew Jackson*, 165.

9. Cat. 44-2, Doc. 17, Case 25, Historic New Orleans Collection.

the ship which he had seized was a French corsair, and asked if war had been declared between France and the United States.

The commodore said "No" and added that he had seen the papers of the corsair, and had found them in order. Mr. Dussac, after having fulfilled his mission, returned aboard. A moment after the commodore had departed from *L'Intrépide*, an American officer from one of the warships boarded the corsair along with several armed soldiers and about 15 sailors. They undid and upset the hold, and made a most unpleasant visit and search. Then they went into the cabin where they opened all of the chests and cabinets, seized diverse papers belonging to the corsair and its officers, retained some and dispersed the others. In vain the lieutenant pointed out to them that the acts they had committed aboard bore the aspects of marked hostility. They continued their visit and took possession of the ship. In consequence Lieutenant Godefroy Bouny declared to them in the name of Captain Pierre Brugman that he protested, as we protest, against Commodore Porter and the commanders of the 3 warships, against their violation of the principles of neutrality, and the insult to the flag of the French nation of an armed force seizing a French corsair without any legitimate and previously declared motive.[10]

Porter gave the officers and crew of *L'Epine* the same rough treatment, with one variation. Six of *L'Epine*'s sailors, all free men of color, were "transported aboard a brig of the United States of America commanded by Mr. Reede, immediately following the seizure of said corsair." The free men of color were subjected to

> odious and vexatious treatment aboard the aforesaid American brig. The commanding officer of the brig in question did order them to *work* aboard the said brig; the deponents told him that they were French sailors, carried by force from a French corsair; that their belonging to a ship of France did not permit their serving aboard foreign ships, and that if they were considered prisoners of war, such service should still not be required of them; that because of this retort, the American officer became enraged and set about striking the deponents and thereupon, with all possible means of violence by said officer and by the American crew, the officer forced the deponents to obey his will . . . and to add insult to injury, the Americans constantly encouraged four English negro slaves, prisoners of the French corsair *L'Epine*, the which four negroes had been brought aboard the aforesaid brig, to insult the said deponents; that the deponents were beaten by these slaves under the eyes of the Americans.[11]

10. Cat. 44-2, Doc. 3, Case 25, Historic New Orleans Collection.
11. Cat. 44-2, Doc. 14, Case 25, Historic New Orleans Collection.

Lieutenant Reed detained these six sailors and one from the *Duc de Montebello* from April 17 until May 10, when all seven were returned to *L'Epine* at New Orleans. Two days later, on May 12, the seven appeared before Pierre François Missonet, one of the justices of the peace for the city and parish of New Orleans, and declared under oath how they had been mistreated.

With the *Duc de Montebello*, *L'Intrépide*, and *L'Epine* safely "moored to the levee under the guns of the navy," Commodore Porter proceeded to libel them for violation of the third section of the Nonintercourse Act. Later, he boasted that through his efforts "all three of the prizes were condemned and sold, and the proceeds divided among the captors, after taking out the largest share in fees to the lawyers and officers of the court, in which distribution the district attorney was not too conscientious to participate. Thus was broken up a formidable nest of pirates (for they were nothing better), through the untiring energy of a fearless officer."[12]

This boast was not entirely true. The *Duc de Montebello*, its tackle, apparel, furniture, boats, cargo, and appurtenances were forfeited to the United States. Porter's share of the spoils was $25,000, from which he paid his lawyer, Edward Livingston, 5 percent.[13] The other two vessels escaped from Porter's clutches.

The *Louisiana Gazette* reported on April 25 that *L'Intrépide* "came into our river according to custom in DISTRESS, was libeled by the District Attorney, and yesterday, the honorable Judge of the District Court ordered her to be liberated on the owners or claimants giving bond to the amount of 1500 dollars, which was done immediately—and once more the French colors are displayed at her mast head. It is presumable she will soon go to sea on a cruise and if fortunate will return again in DISTRESS. 'Hail Columbia, happy land!!!'"

The same paper reported on May 10 that *L'Epine* with her cargo "has been delivered to the claimants by order of the district attorney, by and with the consent of the collector. This appears extraordinary as she of all the Napoleon fleet of privateers that has entered our waters, is marked

---

12. David D. Porter, *Memoir of Commodore David Porter of the United States Navy* (Albany, N.Y., 1875), 80.
13. Stanley Faye, "Privateers of Guadeloupe and Their Establishment in Barataria," *Louisiana Historical Quarterly*, XXIII (1940), 437.

with the strongest proof of guilt. Among her papers were found orders to *sham distress* as soon as she should have made successful captures, and under that pretext to enter the River Mississippi."

L'Epine's captain, Marcellin Batigne, had one little affair to settle before he could sail. The owner of the ship *John* had brought suit against Batigne "for goods plundered from the *John* at sea," and laid his damages at something near one thousand dollars—the captain, rather than hazard a trial, paid six hundred dollars to get an acquittal.[14]

Meanwhile, the French consulate had prepared two crew lists for Captain Batigne. The list that Batigne showed when he left New Orleans said that *L'Epine* had a crew of fourteen French sailors from Guadeloupe. This was a reasonable number since *L'Epine* was only a fifty-two-ton "pilot built schooner." The other list, postdated June 2, said the crew included thirty-two Louisianians. *L'Epine* left New Orleans on May 29, picked up the Louisianians downriver, passed the Balize on June 3, and sailed into the Gulf to capture more prizes and return again another day with a cargo of one hundred seventy African slaves.[15] "Hail Columbia, happy land!"

Since customhouse officials refused to give clearance to *L'Intrépide*, it sailed without one on May 29, the same day *L'Epine* left New Orleans. *L'Intrépide* got safely into the Gulf and was about three hundred miles southeast of the mouth of the Mississippi when its crew spotted a ship to leeward. The privateer gave chase and captured the brig *Los Tres Hermanos* from Campeche, bound for Havana with a cargo of logwood. After examining the ship's papers and cargo, Beluche and four of his officers agreed that their prize was not worth sending to a French port. They transported its crew to *L'Intrépide* and then burned *Los Tres Hermanos*.[16]

L'Intrépide's next prize, *La Ynvicta España*, was worth keeping. It was bound from Cádiz to Vera Cruz with a cargo of iron, wine, and drygoods valued at $600,000. Beluche steered clear of the Mississippi with his prize and headed for Grande Terre, where he unloaded the cargo. Before long, New Orleans ladies rejoiced and honest merchants

---

14. New Orleans *Louisiana Gazette*, July 2, 1810.
15. Faye, "Privateers of Guadeloupe," 437–38; SFA, *Conspicuous Cases*, Book A, Cases No. 378, 379, 380, 381, 401, 402.
16. Cat. 44-2, Doc. 4, Case 25, Historic New Orleans Collection.

groaned when the price of silk stockings from Cádiz fell to nine dollars a dozen and pig iron was offered at one dollar a hundredweight on the coast.[17]

After unloading at Grande Terre, Beluche's two ships were cruising westward past the mouth of Bayou Lafourche and the islands that partially close Timbalier Bay when, on August 2, *L'Intrépide* sprang a leak. Six days later, on August 8, the vessel was moored in three fathoms of water over a bottom of shells and sand, hard on the coast of Louisiana about two leagues from Cat Island (which is today under water), when the wind began to blow with the appearance of a storm. It was hurricane season, and Beluche and some of his officers agreed that it was impossible to remain moored because of *L'Intrépide*'s state of distress. Therefore, as they later reported:

> With the intention of entering the Passage between Cat Island and Wine Island, the captain ordered the ship made ready, which was done, but the wind growing ever stronger and the sea heavier, and not being able to see the buoys which we had set up to find the entrance, we ran aground starboard of the Pass. The sea breaking from astern forward, the corsair was covered and we had five feet of water in the hold. Our first thought was to save the ship's papers and provisions necessary in an uninhabited place. The captain ordered officer Coucaréde to take the dinghy loaded with several barrels of beef and biscuit and deliver them to Cat Island, about a quarter of a league distant, and to return promptly to save the crew; the which was executed with the help of a bateaux towed by the dinghy. The same day about six hours after noon the whole crew was safe on Cat Island where we prepared the present in triplicate, the same day, month, and year as elsewhere stated.[18]

On August 8, the three-masted *Ynvicta España* had moored three leagues from Cat Island in five fathoms of water. When *L'Intrépide* sailed toward the pass, *La Ynvicta España* could not follow because it drew too much water. The crew prepared to ride out the storm, but the weather grew worse. The anchor pulled loose, and the mainmast, foremast, and rudder broke. Then, as the crew later reported: "We embarked in the longboat, in spite of our distance from land. Consequently we made for Cat Island, and after fighting for five hours against the sea

17. Faye, "Privateers of Guadeloupe," 442.
18. Cat. 44-2, Doc. 8, Case 25, Historic New Orleans Collection.

that twice swamped our longboat and put us in the greatest danger, we arrived at the said island where we found the crew of the corsair."[19]

Three days later, a Swedish schooner appeared off Cat Island. Lieutenant Bouny went aboard and invited the captain to come to the camp of those on shore. There he told Beluche and his officers that he was going to New Orleans. They asked him to take eighteen bales of drygoods that they had been able to salvage. The captain paid them $4,500 and sailed away with the bales. "Considering the state of distress in which the crew was," half of the money was immediately divided among them.

Beluche and his officers prepared a report in triplicate on August 15 which said: "We the undersigned captain, officers, and boatswain of the privateer *L'Intrépide*, camped on Cat Island since the sinking of said privateer, saw our prize *La Ynvicta España* under way at 9 A.M., being driven by the wind. We were unable to do anything to save the said prize. We did not have any boats strong enough to take to sea. Moreover, it being impossible to manoeuver a ship without a rudder, foremast, and mainmast, we recognized the futility of any effort on our part to save our prize."[20]

Cat Island had never been inhabited. Who could testify that any part of the reports prepared on Cat Island was untrue?

During the next four years, privateers in greater numbers than ever brought their prizes to Barataria—as the region comprising Grande Terre, Grand Isle, and the adjacent waterways was called. Arsène Lacarrière Latour described this heyday of smuggling:

> From all parts of Lower Louisiana people resorted to Barataria, without being at all solicitous to conceal the object of their journey. In the streets of New Orleans it was usual for traders to give and receive orders for purchasing goods at Barataria, with as little secrecy as similar orders are given for Philadelphia or New York. The most respectable inhabitants of the state, especially those living in the country, were in the habit of purchasing goods coming from Barataria. The frequent seizures made of those goods, were but an ineffectual remedy of the evil, as the great profit yielded by such parcels as escaped the vigilance of the custom-house officers, indemnified the traders for the loss of what they had paid for the goods seized; their price

19. Cat. 44-2, Doc. 9, Case 25, Historic New Orleans Collection.
20. Cat. 44-2, Doc. 12, Case 25, Historic New Orleans Collection.

being always very moderate, by the reason of the quantity of prizes brought in, and the impatience of the captors to turn them into money, and sail on a new cruise.[21]

Beluche was one of those always impatient to sail on the next cruise. He let his lawyers or others haggle about prices and get him out of legal snarls. When he sailed again, it was not as a privateer but as a properly registered shipmaster. This fact does not mean, however, that he abstained from smuggling.

Jean Blanque, owner of the next schooner on which Beluche sailed, was one of the most powerful persons in New Orleans. Governor Claiborne explained to President James Madison on March 4, 1810, that he had nominated Jean Blanque as a member of the Territorial Legislative Council because "he is a merchant in high credit. He is a man of genius and education. He possesses considerable influence in the city and vicinity of New Orleans. He is a member of the City Council, Director of the Louisiana Bank, and for the last three years a member of the House of Representatives of the Territory."[22]

The 128 61/95-ton schooner *Jenny* was registered as belonging to Jean Blanque on November 13, 1810, only three days before Beluche cleared it for Saint Domingue. Six of Beluche's eight crewmen were residents of New Orleans, one was from Charleston, and one from Baltimore. Henri Barbet, supercargo, was on board when the *Jenny* left New Orleans on November 16, 1810. Barbet's job was to dispose of the cargo, which consisted of 189 barrels of flour, two hogsheads containing 170 bearskins, eleven ostrich feathers with their boxes, thirty-six pairs of "coite" (?), twenty-four bunches of rooster feathers, thirty-two dozen inferior (feathers?), twenty-two hats, and a box containing 309 vests.[23]

---

21. Latour, *Historical Memoir*, 15.

22. Carter (comp. and ed.), *Territorial Papers*, IX, 870. Blanque had come to Louisiana in 1803 with Colonial Prefect Laussat. He lived at his villa fronting the Mississippi just below New Orleans and bought another home at 409 Royal Street when he married Marie Delphine Macarty, the widow of Don Ramón López de Angulo, on June 16, 1808. Stanley Clisby Arthur, *Old New Orleans* (New Orleans, 1966), 33, 90.

23. Place and date of building of the *Jenny* are not shown. The ship's statistics: 86' x 20'3" x 8'2"; one deck, two masts, square stern (SFA, *Ship Registers*, I, 72). See also SFA, *Crew Lists*, III, 519; testimony of Barbet, December 3, 1814, in SFA, *Conspicuous Cases*, Book B, Case No. 767.

The *Jenny*, "being unable to reach the port of Santo Domingo [*sic*], entered that of Aux Cayes where all of the flour and coite, 41 bear skins, 49 vests and all but 45 rooster feathers were sold." The remainder of the cargo was left in the care of Mr. Avignon, a merchant of Aux Cayes. Part of it was sold at Port-au-Prince for sixteen sacks of coffee weighing 1,514 pounds, seven hampers of assorted crockery, and twenty-two sacks of ginger.[24]

Beluche returned to New Orleans and canceled this voyage on January 30, 1811. Before he sailed again in the *Jenny*, it had a new owner, Peter Lauve. The *Jenny* was registered in Lauve's name on April 4, 1811; the next day it cleared for Bordeaux with eighteen crewmen listed, although when it left New Orleans only fourteen were on board. The *Jenny*'s cargo on this first run to Bordeaux may have been the $2,000,000 that Sauvinet sent to Napoleon for his Russian campaign. The money seems to have been delivered safely, since this voyage was made without incident. Beluche canceled the voyage in New Orleans on January 10, 1812.[25]

The *Jenny* sailed again for Bordeaux on March 5, 1812, with a sixteen-man crew. We know something of the cargo on this voyage from a letter that Paul Lanusse wrote to the firm of J. and J. D. Forcade in Bordeaux. In the letter, Lanusse said that he had shipped two hundred barrels of sugar in the *Jenny*, and that current prices were: "raw sugar, 7 to 7½ per ton; cotton 6½ to 7½ ditto; Campeche wood, 35 to 40$ per ton; coffee, 16 to 17 per ton." This indicated that the *Jenny* may have carried cotton, Campeche wood, and coffee as well as the sugar. Unfortunately, Lanusse lost his sugar, all of which was "destined for his mother."[26]

The British captured the *Jenny* and on May 8 "detained" it in Plymouth. Many U.S. vessels had also been captured and detained, and these actions and others caused the United States to declare war on Great Britain on June 18, 1812. That same day, "the Senate and the

---

24. Barbet testimony.
25. SFA, *Ship Registers*, I, 72; Isidro A. Beluche Mora, *Abordajes Biografica Esquemática de Renato Beluche* (Caracas, 1960), 10, 14; Isidro A. Beluche Mora, "Privateers of Cartagena," *Louisiana Historical Quarterly*, XXXIX (1956), 89; SFA, *Crew Lists*, IV, 79.
26. SFA, *Crew Lists*, IV, 280; Ms. 97, F4-106-L, Historic New Orleans Collection.

House of Representatives of the United States in Congress assembled authorized the President of the United States to issue to private armed vessels of the United States, commissions or letters of marque and general reprisal in such form as he should think proper . . . against vessels, goods and effects of the government of said United Kingdom of Great Britain and Ireland and the dependencies thereof."[27]

By virtue of this act, six United States letters of marque and general reprisal were issued in New Orleans. Stephen Debon secured one of them for his schooner *Spy* and gave Beluche command of the vessel. The *Spy* is not mentioned in the ship registers or the crew lists, and Beluche is not cited in either of these sources after March 5, 1812.

On November 20, 1812, Debon lodged a formal protest against Beluche before Notary Stephen de Quiñones. In the protest, Debon declared that he was the owner of the corsair *Spy* and that it had cleared port with all the requisite formalities. Moreover, Debon charged that Beluche had taken a prize and unloaded its merchandise at Barataria against the orders and instructions that he had given Beluche not to contravene in any way the laws of the United States.[28]

Beluche may have sent more than one prize to Barataria before Debon lodged his protest. However, after Beluche captured the 332-ton *Jane*, laden with mahogany and logwood from British Honduras, he sent this prize to New Orleans. The *Louisiana Gazette* of Thursday, January 14, 1813, reported: "The ship Jane of Grenock [*sic*], Scotland, 12 guns and 12 men, prize to the Privateer schooner Spy, of this port, came up to the city on Tuesday evening last. She is a handsome new ship, and is the first valuable prize that has been brought into this port. Her cargo is mahogany and logwood (35 to 40$ per ton). She was taken a few leagues to the windward of Cape Antonio, on her return voyage from the Bay of Honduras." Tuesday, the day the *Jane* arrived in New Orleans, was January 12. John R. Grymes, "as lawful proctor of Rene Beluche," had libeled the *Jane* the day before, Monday, January

---

27. New Orleans *Louisiana Gazette*, July 21, 1812; SFA, *Conspicuous Cases*, Book B, Case No. 552.
28. Notarial Records of S. de Quiñones, XIII, 1811–12, No. 667 in Notarial Records of Orleans Parish, Louisiana State Archives, Baton Rouge. Quiñones served as notary from 1805 to 1815.

11, as a prize for and in behalf of Beluche, his crew and all others interested.[29]

George Milne, a British subject and master of the *Jane*, testified on January 22, 1813, that Messrs. Rogers Steward and Sons, natives of north Britain residing near Greenock, were the owners of the *Jane* at the time of its capture; that they were insured for the passage from British Honduras to Greenock; that "the whole of the said cargo of mahogany and logwood was taken on board from the shore at Honduras in the month of August and September last"; and that Beluche captured the vessel on November 17. In answer to interrogatories, Milne said that he did not know whether any bill of sale was made to the owners; that all the cargo was put on board at the port of Honduras; that none of the *Jane*'s papers were destroyed, canceled, or concealed by anyone on board; that he had sustained a small loss by the capture, which he estimated to be $45; that the hull was not broken during the voyage in which he was taken, but that it was broken by the captors after arriving at the Balize "for the purpose of lightening the vessel in order to get her over the bar" and into the Mississippi River.[30]

Dominick Augustine Hall, judge of the U.S. District Court for Louisiana, pronounced his verdict on February 1, twenty days after Grymes had libeled the *Jane*, its tackle, apparel and furniture, guns, and cargo, for Beluche, his crew, and all others interested. Judge Hall's verdict was that "the said ship *Jane*, her tackle, apparel and furniture, guns and cargo, be adjudged and condemned as good and lawful prize to the said Reyne Beluche, commander of the said private armed schooner *Spy*, by my definitive sentence or final decree which I read and promulge by these present."[31]

Beluche was not present. He had sent the *Jane* to New Orleans; he himself had sailed southeast across the Caribbean to Cartagena on the north coast of South America. Beluche published a pamphlet later in which he tells us that he had begun to serve in the Cartagenan navy in

---

29. Beluche was the only one of the six privateers with commissions issued at New Orleans who sent a prize to that city (Edgar Stanton Maclay, *A History of American Privateers* [New York, 1899], 322); SFA, *Conspicuous Cases*, Book B, Case No. 552.
30. SFA, *Conspicuous Cases*, Book B, Case No. 552.
31. Ibid.

1812.[32] The prize that Beluche had sent to Barataria—the one that caused Debon to make a formal protest against him—must have been captured under a Cartagenan letter of marque and reprisal against the ships of Spain. It was not unusual for privateers to sail with more than one commission. Since the United States was at peace with Spain, if Beluche had sent that prize to New Orleans, officials there would have confiscated it.

Beluche's capture of the *Jane* demonstrates that the *Spy* was a good schooner, fast and easily maneuvered. The *Spy* disappears from records after November 17, 1812 (except for Beluche's libel against the *Jane*, which was still pending), and the schooner *La Popa*, very much like the *Spy*, takes its place.[33] Beluche named this vessel for the highest hill behind Cartagena, a landmark that can be seen far out at sea.

---

32. Renato Beluche, *Contesta a las falsas imputaciones con que had intentado manchar su honor el Sr. general de la misma José Padilla en las notas que contiene el papel intitulado "Al Mundo Imparcial"* (Caracas, 1824), 3.

33. Renato Beluche, Hoja de Servicio, in Secretaria de Guerra y Marina, Papeles Sin Clasificación, Archivo Nacional de Colombia, Bogotá.

CHAPTER 5

Privateer for Cartagena

The city of Cartagena faces Panamá on a north-south part of the Caribbean coast in the present state of Colombia. After Francis Drake looted Cartagena in 1586, the Italian engineer Juan Bautista Antonelli planned the military architecture that converted Cartagena into the most strongly fortified city in the Western Hemisphere. Its purpose was to protect the approaches to Panamá and thus keep the Pacific a Spanish lake.[1] This fortified bastion was a parasite and could not support itself. Money from the viceroy at Bogotá maintained Cartagena's garrison and navy, while grain from the neighboring savannas of the Rio Sinú and meat from other valleys fed its inhabitants.

Cartagena, capital of the Province of Cartagena, was eighty miles southwest of the mouth of the Magdalena River. Santa Marta, capital of the Province of Santa Marta, was fifty miles east of the Magdalena's mouth. The lower Magdalena was the boundary between the two provinces, which were part of the Viceroyalty of New Granada, the capital of which was Bogotá. The main highway between the coast and Bogotá began at Barranquilla, the Magdalena's port city.

Cartagena expelled its royal governor in June, 1810. Two months later, Bogotá sent the viceroy down the Magdalena to be shipped to Spain. Then these two cities vied with each other to dominate the twenty-two provinces of New Granada. The Bogotá junta called itself "supreme" and wanted to control a centralized government. The junta of Cartagena championed a federation of states and tried to force royal-

---

1. Enrique Marco Dorta, *Cartagena de Indias: La ciudad y sus monumentos* (Seville, 1951), 9.

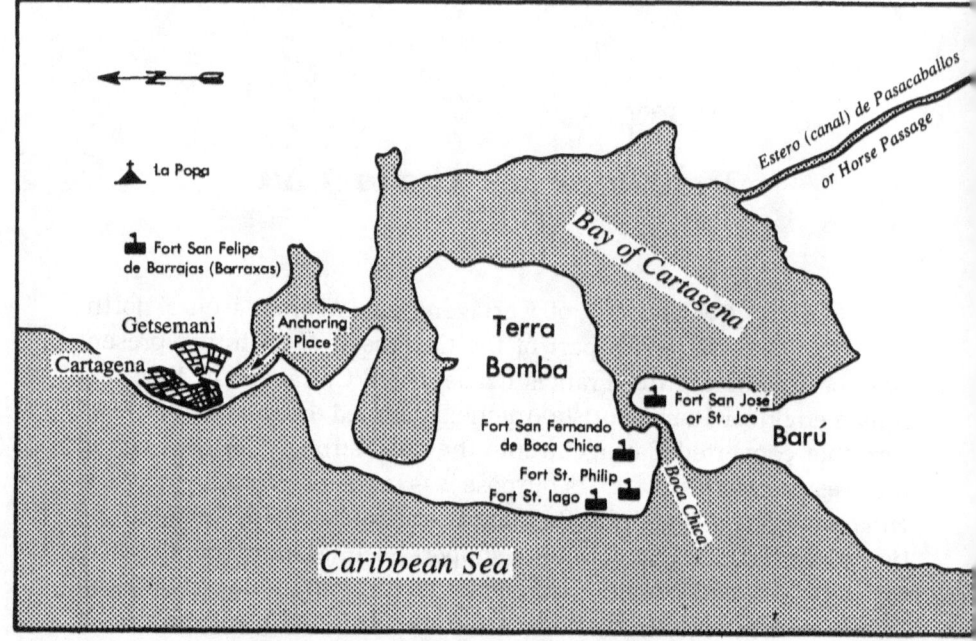

Cartagena

ist Santa Marta into the union by establishing a customhouse at Barranca on the west bank of the river to collect duties as though Santa Marta were a foreign nation.

Santa Marta retaliated and established a customhouse at Tenerife on the east bank of the Magdalena, fortified several towns along the river, and cut all Cartagena's communications with the interior. At the same time, royalist Panamá abetted an uprising against Cartagena in its territory along the Rio Sinú. The result was that Cartagena's food and money supply lines were cut. This would have been fatal if the city had not found a solution to its isolation.

On November 11, 1811, the Cartagena junta declared the independence of the Province of Cartagena. Soon thereafter, the president, Manuel Rodríguez Toríces, solved the supply problem by making Cartagena a privateer base and issuing letters of marque at a time when no other bases were available in the Caribbean. England had captured the French bases, and French letters of marque had not been valid for the past six months. Smugglers and French privateers hastened to Cartagena for licenses to prey on Spanish shipping. They sent many prizes with food, money, and war matériel to Cartagena, but they also sent many to Smugglers' Anchorage at Grande Terre and to other anchorages on the Louisiana coast.

Cartagena was not the first province on the Spanish Main to throw out its royal governor and declare its independence. On Holy Thursday, April 19, 1810, patriots in Caracas had shipped the captain-general and other officials to the United States and established a junta to rule in the name of Ferdinand, heir to the throne of Spain and Napoleon's prisoner. The junta then sent agents to invite the other provinces of the Captaincy General of Venezuela to follow the example of Caracas. The provinces of Maracaibo, Coro, and Guayana refused to join the patriots, but seven provinces did join them: Mérida, Trujillo, Barinas, Barcelona, Cumaná, and the island of Margarita. The seven stars on Venezuela's flag today represent those seven provinces. They elected delegates to a congress in Caracas that, on July 5, 1811, declared the independence of the Republic of Venezuela.

Most of the patriot leaders had military titles; but these represented authority and privilege, not skill in military science, because Spain did not want its colonial aristocrats to acquire military expertise. Moreover, no weapons or ammunition were manufactured in Venezuela. Before the revolution began, the captain-general had depended on France, Spain's ally, to send officers and troops from its Caribbean islands in time of crisis, and many French officers and troops had come between 1803 and 1810 as refugees from the French islands that England captured during those years.

By March of 1812, the patriots were losing their bases on the Orinoco River, and a royalist operation that had begun on the coast at Coro was gaining momentum when, on Holy Thursday, March 26, 1812, an earthquake zigzagged through the heart of patriot-held territory. Frightened survivors and troops deserted to the royalists, and the Republic of Venezuela collapsed at the end of July.

Pierre Labatut was one of the first French officers who escaped to Cartagena. He was commander-in-chief of Cartagena's Magdalena front against Santa Marta when Simón Bolívar, a Venezuelan aristocrat who was two and a half years younger than Beluche, arrived. Labatut sent Bolívar with seventy men to guard Barranca, Cartagena's base on the left bank of the Magdalena.

At Barranca, Bolívar enlisted two hundred men, mostly teenagers, and moved south to Tenerife on the right bank of the Magdalena. On December 24, 1812, when the royalists saw Bolívar on the edge of town, they were so surprised that they fled toward the coast, leaving behind their boats and military supplies. Thus Bolívar, who had no training in military science, established the pattern of his strategy: move quickly; surprise the enemy; get war matériel from him; and recruit en route, especially from the enemy.

Bolívar continued to move up the river and in fifteen days had opened the Magdalena to navigation. He also opened a corridor to Cúcuta, and beyond Cúcuta lay the natural entry route through the mountains to Venezuela. Bolívar's force left Cúcuta on May 14, 1813, and grew as he advanced through Mérida, Trujillo, Guanare, and Barinas. As he approached Valencia, the royalists fled to Puerto Cabello, leaving behind cannon, munitions, food, and a considerable number of horses. Bolívar was in Caracas by August 6, and two days later he reestablished the Republic of Venezuela, although the area of that republic was limited to the invasion route by which he had come.

Meanwhile, in Cartagena at least one native son, Rafael Tono, and enough privateers were present to transport Labatut and his troops to Santa Marta by way of the Ciénaga, a lake formed by one mouth of the Magdalena as it enters the sea. This back-door approach caused the royalist governor and officers to panic. Without firing a shot they embarked for Portobelo, Panamá's eastern port.[2]

That night, January 6, 1813, Labatut wrote a letter to President Rodríguez Toríces in which he reported that the royalists had burned their depot and spiked their guns before fleeing to their warships and transports loaded with wealth and jewels, even those of the cathedral. At the end of the letter, he chided the president for letting this wealth

---

2. Francisco Alejandro Vargas, *Nuestros Próceres Navales* (Caracas, 1964), 217; Kingston (Jamaica) *Royal Gazette*, March 8–13, 1813.

escape. Labatut wrote, "If the ships you offered me had been ready, I could have enriched the State by two million pesos."[3]

All Labatut could think about was wealth. With Cartagena's paper money, which Santa Martans detested, he was the first to buy the confiscated property of royalists who had fled. He acted like a dictator, imprisoning many whose support he could have had if he had not been obsessed with the desire for quick riches, and failed to see that a rebellion was growing against him and that Santa Martans wanted to return to royalist control. He was still collecting loot when a Spanish sloop of war was sighted on February 8. Tono ordered the Spanish flag raised over the fort, so the captain of the sloop of war *Indagadora* entered the port without taking any precautions. He was forced to surrender, and Tono took command of the *Indagadora*.[4]

Labatut could have crushed the royalists, but he thought only of escaping to Cartagena with his loot. He abandoned his garrison and 1,200 muskets that he had brought when he entered the city.[5]

President Rodríguez Toríces was anxious to retake Santa Marta before reinforcements arrived there from Cuba. Fortunately, Beluche and other privateers had brought into port four schooners carrying troops, arms, and munitions that they had captured soon after the schooners left Portobelo for Santa Marta. Rodríguez Toríces rounded up nearly a thousand troops, gave the French officer Luis Fernando Chatillon command of them, and went with the expedition "to give promptly those orders which circumstances might demand."

The expedition embarked on one brig, two schooners (one of which was Beluche's), and some smaller vessels. On May 10 the first attempt to land troops on the beach near San Juan de la Ciénaga was unsuccessful. That night, royalist lieutenant Tomás Pacheco prepared an ambush on the outskirts of San Juan. He hid six hundred Indians armed with machetes in the brush and placed two cannon on each side of the road. Chatillon debarked in the early morning and moved

---

3. Manuel Ezequiel Corráles (ed.), *Documentos para la historia de la Provincia de Cartagena* (2 vols.; Bogotá, 1883), I, 556.
4. *Ibid.*
5. José Manuel Restrepo, *Historia de la Revolución de la República de Colombia en la América Meridional* (5 vols.; Besanzon, 1858), I, 204–206.

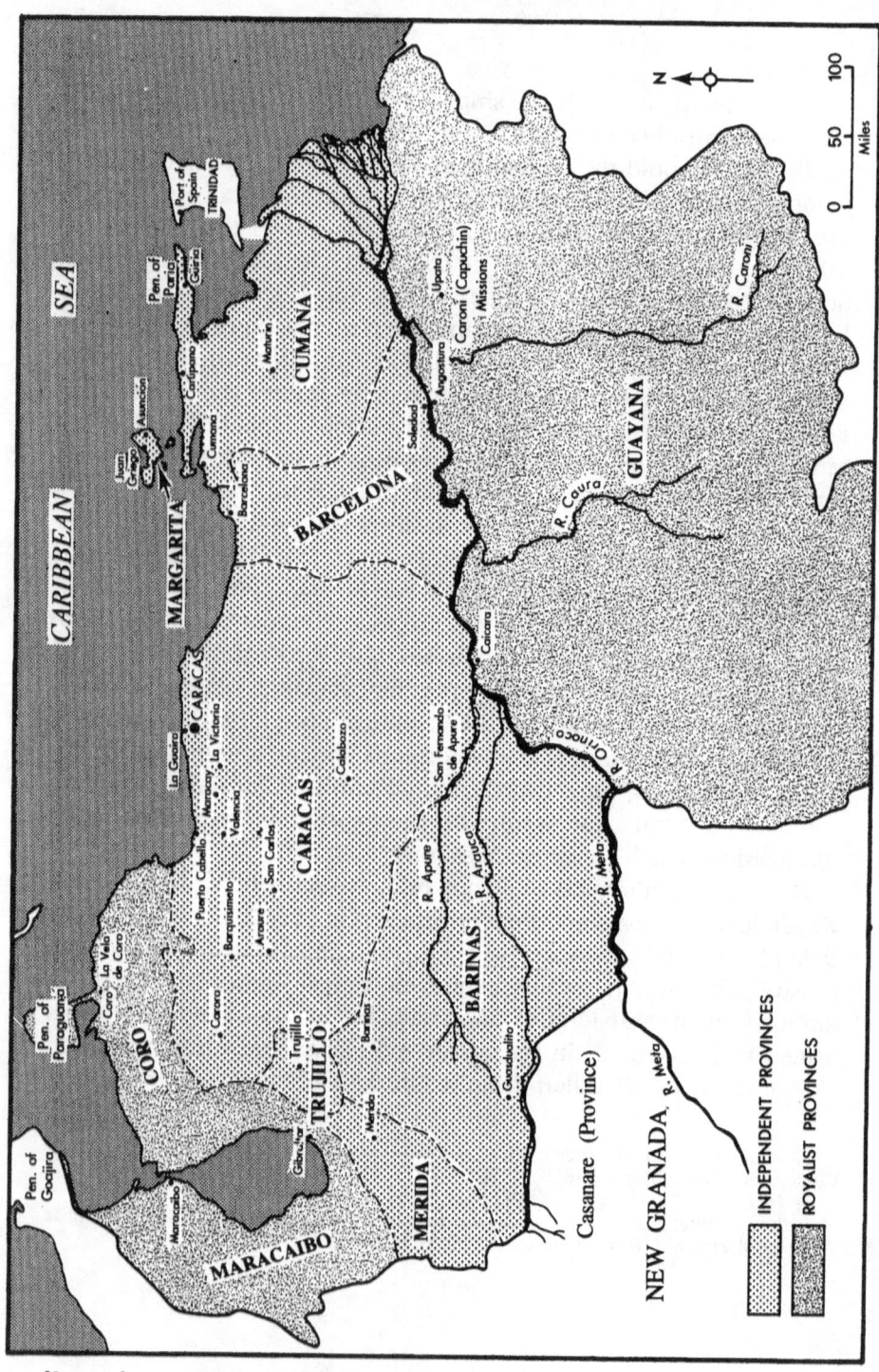

Venezuela's Confederation of Independent Provinces, 1810

toward the town. Pacheco met him with sixty musketmen and 160 men armed with machetes. When Chatillon opened fire, Pacheco's cannon responded. A shot from one of them fell on Chatillon's powder box, which exploded and killed Chatillon and some of his troops. Indians slaughtered the rest.[6]

Royalists fired on the privateers, but Beluche returned their fire and protected the squadron as it sailed back to Cartagena with Rodríguez Toríces and the remnant of the expedition. For this service Beluche was rewarded with the rank of lieutenant in Cartagena's navy.[7]

Rodríguez Toríces let Labatut command a third expedition in August knowing that resistance at Santa Marta would be much stronger because Field Marshal Francisco Montalvo had arrived there with reinforcements. Moreover, privateers were bringing so much loot to Cartagena, including hard money taken from Spanish prizes, that the president did not want to leave that prosperous city.

A fleet of privateers, including Beluche, transported this expedition. Eighteen privateers made a thrust at the Morro of Santa Marta while the rest of the privateers carried troops across the Ciénaga for a land attack. Spanish fire prevented their landing. The next day, August 15, 1813, Labatut tried again to land troops, but the fire of the royalists was so heavy that he ordered the expedition to return to Cartagena. There Labatut was dismissed and expelled to the Antilles.[8]

By this time Beluche had a second schooner to enroll in the service of Cartagena.[9] He named it the *Piñérez* for the Piñérez brothers—Gabriel the vice-president of Cartagena, and his brother Vicente—who favored the privateers in every way they could. For instance, they opposed the heavy duties that Rodríguez Toríces had levied on prize merchandise. Charles Lominé, a French privateer who had been operating out of Savannah and Charleston, usually commanded the *Piñérez* for Beluche.

On October 2, 1813, Beluche, commanding *La Popa*, and Lominé, commanding the *Piñérez*, captured the 1020-ton merchantman *La Ca-*

6. Mariano Torrente, *Historia de la Revolución Hispano-Americana* (3 vols.; Madrid, 1829), I, 399–400.
7. Beluche's Hoja de Servicio; Beluche, *Contesta a las falsas imputaciones*, 3.
8. Restrepo, *Historia de la Revolución de Colombia*, I, 224–25.
9. Beluche's Hoja de Servicio.

ridad, alias *La Cubana*. *La Caridad* belonged to Christobal Iuando, a Spanish subject and an inhabitant of Sántiago in Cuba. Iuando later testified in the federal district court of New Orleans that *La Caridad*, while on a voyage from New Haven to Cuba, "loaded with provisions and pursuing a lawful commerce on the high seas and in view of the said island, near Punta de Maisy [on the eastern tip of Cuba where ships enter the Windward Passage to get to Santiago], was pursued by two vessels of a hostile and piratical character which on getting within range of cannon shot fired upon her, first hoisting American colors and afterwards a strange flag, and as the claimant believes, the flag of the insurgents of Cartagena." Iuando further testified that the captor, or others, converted *La Caridad* into a sea rover on the high seas, "frequenting the inlet or harbor of Barataria in the State or district of Louisiana in the United States of America, and was for a while called the *Atalanta*, that afterwards she was and is now called by the name of *General Bolívar*."[10]

Beluche took his prize to Cartagena, enrolled it in the service of that nation under the name *General Bolívar*, and gave its command to Joseph Clement. The ship needed repairs, so its first destination was New Orleans. Beluche's instructions to Clement, dated Cartagena, March 3, 1814, said: "As soon as you arrive in New Orleans you will call upon Mr. [Joseph] Carpentier who will advance you the necessary funds to repair the Privateer which work you will speed up with all possible diligence and put back to sea and hurry back to Cartagena."[11]

---

10. SFA, *Conspicuous Cases*, Book B, Case No. 760.
11. *Ibid*.

The author and her escort on Taboga, August 5, 1954, in front of the house of Isidro Beluche's father.

The author and Semíramis Beluche on the site of Renato Beluche's home on Taboga.

Site of the house where Renato Beluche lived on Taboga.

The author with Beluche descendants at a banquet in Panama, August 5, 1954. *Clockwise, from extreme right:* Jack de Grummond, Emma M. de Suárez, Benito Suárez, Raquel de Beluche, Isidro Beluche Mora, Waldo A. Suárez, Semíramis Beluche, Dais Sandoval, Ramona H. de Beluche, Buenaventura Antonio Beluche, the author, Pablo Enrique Beluche, Rita H. de Beluche.

The author at a reunion of Beluche descendants in Caracas, April 25, 1955. *Left to right:* José Antonio Olavarría y Braun, María Enriqueta Altuna Cabrera, the author, Oscar Ruíz Beluche, Enriqueta Martínez Olavarría, Marisa Nava Dominguez Olavarría.

Renato Beluche, wearing the Estrella de Libertadores.
Courtesy La Galería de los Próceres, Caracas

Beluche family plot in Rancho Grande Cemetery, Puerto Cabello.

CHAPTER 6

Patterson and the Baratarians

During the spring and summer of 1814, Beluche in *La Popa*, Clement in Beluche's *General Bolívar*, and Lominé in Beluche's *Piñérez* continued to sail as privateers of Cartagena. Some of their prizes they sent to Grande Terre and some to Cartagena. In Europe, Napoleon's empire had collapsed; he abdicated in April, and France and England were at peace. This meant that veteran British troops were released for an all-out effort against the United States.

Vice-Admiral Sir Alexander Cochrane, commander of the British North American Naval Station, maintained the blockade of the Atlantic Coast and the mouth of the Mississippi River while waiting for reinforcements to arrive at Bermuda. The grand strategy for the last half of 1814 was to increase the harassment of the Chesapeake Bay area during August, September, and October so that there could be no build-up of military strength in Louisiana; in November, when the hurricane season was over, the greatest amphibious force England had ever sent to America would concentrate at Negril Bay on the west coast of Jamaica, and in December, this force would take New Orleans.

Because of the British blockade, warehouses in New Orleans were full of cotton, flour, pork, cordage, hempen yarn, cotton bagging, whiskey, and other produce of the lower Mississippi Valley. The 32,000,000 pounds of cotton alone would be worth over $14,000,000 in England;[1] the food would feed all the British West Indies, which had never been able to feed themselves; and possession of New Orleans, key to the Mississippi Valley, would unite Canada with the Gulf of Mexico.

Great Britain had never recognized the Louisiana Purchase as legiti-

1. *Niles' Weekly Register* (Baltimore), VII (February 18, 1815), 390, and VIII (April 15, 1815), 113–14.

mate, and in August its peace commissioners at Ghent in Belgium made demands that stunned the United States commissioners. One demand was based on the principle of *uti possidetis*—that is, keep what you have according to the war map at the time of negotiation, and get as much more as possible. The United States commissioners did not know that before long the British expected to be in possession of New Orleans "in order to insure us the enjoyment of our privileges to navigate the Mississippi."[2]

While waiting at Bermuda for troops from England, Cochrane sent Captain Hugh Pigot in the *Orpheus* to contact Creek refugees in Florida, who had fled there after Major General Andrew Jackson had broken the power of the Creek nation. Pigot anchored the *Orpheus* at the mouth of the Apalachicola River on May 10. During the next two weeks, he made allies of the Creeks and Choctaws and arranged for their instruction in the use of the bayonet. Pigot then reported to Cochrane that 2,800 Creek warriors were ready to fight with the British. They could move overland with these allies from Pensacola to Baton Rouge, capture it, then descend on New Orleans.[3]

Apalachicola was too small a base from which to operate. Pensacola was much larger and had the best harbor on the whole Gulf Coast. Cochrane's next move was, therefore, to send Major Edward Nicholls with marines to organize and train Indians at Pensacola and, at the same time, to discover how vulnerable New Orleans might be.

Captain Henry Percy's squadron transported Nicholls, a surgeon, fourteen officers, and ninety-seven marines to Pensacola. The Spanish governor, Mateo Gonzalez Manrique, made no resistance as Nicholls and his marines occupied the forts. The British were well supplied with guns, ammunition, and food—items that were scarce in Spanish Pensacola.

Mobile, sixty miles west of Pensacola, was headquarters for Military

---

2. Samuel Flagg Bemis, *John Quincy Adams and the Foundations of American Foreign Policy* (New York, 1949), 198; Frank Lawrence Owsley, Jr., *Struggle for the Gulf Border-lands: The Creek War and the Battle of New Orleans 1812–1815* (Gainesville, Fla., 1981), 178–80, 192–93; a London pamphlet entitled "Compendious view of the points to be discussed in treating with the United States," quoted in *Niles' Weekly Register*, VII (December 10, 1814), 218.
3. John K. Mahon, *The War of 1812* (Gainesville, Fla., 1972), 341–47.

District No. 7 of the United States. This district included Louisiana, the Mississippi Territory, Tennessee, and part of Georgia. The command of Military District No. 7 had been given to Andrew Jackson as he was ending the Creek War. After signing a treaty with the Creeks on August 9, Jackson headed for Mobile. He arrived there on August 15 and found that Fort Bowyer, thirty miles across the bay, had been abandoned. If the British got past Fort Bowyer at the tip of the narrow peninsula that almost closes Mobile Bay from the Gulf, they could penetrate via the Alabama and Tombigbee river systems for hundreds of miles into the United States.

Jackson sent Major William Lawrence with 160 men to repair and hold the fort. While they did so, some of Cochrane's forces were burning Washington, the capital of the United States; and Captain Percy landed Nicholls and his marines at Pensacola. Jackson did not know until August 27 that Nicholls and Percy were there. He immediately wrote to Governor William Blount of the Mississippi Territory, reporting the British presence at Pensacola and requesting that he "cause to be organized, equipped, and brought into the field without delay, the whole quota of Militia of your State."[4]

Two months passed before Jackson had enough militiamen to drive the British from Florida. Meanwhile, Nicholls and Percy sent a mission to Jean Laffite, leader of the Baratarians. The British needed command of the bay and bayou approaches through Barataria to New Orleans, and they needed the Baratarians, their knowledge of the terrain, their skill in operating vessels, and the use of their small craft to help land invasion troops from transports. This help is what Nicholls, "Commander of his Britanic Majesty's forces in the Floridas," wanted and expected to get when he wrote to Laffite on August 31, 1814: "I call on you, with your brave followers, to enter into the service of Great Britain, in which you shall have the rank of captain; lands will be given to you all, in proportion to your respective ranks, on a peace taking place."[5] Percy, "captain of his majesty's ship *Hermes*, and senior officer in the Gulf of Mexico," also wrote a letter to Laffite. It was an ultimatum and said that if Laffite and the Baratarians did not accept Ni-

4. Bassett (ed.), *Correspondence of Andrew Jackson*, II, 34.
5. Latour, *Historical Memoir*, vii–x.

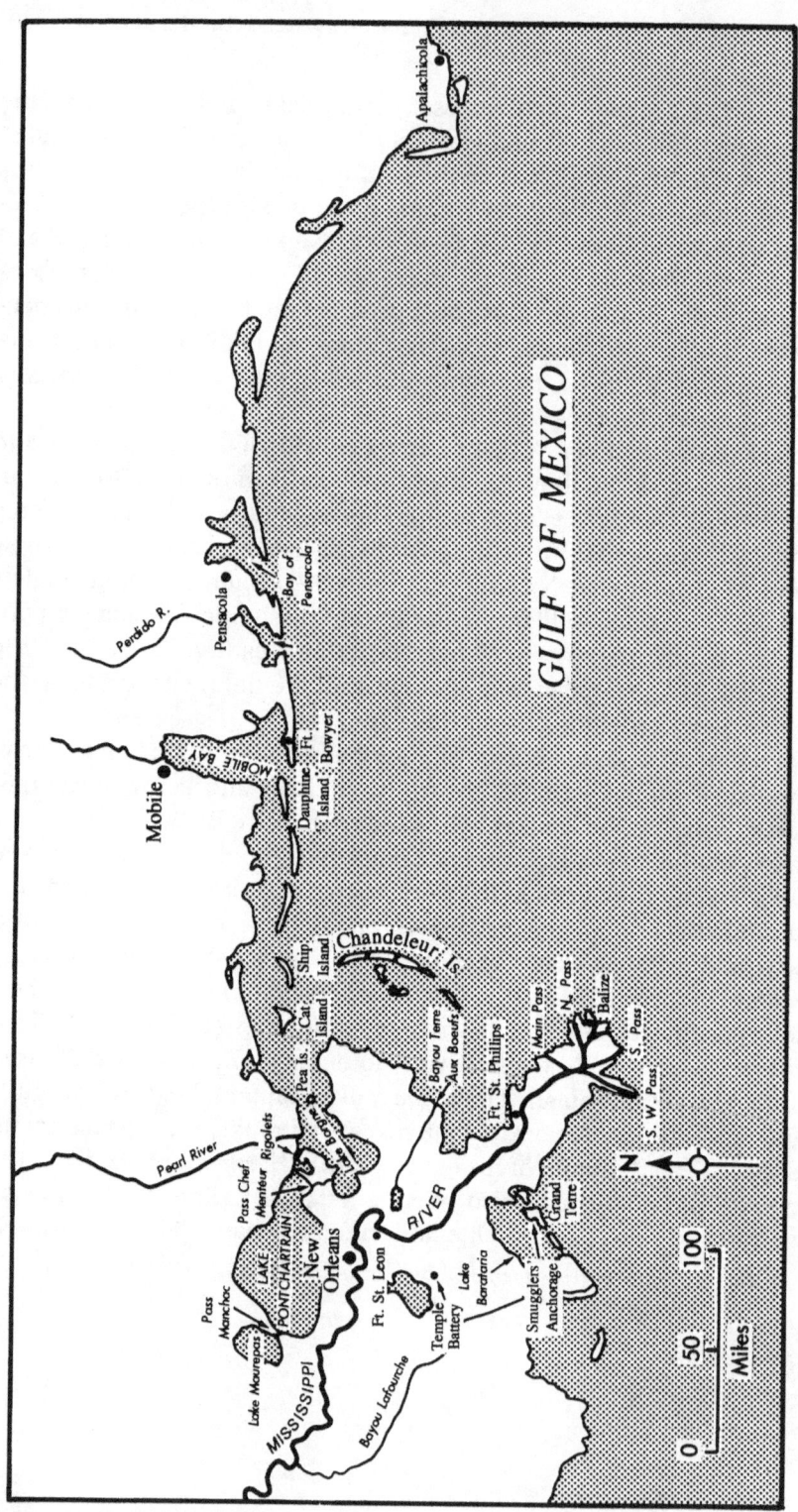

Theater of British Invasion of Louisiana and the Gulf Coast

cholls' offer, the British would completely destroy Barataria and all their vessels.

Nicholls and Percy dispatched Captain Nicholas Lockyer and "a captain M'Williams" in the sloop *Sophia* to deliver the letters and the proclamation to Laffite. They were directed to waste no time at Barataria but to return immediately after delivering the messages and take part in the capture of Fort Bowyer and Mobile.

The *Sophia* entered Barataria Pass on September 3, fired a gun at a vessel about to enter, and caused it to ground. The *Sophia* then anchored, and Lockyer and M'Williams got in a small boat and rowed toward Smugglers' Anchorage, flying the British flag and a flag of truce. Jean Laffite rowed out to meet them but did not make known his identity until both boats had reached shore. A threatening crowd of Baratarians watched every move. Laffite detained the two men until the next day, then had them escorted to the *Sophia* with a letter to Lockyer that said: "The confusion which prevailed in our camp yesterday and this morning has prevented me from answering in a precise manner to the object of your mission. If you could grant me a fortnight, I would be entirely at your disposal at the end of that time."[6]

The *Sophia* was barely outside the pass and headed for Pensacola when Jean Laffite wrote a letter to Jean Blanque in New Orleans. Beluche and other Baratarians sailed Blanque's ships, and his judgment and influence were respected by everyone in New Orleans, including Governor Claiborne. The letter was dated "Barataria, 4th September, 1814," and said:

> Though proscribed by my adoptive country, I will never let slip any occasion of serving her, or of proving that she has never ceased to be dear to me. Of this you will here see a convincing proof. Yesterday, the 3d of September, there appeared here, under a flag of truce, a boat coming from an English brig, at anchor about two leagues from the pass. Mr. Nicholas Lockyer, a British officer of high rank, delivered me the following papers, two directed to me, a proclamation, and the admiral's instructions to that officer, all herewith enclosed. . . . I make you the depository of the secret on which perhaps depends the tranquility of our country; please to make use of it as your judgment may direct.[7]

6. *Ibid.*, xi–xii.
7. *Ibid.*, xii–xiii.

At the end of this letter Laffite said that he had asked the British envoys to return in fifteen days for his answer but that he hoped to hear from Jean Blanque before they came.

Then Laffite wrote another letter, this one to Governor Claiborne. He made a packet of the two letters and the British correspondence and gave the packet to Raymond Ranchier to deliver to Jean Blanque. Ranchier traveled by "courier pirogue" across Barataria Bay, up the bayous, and through the canal to the Mississippi and New Orleans. Travel time via this route was usually three days, but Ranchier may have delivered the packet to Jean Blanque in less time than that. Blanque read the communiqués, then took the packet to Governor Claiborne. The governor opened his letter and read:

> In the firm persuasion that the choice made of you to fill the office of first magistrate of this state, was dictated by the esteem of your fellow-citizens, and was conferred on merit, I confidently address you on an affair on which may depend the safety of this country.
>
> I offer to you to restore to this state several citizens, who perhaps in your eyes have lost that sacred title. I offer you them . . . ready to exert their utmost efforts in defense of this country. This point of Louisiana, which I occupy, is of great importance in the present crisis. I tender my services to defend it; and the only reward I ask is that a stop be put to the proscription against me and my adherents, by an act of oblivion for all that has been done hitherto . . . Should your answer not be favourable to my ardent desires, I declare to you that I will instantly leave the country, to avoid the imputation of having cooperated towards an invasion on this point.[8]

Claiborne was in a dilemma. The secretary of the navy had sent Commodore Patterson to disperse the Baratarians. This mission meant that their base at Barataria had to be destroyed. The U.S.S. *Carolina* had arrived on August 10 to join gunboats in this destruction, and the War Department had ordered Colonel George T. Ross, infantry commander in New Orleans, to cooperate with Patterson. This amphibious expedition was almost ready to sail against Barataria.

The governor wanted to stop the expedition and accept the offer of the Baratarians, in part because of his wife Susana[9] (Beluche's

---

8. *Ibid.*, xiii–xv.

9. Clarisse Duralde, Claiborne's second wife, died of yellow fever on November 29, 1809. Claiborne and Susana Bosque were married on November 8, 1812, when Susana

cousin). Susana and Beluche may both have been related to the Laffites through the Laporte family, and there were many ties between their families and the other Baratarians.

Claiborne had no authority over federal officials, however, because he was no longer the federal governor of a territory. Louisiana had been admitted to the United States as the eighteenth state on April 8, 1812, and soon thereafter Louisiana voters had elected Claiborne governor. As a state governor he could not order Patterson and Ross, who were acting under federal authority, to stop their preparations against the Baratarians, but perhaps he could get their cooperation. He invited them to attend a meeting of the principal officers of the navy and militia in the hope that the dilemma could be resolved.

General Jacques Villeré, commander of the Louisiana militia, was present at that meeting. Claiborne presided, and after reading aloud the Laffite correspondence, he asked two questions: Are the letters genuine? Is it proper for the governor to enter into any correspondence with Laffite and his associates?[10] Only General Villeré spoke in favor of the Baratarians, arguing that the governor should accept their offer. The rest voted that the governor should have no dealings with them. Nevertheless, Claiborne did send copies of the letters and of Nicholls' proclamation to Andrew Jackson at Mobile, while the Patterson-Ross expedition proceeded as the secretaries of the navy and war had ordered.

Ranchier, Villeré, and Susana may have conferred before Ranchier reported to Jean Laffite at Grande Terre that Patterson was coming. Jean left Dominique You in command at Grande Terre while he and Pierre disappeared on the German Coast along the Mississippi above New Orleans.

Patterson, Ross, and seventy men of the 44th Infantry Regiment boarded the *Carolina* on September 11 and sailed downriver. The *Carolina* "formed a junction" with six gun vessels and the tender *Sea*

---

was sixteen years old. Act 494, Funerals Book 1803–15, p. 100b, Act 337, Marriage Book 3, 1806–21, p. 117b, both in St. Louis Cathedral Archives; Jane Lucas De Grummond, "Cayetana Susana Bosque Y Fanqui, 'A Notable Woman,'" *Louisiana History*, XXIII (1982), 277–294.

10. Latour, *Historical Memoir*, 253.

Horse at the Balize on September 13, and this fleet sailed out of Southwest Pass on the evening of September 15. At half-past eight o'clock the next morning, it was at Grande Terre. Patterson reported that an hour later "he perceived the pirates forming their vessels, ten in number, including prizes, into a line of battle near the entrance of the harbor, and making every preparation to offer me battle."[11]

He was mistaken. Dominique You thought at first that the British had returned to carry out Percy's ultimatum; but, as Patterson's gunboats and his tender *Sea Horse* formed in battle order (the *Carolina* was anchored outside the pass because it drew too much water to enter the bay), Dominique knew that he was confronting vessels of the U.S. Navy and refused to fight. This did not mean that all the Baratarians intended to surrender.

Several hundred of them—Patterson estimated between eight hundred and a thousand men—abandoned their vessels and rowed away in small boats. Patterson sent his launch, two gun vessels, and some small boats in pursuit, but the fleeing Baratarians escaped. Those who remained with Dominique did not try to get away and made no resistance as they were captured.

Patterson reported that at noon he took possession of all their vessels in the harbor, "consisting of six schooners and one felucca, cruizers and prizes of the pirates, one brig, a prize, and two armed schooners under the Carthagenian flag [one of these was Beluche's *La Popa*], both in line of battle, with armed vessels of the pirates, and apparently with an intention to aid them in any resistance they might make against me. Colonel Ross at the same time landed, and with his command took possession of their establishment on shore."[12]

Patterson and Ross took Dominique You and eighty Baratarians prisoner and spent one week loading all the loot stored on Grande Terre. During that week, on September 20, the *Carolina* made the signal of "a strange sail in sight to the eastward." It was Beluche's privateer, the *General Bolívar*, with Joseph Clement commanding. The *Carolina* weighed anchor and made chase. The two vessels fired at each other

---

11. Goodrich, "Our Navy and the West Indian Pirates," 1470.
12. *Ibid.*, 1471.

during the chase, and gunboats opened fire across the island on the *General Bolívar*. After two hours the privateer grounded and hauled down its colors. The next day Patterson sent out a small prize schooner to remove the *General Bolívar*'s armament: "one long brass 18 pounder, one long brass 6 pounder, two 12 pound carronades, some arms, etc., and twenty-one packages of dry goods."[13]

On the afternoon of September 23, Patterson left Grande Terre with the whole squadron, "in all seventeen vessels—but during the night one schooner under Carthagenian colors escaped." This had to be *La Popa*, for Nolte tells us that Beluche escaped to reappear later when needed.[14]

Patterson's squadron, minus one Carthagenian privateer, entered Southwest Pass on September 24 and spent seven days ascending the Mississippi River to New Orleans. Three weeks earlier, Ranchier, Laffite's messenger to Jean Blanque, had reached New Orleans in less than three days by the Barataria route, which the British wanted for their approach to the city.

Meanwhile, Major Lawrence and his little band at Fort Bowyer had caused the British to lose a flagship and return humiliated to Pensacola when Percy and Nicholls attacked the fort on September 16. This defeat came as a surprise to British sympathizers in Mobile and "convinced Jackson of the need to drive the British menace from Pensacola, which he knew to be the center of the very keen British intelligence system in the Gulf Coast area."[15]

On September 21, the packet of Laffite correspondence that Claiborne had sent reached Jackson at Mobile. Jackson read the letters and then Nicholls' proclamation and immediately dictated his own proclamation to the Louisianians. It said:

> The base the perfidious Britons have attempted to invade your Country. They have had the temerity to attack Fort Bowyer with their incongruous horde of Indian and Negro assassins—they seem to have forgotten that this Fort was defended by freemen. They were not long indulged in their error.

---

13. *Ibid.*, 1471–72.
14. Nolte, *Fifty Years in Both Hemispheres*, 208–209.
15. Wilburt S. Brown, *The Amphibious Campaign for West Florida and Louisiana, 1814–1815* (University, Ala., 1968), 45–46.

> The gallant Lawrence with his little Spartan band, has given them a lecture that will last for ages: he has taught them what Men can do, when fighting for their liberty, when contending against Slaves. . . .
>
> I ask you, Louisianians, can we place any confidence in the honour of Men who have courted an alliance with pirates and Robbers? Have not these Noble Britons . . . dared to insult you by calling on you to associate, as Brethren with them, and this hellish Banditti.[16]

"Hellish Banditti"—that was Jackson's opinion of the Baratarians who had contributed as greatly to the security of the United States by refusing to cooperate with the British as had Major Lawrence and his men by driving them away from Fort Bowyer.

Barataria was now a well-supplied United States base, and Patterson had brought the big guns of the Baratarians to New Orleans. Of course, he did not know that they would be used to defend the city against the British. If Dominique You had turned those guns against Patterson and if Jean Laffite had sided with the British, their troops could have moved easily and rapidly in three days to a point above New Orleans. Then the Crescent City would have been cut off from all communication with the interior, and troops that the governors of Tennessee and Kentucky were assembling to send down the Mississippi to New Orleans might not have been able to get past the British.

Claiborne and others were urging Jackson to hasten to New Orleans, but he could not do so until he had driven the British from Pensacola and until he was sure they could not break through any part of West Florida for an attack from above New Orleans. Jackson was preparing to attack Pensacola's Fort Barrancas when a series of explosions destroyed the fort. Percy, Nicholls, and their marines and troops escaped before Jackson arrived at the ruins.

The invaders sailed to Apalachicola, which was too small to accommodate many troops, but Jackson wanted to be sure that they would not break through Creek territory. He sent Major Uriah Blue with a thousand mounted men to scour the country between Pensacola and Apalachicola for hostile Creeks, "destroying or making prisoners of all the men, preserving the Women and Children as prisoners of War, taking all cattle or Corn . . . and applying it to the Use of the troops

---

16. Bassett (ed.), *Correspondence of Andrew Jackson*, II, 57–58.

under his command, burning and destroying all Villages that may be found."[17]

With Blue covering the front east of Pensacola, and with Governor Gonzalez Manrique's promise that he would not let the British use Pensacola, Jackson proceeded to the Mobile area. Some Georgia troops had arrived there, and these Jackson sent to Lawrence at Fort Bowyer. He dispatched the 44th Regiment of regulars to New Orleans, Colonel John Coffee and his Tennessee Mounted Volunteers to the Baton Rouge area to protect New Orleans from a possible breakthrough at Mobile or Pascagoula, and Major Thomas Hinds and his Mississippi Dragoons to an area near Coffee where he could find forage. These dispositions Jackson reported from Mobile to the secretary of war on November 20, and added: "I leave this for N. Orleans on the 22d Inst. . . . I travel by land to have a view of the points at which the enemy might effect a landing . . . I have been indisposed of late [dysentery], but will hope to keep the field."[18]

Meanwhile, Cochrane's invasion force continued to concentrate at Negril Bay on the west coast of Jamaica. There, "seventy or eighty sail of vessels lay so closely wedged together that to walk across the decks, from one to the other, seemed at a little distance to be far from impracticable."[19] Fifty of these vessels were warships and transports; the rest were merchant vessels chartered to carry to England the produce stored in warehouses at New Orleans. Approximately 6,000 troops, as many or more sailors, and 1,500 marines were ready to sail on these vessels to New Orleans.

The van of Cochrane's armada left Negril Bay on November 25. It was approaching the western tip of Cuba when Jackson and his escort arrived in New Orleans on December 1. He found confusion and crosscurrents there. An eyewitness tells us:

> Hitherto partial attempts had been made to adopt measures of defence; the legislature had appointed a joint committee of both houses, to concert with the governor, commodore Patterson, and the military commandant,

17. General Orders, November 16, 1814, in *ibid.*, II, 100.
18. Jackson to Monroe, November 20, 1814, in *ibid.*, II, 101–102.
19. *A Subaltern in America: Comprising His Narrative of the Campaign of the British Army at Baltimore, Washington, and During the Late War* (Philadelphia, 1833), 187–88.

such measures as they should deem most expedient; but nothing had been done [Patterson was busy prosecuting Baratarians in court, where he had libeled their ships and goods.]

There was wanting that concentration of power, so necessary for the success of military operations. The citizens, having very little confidence in their civil and military authorities for the defence of the country, were filled with distrust and apprehension.

Citizens were despondent because the legislature was wasting time in idle discussions and consuming state money that should have been employed in defense measures. Credit was annihilated; banks had suspended note payments, issued paper money, and refused to pay specie, and wealthy men had withdrawn their funds "which they no longer lent out without usurious interest of three or four per cent per month. . . . Everyone was distressed."[20]

Patterson's naval force was pitiful, but it could have been respectable. He had six gunboats and two larger vessels: the schooner *Carolina*, length 84 feet and beam 24 feet, carrying twelve 12-pounder carronades and three long nines; and the ship sloop *Louisiana*, length 100 feet and beam 28 feet, carrying sixteen guns—four 24-pounders, eight 12-pounders, and four 6-pounders. Five of the gunboats were stationed on Lake Borgne, the other at Fort St. Philip on the east bank of the Mississippi River fifty miles from its mouth.[21]

The *Louisiana* was useless because Patterson could not get a single sailor to man it. Moreover, he needed replacements on the *Carolina* and the gunboats. There were many Baratarian seamen in New Orleans who had come because that was where their ships were impounded, where their hero Dominique You and their friends were in jail in irons, and where some had been called to testify in court.[22] They were also in New Orleans because they had no base from which to operate—Patterson had taken it from them. As far as the Baratarians were concerned, Patterson could sail his own damn ships.

Jackson had no authority over Patterson. As one historian explains: "No officer in either service had the authority to give orders to an officer in the other service. Thus, if land and sea commanders of the

20. Latour, *Historical Memoir*, 53.
21. Brown, *Amphibious Campaign*, 73.
22. S.F.A., *Conspicuous Cases*, Book B, Cases No. 746 and 760.

United States forces arrived at any sort of cooperation, they had to do so through diplomatic relations carried on between them as if each were sovereign."[23]

So Jackson let Patterson stew in his own juice until events made him amenable to cooperation. Jackson had too much to do to worry about Patterson.

23. John K. Mahon, "The United States Army in the Gulf Coast Region," in William S. Coker (ed.), *The Military Presence on the Gulf Coast* (Pensacola, 1978), 86.

CHAPTER 7

The British Invade Louisiana

A welcoming committee, including Governor Claiborne, Mayor Nicholas Girod, and members of the two defense committees, led Jackson to his headquarters at 106 Royal Street. Crowds had already filled the street, and Jackson spoke to them in English, but Edward Livingston, lawyer for the Baratarians and chairman of the citizens' defense committee, translated what Jackson said into French.

The effect was electric. Everyone sensed that here was a man who had the energy "to give a great impulse to the population of Louisiana." Bernard de Marigny, who was in the crowd, reported: "Never was a general received with more enthusiasm. His military reputation, his well known firmness of character contributed to call forth a spontaneous movement. From all quarters the cry was 'To arms.' The whole population arose in a body. It would be impossible for our detractors to cite a single Louisianian, a single Creole, or a single naturalized Frenchman, who in the moment of danger, abandoned the country or refused to fight."[1]

After the speech, Jackson went to work. He studied maps and conferred with Latour and other engineers about approaches to New Orleans that the British might use. Jackson had already detailed forces to cover the West Florida flank, but there were five other routes the English might use: (1) they might try to come through the bays and bayous of Barataria; (2) they might try to come up the Mississippi River, in spite of its strong current; (3) east of the Mississippi they could come up the bayous leading to English Turn, or up Bayou Bienvenu and its

---

1. Bernard de Marigny de Mandeville, "Reflections on the Campaign of General Andrew Jackson in Louisiana 1814 and 1815" (typescript in Jackson Barracks, New Orleans), 2.

branches to a position closer to New Orleans; (4) after entering Lake Borgne, the invaders could come through Pass Chef Menteur to its confluence with Bayou Savage, where a narrow ridge of dry ground known as the Gentilly Road led directly to New Orleans; (5) from Lake Borgne they could go through Pass Rigolets, then across Lake Pontchartrain to Bayou St. John, and up that bayou to New Orleans.

Jackson made his decisions quickly. He sent Major Michael Reynolds to Barataria to take charge of establishing defenses west of the Mississippi and of obstructing the bayous there. Reynolds made his headquarters at "The Temple," the center of Barataria, which was also in the center of the area where Jean Laffite had his munitions depots.

The task of obstructing all the bayous east of the Mississippi was given to Governor Claiborne, who assigned the job to the commander of the Louisiana militia, General Jacques Villeré, whose plantation was nine miles below New Orleans. Its drainage canal emptied into Bayou Manzant, as did the canals of the two plantations immediately above Villeré's, the Lacoste and de la Ronde plantations. Canals helped make Bayou Manzant the main branch of Bayou Bienvenu, which empties into Lake Borgne. Bayou Bienvenu was then from 110 to 150 yards wide; it had six feet of water at the bar at common tides, nine feet at spring tides, and within the bar there was enough water for vessels of from two hundred to three hundred tons.[2]

Lake Borgne, unmolested by large boats because it was too shallow for them, was an ideal fishing ground. A mile or so from the mouth of Bayou Bienvenu was a village of twelve very large cabins, where thirty or more Spanish, Portuguese, and Italian fishermen lived. They went out on Lake Borgne in their small boats to fish, on some trips remaining out for two or three days. Then they would take their catch up Bayou Bienvenu, Bayou Manzant, and any one of the three canals (Villeré's, Lacoste's, or de la Ronde's) to the River Road. There the fish would be loaded on wagons and taken to market in New Orleans. Latour tells us that "Villeré, Lacoste and La Ronde permitted those fishermen to enjoy the gratuitous use of their canals, and constantly afforded relief to such of those wretches as happened to fall sick."[3]

2. Latour, *Historical Memoir*, 78–80.
3. *Ibid.*, 82.

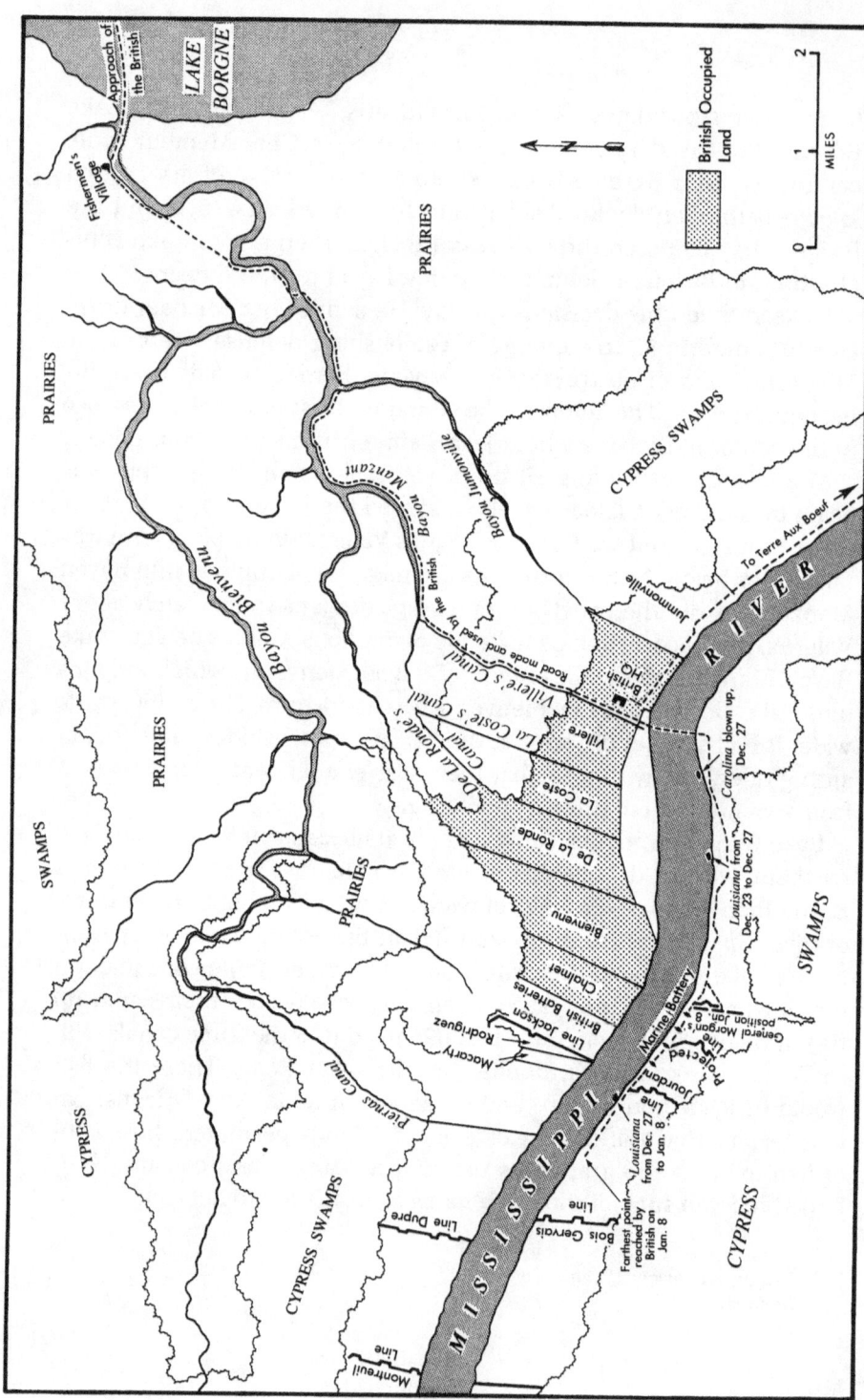

British Advances, December 23, 1814, to January 8, 1815

Above the de la Ronde plantation was the Bienvenu plantation, and above that was Chalmette, the plantation where Renato Beluche had lived as a boy. The firm land or plain between the Mississippi River and the swamps on de la Ronde was three times as wide as on Chalmette, and on Bienvenu it was twice as wide as on Chalmette. Chalmette was a narrow plain, a bottleneck, flanked on one side by the river and on the other by impenetrable cypress swamps. Beluche knew all the bayous that drained the plantations above and below Chalmette. He knew the owners of these plantations, the smugglers who used their bayous, and he knew Henri, baron de St. Gême. This aristocratic Frenchman was the friend and partner of Dominique You, friend of his lawyer Livingston, of Beluche, and of the Baratarians, who sailed St. Gême's ships. In fact, one of the ships that Patterson seized at Grande Terre, the *Cassadore*, belonged to St. Gême, and he too was being indicted in the federal district court of New Orleans.[4]

In 1808 the famous tactician General Jean Victor Moreau had visited New Orleans and "met with a reception of the best New Orleans kind." The governor, the militia, the civil authorities, and the people "turned out en masse to make the solemnity imposing." General Moreau was fond of riding horseback, and St. Gême, "an intrepid hunter who knew all the localities in the environment of New Orleans," furnished the mounts and rode with him.[5]

One day they were riding across the plantations below New Orleans, and when they came to the canal on the triangular Rodriguez plantation, wedged between Macarty and Chalmette, Moreau was fascinated with its possibilities as a bulwark if fortified as an entrenched camp. Sitting erect upon his horse at the canal, he pointed out to St. Gême how the plain there (just above the Chalmette bottleneck) was wider than on Chalmette, and how batteries on earthworks at the canal ex-

---

4. The grand jurors made their presentment against St. Gême on October 19, 1814. It was the only paper in the case. S.F.A., *Conspicuous Cases*, Case No. 786. Verdict: *nolle prosequi*. Survey of Federal Archives in Louisiana, *Synopsis of Cases in the U.S. District Court for the Eastern District of Louisiana, Cases No. 1 to No. 3000* (Baton Rouge, 1941).

5. Moreau arrived toward the end of January and left on March 3. New Orleans *Louisiana Gazette*, January 22 and March 4, 1808. Sources for Moreau and St. Gême are Castellanos. *New Orleans As It Was*, 71–72; Grace King, *Creole Families of New Orleans* (New York, 1921), 443–45; Marigny, "Reflections on the Campaign," 12; and Nolte, *Fifty Years in Both Hemispheres*, 213.

tending to and into the swamp would shield troops behind them, preventing an enemy approaching across the plantations below from advancing farther than the upper end of Chalmette.

Thomas P. Abernethy tells us that Baratarians advised the British where to land in December, 1815;[6] but some of the plantation owners had to cooperate with them. The logic of the situation could not escape Beluche, St. Gême, Dominique, Jacques Villeré and his son Gabriel, Pierre Lacoste, Denis de la Ronde, and others: Jackson had no navy with which to attack the British at sea; they were going to land somewhere, and Jackson had to attack after they landed. Therefore, the British had to be decoyed to a position most advantageous to the Americans—where the British would be like sitting ducks.

While these ideas were germinating, Jackson was not idle. He had to see everything for himself. On December 2, he reviewed the five uniformed companies of Major Jean Plauché's Bataillon d'Orléans (including Major St. Gême's company of Dragons à Pied)—about 600 men; Major Pierre Lacoste's battalion of free men of color—not more than 256 men; Major Louis Daquin's battalion of free men of color from Saint Domingue—200 men; and Captain Thomas Beale's rifle company of lawyers and merchants—62 men.[7]

Letter-writing, map study, and conferences occupied Jackson for the rest of the day. His inspector general, engineers, and officers told him that the old fort at the Balize could not be strengthened enough to keep the British from entering the Mississippi. They all advised Jackson that Fort St. Philip, fifty miles from the mouth of the river, was the key to the defense of the Mississippi.

The next day Jackson began a reconnaissance of both banks of the river as far south as Fort St. Philip. He inspected that fort and old Fort

6. Unfortunately, Abernethy cites no source for this information. Thomas P. Abernethy, *The South in the New Nation, 1789–1819* (Baton Rouge, 1976), 384.

7. The Louisiana legislature on September 6, 1812, passed an act giving the governor authority to organize a corps of free men of color from among the Creoles "and such as shall have paid a State tax . . . their commander shall be a white man. Said Corps shall not consist of more than four companies, each of which, officers included, shall not consist of more than sixty-four men." "Legislative Acts of Louisiana Militia 1805–1824" (typescript in Jackson Barracks, New Orleans), 2–3. Captain Joseph Savary, a free man of color from Saint Domingue, had organized the Saint Domingue battalion, but according to the act of September 6, 1812, a black man could not command this battalion. The command was given to a white man, Major Louis Daquin. Latour, *Historical Memoir*, 105; Bassett (ed.) *Correspondence of Andrew Jackson*, II, 127.

Bourbon on the opposite bank of the river a short distance below St. Philip. Then he ordered improvements that would expose the British, if they came up the river, to a cross fire of guns from St. Philip, Bourbon, and a battery one mile above St. Philip.

When Jackson returned to New Orleans on December 9, Cochrane's fleet was opposite the Chandeleur Islands; two days later, December 11, Thomas Ap Catesby ("Tac") Jones's gunboats on Lake Borgne sighted them as they began to anchor between Cat and Ship Island. That night Jones wrote to Patterson: "Sir—I hasten to inform you that the enemy at Ship Island are increasing to an alarming force; at sunsett this evening there was from twenty to thirty sails in sight; six ships (four supposed to be of the line) many brigs, schooners and sloops, etc. and others hourly joining them. New Orleans is unquestionably their object; the attack will be made through the lakes; their small vessels appear to be well calculated for that service. . . . I fear the enemy's force is too strong for us to make any stand against him, east of the Malheureux Islands."[8]

The next morning, December 12, Jackson began a three-day reconnaissance of the Gentilly-Chef Menteur-Rigolets sector. In New Orleans, the federal district court was in session as usual. On December 13 Joseph Carpentier testified that Beluche's *General Bolívar* was "commissioned as a private vessel of war according to the laws of the Republic of Carthagena with whom the United States are at peace, and duly authorized by the Government of the said Republic to sail against its enemies and that the schooner *General Bolívar* had been unlawfully captured, seized and taken from the possession of the Captain, officers and crew of the said schooner by the libellant [Patterson]."[9]

Patterson received Tac Jones's letter the next day, December 14, and almost panicked. He had to have seamen. He conferred with the governor, showing him Jones's letter, then Claiborne and Patterson each wrote a letter. Claiborne's was to "Gentlemen of the senate and house of representatives." It recommended the suspension of the writ of habeas corpus so that Patterson could impress seamen for manning the

8. *Official Journal of the Proceedings of the House of Representatives of the State of Louisiana* (New Orleans, 1814), 35.
9. S.F.A., *Conspicuous Cases*, Case No. 760.

vessels of the United States under his orders. Patterson's letter was addressed to Claiborne:

> Sir—I do myself the honor to inclose you a copy of a letter [Jones's] just received by express from the eastward, by which you will learn the arrival of the enemy in great force, with a species of vessels well adapted for their approach to this city, by way of the lakes, and which must be met with such vessels as I have under my command, beyond the Rigolets. But I am greatly in need of seamen who can only be obtained by coercive measures; I therefore beg leave to suggest to you the necessity of recommending to the legislature, a suspension of the writ of Habeas Corpus during the period of danger from the enemy, by which I shall be enabled to procure such seamen as may be in the city, or on board of the merchant vessels and barges in port.[10]

Claiborne sent the three letters to the legislature. A message from the Senate to the House suggested that the letters be referred to a joint committee of both houses, which was done that same day, December 14. While the committee considered the matter, the British captured Tac Jones, his men, and his gunboats. The committee of course was not aware of this event, and before the end of the day it reported that "it is unnecessary, and inexpedient at this time to suspend the writ of Habeas Corpus." The Baratarians had many friends in the legislature.

The capture of the gunboats was not known in New Orleans until the next day, December 15. Jackson was at Chef Menteur when he was informed and hurried back to the city. There, Bernard de Marigny, chairman of the legislature's defense committee, members of that committee, and Jacques Villeré confronted him, resolved "to destroy the antipathy that he had conceived against the Baratarians, . . . men accustomed to the use of arms, to war, among whom were some excellent cannoniers and bombardiers."[11]

Jackson's answer to their pleas was: "These men are being prosecuted by the civil officers of the United States. I cannot do anything in this matter." Marigny and the others "retired saddened by such a decision." They felt they had failed, but had they? Did not Jackson's reply tell them what had to be done? After all, Jackson needed men, arms,

---

10. *Journal of the House*, 35–36.
11. Marigny, "Reflections on the Campaign," 3–4.

and ammunition. He had no flints, no powder, no shot for the cannon that Patterson had brought from Barataria, and he needed expert cannoniers.[12]

Marigny and Joseph Roffignac went to the house of the Honorable Dominick Augustin Hall, since 1804 judge of the admiralty court in New Orleans. Judge Hall said, "I am general in these circumstances. Present at once a resolution in the Legislature demanding that the procedures against these men be suspended for four months and I will immediately give my orders to the District Attorney of the United States."[13] Such a resolution was presented to both houses, and they began work on an act "to provide the means of enrolling all seafaring persons now in this state who are not in the service of the United States."

While the legislature worked on the bill, Admiral Cochrane's sailors began rowing troops from the anchorage at Ship Island to Pea Island, a small swampy spot at the mouth of the Pearl River, thirty miles west of the anchorage and twenty miles from the mouth of Bayou Bienvenu. Cochrane's objective in moving the troops to Pea Island was to attack Fort Petites Coquilles guarding the Rigolets, then sail across Lake Pontchartrain, up Bayou St. John, and attack New Orleans from the rear.[14] Within the next few days, however, misinformation, fishermen, and "five or six French Americans" made him consider another approach.

During the gunboat battle on Lake Borgne (December 14), the British suffered seventeen killed and seventy-seven wounded, the Americans six killed and thirty-five wounded. Tac Jones and two of his officers were among the wounded. All the surviving Americans were taken to the anchorage off Ship Island, where they were imprisoned on the *Gorgon*, a large storeship. When Tac Jones was questioned about Fort Petites Coquilles, he said that it had forty pieces of artillery and a

12. *Ibid.*
13. *Ibid.*
14. John Henry Cooke, *A Narrative of Events in the South of France and of the Attack on New Orleans in 1814 and 1815* (London, 1835), 182. Mahon gives the distance between Pea Island and the mouth of Bayou Bienvenu as twenty-four miles (*War of 1812*, 356). Cochrane's chief of staff, Sir Edward Codrington, as late as December 16 expected to attack at Petites Coquilles (Brown, *Amphibious Campaign*, 172).

garrison of five hundred men. Cochrane's spies had told him that the fort had only eight guns and a garrison of fifty men.[15]

As soon as Patterson heard of the capture of the gunboats, he sent purser Thomas Shields and Dr. Robert Morrell to Cochrane under a flag of truce. Shields was to negotiate the release of the prisoners, and Morrell was to take care of Tac Jones and the other wounded. Cochrane did not let them see the prisoners; he thought the two had come as spies and detained them. He observed that Shields was deaf and had the two men placed in a room where they could easily be heard. Morrell and Shields suspected as much; and when all was quiet, they began to talk in loud voices, congratulating themselves on not having given the British any information. Then Shields said: "How greatly these gentlemen will be disappointed in their expectations, for Jackson with the 20,000 troops he now has, and the reinforcements from Kentucky which must speedily reach him, will be able to destroy any force which can be landed from these ships."[16]

Cochrane and Major General John Keane, commander of the land forces, joined the advance at Pea Island on December 17. Fishermen from the village near the mouth of Bayou Bienvenu were there trying to sell the fish they had caught on Lake Borgne, so when questioned, they were friendly. They described Bayou Bienvenu, how easy it was to navigate to Villeré's or Lacoste's or de la Ronde's canal, and how they got their fish to New Orleans.

These fishermen were the decoys. On the night of December 18, they disguised two British officers, Lieutenant John Peddie and Captain Robert Spencer, as fishermen. Then, "with a smuggler as their guide," these officers "pulled up the bayou in a canoe, and advanced to the highroad (River Road), without seeing any persons, or preparations." On their return to Pea Island, they reported the route completely unobstructed and unguarded.[17]

The final persuasion came on December 21. That day, "about five or six French Americans, natives of New Orleans or neighborhood, ar-

15. Mahon, *War of 1812*, 355–56; William James, *A Full and Correct Account of the Military Occurrences of the Late War Between Great Britain and the United States of America* (2 vols.; London, 1818), II, 358.
16. John Henry Eaton, *Life of Andrew Jackson* (Philadelphia, 1824), 287–89.
17. James, *A Full and Correct Account*, II, 358.

rived as friends." When questioned, they declared that "they had come over to the side which they believed to be the strongest. . . . They spoke of General Jackson as an able man; but one so hated on account of his tyranny and violence, that not one inhabitant of the State would adhere to his standard, after they beheld the British flag unfurled."[18]

At eleven o'clock the next morning, December 22, the British advance force of 1,600 men under Colonel William Thornton embarked in rowboats and headed for the mouth of Bayou Bienvenu. Two of the French-American deserters were their guides. The remainder of the troops would embark later in the captured gunboats and other sailing craft, move across Lake Borgne until they grounded, and after the 1,600 troops had landed, the rowboats would go to the sailboats and ferry the troops from them to Bayou Bienvenu.[19]

Meanwhile, Jackson's adjutant general had sent these orders to General Coffee above Baton Rouge: "Immediately on receipt hereof move your command day and night to this place . . . despatch an order to Major Hinds, commanding Mississippi Dragoons, to hasten in like manner his movements to this point." Coffee received these orders at eight o'clock on the night of December 16. At four o'clock the next morning, he wrote Jackson: "I shall move my command this morning at sunrise, no time will be lost by me until I reach New Orleans . . . I have despatched an express to Genl. Carroll." General William Carroll and his Tennessee Volunteers were on the Mississippi River below Natchez. Major John Thomas, with the Kentucky militia, was much farther up the river.[20]

In New Orleans, the speaker of the House of Representatives and the president of the Senate signed the following resolution on December 19:

> Whereas in the Present state of Public affairs it is of the greatest importance to procure seamen for the Service of the United States, and whereas many Persons who have served on board or been concerned in, or connected with privateers lately resorting to Barataria in this state, are deterred from

18. William Surtees, *Twenty-Five Years in the Rifle Brigade* (London, 1833), 339; *A Subaltern in America*, 205–206.
19. Latour, *Historical Memoir*, clxi; Brown, *Amphibious Campaign*, 95.
20. The orders and Coffee's reply in Bassett (ed.), *Correspondence of Andrew Jackson*, II, 117.

offering their services for fear of persecution as violators of the Revenue Laws of the United States.

Wherefore Be it Resolved by the senate and house of Representatives of the state of Louisiana in general assembly convened, that the commanding officer of the District be requested to use his endeavours to procure an amnesty for all of the Persons above described who are now actually in service, or who shall within thirty days enrole themselves to serve in the land service or in the navy of the United States or other ways when directed by the commanding officer, for the defence of the state during the Present occasion, or while the Enemy shall remain on the coast, and shall continue in such service according to the time of their engagement, and that this Legislature will earnestly recommend to the President of the United States to grant a full pardon to all such Persons for any offence they may have committed against the laws of the United States as aforesaid.

And Be it further Resolved that the Governor of the state and the said commanding General be requested to use their endeavours to procure the Attorney of the United States with the leave of the court to enter a nolle prosequi against all such persons now confined for any of the offences aforesaid on the Conditions above stated.[21]

The Baratarians in jail were released. Jean Laffite appeared before Jackson and offered his services, those of the Baratarians, and all the ammunition he could possibly use. Jackson accepted the offer with grace and immediately authorized Laffite to organize the delivery of powder from his depots in Barataria to Jackson's magazines. Lieutenant Charles Thompson signed on a crew of 170 Baratarians for the *Louisiana*, and Master Commandant John Henley found all the replacements he needed for the *Carolina*.

Beluche, Dominique You, and three Baratarian artillery companies appeared as if by magic. These companies had been raised by Captain Thomas Songis, Captain John Colson, and Captain François Legaud. Jackson sent Legaud's company to Fort St. Philip and Songis' company to Fort Petites Coquilles at the Rigolets. Beluche, Dominique You, and Colson's company went to Fort St. John, where Captain Plauché's five companies of the Bataillon d'Orléans and Beale's Rifles were already stationed.[22] If the British broke through at the Rigolets, Jackson

---

21. *Journal of the House*, 41–45; *Official Journal of the Senate During the First Session of the Second Legislature of the State of Louisiana* (New Orleans, 1814), 27–32.
22. Latour, *Historical Memoir*, 72.

wanted to be sure they could not get past Fort St. John and into Bayou St. John.

Lacoste, his battalion of free men of color, and the Feliciana Dragoons (from the parishes above Baton Rouge) of the Louisiana militia were in the Gentilly sector at the confluence of Bayou Savage and Chef Menteur, watching British movements and covering the road to the city. Daquin and the free men of color from Saint Domingue were in New Orleans. Jackson wanted them near headquarters, since they were veteran fighters. General Jacques Villeré was on the Acadian Coast[23] above New Orleans, commanding the militia companies there. General David Morgan was in command of the troops at English Turn, and Colonel Denis de la Ronde on the plantations drained by Bayou Bienvenu. The Regulars (7th and 44th United States Infantry) were at Fort St. Charles on the lower river corner of the city and in barracks nearby.

General Coffee had left Sandy Creek at sunrise on December 17 with 1,250 men. More than a third of them could not maintain the pace he set during the next three cold, rainy days, but Coffee and 800 of his Tennessee Mounted went into camp four miles above New Orleans on the morning of December 20. The next day, Carroll and 3,000 Tennessee Volunteers stepped out of their boats and camped with Coffee. Major Hinds arrived soon after Carroll with 107 Mississippi Dragoons.

On the night of December 21, Colonel de la Ronde instructed his son-in-law, Major Gabriel Villeré, to send a picket of twelve men to the fishermen's village. From this base they were to watch for the British. The picket found only one fisherman at the village, a sick man. He said that all the rest had left the day before and were somewhere on the lake. A few men rowed into the lake but saw nothing. On their return their sergeant posted a sentinel, and the rest slept in one of the cabins.

At daybreak, December 22, three fishermen went two miles into the lake to reconnoiter and returned again with nothing to report. Every two hours, fresh parties were sent out and saw nothing, because the first boats of the British advance did not leave Pea Island until 11 A.M.

---

23. "Coast" meant the natural levees bordering the Mississippi. St. James Parish on the right bank and Ascension Parish on the left bank were known as the Acadian Coast. Fred B. Kniffen, *Louisiana: Its Land and People* (Baton Rouge, 1974), 7.

William Surtees, who was with the British rifle brigade that went part way in the sailboats, recalled that they did not push off until 2 P.M.[24]

Late in the afternoon, someone saw sails on Lake Borgne off Terre aux Boeufs. He hurried to tell de la Ronde, who immediately sent a courier to Jackson. Shortly after midnight, the sentinel at Fishermen's Village heard a noise and alerted those in the cabins. "By the last gleams of the setting moon," they saw barges full of men coming up the bayou. Several of the pickets tried to escape, but only one, "Mr. A. Rey," succeeded.[25]

The British put their prisoners in one of the huts with a guard at the door. About an hour later, one of the prisoners, Joe Ducros, was taken to General Keane and Admiral Cochrane. They asked him how many men Jackson had. Joe said that there were 12,000 to 15,000 troops in New Orleans, and 3,000 to 4,000 more at English Turn. When Cochrane and Keane went to the hut, they questioned the other prisoners and received the same answer.

It was four o'clock on the morning of December 23 when the first boats reached Villeré Canal. After seventeen hours seated in boats where they could hardly move, chilled to the bone with winter rain and cold, the first troops who debarked had to wait for the rest. Surtees' unit arrived about an hour after daylight.[26]

The whole advance of 1,600 men was on the move by 10 A.M. An hour later, they surprised and captured the militiamen at Villeré's house, but Gabriel Villeré escaped to the swamp, ran along its edge to de la Ronde's plantation, and found his father-in-law. They raced to the river, crossed in a small boat, secured horses and rode up the riverbank until they were opposite New Orleans. Then they recrossed the river and reported to Jackson.[27]

Jackson already knew that the British were on the Villeré plantation. De la Ronde's courier had reached him the night before, and this morning Jackson had sent Latour and Howell Tatum to find out if the report was true. When these two engineers reached the boundary be-

24. Surtees, *Twenty-Five Years in the Rifle Brigade*, 340.
25. Latour, *Historical Memoir*, 85–86.
26. Surtees, *Twenty-Five Years in the Rifle Brigade*, 342; Mahon, *War of 1812*, 358.
27. Latour, *Historical Memoir*, 87; Alexander Walker, *Jackson and New Orleans* (New York, 1856), 126–28.

tween the Bienvenu and de la Ronde plantations, they met several people fleeing toward the city who confirmed the report. Tatum immediately returned to town while Latour approached "within rifleshot of those troops, and judged that their number must amount to sixteen or eighteen hundred men. It was then half past one P.M., and within twenty-five minutes after, General Jackson was informed of the enemy's position."[28]

Jackson said to those around him, "Gentlemen, we must attack tonight."

He sent for the troops camped four miles above the city and for Beale's Rifles and Plauché's battalion at Fort St. John. Patterson was at Fort St. John examining batteries that were being erected under the direction of Captain John Henley of the *Carolina*. Patterson and Henley hurried to their ships in the Mississippi River, and Beale's Rifles and Plauché's battalion hurried to Jackson. This left Beluche, Dominique You, and their gun crews to hold Fort St. John.

Hinds, Coffee, and Carroll were the first to arrive at the designated point, Fort St. Charles. Jackson wanted another check on the strength of the enemy, so he ordered Hinds and some of his dragoons to make a reconnaissance. Inspector General Arthur P. Haynes went with them.

The afternoon was sunny and hot. Some of the enemy troops were cooking; others were bathing or sunning themselves. One company was on guard a mile in advance of the camp. About three o'clock, Hinds's dragoons appeared and fired some shots at those on guard, who fired back. The sound of this shooting "caused the whole of the troops to fall in line until the cause of the alarm was ascertained." Haynes made a quick estimate of the number of the enemy before he retired with Hinds.

The British thought that they had routed the dragoons and "set about their cooking again with great glee."[29] Their overconfidence was in part due to their belief that, since the Americans had not attacked at Washington and Baltimore, they would not attack here. The British were mistaken.

---

28. Latour, *Historical Memoir*, 88.
29. Surtees, *Twenty-Five Years in the Rifle Brigade*, 344.

CHAPTER 8

Sitting Ducks

Jackson feared that the force at Villeré's might be a feint to divert him from a stronger force that might already have gained a base near Chef Menteur, so he sent Carroll with his Tennesseans and Claiborne with three militia regiments to strengthen the Gentilly sector. All the other troops filed by Fort St. Charles, where they were fully provided with powder and ball. Jean Laffite had delivered this ammunition to Jackson's depot on the west bank of the Mississippi, and the *Louisiana* had ferried a plentiful supply across the river to Fort St. Charles.[1]

At 2:30 P.M., a detachment of artillery with two field pieces, the 7th Infantry, and a detachment of marines left Fort St. Charles and marched down the River Road. Their orders were to halt at Montreuil's, the third plantation below the city, until they received the command to advance. Coffee's mounted, Beale's Rifles, and Hinds's Dragoons were the next to leave. They went down the River Road to Rodriguez Canal, marched left to the edge of the swamp, then crossed Chalmette and Bienvenu to the de la Ronde plantation. Coffee was in command of this left flank.

The 44th Infantry, Pierre Jugeant and his Choctaws (eighteen men), Daquin's free men of color, and Plauché's battalion were the last to leave Fort St. Charles. According to Latour, Jackson had 1,399 men in the flank he would command along the river, and Coffee had 732 men—that is, a total of 2,131 men against the enemy, whose number increased from 1,688 men during the battle to 2,050 men, and to 5,050

---

1. Eaton, *Life of Jackson*, 309; Nolte, *Fifty Years in Both Hemispheres*, 210.

men by Christmas morning. But the British had no support on the river, and Jackson did.[2]

Patterson and Henley arrived about 4 P.M. at the docks where the *Carolina* and *Louisiana* were anchored. The *Carolina* carried 95 men and forty-four guns, the *Louisiana* 170 men and twenty-two guns. There were no better cannoneers anywhere than the Baratarians who served the guns on these two vessels. Lieutenant C. B. Thompson commanded the *Louisiana*, and Henley commanded the *Carolina*. Patterson ordered Thompson to follow the *Carolina*, then Patterson and Henley boarded the *Carolina* and, the wind being calm, dropped down-river with the current. At 6:30 P.M., when the two ships were opposite Jackson's flank, Edward Livingston came out to the *Carolina* with a "request" from Jackson that Patterson anchor abreast of the enemy's camp (two miles below Jackson's position) and open fire. His first broadsides would be the signal for Jackson and Coffee to attack.[3]

The *Carolina* moved downstream. The *Louisiana*, being less manageable in the calm than the *Carolina*, had to anchor after an advance of one mile, but the *Carolina* was able to ride the current for another mile. The calm continuing, Commander Henley got out his sweeps, anchored, and sheered close in shore abreast the British camp, where most of the troops were sleeping. At 7:30 P.M., the *Carolina*'s guns opened fire. "Round after round, and ball after ball, were vomited forth, driving the troops into most dire confusion." For the next two hours, the *Carolina* did "more mischief than 1,000 men could have done."[4]

A half hour after the *Carolina*'s opening broadsides, Jackson reached Captain William Hallen and his eighty men—the foremost British picket. Jackson drove Hallen back 150 yards, then Colonel William Thornton ordered the 85th and 95th regiments (eight hundred men) to support Hallen. This checked Jackson's advance, as did gunsmoke

---

2. Latour, *Historical Memoir*, 105; James, *A Full and Correct Account*, II, 355, 361–63.
3. Mahon, *War of 1812*, 358, 361; Patterson's report to the Secretary of War, December 28, 1814, in Latour, *Historical Memoir*, xliii–xliv.
4. Cooke, *Narrative of Events*, 191–92; Surtees, *Twenty-Five Years in the Rifle Brigade*, 351–52.

and heavy fog from the river, which settled over the battlefield and made it difficult to distinguish friend from foe. Jackson withdrew "after a severe conflict of upwards of an hour."[5]

Coffee, meanwhile, had driven the outposts of the enemy's right flank back to the Lacoste plantation and then to the river. They took refuge behind an old levee as several companies of the 21st and 93rd Regiments arrived from Lake Borgne to reinforce them. Fearful of a bayonet charge and fire from the *Carolina,* Coffee withdrew to the gardens of the de la Ronde plantation. His flank had been in the battle an hour longer than Jackson's.

Both sides checked their losses after the firing ceased and took care of their wounded. American losses were 24 killed, 115 wounded, 74 missing: total number of casualties, 213. British losses were 46 killed, 167 wounded, and 62 missing: total casualties, 275.[6]

Jackson intended to spend the night in the field and then renew the attack at dawn, and he sent an order to Carroll at Gentilly to come with his volunteers to help. Livingston was uneasy about such an attack. He advised Jackson to consult with Major St. Gême, who persuaded Jackson that Major General Keane, by early morning, might have six thousand seasoned veterans, all skilled in the use of the bayonet, at his command. In the open field, these troops could surround, defeat, and capture Jackson and his small force of raw levies. Then St. Gême explained why Rodriguez Canal was the line that General Moreau had indicated "as the best one adapted to a defense of the city, particularly by unpractised troops."[7]

Jackson heeded St. Gême's advice and requisitioned every spade, shovel, pickaxe, crowbar, wheelbarrow, and cart in New Orleans and the surrounding areas. It was 4 A.M., December 24, when Jackson began to withdraw his army from de la Ronde across Bienvenu, Chalmette, and Rodriguez plantations to the Macarty plantation. At that moment, it was noon in Ghent, Belgium, where commissioners of the

---

5. Jackson's report to the Secretary of War, December 26, 1815, in Latour, *Historical Memoir,* xliv.
6. Latour, *Historical Memoir,* 102–103; James, *A Full and Complete Account,* II, 362.
7. Nolte, *Fifty Years in Both Hemispheres,* 213; Marigny, "Reflections on the Campaign," 12.

United States and Great Britain were celebrating their signing of a peace treaty. And in the Gulf of Mexico, Sir Edward Pakenham's fleet was approaching Ship Island, where Cochrane's big ships were anchored. Pakenham was to take command of the land forces. His instructions were that, if a treaty were signed at Ghent, it would not apply to Louisiana until he, Pakenham, received confirmation from the prince regent. The British government meant to have Louisiana and control of the Mississippi River.[8]

Rodriguez Canal had long been abandoned, "so that its banks had fallen in and raised its bottom, which was covered with grass, presenting rather the appearance of an old drainage ditch than a canal."[9] The tools Jackson had requisitioned arrived almost as soon as the troops were ready to use them, and owners of slaves sent them to help with the digging. Earth from the ditch was thrown on the upper side, leaving the bank on the Chalmette side as it was, a little elevated above the soil and forming a kind of glacis. After the ditch had been deepened three feet, the diggers struck water, and the wet soil thrown on the bank began sliding back into the canal. All the fence posts in the area and cypress logs (cut from trees on the edge of the swamp) were laid crib-fashion, and dry dirt was hauled from the rear to thicken the watery mud thrown into the cribs. This work continued unimpeded day and night.

The enemy could not come near. Jackson had left the Mississippi and Feliciana dragoons and the 7th Regiment at de la Ronde's to observe enemy movements and drive back any forward thrust. Jugeant's Choctaws operated in the cypress woods, even into the swamp, sniping at any enemy who ventured to use this route.[10]

The River Road was not accessible to the British troops because of

---

8. James Parton, *The Life of Andrew Jackson* (3 vols.; Boston and New York, 1888), II, 105, 109–10. Heavy reinforcements from Canada were on their way to Pakenham. They arrived on January 9, and on that day five regiments were dispatched from Cork—seven days after an English chargé had sailed to New York with a ratified copy of the Treaty of Ghent. "As late as February 28, 1815, the British Prime Minister wrote to Wellington that he was hoping momentarily to receive news of a great victory . . . towards which victory the British government had done everything possible." Brown, *Amphibious Campaign*, 166.

9. James, *A Full and Complete Account*, II, 365.

10. Brown, *Amphibious Campaign*, 109.

fire from the *Carolina* and the *Louisiana*. After the firing had stopped on the night of December 23, the *Carolina* had weighed, as Patterson reported, "and swept across the river, in hopes of a breeze the next morning . . . but was disappointed on the 24th by a light air . . . which toward evening, hauled toward northwest and blew a heavy gale, compelling me to remain the 24th, 25th, and 26th at anchor in a position abreast of the enemy camp."[11] Patterson was worried about his immobility, but his gunners fired at any enemy movement by day and any enemy campfire that might be lit at night.

On December 24, Jackson had Latour cut several trenches in the levee so that water from the Mississippi flooded the ground on Chalmette in front of his line. This prevented British troops from making any reconnaissance, but Hinds and his horsemen could cross Chalmette and patrol the British camp. That night Hinds reported that the enemy had moved up from the Villeré plantation to Lacoste and de la Ronde.

The next day—Christmas—Hinds reported that a new commander had arrived at the British camp, someone very important, perhaps the duke of Wellington. It was not the "Iron Duke" himself, but his wife's brother, General Pakenham. Major General Samuel Gibbs, his second in command, and three thousand reinforcements came with Pakenham.

Pakenham surveyed the British position and looked toward Jackson's line, but all he could see was Hinds's horsemen galloping over cane-stubble fields. The new commander called a staff meeting and was persuaded that he must first get rid of the *Carolina* that was tormenting his army. Its sides "day and night vomited iron harbingers into the bivouac of the British, so that the city of New Orleans and General Jackson now became a secondary consideration, and the discussion was how to get rid of this watery dragon."[12]

And so Sir Edward, instead of immediately advancing along the edge of the woods and attacking the left end of Jackson's line, where there were no breastworks, let his whole army wait two days for guns from the ships. During that time, Jackson's "barricade was rising out

11. Patterson to Secretary of War, December 28, 1814, in Latour, *Historical Memoir*, xlii–xliii.
12. Cooke, *Narrative of Events*, 200–201.

of the earth like enchantment as a real stoppage to take the place of an imaginary one."[13]

Pakenham sent to the big ships anchored between Cat and Ship islands for two 9-pounders, four 6-pounders, two 5½-inch howitzers, a 5½-inch mortar, furnaces for heating shot, and ammunition. His sailors had a long haul—almost twenty miles to the mouth of Bayou Bienvenu and sixty more to the big ships. Meanwhile, Jackson kept his ditchdiggers busy that Christmas day and sent orders to General Morgan to evacuate his post below the enemy. Morgan was to cross the river, leave a hundred men at Fort St. Leon, then move up the west bank of the river with the rest of his troops and camp on the plantation of Dr. William Flood, opposite Jackson's line.

The next day, December 26, Jackson ordered Morgan to send his chief engineer Barthélemi Lafon with a detail to cut trenches in the levee on the Jumonville plantation below the British and as close to their position as possible. The objective was to make an island of the enemy camp. This would secure Jackson from attack and force the British to evacuate. "Old Man River" cooperated for a few hours, long enough to fill Villeré Canal and also to aid the British sailors who, after incredible toil in December rain and cold, arrived that night with the guns that were to destroy the *Carolina* first and then the *Louisiana*. There was no rest for those sailors; they were promptly sent back to the ships for more guns.

Patterson had gone ashore that afternoon, December 26, to consult with Jackson at "his request." This left Captain Henley to deal with the battery of nine guns that the British erected that night opposite the *Carolina*, "at the most advantageous angle of the levee" for the purpose of firing hot shot into the *Carolina*. While enemy furnaces were getting hot, Henley "made every possible exertion to move the *Carolina* higher up the river . . . without success; the wind blowing fresh and too scant to get under way, and the current too rapid to move her by warping, which I had endeavoured to do."[14]

The Macarty mansion—Jackson's headquarters—was near the river and a hundred yards behind his ditch. At daylight on December 27,

---

13. *Ibid.*, 203–204.
14. Henley to Patterson, December 28, 1814, in Latour, *Historical Memoir*, xlvii.

Jackson was standing at his best observation post, a second-story window. He saw the *Carolina*, then he focused on the *Louisiana*, which was closer to Jackson's line but still only one mile above the *Carolina*, and within range of the enemy battery. Suddenly Jackson saw, then heard, the guns of that battery concentrate their hot shot and shells on the *Carolina*. The second shot fired by the enemy lodged "in the schooner's main hold under her cables, and in such a situation as not to be come at, and fired her, which progressed rapidly; finding that hot shot were passing through her cabin and filling room, which contained a considerable quantity of powder; . . . and expecting every moment that she would blow up," Henley gave orders for the crew to abandon the ship, "which was effected, with the loss of one killed and six wounded." A short time after the crew was safely on the west bank, Henley "had the extreme mortification of seeing the *Carolina* blow up."[15]

Then the British aimed their hot shot and shells at the *Louisiana*, a floating powder depot, but it was already on its way to safety. One hundred Baratarians of the crew had gotten into small boats with tow lines and were pulling the ship out of the danger zone. It was finally anchored on the west bank near Dr. Flood's canal.[16]

The river was falling rapidly, and no more water came through the trenches to impede the British. During the day, a light freeze helped to firm the ground. Pakenham prepared to storm Jackson's line. He divided his army into two columns under General Samuel Gibbs and Major General John Keane: Gibbs was to advance along the cypress wood, and Keane to lead his column up the River Road. Before the day was over, sailors had brought a few more heavy guns, ammunition, and stores from the ships.

December 27 was also a busy day for Jackson's army. All day long, troops and slaves worked on the breastworks making them longer and higher. More batteries were installed behind them, so that four were ready by the early morning of December 28. Sources are vague about batteries No. 1 and No. 2. Battery No. 1 on the river end of Jackson's line had two guns. Battery No. 2, a hundred yards left of No. 1, had a

---

15. *Ibid.*, xlvii–xlviii.
16. Latour, *Historical Memoir*, 118.

howitzer, either a 6-pounder or a 12-pounder. Battery No. 3, a 24-pounder, was fifty yards left of No. 2; and No. 4, another 24-pounder, was twenty-five yards left of No. 3. Jackson's troops were stationed behind the gunners and across the rest of the line, with Beale's Rifles on the river end and the Tennesseans of Carroll and Coffee on the swamp end and in the swamp.

Early on the morning of December 28, Hinds reported that the British were advancing, forcing Jackson's outposts to draw back. Jackson sent for Beluche and Dominique You to come from Fort St. John and man the 24-pounder at battery No. 3. Then Jackson ordered Colonel William MacRea to fire and blow up the buildings on Chalmette and Bienvenu so they could not protect the enemy from artillery fire.

From his observation post, Jackson saw the day dawn frosty and clear. He saw Beluche, Dominique, and their gun crew coming on the run. Behind them came two gun crews that had served the *Carolina*: Lieutenant Charles Crawley and his crew took charge of the howitzer at No. 2; Lieutenant Otto Norris and his crew, the 24-pounder at No. 4. Looking toward the river, Jackson saw the *Louisiana* move a short distance downstream and anchor so that its guns commanded the field in front of his line. Jackson looked toward the enemy. He saw one column—Keane's—coming from behind the buildings on Bienvenu, MacRea and his company fleeing from the first row of buildings on Chalmette, in which they had placed explosives, and Gibbs's column advancing parallel to Keane's but near the swamp.

When the two columns reached Chalmette, the field artillery at the head of Keane's column opened up with shot, shells, and rockets, and the river battery that had destroyed the *Carolina* fired shells and hot shot at the *Louisiana*. Lieutenant Thompson and Jackson's gun crews waited until the enemy was on Chalmette, then the *Louisiana*'s guns and the line batteries fired. Buildings on Chalmette exploded, and Keane ordered his men to take cover in ditches.

Gibbs's column had better luck. It was out of range of the *Louisiana*, and Jackson had no batteries on this half of his line. As Gibbs's advance approached the left end, Carroll sent Colonel James Henderson with two hundred Tennesseans to drive it back. Henderson was killed, and six of his men were killed or wounded. The rest retreated, but the British did not pursue. Pakenham had ordered the whole army to withdraw when he saw Keane's troops flat in the mud. Gibbs's line did file to the rear, but Keane's could not. His men lay in the mud for seven hours—that is, until the cannoneers relented and ceased firing.

The British reported their losses that day as forty or fifty men killed or wounded. An unofficial report of Keane's losses was one man in twelve of all ranks. Jackson's losses were nine men killed and nine men wounded. Patterson, in a letter to the secretary of the navy, said: "Many of their [the British] shot passed over the *Louisiana*, and their shells burst over her decks, which were strewed with fragments; yet, after an incessant cannonading of upwards of seven hours, during which time 800 shot were fired from the ship, one man only was wounded slightly, by the piece of a shell, and one shot passed between the bowsprit and heel of the jib-boom. . . . The crew of the Louisiana is composed of men of all nations, English excepted . . . yet I never knew guns better served, or a more animated fire, than was supported from her."[17]

Cochrane and Pakenham agreed that now they must bring heavy guns from the ships, concentrate their fire on Jackson's line to silence his batteries, blast an opening in his breastworks, rush infantry through the breach, and overwhelm Jackson's army. Pakenham set a deadline: navy guns must be in place and the army ready to move at dawn on Sunday, January 1, 1815.

This gave Jackson three days to mount a total of twelve effective guns, strengthen his parapets, prolong his line into the cypress swamp, and arrange his tents in proper order. The British had no tents, and they could not have campfires because these became immediate targets for the guns of the *Louisiana* and of Jackson's line batteries.

Hinds's dragoons, including those of Feliciana, Jugeant's Choctaws, and the Tennessee riflemen (whom the British called "dirty shirts"), never gave the enemy five minutes rest day or night. An eyewitness said: "The Tennessee riflemen are constantly shooting their British picket guards, and every night kill more or less of them. The deserters say that there would be a great many more desert, if they were not afraid of '*those fellows with dirty shirts*,' but as soon as they see any coming up to them, they shoot them with their rifles, so that many

---

17. Brown, *Amphibious Campaign*, 116; Patterson's letter was dated U.S. Ship *Louisiana*, 4 miles below New Orleans, December 29, 1814, in Latour, *Historical Memoir*, xlix–1.

of the deserters cannot get near enough to our pickets to cry out 'a friend.'"[18]

On December 29, Patterson sent to the New Orleans Navy Yard for a 24-pounder from one of the captured Baratarian ships, installed the gun on the west bank of the Mississippi River opposite Jackson's line, "in a position where it could most annoy the enemy when throwing up works on the levee or in the field." The next day, the gun proved so effective that on December 31 Patterson landed two 12-pounders from the *Louisiana* and mounted them on the levee "to harass the flank of the enemy and to aid our right."[19]

This marine battery and the guns of the *Louisiana* kept the British from completing their batteries until the night of December 31–January 1. By dawn they had six batteries ready for action. According to Lieutenant Peddie's sketch showing redoubts and batteries (on which figures No. 1 and No. 2 are redoubts), batteries No. 8 and No. 7 were on the new road—that is, on top of the new levee. Seven British guns were mounted to bear on the *Louisiana* and Patterson's marine battery. Facing Jackson's line and 500 to 800 yards from it (authorities differ about the distance), were the following batteries:

> No. 6—near the new levee; 2 guns (Fortescue says it had four 18-pounders).
> No. 5—50 yards to the right of No. 6; 6 guns (six 18-pounders).
> No. 4—to the right of No. 5 and left of the old levee road; 4 guns (four 24-pound carronades).
> No. 3—to the right of the old levee road; 5 guns (probably field pieces and howitzers).[20]

The seventeen guns of these four batteries were mounted to bear on the twelve effective guns of the batteries on Jackson's line. These batteries were:

> No. 1—on the new levee or road, 70 (75?) feet from the river; 3 guns (two 12-pounders and one 6-inch howitzer). Captain Humphreys and

---

18. J. W. Fortescue, *A History of the British Army* (13 vols.; London, 1899–1930), X, 164; Letter to "Dear Brother," December 30, 1814, in Boston *Daily Advertiser and Repertory*, February 4, 1815.
19. Patterson to Secretary of Navy, January 2, 1815, in Latour, *Historical Memoir*, 1–li.
20. Adams, *History of the United States*, VIII, 360–61; Fortescue, *History of the British Army*, X, 164.

regular artillerymen served the two 12-pounders; St. Gême and some of his dragoons, the howitzer.

No. 2—50 yards from No. 1; one gun (a 24-pounder), served by Lieutenant Norris and seamen from the late *Carolina*.

No. 3—50 yards from No. 2; 2 guns (24-pounders). Beluche commanded one, Dominique You the other, each with a Baratarian crew.

No. 4—20 (25?) yards from No. 3; 1 gun (a 32-pounder), Jackson's largest gun, served by Lieutenant Crawley and seamen from the late *Carolina*.

No. 5—190 (200?) yards from No. 4; 2 guns (two 6-pounders). Colonel William D. Perry commanded one, Lieutenant John Kerr the other, each with crews of regular artillerymen.

No. 6—36 (50?) yards from No. 5; 1 gun (a 12-pounder). General Garrigues Flaujeac (one of the four members of the legislature who served at the front) commanded its crew, Lieutenant Etienne Bertel and his company of Francs.

No. 7—190 (200?) yards from No. 6; 2 guns (a long brass 18-pound culverine and a 6-pounder). Lieutenant Samuel Spotts and Lieutenant Louis Chaveau commanded the regular artillerymen who served as its crew.

No. 8—60 (50?) yards from No. 7 and on the edge of the woods; 1 gun (one small brass carronade with imperfect carriage, therefore not very effective). The name of the corporal commanding it was not recorded.[21]

Believing that sugar would be as effective as sand in stopping cannon balls, the British had used hogsheads filled with sugar in building embrasures for their guns. Jackson's work crews had used cotton bales for the embrasures of some of his guns. As Pakenham's deadline approached, his guns were ready for action, but his veteran artillerymen knew that they did not have enough ammunition.

Pakenham's troops were hungry because the small boats bringing in guns and ammunition had room for only a fraction of the daily food supply. Thanks to the British blockade of the mouth of the Mississippi, warehouses in New Orleans were full of flour, cornmeal, and meat, and a wagon train each day brought bread, cornbread, bacon, sweet potatoes, other food, coffee, and whiskey to Jackson's camp.

The British expected to dine in New Orleans, land of plenty, on the

---

21. First distance from Latour; distances in parentheses are from Brown. Latour, *Historical Memoir*, 147–48; Brown, *Amphibious Campaign*, 137.

night of January 1. Pakenham's hungry troops were in position before dawn, a hundred yards behind the batteries, anxiously waiting for the sun to rise, "but the sun was slow of making its appearance; a heavy mist obscured him, and the morning was far advanced when it cleared away."[22] Jackson, too, was up early. The fog limited visibility to a few feet, and Old Hickory knew that there could be no enemy action until the fog lifted. It was Sunday, New Year's Day, and visitors from New Orleans began to arrive at his camp. Jackson ordered a military parade, then went to Macarty House to rest.

The instant the fog lifted (at ten o'clock), British gunners at batteries No. 6 and No. 5 opened fire on Macarty House. Those at No. 4 and No. 3 fired at Beluche's, Dominique's, and Crawley's guns, which is where Pakenham's infantry expected to break through. In less than ten minutes, upwards of a hundred balls, rockets, and shells struck Macarty House and drove everybody out, including Jackson. No one was hurt because, as Sir Edward Codrington reported, "our firing too high was not made out until we had expended too much of our hardly-collected ammunition to push the matter further."[23]

Patterson's marine battery opened fire. When Jackson's batteries answered, they hit their targets and fired round after round with inexorable regularity. The 24-pounders of Beluche and Dominique You did the most damage, firing "alternately with great deliberation and with unvarying effect." Shot from Jackson's guns "penetrated the sugar-hogsheads as if they had been empty casks," reported the subaltern, "dismounting our guns and killing our artillerymen. Our fire slackened every moment; that of the Americans became every moment more terrible, till at length, after more than two hours and a half of firing, our batteries were silenced. The American works remained as little injured as ever, and we were completely foiled."[24]

The subaltern's report was not quite accurate. Dominique You's gun carriage and that of Crawley were broken, as was the fore-train of Flaujeac's 12-pounder; two caissons were blown up, and some cotton

---

22. *A Subaltern in America*, 249.
23. Lady Jane B. Bouchier (ed.), *Memoir of Admiral Edward Codrington* (2 vols.; London, 1873), I, 334. Lady Jane was Codrington's daughter.
24. Augustus C. Buell, *History of Andrew Jackson* (2 vols.; New York, 1904), I, 419 (Buell's reference was Captain B. E. Hill's report); *A Subaltern in America*, 249.

bales were knocked loose and set on fire. Damaged guns were quickly repaired, more powder was brought to the line, and all cotton bales were taken off the works and thrown in the rear, "where the men broke them open and used the layers of which they were composed for mattresses."[25]

The British were not so lucky with their shattered sugar hogsheads. "The constant drizzling rain dissolved their contents, making where they lay soft, sticky and sweet mud-holes." As soon as darkness fell, Pakenham sent troops and seamen to retrieve the guns that had been supported by the hogsheads. The labor of dragging those crippled guns "out of the soft soil into which they had sunk, was more extreme by far than anyone expected to find it; indeed," reported the subaltern, "it was not until four o'clock in the morning that our task came to a conclusion."[26]

Twice, on December 28 and on New Year's Day, British artillery had failed to blast an opening in Jackson's earthworks, so Pakenham's army had not yet had a chance to show what it could do. He had 5,000 veterans well armed with muskets, rifles, and bayonets, but he decided to wait until General Lambert arrived with two regiments, "mustering under arms upwards of 1700 bayonets," before storming the enemy line. Since the night attack of December 23, Jackson had shown no inclination to come out on the open plain and do battle against British bayonets. Therefore, Pakenham concluded, Jackson must be afraid of them.[27]

Jackson was. His militia was not well armed. "On the first intimation" that the British intended to invade Louisiana, he had informed the secretary of war that he needed both arms and ordnance and suggested that they be sent immediately, and Secretary Monroe had ordered "an ample supply to be embarked from Pittsburgh." Since no steamboat was available, the contractor delivered the arms and ordnance "to the captain of a large flat bottomed boat which moved slowly

---

25. Latour, *Historical Memoir*, 133–34; Buell, *History of Andrew Jackson*, I, 425. Buell quoted from "Kentucky at New Orleans," a pamphlet written by John Richard Ogilvy, one of General John Adair's militiamen.
26. *A Subaltern in America*, 251.
27. Cooke, *Narrative of Events*, 215.

and stopped along the way to trade off the articles with which she was laden."[28] The flatboat was somewhere near Natchez on New Year's Day.

Major General John Thomas arrived at Jackson's headquarters on Wednesday, January 4, with about 2,250 thinly clothed Kentucky militiamen. Northern campaigns had drained Kentucky of firearms and supplies; only 550 of the Kentuckians had arms, and all were in need of warm clothes and blankets. Jackson was stunned. The next day he sent Brigadier General John Adair with the armed men and 200 men without arms to support Carroll on the front line.[29]

Jackson had established a second line on the Dupré plantation two miles behind his earthworks, and a third one on the Montreuil plantation, a mile and a half behind the Dupré line. He stationed the rest of the unarmed Kentuckians with 300 unarmed Louisiana militiamen on his second line, where they could "add to his appearance and numbers, without at all increasing his strength."[30]

Old Hickory could not meet British bayonets in force on an open field, so he had to depend on artillery, musketmen, and riflemen *behind* his earthworks. Therefore, he had to wait for the British to take the offensive. While he was waiting, Pakenham heeded some advice from Admiral Cochrane: extend Villeré Canal through the levee to the river; send troops across the Mississippi River at night; advance up the river, seize Patterson's guns, turn them on Jackson's line before dawn, and be ready to open fire at Pakenham's rocket signal.[31]

Morgan, as well as Patterson, was responsible for the defense of the west bank. Fearing that the British might make a feint on that side of the Mississippi, Jackson sent Latour on New Year's Day to lay out and fortify a line for Morgan. He chose Bois Gervais Canal (three miles below New Orleans, two miles above Patterson's marine batteries) and set 150 slaves to throwing up an earthwork.

During the next few days, Patterson took more guns and their crews from the *Louisiana*, which, after December 31, did not drop down-

---

28. John Reid and John Henry Eaton, *The Life of Andrew Jackson* (Philadelphia, 1817), 271–72.
29. Latour, *Historical Memoir*, 141.
30. Reid and Eaton, *Life of Jackson*, 333.
31. Fortescue, *History of the British Army*, X, 166.

river but remained above Patterson's position on the levee, out of range of enemy hot shot. When Jackson sent Latour to aid Morgan, this time to locate a forward position for him, Latour chose one that began midway between the nine guns that Patterson now had strung out for a mile along the levee road. Patterson and Morgan conferred and rejected this line, even though it was only 900 yards from the river bank to impassable woods. They chose one below Patterson's nine guns, where the distance was 2,000 yards from the river to the woods in a line along the shallow Raguet Canal. By Saturday evening, January 7, only 200 yards of earthwork had been thrown up from the river into the plain. Nine-tenths of the line had no protection.[32]

That Saturday afternoon, at Jackson's request, Patterson went down-river and verified the report that the British had indeed extended Villeré Canal to the river, "and from the number of men, soldiers and seamen, I [Patterson] apprehend they will get their Boats in the River tonight." When Patterson returned, he had a 12-pounder and two 6-pounder brass field pieces mounted on Morgan's 200-yard line. Patterson's nine guns on the levee were mounted "with a view to aid the right of General Jackson's lines on the opposite shore, and to flank the enemy should they attempt to march up the road leading along the levee." These guns were not swivel guns, and they could fire in one direction only—across the river. They could not cover Patterson's gunners or Morgan's militia against attack from below. Some of the captured Baratarian guns, however, were swivel guns.[33]

In the report of his reconnaissance down-river, Patterson "recommended" to Jackson that he send reinforcements to him and Morgan. Jackson received the report about 7 P.M. General Thomas was too ill to exercise command, so Jackson ordered Adair to send 400 Kentucky militia to reinforce Morgan. Adair gave this job to Colonel John Davis, who marched the unarmed militiamen to New Orleans, where they were to get arms. There, 170 of the men were armed with muskets, many without flints, and with old Spanish shotguns and fowling pieces. The 230 Kentuckians without arms returned to camp.[34]

32. Latour, *Historical Memoir*, 166–68; Brown, *Amphibious Campaign*, 135–38.
33. Patterson to Jackson, January 8, 1815, in Bassett (ed.), *Correspondence of Andrew Jackson*, II, 132; Patterson to Secretary of the Navy, January 13, 1815, in Latour, *Historical Memoir*, lxi.
34. Latour, *Historical Memoir*, 170–71.

Davis and the 170 armed militia crossed the river on a ferry, then marched five miles, sometimes knee-deep in mud, and reached Morgan's camp at 4 A.M. on Sunday, January 8. Morgan was glad to see them. The night before, he had sent Major Jean Arnaud with 85 poorly armed Louisiana militia and 15 men without arms down-river to keep the British from landing. Morgan now sent Davis with his men to join Arnaud somewhere below Morgan's 200-yard line.

On the other side of the river, Jackson's ramparts on Rodriguez Canal stretched in a fairly straight line on firm ground from the river to fifty yards beyond battery No. 8, a distance of 700 yards. Beyond that, the line plunged 750 yards into the woods to where enormous holes full of water made it necessary to turn the line 90 degrees and extend it back 200 yards. Day and night, General Coffee's Tennesseans guarded the 750-yard sector and the 200-yard end, working in mud and water, sleeping when they could in tents pitched on small isles surrounded by more mud and water.[35]

Jackson had agreed, against his better judgment, that a redoubt should be placed in front of his line on the river end to rake any column coming up the levee road. This decision was made on January 5, as the last of Lambert's "1700 bayonets" were arriving at the British camp. On the night of January 6, a deserter from Jackson's line "unfolded to the British the situation of the American line; the late reinforcements we [Jackson's army] had received, and the unarmed condition of many of the troops; and pointing to the center of Carroll's division [all the troops from battery No. 6 to 50 yards beyond battery No. 8] as a place occupied by militia alone, recommended it as the point where an attack might most safely be made."[36]

That night, while six 18-pounders were being mounted to take care of Jackson's first four batteries, Pakenham called his last council of war. Pakenham, Cochrane, and their officers reviewed tactics for their simultaneous attacks, which were to begin the next day before dawn. There was one exception: Thornton's 1,200 men were to start across the river before this council of war ended—that is, they were to be on

35. *Ibid.*, 149–50.
36. Brown, *Amphibious Campaign*, 129; Reid and Eaton, *Life of Jackson*, 334–35. This man was the only deserter from Jackson's army, according to S. Putnam Waldo, *Memoirs of Andrew Jackson, Major–General of the Army of the United States and Commander-in-Chief of the Division of the South* (Hartford, 1819), 244.

their way by 9 P.M. Cochrane's sailors were even now dragging fifty boats up Villeré Canal for them.

Major General Gibbs, with 2,200 men, was to lead the main assault against Carroll's center. Under cover of darkness, his troops were to advance to within 200 yards of batteries No. 6 and No. 7. Lieutenant Colonel Thomas Mullins, commander of the 44th Regiment, with 300 of his men carrying fascines (bundles of fresh, therefore heavy, sugar cane) to fill the ditch and ladders for scaling Jackson's slippery earthworks, were to be at the head of Gibbs's column.

In order to keep Coffee and Jugeant's Choctaws from striking Gibbs's right flank, 200 artillerists and 500 black troops of the First West India Regiment were to advance along the edge of the swamp. Major General Keane's column of 1,200 men was in two sections. Colonel Robert Rennie, with the smaller section, was to advance along the levee road and take Jackson's unfinished redoubt. Keane and the bulk of his brigade were to advance on Rennie's right and, according to circumstances, aid Rennie or oblique right to support Gibbs. Major General Lambert with 1,400 reserves was to remain in the center of the rear.

Thus, a total of 5,300 men was to assault Jackson's line before daylight; and Thornton's 1,200 men were to capture Patterson's guns and be ready to fire when they saw Pakenham's rocket signal. Seamen and troops detailed for other duties swelled the total of the attacking force to 8,000 men.[37]

Thornton, his troops, and the seamen were ready to cross the river at 9 P.M., but there were no boats. A dam had broken, the sides of the newly dug river end of Villeré Canal had caved in, and all the boats were blocked a quarter of a mile from the river. By 5 A.M. on January 8, tired sailors had been able to drag only enough boats to the river for 298 troops and 100 seamen. So, as Thornton reported: "We were unable to proceed across the river until eight hours after the time appointed. . . . The current was so strong, and the difficulty, in consequence of keeping the boats together, so great, that we only reached this side of the river at daybreak."[38] The current forced his boats downriver so that he landed about three miles below Morgan's line.

---

37. James, *A Full and Faithful Account*, II, 373–74; Adams, *History of the United States*, VIII, 372–73; Bassett, *Life of Jackson*, 192–93.

38. Thornton's report to Pakenham, January 8, 1815, in Latour, *Historical Memoir*, clvii.

Jackson began to review his line at 1 A.M. that Sunday morning. He started at the river end, where a company of the 7th Regiment and Beale's Rifles protected the redoubt. From battery No. 1 to No. 6 were the rest of the 7th Regiment, Plauché's battalion, Lacoste's and Daquin's troops, then the 44th Regiment—total number of regulars and militia, about 1,400 men. Colonel Ross commanded this part of the line. Carroll's command began with 50 marines to the right of No. 6. From No. 6 to 50 yards beyond No. 8 (where the line entered the woods) were 1,400 Tennessee riflemen and Adair's 525 Kentucky riflemen. Coffee commanded the rest of the line, the swamp part. He had about 800 Tennesseans and Jugeant's Choctaws.[39]

Thus, Jackson had between 4,000 and 4,500 sharpshooters behind his earthworks, ready to battle Pakenham's assault force of 5,300 men equipped with European rifles. These were heavier and shorter than the American long rifle and used heavier bullets: twenty to the pound. The American rifle used forty to sixty bullets to the pound. The smaller American projectile, with less air resistance to overcome, developed more velocity and striking power than the heavier British one. A British sharpshooter could qualify by hitting a target four feet in diameter at two hundred yards. At that distance, Jackson's sharpshooters could hit a deer between the eyes, or a duck; and at a distance of three hundred yards, they could hit the target 50 percent of the time.[40]

Pakenham's troops fell in at four o'clock and moved forward under cover of darkness. Mullins led Gibbs's column. He halted his 300 men at the first redoubt to pick up the fascines and ladders, but no engineer officer came to point out the equipment. A commanding officer, even of a regiment, is only a secondary person to the engineer department on such an occasion.[41] Mullins and his 300 men resumed the lead without fascines and ladders. The column halted six hundred yards from Jackson's earthworks, waiting for the starting signal. Gibbs rode to the front, where he discovered the 44th Regiment did not have the fascines and ladders. He sent Mullins and his men back for them, more than a quarter of a mile. Pakenham was on his way to the levee

---

39. Latour, *Historical Memoir*, 147–52; Brown, *Amphibious Campaign*, 137.
40. Lynn Montross, *War Through the Ages* (New York, 1960), 426–28, 563; Buell, *History of Andrew Jackson*, I, 73–74, II, 11.
41. Cooke, *Narrative of Events*, 247.

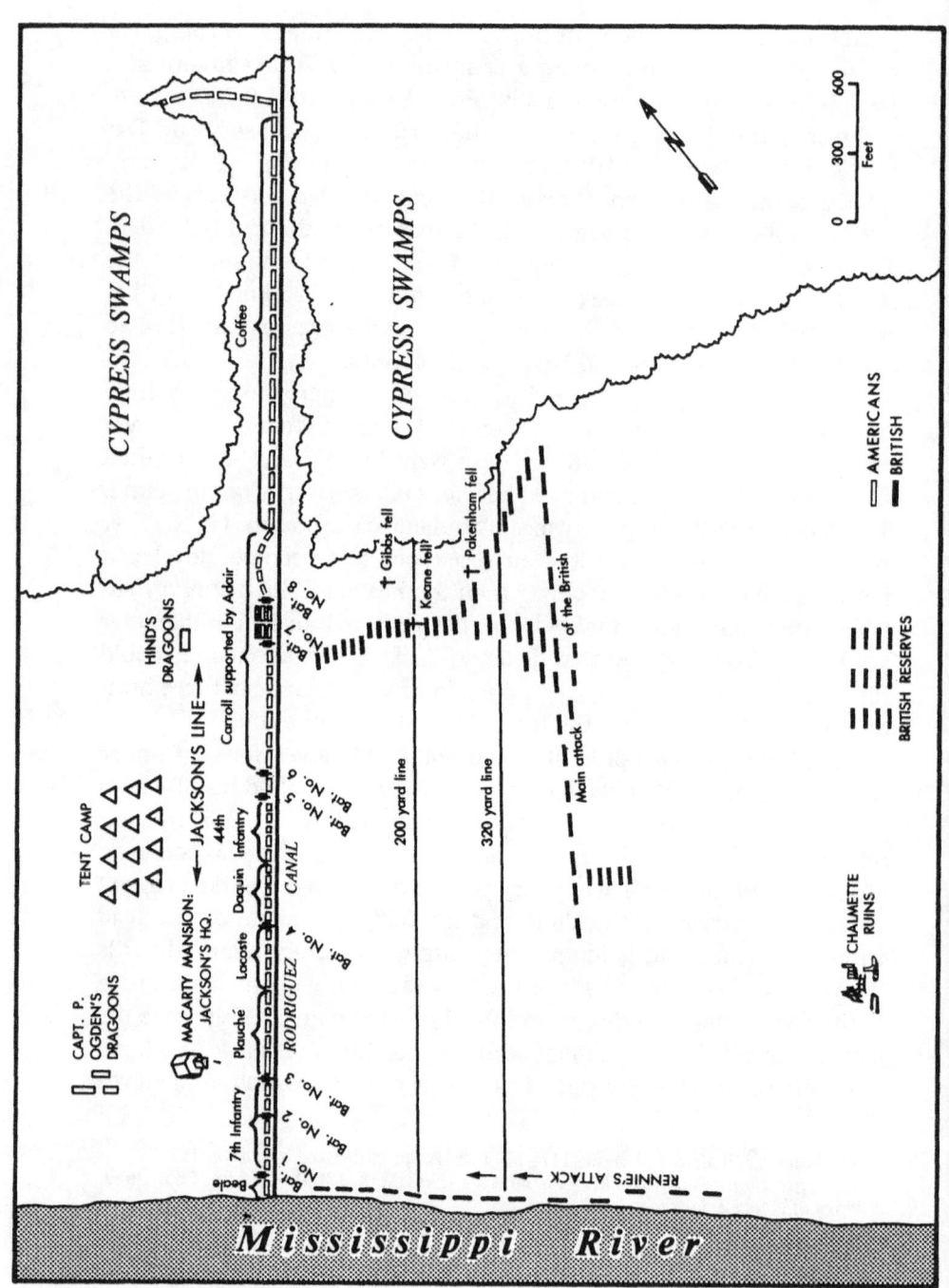

Last Round in the Battle of New Orleans, January 8, 1815

end of his line when this mishap was reported to him. Perhaps that is why he ordered Keane to forget about Rennie and support Gibbs.

At six o'clock Pakenham climbed to the top of the levee. There was a little daylight, but because of mist and fog he could not see across the river. He supposed that Thornton had landed just below Morgan's line and was ready to attack. If the battle did not start now, wind might lift the fog and Keane's column would no longer be protected from Patterson's batteries. So Pakenham ordered two rockets fired as the attack signal: one toward the river for Thornton and Keane, and one toward Carroll's position for Gibbs.

Jackson and several of his officers were standing on the parapet near battery No. 7. Through the mist they saw the sputtering trail of bluish light that the second rocket made. "That is their signal for advance," said Jackson.[42] He ordered the others off the parapet but remained there himself for a while longer.

Carroll's and Adair's men were formed four deep in open order with plenty of room to move to and fro. The first row was on the fire step at the parapet. After it fired, it was to step to the rear and reload so that, by the time the other three rows had fired and stepped back, the first row would be ready to fire again.

Jackson's gun crews had piled balls and grapeshot (a cluster, usually nine, of small iron balls) beside their loaded cannon. A capricious wind lifted the fog in patches. Gun crews and sharpshooters saw Keane and his 93rd Highlanders obliquing right to aid Gibbs, and Gibbs's sixty-man-wide column moving forward like deer or ducks approaching a blind. They were 500 yards from the earthworks.

Battery No. 6, with old General Flaujeac commanding, opened fire; the other seven batteries fired an instant later. Jackson's sharpshooters waited. Pakenham's 18-pounders replied, and Patterson's gunners across the river fired blind at their flashes. Then the fog lifted.

Cannon balls and grapeshot raked the British columns, knocking down whole files of troops; but the thinning columns advanced. When they were 350 yards from the earthworks, Kentucky and Tennessee riflemen fired. Redcoats fell like rain, including Gibbs. Pakenham galloped to rally the fleeing column, and grapeshot killed him at the 300-

---

42. Buell, *History of Andrew Jackson*, II, 12, 19.

yard line. Keane fell badly wounded, and his column was almost annihilated. On the left, two out of three of Rennie's men fell before survivors took the unfinished redoubt. Beale's Rifles killed Rennie and a few others, the rest of the British fleeing as best they could. Lambert, now the commander-in-chief, brought up the reserves. At the 250-yard line, they bolted and fled.

This battle lasted twenty-five minutes, but Jackson's rifle fire did not cease until 8:30 A.M. Then Jackson looked across the river and saw Morgan's troops retreating and redcoats advancing against Patterson's unprotected rear. By the time Thornton's troops debarked about three miles below Morgan's line, the main battle was over, but Thornton had no way of knowing this. He pushed his troops forward, and three gunboats (boats with carronades) advanced along the bank with them toward Arnaud's camp.

Arnaud's 100 men were recent recruits, untrained and badly armed. They resented being given an impossible task. How could they prevent the British landing? They had advanced on Saturday afternoon to a position opposite Villeré Canal and had remained there until midnight. Then, the British not having appeared, Arnaud posted a sentinel and led the rest of the men to camp, one mile below Morgan's earthworks, where they all went to sleep. Their courage was not revived when Davis arrived at daybreak with 170 tired Kentucky recruits, also untrained and badly armed. There was no rapport between the Louisiana militiamen and those of Kentucky. Arnaud's Frenchmen could not understand Davis, who was now in command.

Shortly after 7 A.M., Arnaud's sentinel ran into camp and pointed toward the advancing redcoats. Then the gunboats fired grapeshot. Davis barked an order that someone translated as "Sauve qui peut" (Save himself who can), and Arnaud and his men fled to the woods. The Kentuckians fired a few volleys and ran to Morgan's line. Morgan's Louisiana militiamen were behind the 200-yard earthworks, so Morgan posted the Kentuckians to his right along 300 yards of the unprotected mile of his line.[43]

Thornton outflanked the Kentuckians, and they fled toward the

---

43. Gayarré, *History of Louisiana*, IV, 484. "In taking to his heels the untrained man is justified by the traditions of thirty centuries" (Montross, *War Through the Ages*, 562).

earthworks at Bois Gervais Canal. Grapeshot from the gunboats persuaded Morgan's militia to join them. Patterson's gunners spiked their cannon, ran to the *Louisiana*, and pulled the ship upstream out of danger. Militiamen held behind the earthworks, and Thornton advanced no farther than the canal.

The artillery on Jackson's line blasted away until two o'clock in the afternoon. Then, as the guns cooled and the dense smoke from their firing rolled off the battlefield, Jackson's gunners and sharpshooters climbed the parapet and looked at the plain in front of them. It was covered with dead and wounded, and with those who had fallen paralyzed by fear alone. Later, Jackson said: "I never had so grand and awful an idea of the resurrection. I saw in the distance more than five hundred Britons emerging from the heaps of their dead comrades, and still more distinctly visible as the field became clearer, coming forward and surrendering as prisoners of war to our soldiers. They had fallen at our first fire upon them, without having received so much as a scratch, and lay prostrate, as if dead, until the close of the action."[44]

Lambert requested and Jackson granted a truce so the English could bury their dead, and Jackson sent troops to help them. Most of the dead were buried on Bienvenu Plantation, and about three hundred of the wounded were carried into the American camp. The remains of Pakenham and Gibbs were disemboweled, put in casks of rum, and sent home to England.

The official report of British losses for January 8 on both banks of the Mississippi was 290 killed, 1,262 wounded, 484 missing: total casualties, 2,036. Losses on Jackson's line were 7 killed and 6 wounded; losses across the river were 6 killed, 33 wounded, and 19 missing: total casualties, 71.[45]

England had tried to gain possession of the Mississippi Valley and control of the Gulf of Mexico's northern coast ever since 1698, when Daniel Coxe had sailed from Britain with a small invasion fleet. Bienville, coming down the Mississippi River with a few Frenchmen, had foiled this first attempt in September, 1699, at English Turn. Now

44. Parton, *Life of Jackson*, II, 208–209.
45. Lambert to Bathurst, January 10, 1815, Jackson to Secretary of War, January 19, 1815, both in Latour, *Historical Memoir*, cliii–cliv, lix–lx.

Jackson and his polyglot army of militia and a few regulars foiled Great Britain's last and largest invasion attempt.

After Jackson received official notice from Washington that the Treaty of Ghent had been signed, he disbanded his army; but before the officers went home, those of the Louisiana militia gave a banquet for the officers of the Kentucky, Tennessee, and Mississippi militias. Father William Dubourg, administrator of the Diocese of New Orleans, made the welcoming address. He ended it by expressing sorrow "that such an awful battle had been fought and so many souls sent unprepared into the presence of the Creator two weeks after the treaty of peace had been signed on the other side of the ocean." The guest officers chose Captain Henry Garland, one of Coffee's mounted volunteers, to speak for them because he could do so in French. He made some introductory remarks, then said:

> The British Cabinet believed that Louisiana was defenceless. There is a graveyard down yonder that the simple colored people never go near at night and that they call "God's Acre." That graveyard tells better than words can, the error of the British Cabinet. They say "dead men tell no tales." But "God's Acre" down yonder tells more tales of English arrogance and folly than could be told by all the orators from Demosthenes to our times!
>
> The most Reverend Prelate suggested that it was a pity that such an awful battle should have been fought after the treaty was signed. I do not agree with him. It needed that battle to make the treaty good. . . .
>
> The treaty as written did not mean anything. It says that the territorial *status quo ante bellum* shall be observed. But the British Cabinet held l'arrière pensée about that. They never admitted Napoleon's right to convey Louisiana to us through President Jefferson. They did not mean to include the Louisiana Purchase in the territorial *status quo ante bellum*!
>
> The treaty signed in ink the 24th of December was a cheat. But the treaty that pioneers of Kentucky and Tennessee punctuated with rifle-bullets the 8th of January will stand. . . . The British soldiers who lay down to die the 8th of January on Chalmette plain were sincere and honest. It was in their life-blood that the real treaty was written; not in the ink of Ghent. . . .
>
> Most people say that our American Republic was born the Fourth day of July, 1776, at Philadelphia. This is not true. It was only begotten then. It was born when Cornwallis yielded at Yorktown. But it was never confirmed, as they say in the religion of the Holy Saviour, until the 8th of last January!
>
> That day saw not merely the repulse and destruction of a British army, but it taught the whole world a lesson never to be forgot. It needs not the gift of

prophecy to foresee that the battle fought by Andrew Jackson and his "backwoods rabble" there did more than repulse cowardly and treacherous invasion. It taught all the princes and kings and emperors on the face of the earth that they must let our young Republic alone![46]

46. Quoted in Buell, *History of Andrew Jackson*, II, 79–83.

CHAPTER 9

Cartagena, 1815

General Lambert's engineers built a road to Lake Borgne because he did not have enough boats to carry off his troops in a body. The road was completed on January 18. That night, as soon as darkness concealed their motion, regiment after regiment stole away, leaving behind a pungent graveyard.

Rains had caused dead bodies covered with Louisiana mud to rise to the surface, and legs, arms, and heads appeared in many places above ground. The effluvium was unbearable. As soon as the British were gone, Jackson prepared to move the main part of his army to New Orleans.

On Saturday, January 21, his troops were drawn up behind the earthworks, ready to march as soon as Jackson's address and general orders were read at the head of each corps. The address began: "The enemy has retreated, and your general has now the leisure to proclaim to the world what he has noticed with admiration and pride—your undaunted courage, your patriotism and patience, under hardships and fatigues." Then Jackson proudly described each round of the battle from the night of December 23 to the last round on January 8, and the results of this short and decisive campaign.

In the general orders, Jackson praised every corps: the regulars, Tennesseans, cavalry of the Mississippi Territory, the Kentucky militia, Jugeant and his Choctaws, the Louisiana militia, the two volunteer corps of free people of color, distinguished foreigners, the Baratarians, men of the United States Navy, and all his staff and aides. Of the Baratarians, Jackson said:

> They performed their duty with zeal and bravery. . . . Captains Dominique and Belluche, lately commanding privateers of Barataria, with part of their former crews and many brave citizens of New Orleans, were stationed

at Nos. 3 and 4. The general cannot avoid giving his warm approbation of the manner in which these gentlemen have uniformly conducted themselves while under his command, and of the gallantry with which they have redeemed the pledge they gave at the opening of the campaign to defend the country. The brothers Laffite have exhibited the same courage and fidelity; and the general promises that the government shall be duly apprised of their conduct.[1]

Beluche was not present to hear himself praised. As soon as the battle was over, he had slipped away to wherever it was that he had anchored *La Popa*. The very day that Jackson was praising Beluche, January 21, 1815, the privateer captured *La Caridad*, a Spanish merchant vessel, off the coast of Santiago, Cuba. He put a prizemaster and crew on board the *Caridad* (which indicates that a number of Baratarians must have slipped away with Beluche) and ordered them to proceed to Cartagena.[2]

Four days later, the "American private armed vessel *Harrison*" fell in with the *Caridad*. Suspecting the *Caridad*'s cargo to be British, the captain of the *Harrison* took possession of the cargo and transferred it to his own vessel, then sailed to Wilmington, North Carolina, where he proceeded against it in the circuit court. Salvador Bages and others—Spanish subjects domiciled at Santiago—interposed a claim, alleging that the ship was a Spanish ship and, with its cargo, their property, was captured on the high seas by an armed vessel "cruising under the pretended colours of Cartagena."[3]

Using the alias Pedro Brugman, Beluche had his lawyer file a cross claim in behalf of himself and others. His lawyer proved to the satisfaction of the circuit court that *La Popa* had been "commissioned by the sovereign authority of the independent State of Cartagena, and furnished with letters of marque and reprisal, authorizing her to capture, on the high seas, the property of the enemies of said State." The circuit court decreed that the goods be restored to the possession of Pedro Brugman. Salvador Bages, for himself and the original Spanish owners, appealed to the Supreme Court, which upheld the decree of the circuit court on the following grounds:

1. Latour, *Historical Memoir*, clxxxii–cxc.
2. Henry Wheaton, *Reports of Cases Argued and Adjudged in the Supreme Court of the United States* (12 vols.; New York, 1816–27), IV, 497–99.
3. Ibid.

There is no doubt that the property was Spanish, nor that the privateer *La Popa* was commissioned as a cruiser. . . . The only question in this case is, whether an original Spanish owner is entitled to the aid of the Courts of this country, to restore to him property of which he has been dispossessed by capture, under a commission derived from the revolted colonies? . . .

War notoriously exists, and is recognized by our government to exist, between Spain and her colonies. . . . No neutral nation can act against either, without taking part with the other in the war. All that the law of nations requires of us, is strict and impartial neutrality. And no friendly nation ought to demand of the Courts of this country to do an act which may involve it in a war with the victor. Our duty is, whether the property of either is brought innocently within our jurisdiction, to leave things as we find them.[4]

Beluche was too busy in the Gulf and Caribbean to be bothered about what was going on in the courts of North Carolina. Soon after he had captured the *Caridad*, the eighteen-gun English brig *Forester* hauled *La Popa* into the harbor of Kingston, Jamaica, on allegation of having plundered an English vessel. Beluche was tried and acquitted in the vice-admiralty court at Spanish Town (then the capital of Jamaica) on Thursday, March 16, 1815.[5]

While being detained, Beluche had *La Popa* hove down, repaired, and refilled, and he signed on more than twenty seamen. Five of these were United States prisoners of war whom the English had recently released. "Before these sailors shipped at Kingston, the crew of *La Popa* were almost all black."[6]

When *La Popa*, with Cartagenan letters of marque and reprisal, was released, Beluche sailed westward and cruised off the Mexican coast near Punta Delgado. By the end of May he had captured nine valuable prizes. Then he changed *La Popa*'s cruising ground "and captured, between Matanzas and the Havana, a ship from St. Andero (Spain), a brig from New Providence, and a schooner bound to the Havana and ordered them for Cartagena."[7]

Beluche was cruising off the western tip of Cuba, between Cabo San Antonio and Cabo Corrientes, when he captured the *Cleopatra* on July 7. This merchant ship and its cargo, mostly of "wine, oil, flour,

4. *Ibid.*, IV, 499–502.
5. Kingston *Royal Gazette*, March 18–25, 1815.
6. Testimony of James Kelly, in SFA, *Conspicuous Cases*, Case No. 857.
7. Shipping Intelligence, Kingston *Royal Gazette*, September 2–9, 1815.

silks and perfumery," belonged to Ronaldo Tejada of Cádiz and other Spanish subjects and was engaged in lawful commerce between Cuban ports when *La Popa* captured it. Crewmen of *La Popa* transferred silk, laces, veils, and other articles from the *Cleopatra* to *La Popa*, then Beluche put Jean Marie Callet, prizemaster, and a prize crew on board with orders to take the *Cleopatra* to Cartagena for condemnation. Soon after separating from *La Popa*, the *Cleopatra* met with contrary winds. The vessel "being in bad trim for sailing, and being in want of provisions and water," Callet determined to put into New Orleans for refreshment.[8]

On July 26, William Somers, pilot at the Balize, discovered a vessel bearing south-southwest from the blockhouse. Somers rowed out to the vessel and found it to be the *Cleopatra*. Prizemaster Callet said he needed a pilot to enter the river and get to New Orleans, and he asked if any vessel under Cartagenan colors had gone to New Orleans. Somers said that several had. He remained on board the *Cleopatra* for a few days waiting for the wind to beat up against the current so that he could get to the Balize.[9]

Before the wind was favorable, the private armed vessel *Creole* appeared, captured the *Cleopatra*, put a prizemaster and crew on board, and then both ships steered southwest. The captain of the *Creole* and Callet agreed that they would sail for the Sabine River. Several days later, they found themselves at Galveston Bay. Reversing direction, they headed for Cat Island (near Timbalier Bay). On August 11, the *Creole* captured the *General Wale*, a sloop from New Orleans. The three vessels were near Cat Island when Lieutenant Thomas S. Cunningham, commanding the United States schooner *Firebrand* but flying French colors forward and Cartagenan colors aft, rescued the *Cleopatra* and the *General Wale*. The *Creole* escaped up Bayou Teche.[10]

Cunningham escorted the *Cleopatra* to New Orleans and claimed a "reasonable salvage." In spite of the fact that the crew of *La Popa*, then prize crews of the *Cleopatra* and the *Creole*, had looted part of the cargo, this "reasonable salvage" would be a considerable amount. Cun-

8. Libel of Diego Morphy, representing Tejado and the other owners, in SFA, *Conspicuous Cases*, Case No. 857; testimony of Callet, in *ibid*.
9. Testimony of Somers, in *ibid*.
10. Testimony of Cunningham, in *ibid*.

ningham's claim was for 1,953 barrels of flour, 1,830 pipes of red wine, one ullage (cask only partly filled) of the same, 6½ more pipes of red wine, 6 barrels of white wine vinegar, 45 boxes of vermicelli, 15 cases of hats, 13 boxes of glass, 22 barrels of peas, and one box of tooth powder.[11]

In this as in other cases where *La Popa* was involved, some of Beluche's seamen testified that they did not know the name of her captain. Felippe Briones, a Portuguese sailor, said the captain was Monsieur Pierre, and Callet said that Mr. Pierre Brugman was captain of *La Popa* and fourth owner.

After four years of revolution in South America, three provinces on the Caribbean coast of New Granada remained royalist: Panamá, Santa Marta, and Rio Hacha east of Santa Marta. Ten provinces were independent. Nine of these, including Cartagena, had confederated as the United Provinces with their capital at Tunja. The independent province of Cundinamarca in the heart of New Granada, dominated by its capital Santa Fé de Bogotá, refused to join the United Provinces. South of Cundinamarca, the provinces of Quito and Guayaquil and two provinces on the Peruvian frontier were controlled by royalists.

The ease with which the independent provinces had overthrown their Spanish rulers, and the fact that so far Venezuela had been the battleground, gave the United Provinces and Cundinamarca a false sense of security. They had not mobilized except for the troops guarding the Magdalena against Santa Marta and those on the Venezuelan frontier. Even when the royalists destroyed Venezuela's second republic and drove the patriots again into exile, the independent provinces in New Granada showed little interest in military defense against Spain.

When Bolívar and other Venezuelans arrived at Cartagena a second time as exiles on September 19, 1814, two factions were struggling for control of the city. Governor Toríces and his cousin General Manuel Castillo, commander of the troops guarding the frontier against Santa Marta, led one faction; the Piñérez brothers led the other. Foreign residents, and the owners and crews of privateers, favored the Piñérez

11. *Ibid.*

brothers, who opposed the heavy duties that Toríces had levied on prize goods.

Bolívar remained in Cartagena only one day, then he left for Tunja to report to the federal congress there. That body gave him command of local troops and of a patriot army that had escaped from Venezuela. With this force, Bolívar was to overthrow the dictator at Santa Fé de Bogotá and bring Cundinamarca into the federation. The dictator surrendered on December 12, and by January 13, 1815, the congress of the United Provinces had moved to Santa Fé de Bogotá. It named Bolívar captain general of the Armies of the Union, authorized him to get military supplies from Cartagena, take Santa Marta and Rio Hacha, and then begin the liberation of Venezuela.

News of this action produced repercussions in Cartagena, where Manuel Castillo was now the military dictator. Castillo moved his troops from the defense line against Santa Marta into the city of Cartagena, then shipped the Piñérez brothers and other opponents into exile.

While Castillo's troops were in the city, Santa Martan forces penetrated as far south as Ocaña. Bolívar, on his way from Santa Fé de Bogotá to Cartagena, recaptured Ocaña, dispatched troops to drive the royalists north to the sea, and proceeded with the rest to Turbaco on the outskirts of Cartagena.

Castillo refused to meet Bolívar, much less to equip him for a campaign against Santa Marta and other royalist provinces. Fearing that Bolívar might next move his troops to La Popa, Castillo had its water tanks poisoned. La Popa commanded all land approaches to Cartagena, and Bolívar would be in a position there to divert food caravans to feed his army with food intended for the city.

Bolívar did move his Venezuelan troops to La Popa on March 27. When they drank from its tanks, many sickened and died. During the next six weeks, Bolívar tried to negotiate with Castillo and failed, and royalist troops from Santa Marta regained control of the Magdalena River from its mouth south to Mompox. Then news arrived that General Pablo Morillo, with an expedition of 10,500 veterans of the war against Napoleon, had arrived in Venezuela, and that some of those troops were destined for the conquest of Cartagena and the other independent provinces of New Granada.

On May 8, 1815, Bolívar sent his resignation as commander-in-chief to the president of the United Provinces. He explained to his troops: "No tyrant has been vanquished by your arms; they have been stained by the blood of brothers. I leave you. . . . The salvation of the army has imposed this penalty upon me."[12] The next day Bolívar sailed for Kingston, Jamaica.

Castillo did nothing for the defense of Cartagena during the summer of 1815. A strange feeling of optimism pervaded the city as Beluche, Lominé, and other privateers sent in or brought food and ammunition.

The rest of independent New Granada was uneasy. It had no communication with Cartagena, and patriot armies on the Quito and Venezuelan frontiers were in need of weapons and ammunition. The Union Congress sent José María Durán to Europe to buy war matériel. He enlisted the help of Luis Brion, a merchant from Curaçao, who chartered the English corvette *Dardo* and sailed from London with weapons, ammunition, and three printing presses, "the whole on account of the United Provinces of New Granada."[13] When the *Dardo* arrived at the island of St. Thomas, Brion wrote to Bolívar asking how best to dispose of the unpaid-for cargo. Bolívar replied: "New Granada has plenty of money to buy from you everything you bring. The best route for you to take is up the Atrato River as Cartagena now has no communication with the interior, is without money, and has more than enough arms and ammunition."[14]

As Brion approached Cartagena on his way to the mouth of the Atrato, he decided to find out what was happening in that city. On August 1, he anchored under the guns of Fort San Fernando at Boca Chica, the narrow entrance to the bay. Brion found H. L. V. Ducoudray Holstein commanding this fort, two others near it, and Fort San José directly across from San Fernando on the island of Barú. Ducoudray, a Dane by birth, was with the French troops that Napoleon had sent to Venezuela in 1808, and when the first republic of Venezuela fell, he escaped to Cartagena. In the power struggle there, he had sided with the Castillo faction, and Castillo had given him command of the four

---

12. Felipe Larrazábal, *La Vida y Correspondencia general del Libertador Simón Bolívar* (2 vols; New York, 1878), I, 363–64.
13. Kingston *Royal Gazette*, August 5–12, 1815; Restrepo, *Historia de la Revolución de Colombia*, I, 273, 347.
14. Vicente Lecuna (ed.), *Cartas del Libertador* (11 vols.; Caracas, 1929–49), I, 169–72.

forts that guarded Boca Chica. This narrow entrance to the bay was twelve miles south of the city of Cartagena.

There was another entrance to the bay south of Fort San José on the island of Barú. In the seventeenth century, Spaniards had dug a canal through the mangrove swamps of Barú, naming it the Estero (canal) de Pasacaballos. It led from the sea to the Bay of Cartagena. Several gunboats were guarding the canal at this time.

Brion found Ducoudray, Louis Aury (a French privateer who commanded the naval forces of Cartagena), and others turning against Castillo because of his inaction as the Spanish threat increased. General Morillo had sailed from Puerto Cabello in Venezuela on July 12, and ten days later debarked 8,500 royalist troops at Santa Marta. Three thousand five hundred of these troops were conscript Venezuelans. General Tomás Morales crossed the Magdalena River with the Venezuelan troops, then led them behind La Popa, where they began the encirclement of Cartagena on the land side. Inhabitants of the area fled before Morales and found refuge within the walls of Cartagena, where they swelled the city's population to 18,000—an increase of 6,000 mouths to be fed.

Meanwhile, Morillo had established a sea blockade of the walled city and of the eight-mile-long island of Tierra Bomba that shielded the bay from the Caribbean. He could not take the four forts that controlled the Boca Chica entrance to the bay, but he took all of the island of Barú except Fort San José at Boca Chica, and he sent a fleet of light gunboats through the Canal of Pasacaballos.

Aury kept enemy boats from entering the bay until October 3, when he ran out of gunpowder. He begged Brion to let him have ammunition from the *Dardo*, safely anchored at Boca Chica under the guns of Fort San Fernando, but Brion refused. Aury had no money, and Cartagena had no credit.

As Morillo's gunboats entered the bay through Pasacaballos and connected with Morales' land forces, Aury retreated up the bay to the anchorage in front of Cartagena. He went into the city and found the belief spreading that Castillo was guilty of treason, so he helped plan Castillo's overthrow. Francisco Bermúdez, a Venezuelan who commanded the troops on La Popa, sent many of them into the city, where they were hidden for a few days. On October 17, when Castillo ordered communications cut between the city and La Popa, Aury and others arrested him and named Bermúdez to succeed him as military commander.[15]

Morillo tried to take the hill of La Popa, but Bermúdez's troops inflicted so many casualties on his forces that Morillo withdrew. He "contented himself with drawing the line of blockade closer, and awaiting the slower but more certain operation of famine." The death rate was about a hundred a day when, on November 13 or 14, Beluche in *La Popa* beat off two royalist schooners of the blockading squadron, entered Boca Chica, and anchored at Fort San Fernando with a cargo of food.[16]

Within the fort, Beluche found Ducoudray and Brion agreeing that only Bolívar could unite the patriots. Ducoudray thought that Bolívar should come to Cartagena to do this, so this former enemy of Bolívar wrote to him and said: "Dear General, an old soldier of acknowledged republican sentiments invites you to come and place yourself at the head of the government of Cartagena. . . . Captain Pierril [this was one of Beluche's aliases], who commands the *Popa*, has orders to take you and your friends to Boca Chica."[17] Ducoudray never bothered to call Beluche by his right name.

Beluche and Brion were not sure that Bolívar would or should come to Cartagena. As long as a few patriots held that gaping cemetery, the bulk of Morillo's troops would be concentrated in the small area between Santa Marta and Cartagena and could not be used against patriots elsewhere. Brion intended to leave Cartagena when Beluche did and take his cargo of war matériel to the port of Aux Cayes on the southern coast of Haiti.

This republic was a constant reminder to the great powers of a successful slave revolt. Therefore, the great powers had not recognized it, which made Haiti the one place in the Caribbean that could be used without international complications as a base for the invasion of South America. Beluche, Lominé, and other privateers knew its southern

---

15. Kingston *Royal Gazette*, October 21–28 and October 28–November 4, 1815. Colombian historians say that Castillo's arrest took place on October 17.
16. Kingston *Royal Gazette*, January 20–27, 1816; *ibid.*, November 18–25, 1815.
17. H. L. V. Ducoudray-Holstein, *Memoirs of Simón Bolívar* (Boston, 1830), 120.

coast well, especially its coves, where for years they had disposed of legitimate and prize cargo to their associates.

Early in the third week of November, Brion in the *Dardo* and Beluche in *La Popa* evaded the blockading squadron and got safely into the Caribbean. Then the *Dardo* headed for Aux Cayes while Beluche in *La Popa* sailed to Kingston with Ducoudray's letter to Bolívar.

By December, the stench of putrefaction in Cartagena became unbearable. There was no place to bury those who had died, and cadavers were piled up in the streets. The governing junta and its supporters planned to sail away on Aury's vessels with their families, but first they sent the surviving poor, most of whom were women, children, and old men, outside the city. Morillo sent the junta a message saying that he would not drive these starving wretches back into the city, but that it must surrender within three days.

More than two thousand half-famished upper-class citizens boarded the thirteen vessels of Louis Aury's squadron at the city's wharf on the night of December 5, then sailed past royalist batteries and down Cartagena Bay to Fort San Fernando at Boca Chica. No effort was made to stop them, but a few token shots were fired from the enemy guns. Morillo wanted them to get away so he would have two thousand fewer people to feed.

Aury's squadron anchored in front of Fort San Fernando on December 6. That day and the next, officers and their families boarded the vessels with some food from the fort that had been divided among them. Ducoudray was the last officer to leave the fort. By the time he and his family had boarded Aury's flagship *Constitution*, it was nearly midnight, but the squadron could not sail until the wind changed early the next morning, December 8. The refugees hoped that their destination would be Jamaica, but England was technically at peace with Spain and might not let them stay. If so, they would sail on to Haiti.

When the squadron reached the open sea, the wind increased to a gale and separated the vessels. Only three or four of them made it to Kingston, but, not being allowed to stay, they sailed on to Aux Cayes.

CHAPTER 10

The Aux Cayes Expedition

When Beluche arrived in Kingston with Ducoudray's letter, Bolívar resolved not to go to Cartagena but to sail in *La Popa* to Aux Cayes. Both his hot little room and his landlady were becoming unbearable. For six months, Bolívar had been paying his living expenses with money that the English merchant Maxwell Hyslop had given him; now his landlady presented him with a bill of one hundred pesos for "extraordinary expenses." Bolívar had no money, and he was too depressed to ask Hyslop for more.[1]

On Sunday night, December 10, 1815, Bolívar went out to *La Popa*, after instructing his paymaster, Felix Amestoy, and one of his aides to bring his baggage there the next day. So, that Sunday night, Bolívar was not sleeping in his room at the lodging house on the corner of Princess and White streets. The paymaster lay down in Bolívar's hammock, and about ten o'clock a slave named Pío stabbed him to death. Pío was apprehended the next day, and during his examination he confessed that some Spaniards had offered him $2,000 to murder Bolívar. They gave Pío some rum, which he drank, and was intoxicated when he stabbed the man he thought was Bolívar.

The murder of Amestoy delayed Bolívar's departure until December 19. On that day he wrote to Alexandre Pétion, president of Haiti, that for a long time he had wanted to make known the profound esteem he felt for him, and that Pétion's achievements had inspired Bolívar and his compatriots. Circumstances were now causing them to seek refuge in Haiti, and, Bolívar added, "I will hasten to present myself to you as soon as possible after arriving at Aux Cayes."[2]

After Bolívar boarded *La Popa*, Beluche headed toward Aux Cayes.

1. Alfredo Boulton, *Miranda, Bolívar y Sucre* (Caracas, 1959), 44–45.
2. "Sailed from Port Royal, December 19, schooner La Popa," Kingston *Royal Ga-*

In the afternoon, *La Popa* bespoke the Cartagenan privateer *Republicana*, and its captain, Gianni Barbe-en-fume (Johnny Beard-on-Fire or Redbeard) told Beluche that the patriot leaders and their families had escaped from Cartagena on December 5.[3]

La Popa anchored at Aux Cayes on the night before Christmas. In his conference with Brion the next day, Bolívar learned that the *Dardo* was to be returned to its English owners and that its cargo was safely stored in Haiti's arsenal at Aux Cayes.

The day after Christmas, Bolívar left for Port-au-Prince, arriving on December 31, but because it was the holiday season, he was unable to see Pétion until January 2, 1816. That night, Bolívar said in a letter to Brion: "The President impressed me, as he does everyone, very favorably. . . . I have asked that the schooner intended for you be sent to the port where our refugees are, as you suggested."[4]

Bolívar's conference with Pétion extended over a period of three weeks, and when he left Port-au-Prince, Bolívar had Pétion's promise that he would give all possible aid to the patriots. At Aux Cayes, Bolívar found that four vessels of Aury's squadron and a few other ships had debarked a total of six hundred famished men, women, and children. So wretched was their state that two hundred of them died in a few days. The survivors could barely stand on their feet. Haitian families took them into their homes and helped them regain their strength.[5]

During Bolívar's absence, the New Granadan priest Father J. Marimón had acted as though he had authority over the exiles, and the day after Bolívar's return, Father Marimón demanded that all Cartagenan letters of marque be turned over to him. He appointed Brion commander of the fleet and ordered Aury to offer Brion the services of Cartagena's vessels.[6] Just one year before, Marimón had deliberately poisoned the population of Cartagena against Bolívar and let him know that he, Marimón, would never aid but forever oppose him. Moreover,

---

zette, December 16–23, 1815; Fundación John Boulton, *Cartas del Libertador 1803–1830* (Caracas, 1959), 38–39.

3. Salvador de Madariaga, *Bolívar*, (Coral Gables, Fla., 1952), 268.
4. Harold A. Bierck, Jr. (ed.) and Vicente Lecuna (comp.), *Selected Writings of Bolívar* (2 vols.; New York, 1951), I, 129.
5. Vicente Lecuna, *Crónica Razonada de las Guerras de Bolívar* (3 vols.; New York, 1950), I, 417.
6. *Ibid.*, I, 419–21.

Marimón had dominated Castillo, so that Bolívar's campaign against Santa Marta could not get started and Cartagena had fallen to the royalists. Now, in Aux Cayes, Marimón was trying to dominate the refugees. He had to be crushed before his authority became recognized and powerful.

Bolívar called a meeting of the patriots to select a commander-in-chief and to make that commander's authority legal. Among those present were Brion, Aury, Ducoudray, the New Granadan Francisco Antonio Zea, and three Venezuelans, Carlos Soublette, Santiago Mariño, and the mulatto Manuel Piar. Bolívar began the meeting with a speech in which he analyzed the patriots' situation. First, Ferdinand VII's government and Spain lacked the manpower and resources to send enough forces to subjugate all America; therefore, the patriots must take advantage of this weakness, invade Venezuela, and aid the rebellion there before Morillo became strong enough to take all of New Granada. Second, the patriots must elect a supreme chief, then decide where they would make their first base.[7]

Brion jumped to his feet and said: "General Bolívar is a suitable man for such a command. If the majority are in his favor, I will join with my vessels and employ my means and credit to fit out the necessary number of other armed vessels and transports, with provisions, to assist General Bolívar but no body else." What vessel or vessels did Brion have at Aux Cayes? He was bluffing. However, he did have some credit with merchants in St. Thomas and Curaçao and with Maxwell Hyslop in Jamaica, who could command large credits. Brion appears to have been one of Hyslop's agents, and this may have been the reason why his bluff worked.

Louis Aury was against giving Bolívar unlimited power. Aury proposed that Bolívar be a member of a committee of three or five persons who would have joint authority. Moreover, Aury stated, the expedition should sail to Old Providence, and from that island base drive the Spaniards from Cartagena.

Brion instantly attacked both of Aury's proposals and then asked those present: "Do you consent that General Bolívar as Captain-general

7. Sources for the conference: Ducoudray, *Memoirs*, 122–26; Lecuna, *Crónica Razonada*, I, 421–23; Stanley Faye, "Commodore Aury," *Louisiana Historical Quarterly*, XXIV (1941), 15–17, in reprint.

of the armies of Venezuela and New Granada, shall be our only commander—yes or no?"

A few dissented, one of them being Aury. The next day, Aury presented a bill to Father Marimón for advances that he, Aury, had made to the government of Cartagena for the cost to him of the evacuation and of repairs he had made on two vessels in his fleet. The sum due him, he said, was $25,000, but he would accept the Cartagenan schooner *Constitution* as payment for his claims. Marimón, Zea, and other New Granadans consulted together, agreed that Aury should have the *Constitution*, and wrote a transfer of ownership that Marimón and Zea signed.

When Bolívar heard of this proceeding, he sent for Marimón and Zea, reprimanded them, and annulled the award. Then he requested the governor of Aux Cayes to station Haitian troops on the *Constitution* to prevent Aury from taking possession of it.[8] Bolívar next appointed Brion *capitán de navío*, or commodore. Aury refused to serve under Brion and sailed to join the Mexican patriots.

Beluche, meanwhile, was privateering. He had sailed away in *La Popa* after landing Bolívar at Aux Cayes on December 24, 1815, and joined another privateer with a Cartagenan commission, the *Centinela*. They captured two Spanish brigs from Cádiz bound to Havana, laden with silks and other valuable goods. *La Popa* and the *Centinela* had these prizes with them when, on December 28, they detained the *Dos Amigos* off Navassa, a small island between Haiti and Jamaica. The privateers took a few articles from the *Dos Amigos*, then let it sail away.[9]

Then the *Centinela* escorted the captured vessels to Aux Cayes while *La Popa* went prowling along the trade route between Haiti and Jamaica. Near Kingston, Beluche spied the schooner *Rosita*, alias *Pelican*. The *Rosita* had sailed from Santa Marta on December 24, heading for Kingston, where it took on a cargo of dry goods. The ship left Kingston on January 5, 1816. The next day, Beluche captured the *Rosita* and put its crew in chains but left the captain, Don Pedro Bruno, and two supercargos unchained. Putting a prize crew on the ship,

8. Faye, "Commodore Aury," 16–17; Ducoudray, *Memoirs*, 125–26.
9. Kingston *Royal Gazette*, January 6–13, 1816.

Beluche transferred the captain and supercargos to *La Popa* and sailed to Aux Cayes.[10]

He anchored outside that harbor at eight o'clock on the night of January 10. Seeing the *Centinela* within, he signaled it. The *Centinela* came out to *La Popa* and the *Rosita*, and the three vessels sailed east about two leagues to the bay of Haquen or Aquin. There, marks on boxes and bales were erased and new ones put in their places. While this was being done, the value of the cargo was estimated at $40,000. It was landed and sold for $30,000 to a Frenchman who speculated in such merchandise. Then Beluche went back to sea. On this voyage, while on the open sea, he was hailed by a United States schooner. The captain informed Beluche that a Spanish warship from Cartagena was after him, at which Beluche laughed and said, "I would like to meet that warship."[11]

Captain Bruno and the two supercargos of the *Rosita* were still on board *La Popa*. They had observed all these events; and later, after Beluche landed them on the coast of Cuba, Captain Bruno told Spanish authorities that *La Popa* had a crew of one hundred men and was armed with one 16-pound cannon, one 12-pound swivel, twelve small bronze cannon, and fifty muskets.[12]

Beluche sailed from Cuba toward Jamaica on January 28, capturing the *Havannera* off Pedro Point (on the north coast of Jamaica almost at its western end). "His crew plundered her of 44,000 dollars and every other portable article they could lay their hands on, then permitted her to proceed to her port of destination." The Jamaican paper that reported this action said that before Beluche had taken the *Havannera*, he had sunk the *Caridad*, which had sailed from Rio Hacha with a cargo of cattle and logwood. The report did not say what Beluche did with the cargo, but he did remove the *Caridad*'s crew before he sank it.[13] Beluche could always use more sailors to man captured vessels.

Cartagenan commissions were good for only three months, and Beluche's had now expired, so he returned to Aux Cayes to see if Bolívar was ready to sail to Venezuela. As soon as he had a base on Venezuelan

---

10. Corráles (ed.), *Documentos de Cartagena*, II, 296–97.
11. *Ibid.*
12. *Ibid.*
13. Kingston *Royal Gazette*, January 27–February 3 and February 3–10, 1816.

territory, Bolívar was to establish a prize court and issue letters of marque and reprisal.

There was much activity in the bay of Aux Cayes when Beluche arrived and many small vessels coming and going. Wherever their captains could make a landing on islands like St. Barts or St. Thomas in the Lesser Antilles, these ships picked up patriot refugees. One captain had delivered a letter to Josefina Machada in St. Thomas, who had been Bolívar's sweetheart since 1813. Bolívar wanted her to come to Aux Cayes, but Josefina was not ready to return with the messenger. He may have been the one who delivered a letter to Bolívar from Jean Baptiste Bideau (or Videau), who happened to be at St. Thomas.

Bideau, a mulatto, had been born on the island of St. Lucia before the English took it from the French. In his letter, he advised Bolívar that the conquest should begin in Guayana, Venezuela's largest province, which extended south from the Orinoco to Brazil. Guayana was rich in cattle, mules, and food from the Caroní missions and had not suffered from the war. Many of the inhabitants were secretly opposed to the Spaniards and would declare for independence as soon as Bolívar presented himself with a thousand men. General Morillo was unaware of this undercurrent in Guayana and felt so sure of the province that he had only a few troops defending it. Moreover, the Negroes that Bideau knew had possession of Güiria (a port opposite Trinidad on the Gulf of Paria) and Maturín (a river port some distance up the Río Guarapiche, a branch of the Río San Juan that empties into the Gulf of Paria). Bolívar could enter Guayana overland from Güiria or Maturín after privateers had landed him, his army, and war matériel there.[14]

Bolívar, Mariño, and Piar discussed this letter, and all three perceived the merit of Bideau's proposed strategy. Then news from Margarita deflected them from this entry. Margaritans had risen en masse and, directed by Juan Bautista Arismendi, had forced the Spaniards to take refuge in the forts of Santa Rosa, Pampatar, and Porlomar, and within the fortified line of Asunción. They could not sally forth from this fortified area without suffering defeat after defeat.

What the refugees did not know was that Salvador de Moxo, whom Morillo had left in command in Caracas, had formed an armed squad-

14. Ducoudray, *Memoirs*, 193.

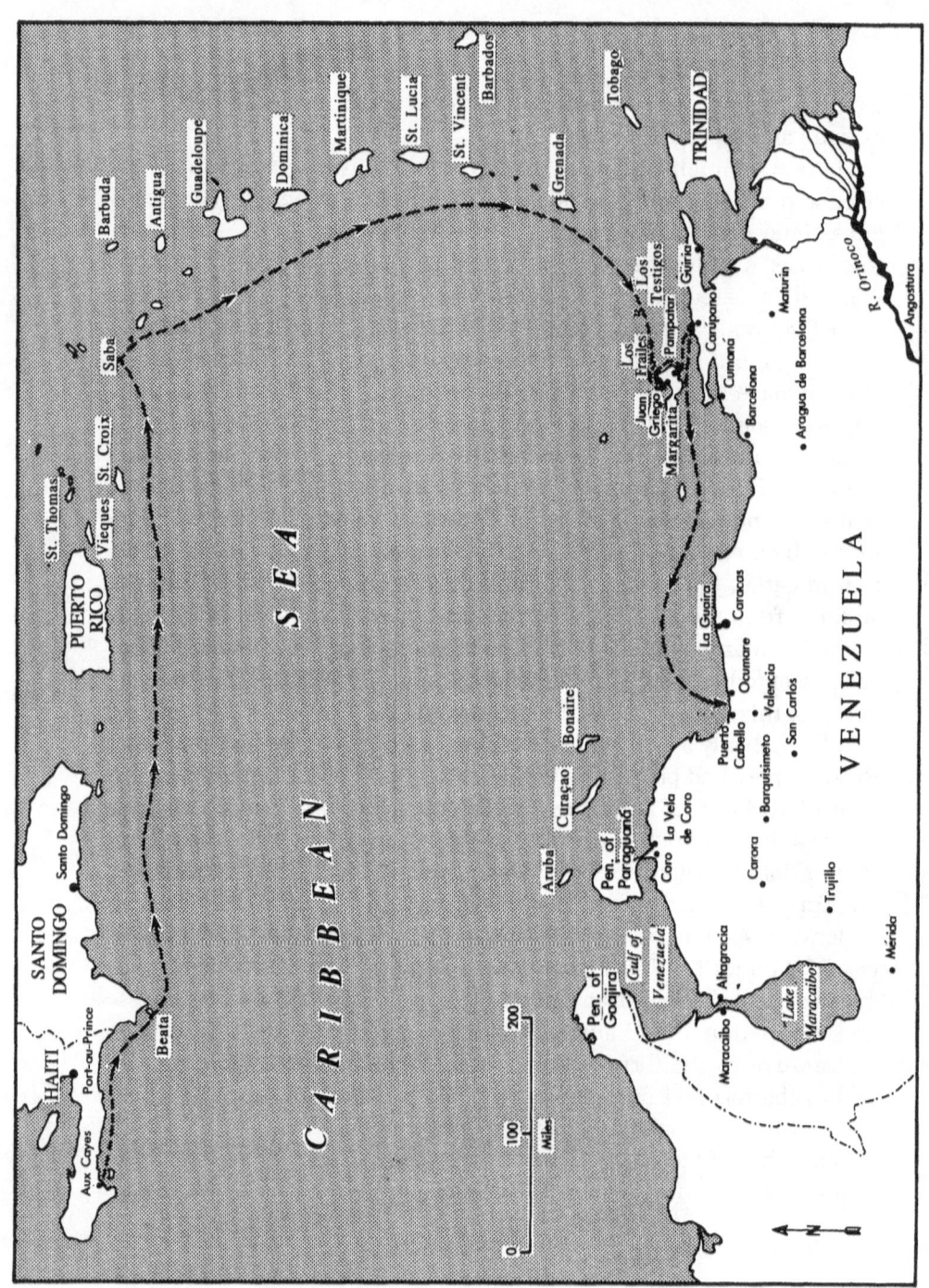

The Aux Cayes Expedition, March 31 to July 17, 1816

ron of five vessels to blockade the island: the 14-gun brig *Intrépido*, and the schooners *Morillo*, *Ferrolana*, *Rosa*, and *Rita*. Moxo put garrisons on board each vessel, and in March this squadron began to blockade Margarita.[15]

Bolívar and his council voted to sail first to Margarita, establish a base there where they could issue privateer commissions, then decide what to do next: attack Caracas, or move on Guayana, or perhaps both. Bolívar appointed Ducoudray chief of staff and asked him to include Carlos Soublette when he organized it. Brion was already in command of the navy. What navy? It was composed of seven schooners: Beluche's *La Popa*, Lominé's *Jupiter* (this had been Beluche's *Piñérez*, but Lominé was now listed as its owner), the *Constitution*, another Cartagenan schooner, and three schooners that President Pétion had sent to Bolívar.[16] These three may have been privateers that, like *La Popa*, needed a new source of letters of marque and reprisal.

Cooperating with Bolívar worked to Pétion's advantage. Privateers, attracted to Bolívar as a new source of commissions, had brought prosperity to Haiti. This prosperity would continue when Bolívar established a base from which to issue letters of marque and reprisal. Each of the seven vessels was well stocked with war matériel because Pétion had ordered the governor of Aux Cayes to let Bolívar have 15,000 pounds of powder, 15,000 pounds of lead, 4,000 muskets with bayonets, and a printing press from Brion's cargo.[17]

Lominé must have felt that luck would be with him because he changed the name of his *Jupiter* to *Feliz*. Beluche changed the name of *La Popa* to *General Bolívar* when it was chosen to be the flagship. This was the best armed and fastest of the seven schooners. When Bolívar, Brion, and Ducoudray boarded, they appropriated the cabin, and Beluche, the captain and owner, shared the deck along with the other officers, the sailors, and baggage. There were no women on board the *General Bolívar* because it was intended to spearhead attack and defense. Ducoudray said that the following persons boarded the schooners:

15. Lecuna, *Crónica Razonada*, I, 398–99.
16. Ducoudray, *Memoirs*, 184.
17. Lecuna, *Crónica Razonada*, I, 429.

six generals, nine colonels, forty-seven lieutenant colonels, a chief of staff, three adjutant generals and their colonels, and eighteen officers of the staff; one commandant of artillery, one intendant general, one secretary general of the intendancy, and a good number of the administration of the army; one commandant general of cavalry, without taking into account that each general had his aide-de-camp, a secretary, servants, and many their mistresses or wives; that each adjutant general and each colonel had his adjutant; that the number of majors, captains, and lieutenants amounted to about 500, and that we had for these epaulets not fifty soldiers. Each lady had either her mother, sister or some other friend male or female, servants and a good deal of baggage, which embarrassed greatly the manoeuvering of the vessels. There were besides a number of families, emigrants from Venezuela, who embarked at Aux Cayes in spite of the entreaties of Brion, who was against the admittance of any female on board the squadron.[18]

Ducoudray also opposed having women along, and on this issue he could maintain a holier-than-thou attitude, since he had left his wife and children in Aux Cayes.

The seven little vessels sailed from Aux Cayes at the end of March, their objective being the liberation of half of South America. They cruised east along the coast and were approaching the island of Beata when a fast-sailing pilot boat hailed the *General Bolívar* and reported that Josefina had arrived at Aux Cayes with her mother and sister. This created a problem. Would the fleet return for Josefina or sail on without her?

Brion and Ducoudray seemed to be the only ones who begrudged Bolívar his sweetheart. They made no attempt to hide their annoyance—and for a very good reason. If Josefina came on board, they would have to move out of the cabin and sleep on deck like Beluche. Eventually they consented to let her travel with the expedition on condition that she stay off the flagship.

So Bolívar appointed Carlos Soublette as Josefina's escort, and Captain Jean Monier sailed the *Constitution* back to Aux Cayes for Josefina, her mother and sister, and all their baggage. When they caught up with the fleet, Bolívar made his toilet in a superb style, and everyone on *La Popa* watched as he departed to visit the *Constitution*. He remained a day and a night and then returned to the flagship.

18. Ducoudray, *Memoirs*, 142.

There was no haste in making love or war on this expedition. Why hurry? Who could tell when or where the Spaniards would be sighted?

"Schooner ahead! Spanish!" yelled the lookout.

Lominé in the *Feliz* gave chase and came alongside the schooner near Santo Domingo City. As grappling hooks of the *Feliz* bit into the schooner, its crew jumped overboard and escaped to shore. They reported that two priests were still on board. The whole city was in alarm until Lominé exchanged the two priests for two cows, and the expedition sailed on.[19]

After passing Puerto Rico, the fleet began island-hopping to pick up patriot refugees, food supplies, and crewmen. The expedition followed the line of the Antilles in order to approach the north coast of Margarita from the east.

Days passed into weeks and weeks into a month as the fleet sailed leisurely along. On May 1, at nightfall, the watch sighted the Testigos Islands. At dawn the squadron changed its course to due west, and by seven o'clock they saw the islands of Los Frailes and at the same time the mountains of Margarita. Two hours later the watch sang out, "Enemy sail to the west! Big schooner and a brig!"

The schooner was swifter than its companion and soon left it behind. Lominé in the *Feliz*, followed by the *Mariño* and *Conejo*, went in pursuit of the schooner, while the rest of the fleet followed behind the flagship. As the distance lessened between it and the brig, Beluche saw that his enemy was the *Intrépido*. When the two vessels were within cannon-shot of each other, Beluche's gun crews fired.

Enemy cannon answered. Some troops on the *Intrépido* jumped into the rigging and fired their muskets. Most of their shots went wild, but one shot hit Brion in the head. He had to be carried below, and with the exception of Bolívar, all the passengers also went below. Bolívar climbed into the longboat, and from this vantage he watched Beluche and his crew fight the Battle of Los Frailes.

They were old hands at boarding and taking command of another vessel. As soon as grappling hooks were in place, Beluche's crew swarmed onto the *Intrépido* and felled anyone who got in their way. They took the quarter-deck and drove to the hold those Spaniards

---

19. Lecuna, *Crónica Razonada*, I, 438–39.

whom they did not kill or who did not jump overboard. When Bolívar boarded the *Intrépido*, he found the captain dead in his cabin, forty-two killed and thirty-one wounded on the decks and in the hold. Beluche's casualties were seven crew members killed and eight wounded.[20]

The vessels that had chased the schooner returned late in the afternoon with their prize. It was the *Rita*; and when Beluche admired its long slim lines, Bolívar awarded the *Rita* to him as a prize of war.[21]

The Battle of Los Frailes ended the blockade of Margarita on its north side. That day, May 2, 1816, Bolívar promoted Brion to admiral and Beluche to commodore. Soublette, who had protected Josefina on the *Constitution* one mile distant from the battle, was promoted to adjutant general colonel. Ducoudray was not promoted.

---

20. Santiago Mariño's May 3 report, in *Niles' Weekly Register*, X (July 13, 1816), 335; Lecuna, *Crónica Razonada*, I, 440–41; Daniel Florencio O'Leary, *Memorias del General O'Leary, publicados por su hijo, Simón B. O'Leary* (32 vols.; Caracas, 1879–1914), XV, 54.
21. Ducoudray's June 8 report, in *Niles' Weekly Register*, X (August 3, 1816), 379.

CHAPTER 11

The *General Arismendi*

After the Battle of Los Frailes, Bolívar's fleet with its two prizes sailed into the harbor of Juan Griego on the north coast of Margarita. A *flechera*[1] with visitors aboard came alongside the *General Bolívar*. The visitors had come to compliment Bolívar and his officers and to invite them ashore. Bolívar embraced the first man who came aboard. He was thin, muscular, and about fifty years old, "though in appearance older; continued anxiety, his hard mode of living, together with several wounds having done more than time to increase the deep furrows which marked his weatherbeaten countenance."[2] The man was Juan Bautista Arismendi.

Bolívar, Arismendi, and their principal officers debarked and rode horseback to Arismendi's headquarters. The next day, Bolívar had cannon, muskets, and ammunition landed for the Margaritans; and Arismendi called a meeting of the most important inhabitants for May 7. Arismendi explained to those assembled the necessity of concentrating the direction of the war and the destiny of the republic in one leader. Then he said: "The patriots who escaped to Aux Cayes have elected Bolívar to be their supreme chief. I, too, recognize General Bolívar, and I entreat you to do the same."[3]

The Margaritans gave unanimous approval, whereupon Arismendi proclaimed Bolívar commander-in-chief of the Republics of Venezuela

---

1. "These boats are fifty feet long, very sharp and low, to admit of their being propelled by paddles dexterously handled by the Indian rowers who, keeping perfect time in the strokes, give in consequence greater impetus to the *flecheras*; hence their name from *flecha*, an arrow." Ramón Páez, *Wild Scenes in South America, or Life in the Llanos of Venezuela* (New York, 1862), 427–28.
2. Captain Cowie, *Recollections of a Service of Three Years During the War-of-Extermination in the Republics of Venezuela and Colombia* (2 vols.; London, 1828), I, 33.
3. Lecuna, *Crónica Razonada*, I, 442–43.

and New Granada. Bolívar accepted the honor with great dignity, immediately ordering that the flag of Cartagena be lowered from his vessels and replaced by that of the Republic of Venezuela. Next, he proclaimed an admiralty court established at Juan Griego, and each of his vessels "was duly commissioned and authorized by the Republic of Venezuela to capture all vessels, their cargoes and all other property belonging to enemies of the said republic."[4] It was at this time that Beluche changed the name of his prize, the *Rita*, to the *General Arismendi*.

When Juan Bautista Pardo, Spanish commander of the eastern end of the island, learned that Bolívar's fleet was in the harbor of Juan Griego, he totally destroyed Asunción, the capital of Margarita. Then Pardo retired with his army to the forts of Pampatar and Porlamar. Beluche and Bolívar appeared before Porlamar on May 17 with five patriot schooners and some *flecheras*, but cannon fire from the forts kept the vessels at a respectful distance. Not having enough manpower to force the issue by land, Bolívar directed the fleet to return to Juan Griego.

He knew his expedition would have to leave Margarita, not because of the royalists, but because of poverty. "We were absolutely destitute of everything," wrote Ducoudray. "The small rocky island was unable to furnish us the necessary provisions; the vessels were in want of rations for the crew, so that each officer and private had a scanty ration, consisting of a little cake of Indian meal, not weighing two ounces, called *arepa*, and two small salted fishes, and nothing else! . . . no money, no clothes, nor anything but great confusion and misery."[5]

On May 25, Bolívar's squadron sailed from Margarita, "and after a long passage of six days, owing to the rapidity of the current," anchored in front of Carúpano in the late afternoon of May 31. At dawn the next morning, Bolívar notified the Spanish commander that unless he surrendered the town, it would be assaulted. When the commander refused to surrender, the patriot squadron fired grapeshot on the beach and the center of town while troops disembarked. In less than two hours, the patriots were in possession of Carúpano. The royalists fled to the west, leaving munitions and provisions behind.

4. SFA, *Conspicuous Cases*, Book D, Case No. 1035.
5. Ducoudray, *Memoirs*, 152.

The victors found Carúpano's stores filled with food and dry goods, and each one helped himself. This development was more than Ducoudray could endure. He went to Bolívar and said: "None of the provisions are being distributed in the regular way. Let me make magazines and station guards and sentries in order to save them, and then distribute regular rations."

Bolívar laughed. "The guards," he said, "would be the first to take what they wanted and the attempt would be useless."

Ducoudray was shocked. This was not the way a victorious army took possession of the spoils of war in Europe. "But if we don't do this," he protested, "the food will be gone in a few days."

"You are right," agreed Bolívar, "and then we will tighten our belts until fortune smiles on us again."[6]

Mariño and Piar persuaded Bolívar to let them advance on Güiria and Maturín to begin the liberation of eastern Venezuela. They asked for and received officers, arms, ammunition, one schooner, and some *flecheras* to convey them along the coast. Once again, Ducoudray was shocked. He told Bolívar that Mariño and Piar would set themselves up as independent dictators, but Bolívar took that risk because these two could occupy Güiria and Maturín and send him recruits.

Officers whom Ducoudray had reprimanded gathered around Josefina, who had gone ashore and moved into a house at Carúpano. They contrived to frustrate every improvement that Ducoudray tried to make. Moreover, Bolívar did not support his efforts to discipline officers and troops and had not promoted Ducoudray to the rank of general. So it was at Carúpano that Ducoudray resigned from Bolívar's army. He sailed to Haiti for his wife and children, then left for the United States.[7]

Bolívar's situation was critical. Some of his men had died, and some had gone with Mariño and Piar. Although Bolívar had been able to round up a few recruits, and Mariño and Piar had sent him some, all of these together amounted only to two hundred troops. These additions gave Bolívar a total of six hundred troops. The Spaniards were concentrating twice that number at Cumaná for an attack by land, and twelve

6. *Ibid.*, 152–53.
7. Lecuna, *Crónica Razonada*, I, 449–50; Ducoudray, *Memoirs*, 157–68.

vessels were ready to attack Bolívar by sea. His fleet and munitions had been depleted to aid Mariño and Piar, and Lominé, one of Bolívar's best captains, had taken the battered *Intrépido* to New Orleans for repairs.

Beluche's crews were restless. They had been inactive and unpaid for two months, and Brion, now apparently recovered from his head wound, wanted to leave Carúpano before all the rations were gone. He did not have enough men to battle the Spanish fleet. Bolívar did not have enough troops to attack Cumaná, and there was not enough food to last while the expedition sailed to Guayana.

Bolívar thought of his coffee and cacao plantations in the valley of San Mateo west of Caracas—there he could get food and recruits. His expedition could land west of La Guayra at Ocumare, where the distance would not be too far inland to his plantations in the mountain valleys that lead east to Caracas.

The expedition sailed on July 2. Four days later, it anchored in the port of Ocumare, and by midday Bolívar's troops had occupied the town of Ocumare, one league from the port, without firing a shot.

Beluche persuaded Brion that unless their unpaid crews had a chance to take prizes soon, many sailors would desert. The captains assured Brion that prizes were available because, as Bolívar advanced east toward Caracas, wealthy royalists would flee to ports on the coast and sail away with their portable wealth, just as rich patriots had done seven months earlier at Cartagena.

Lured by the possibility of loot, crewmen disembarked arms and munitions on the Ocumare beach, took on board food produced by local haciendas, and harried the coast until September, when the ships needed repairs, especially the badly crippled *Constitution*. The *General Arismendi* and the *Constitution* sailed slowly toward New Orleans. The *General Bolívar*, with Brion commanding, went full speed ahead until Brion wrecked it on the Isle of Pines off the southern coast of Cuba.[8]

It was October before Beluche in the *General Arismendi* and Monier in the *Constitution* anchored at New Orleans. They found Lominé

---

8. Dateline Jamaica, September 21, 1816, *Niles' Weekly Register*, XI (November 16, 1816), 489.

there with the repaired *Intrépido*, which Pierre Laffite wanted to buy. Beluche and Monier were glad to sell the formerly Spanish schooner because it lacked speed.[9]

Barshell, a ship carpenter, examined the *Constitution* and reported that it was unfit to navigate the sea. So it lay in the harbor for four or five months before Barshell and his men began to work on it. They took two and a half months to make the repairs, for which Beluche paid Barshell $1,000.[10]

The *Constitution* sailed from New Orleans about the same time that the Spanish schooner *Estrella* left Havana, and it captured the *Estrella* on April 24, 1817, near the mouth of the Bahama Channel. Captain Monier sent J. F. Lamoreaux with a prize crew to take command of the *Estrella*, and Lamoreaux transferred the captain of the *Estrella*, its supercargo Juan Botet, and thirteen of its crewmen to the *Constitution*. They had not been aboard very long when the *Constitution* "upset in a gale of wind and sunk, at the distance of about one or two miles from the *Estrella* by which accident between twenty and thirty of her crew, including Captain Monier, were drowned: and the remainder on board, amounting to about thirty-eight were saved on board the *Estrella*; but the crew of the *Estrella* on board the capturing vessel at the time she sunk, were all drowned excepting Juan Botet and two of the hands who saved themselves by swimming, and were also taken aboard the *Estrella*."[11]

Prizemaster Lamoreaux wanted to sail the *Estrella* either to Charleston or New Orleans but headed for Barataria instead because he had no papers—the *Constitution* had sunk before Lamoreaux could receive his prize commission and necessary instructions. Bad luck pursued him. "Within the waters and jurisdiction of the United States, to wit: Grande Terre or Barataria, the *Estrella* was recaptured by the United States ketch *Surprise* and brought to the port of New Orleans."

The law firm of Ellery and Smith, acting for Gaspar Hernández, a

---

9. Stanley Faye, "The Great Stroke of Pierre Laffite," *Louisiana Historical Quarterly*, XXIII (1940), 42 in reprint.
10. Barshell's testimony, in libel filed May 19, 1817, by Gaspar Hernández, in SFA, *Conspicuous Cases*, Book E, Case No. 1035.
11. Deposition of Miguel Muñez, filed June 2, 1817, in *ibid.*, Book E, Case No. 1035. The remaining quotations with reference to the *Constitution* and the *Estrella* are from the same case.

Spanish merchant resident in Havana and owner of the *Estrella* and its cargo, filed a libel against the schooner and cargo on May 19, 1817. The libel stated that the *Constitution* "had no commission whatever to commit hostilities at sea against the citizens or subjects or property of the King of Spain with whom the United States then were and now are at peace—in violation of the laws of the United States and the law of nations."

Lamoreaux's lawyers filed his claim and answer on May 27. In it, Lamoreaux argued that the *Constitution* was "duly commissioned by the Republic of Venezuela, and authorized to capture all vessels, their cargo and all other property belonging to the enemies of the said republic . . . and the aforesaid schooner *Estrella* at the time of her capture belonged to the enemies of the said republic of Venezuela. . . . He, Lamoreaux, could not produce those papers because they had sunk with the *Constitution*."

Beverly Chew, collector of customs for the port of New Orleans, and three customhouse officers testified during the trial that the *Constitution* had arrived at New Orleans with, and had left with, about twenty crewmen, and that it had not taken on any arms and munitions. Witnesses for Hernández testified that the *Constitution* had indeed taken on arms and munitions at New Orleans, that the "crew numbered between 70 and 75 men, each well armed with muskets, sabers, pistols, etc., and that each sailor received $8 in advance." Moreover, several of the crew who shipped at New Orleans were citizens of the United States.

The district court issued a decree of restitution of the *Estrella*, its tackle, apparel, furniture, and cargo in favor of Hernández. Then Lamoreaux filed a petition of appeal to the Supreme Court on June 16. The Supreme Court met in February, 1818, and "affirmed the decree of the United States District Court for Louisiana District in which the claim of J. F. Lamoreaux, claimant, was dismissed with costs, and the *Estrella*, etc., decreed to be delivered up and restored to Gaspar Hernández, libellant."[12]

---

12. The Supreme Court's affirmation is the last item in Case No. 1035.

CHAPTER 12

Prizes and Prize Money

Beluche had better luck than Lamoreaux and Monier. While carpenters in New Orleans altered the *General Arismendi* to an hermaphrodite brig (square-rigged on the foremast and fore-and-aft rigged on the main), Beluche had agents like "William Young of the city of New Orleans, tavern keeper, residing in the Faubourg Marigny," help him round up a polyglot crew of French, Spanish, Portuguese, Cartagenan, Italian, and American seamen. About thirty of the Americans were from Philadelphia and Baltimore. Crew members were paid off either $12 or $14 in advance.[1]

The four months that carpenters worked on the *General Arismendi* were pleasant ones for Beluche. He was in love with Señora María Mezelle Beaudri Espocita. When he sailed away, Mezelle was with child.[2]

On February 18, 1817, the *General Arismendi* left New Orleans and took on part of its crew, armament, and provisions after it dropped downriver—that is, it loaded within the territorial waters of the United States. Beluche, on leaving the Mississippi, headed south to Yucatán and prowled along the coasts of Campeche, Mexico, Cuba, and as far east as the Bahama Channel.

Who knows how many prizes he made before June 9, when he captured the *Virgin del Mar* and the *Amiable Antonio* near the mouth of

---

1. Testimony of John Shott in *United States* v. *William Young*, in SFA, *Conspicuous Cases*, Book F, Case No. 1246; testimony of Antonio Alticen, Cayetana Mandana, Sebastian Tur, Domingo Castro, and Francisco José Acosta, in *Felipe Fatio* v. *Polacre "Virgin del Mar,"* in *ibid.*, Book D, Case No. 1068.

2. This child was seven years old in 1824, the year her parents were married. She and her four-year-old sister were legitimized at that ceremony. From Marriage Record of Mezelle and Beluche, November 17, 1824, in Parroquia de San José, Padres Agustinos Recolectos, Puerto Cabello.

the Bahama Channel? The sea leaves no trail, and there are written records only of those prizes that were involved in court cases or were reported in newspapers or to Spanish authorities. Beluche put a prizemaster with a five-man crew aboard the *Virgin del Mar* and transferred all but four of its crew members to the *General Arismendi*. One of these four, Antonio Alticen, later declared that "he had many conversations with the prize crew, as well as heard their conversations; . . . that the *General Arismendi* had been provisioned for a four months' cruise which had nearly expired; that they had left port with a crew of about 130 men which had been greatly reduced by manning several prizes; the number of which prizes this deponent does not precisely remember. But he recollects that they mentioned one brig from Campechy, lost afterwards upon the Mexican coast, one schooner from Coruna, one schooner from Tampico, one schooner from Vera Cruz, ransomed for $14,000, and one coasting vessel from Havana."[3]

The *Amiable Antonio* had sailed from Havana on June 8 "laden with a cargo of sugar, coffee, brandy, etc., on a voyage to Santa Cruz in the island of Teneriff." Domingo Castro, boatswain on board the *Amiable Antonio*, testified that Captain Beluche had put a prize crew on board "after taking out the best part of the crew of the *Amiable Antonio*, including this deponent," for service on board the *General Arismendi*, "whose crew had been reduced from 130 to 60 hands by manning the different prizes they had taken during their cruise."[4]

No more was recorded about the *Amiable Antonio*, which means that it escaped capture by any vessel attached to the New Orleans station. The *Virgin del Mar*, however, was not so lucky. It arrived at the mouth of the Mississippi River on June 24 and came to anchor a little inside the Balize. The prizemaster, Alticen, and another sailor went ashore in a small boat, and the prizemaster asked the pilot "to provide him with some hands to assist in navigating the polacre to Galveston." The pilot had no hands to spare, but he suggested that the prizemaster might get some from "Mr. Ever" (*i.e.*, Lieutenant Isaac McKeever), who was on the United States ketch *Surprise*.[5] The prizemaster and

3. Cayetano Mandano, mariner, and Sebastian Tur, cabin boy, made similar declarations. SFA, *Conspicuous Cases*, Book D, Case No. 1068.
4. Francisco José Acosta gave the same testimony, in *ibid*.
5. *Ibid*.

Alticen boarded the *Surprise*. While the prizemaster talked to McKeever, Alticen talked to one of the pilots and "related to him the circumstances of the capture of the polacre." The pilot reported this conversation to his commanding officer, who immediately sent for Captain McKeever. He ordered a midshipman and nine hands to board the *Virgin del Mar* and take it to New Orleans.

There, the firm of Ellery and Smith libeled "the polacre *Virgin del Mar*, her tackle, apparel, furniture and cargo" for the owners, José Antonio Vidal y Pasqual and other Spanish subjects. Beluche's proctor, the firm of Nicholson and Mabin, and J. B. Laporte filed a claim and answer for Beluche in which they "respectfully" showed that the *General Arismendi* had lawfully captured the *Virgin del Mar* "by virtue of a commission granted by the Republic of an independent nation that was and is at this time waging war against Spain." This claim was filed on July 19. A third party entered the case of Pasqual versus the *Virgin del Mar* when John Dick, United States attorney, presented a claim on the part of "Mr. Ever, the commander and officers and crew of the United States ketch Surprise," who wanted salvage.[6]

If the district court followed the precedent set by Case No. 1035 (in which John Dick had restored the *Estrella* and its cargo to the owner), it might award the *Virgin del Mar* and its cargo to Pasqual, the libellant; but it did not have to follow this precedent. The district court might decide that the capture of the *Virgin del Mar* was legitimate; however, since the capturing vessel had been armed and outfitted within the territorial jurisdiction of the United States, the district court might award everything to the salvage crew. Finally, there was a slim chance that the court might decide that Beluche and his crew should have some compensation. After all, the *General Arismendi* had not sunk near the Bahama Channel (as had the *Constitution*) with all the necessary papers. The *General Arismendi*'s papers could be produced in court.

Ellery and Smith for the libellants and John Dick for "Mr. Ever *et al.*" must have bargained out of court with Beluche's proctor and his agent in order to keep either the libellant or "Mr. Ever *et al.*" from being awarded everything. How else could one explain the agreement

6. *Ibid.*

made in court on October 20 that the cargo of the *Virgin del Mar* be sold by the marshal, and the next maneuver, which closed the case? This maneuver was:

> On motion of Mr. Smith one of the proctors for the libellant, and with the consent of Mr. Dick on the part of Mr. Ever the commander and officers and crew of the United States ketch *Surprise,* claiming salvage, [the court] ordered that the said polacre *Virgin del Mar,* her tackle, apparel, and furniture and whatever else she may contain, be restored and delivered up to the libellant by the Marshal. And further that the Marshal pay over one half of the net proceeds of the sale of said cargo of sugar (by the Marshal sold under the order of the court in this case) to the libellant or his proctors and that he pay over the other half thereof to the claimant [Beluche and his crew] or his proctor, deducting before the said distribution from the amount of the said sales all costs and Marshal's expenses, and also deducting the sum of three thousand dollars as salvage to the said commander, the officers and crew of the United States armed ketch *Surprise.*[7]

The loot from Beluche's prizes put a good bit of money into many pockets in New Orleans, especially into those of customhouse officials. The next Beluche prize they seized put a considerable amount of money into the pockets of Dr. Flood, whose plantation was about five miles below New Orleans on the west bank of the Mississippi.

During the summer and fall of 1817, Beluche slipped into New Orleans a number of times to visit Mezelle and to confer with his lawyers. On September 15, he bought two lots in Faubourg Marigny, the first suburb developed below the old city. Beluche sailed from New Orleans early in November. Soon a Jamaican newspaper reported that "the Venezuelan government brig, *Arismendi,* Captain Beluche, of 6 guns and 96 men, in 30 days from New Orleans, bound to Margarita, having carried away her rudder, put into Charleston to refit at the commencement of December."[8]

Beluche may have captured several prizes during the thirty days that it took him to sail from New Orleans to Charleston. He did send at

---

7. *Ibid.*
8. The property Beluche purchased is today 613–17 Esplanada. Friends of the Cabildo, *The Creole Faubourgs* (New Orleans, 1974), 136, Vol. IV of Friends of the Cabildo, *New Orleans Architecture.* See also Spanishtown (Jamaica) *St. Jago de la Vega Gazette,* January 3–10, 1818.

least one prize to Margarita.[9] After the *General Arismendi* was refitted, Beluche sailed to Margarita to renew his commission and left that island on February 2, 1818. Nine days later, on February 11, Beluche captured the slaver *Josefa Segunda* off Cape Tiburón on the south coast of Haiti almost at its western end—that is, not far from the southern coast of Cuba. Marcelino Moran, captain of the *Josefa Segunda*, begged Beluche to put him and his crew ashore, but Beluche permitted only Moran with four sailors to go in a small boat. They made it to Santiago de Cuba by the evening of February 13, and the next day Moran and his first and second mates appeared before a notary public to report their version of what had happened to the ship since it had left Cuba.

According to that report, the *Josefa Segunda* had cleared Havana in July, 1817, bound for the Guinea coast of Africa. There, her captain "purchased 314 Negroes of both sexes, all ages," and was loading them at the port of Maura on the night of December 9 when Englishmen from a sloop of war boarded the ship, damaged some instruments, threw parts of the rigging and equipment into the sea, and then sailed away. Moran steered the crippled *Josefa Segunda* to the island of Principe, where he made temporary repairs, going back out to sea on January 3, 1818. As he neared Cuba, he steered for the south coast, "having been informed that the north of the island was dangerous on account of insurgent privateers cruising there, and also on account of the state of his vessel." The *Josefa Segunda* proceeded without mishap until daybreak on February 11, when Moran sighted a brig to the northeast pursuing him.

The brig "crowded all sail to come up to the *Josefa Segunda* which tried to escape but could not because of the superior sailing of the pursuer. It came up to the *Josefa Segunda* at ¾ past 12 of the same day. The pursuing vessel proved to be the insurgent privateer *General Arismendy*, Captain Beluche. Seeing his superior force, it was thought proper by common consent to strike our flag, in order to avoid the

---

9. Luis Brion to Bolívar, February 23, 1818, in Enrique Ortega Ricaurte, *Luis Brion de la Orden de Libertadores, Primer Almirante de la República de Colombia y General en Jefe de sus ejércitos 1782–1821* (Bogotá, 1953), 39.

atrocities which this class of pirates usually commit. A prize crew came on board and put my crew in irons in the hold. The crew of the *General Arismendy* numbered 144 men, the greatest part blacks and mulattoes—and her armament one brass 18, two brass culverin (9 pounder) and four 18 carronades, musketry, etc."[10]

François Raimond was the prizemaster that Beluche had "duly commissioned" to take command of the *Josefa Segunda*. Raimond and his prize crew found "from 200 to 300 slaves on board, some of whom were dead." The *Josefa Segunda* and the *General Arismendi* sailed together along the south coast of Cuba for several days, during which time Spaniards came on board the *Josefa Segunda* to buy slaves. Raimond had sold about fifteen or twenty of them by February 23.[11]

At the end of February, Beluche gave Raimond orders in writing to sail the *Josefa Segunda* to Margarita. Forty-nine days later, on April 18, the slaver was at the mouth of the Mississippi River, many miles farther away from Margarita than it had been at the end of February. Beluche had taken only nine days to sail from Margarita to the waters near Cuba where he had captured the *Josefa Segunda*. True, the prevailing winds had favored Beluche, and Raimond would have had to sail against those winds to get to Margarita, and for that long voyage he needed provisions. But why did the *Josefa Segunda* have to go to New Orleans for provisions "when so many ports, more contiguous, and where supplies might have been obtained, were passed on her way to the Balize, without a single effort to procure a supply at any of them? Why not go to Kingston, in Jamaica, which was in the neighborhood of the place where the capture was made, and to which port the Privateer *General Arismendi* went after making the capture?"[12]

Customhouse officers at the Balize seized the *Josefa Segunda* on April 24 and conducted it to New Orleans. John Dick, district attorney for the United States, filed a libel in the United States district court on April 29 for the United States against the *Josefa Segunda*, its tackle, apparel, furniture, and cargo. On May 1, Beverly Chew, collector of

---

10. SFA, *Conspicuous Cases*, Book E, Case No. 1183; testimony of Marcelino Moran, in *ibid*.
11. Protest of François Raimond, in *ibid*.
12. James Brown Scott (ed.), *Prize Cases Decided in the United States Supreme Court, 1789–1918* (3 vols.; London, 1923), II, 1093.

customs, ordered the Negroes to be delivered "to Dr. Flood at his plantation below as soon as he is ready to receive them and upon his giving receipts with proper assurance therein of his being responsible for their custody. They will remain afterwards at Dr. Flood's plantation for safe keeping, none of them to be removed thence unless by course of law or by direction of the Collector, the Naval Officer, or the Surveyor."[13]

The seventh section of the Act of Congress prohibiting the importation of slaves into the United States after the first day of January, 1808, provides that

> any vessel hovering on the coast thereof, having on board any negro, mulatto, or persons of colour, for the purpose of selling them as slaves, shall be forfeited to the use of the United States and may be seized, prosecuted and condemned . . . and the proceeds of all such ships and vessels, their tackle, apparel and furniture, and the goods and effects shall be divided equally between the United States and the officers and men who shall make such seizure . . . provided that the officers and men to be entitled to one half of the proceeds aforesaid shall *safe-keep* every negro, mulatto, or person of colour, found on board of any ship or vessel so seized by them.[14]

Chew, by his order that the slaves shall be delivered to Dr. Flood for "safe-keeping," staked out his claim, that of Naval Officer Edwin Lorrain, and that of Surveyor of the Port William Emerson to one-half of the net proceeds from the sale of the *Josefa Segunda* and its cargo. These three men had never seen the *Josefa Segunda* until after it docked at the customhouse anchorage, but they intended to keep all other customs officers and the men they commanded from getting any part of the proceeds. At least eleven such officers were on the *Josefa Segunda* when it arrived at New Orleans, as is shown in the protest that Raimond made on May 4:

> By this public act of protest be it known that this day before me, Carlisle Pollock, notary public, in and for the city of New Orleans, came François Raimond, commander of the Spanish brig *Josefa Segunda*, prize of the Venezuelan Republican brig of War *General Arismendi*, Rene Beluche commander, who having been duly sworn to declare the truth, deposed that on 11th February last, he got orders from Capt. Beluche to take charge of said

---

13. SFA, *Conspicuous Cases*, Book E. Case No. 1183.
14. Scott (ed.), *Prize Cases*, II, 1092.

prize, and a cargo of negroes on board, which had been captured off Cape Tiberoni. That when he took charge of said vessel, there was a total want of provisions. The two vessels kept company steering for Cuba in hope to procure there some supplies, but got only a very trifling quantity; and to prevent slaves perishing of want, Capt. Beluche ordered this appearer to make the best of his way to the Island of Margarita, which order was endorsed on the copy of the Brig's commission.

The prize having afterwards experienced violent weather and contrary winds, and suffered much in her spars, sails, and riggings; and this appearer being convinced that the slaves and the 12 persons composing his crew were in danger of dying of hunger, the provisions being nearly exhausted, endeavored to make the Jardines de la Reine in Cuba, to procure water and provisions, but he could obtain only a very short supply; and forced by these imperious circumstances, he steered for the Mississippi and entered the river on the 18th of April, in the morning without having touched at any other part of the United States. . . .

That after arrival at Balize the prize was boarded by Mr. Roberts a custom house officer, who after having ascertained the fact of her having no fresh water, placed a keeper on board the brig at the desire of this appearer who thereby sought to remove or prevent all suspicion of an intention to violate laws of the United States. This appearer then purchased of Holland and Silva and Company, Branch Pilots, provisions for his immediate consumption, sent a boat on the 19th to Mr. J. B. Laporte of this city, merchant, for a supply of provisions, a boat, an anchor, cable, and some cordage of which he stood in need. His boat returned on the 24th April, with 6 bags of Rice and a letter from Mr. Laporte directing this appearer to wait until he should receive articles he had demanded, and then proceed to his port of destination.

That on the night of 24th, 25th at 11 P.M. two boat loads of fully armed soldiers boarded the prize as if she had been an enemy's vessel; . . . and Mr. Gardner, a Custom House officer, took command of the prize and proceeded up the river. They arrived at Fort Saint Philip on 25th at noon, and this appearer waited on the commanding officer for relief, but was informed by him that the vessel, having been seized by Custom House, he could not interfere.

Mr. Roberts, before mentioned, was present and took the Prize's papers, and refused to give any receipt for same until commander of Fort explained that it was fit he should do so. . . . The same day 3 other Custom House officers came on board, and the next day came some others, so that when they set out from the Fort, they had *eleven Custom House officers on board.*

From that moment this appearer was considered as a prisoner, but no warrant or order was signified; he was prevented from working the vessel and from all communications with the patrons of the pirogues which had brought the articles ordered from town. And such vigor was used by these

Custom House people, that a letter from Mr. Laporte to this appearer was detained, without his being even informed that it had been received. The said Custom House officers refused to give biscuits sent from town to the prize crew, on the pretext that they had been furnished by the Collector tho' from the Custom House permit it was apparent they had been sent by a merchant.

On the first of this month, the prize, then in charge of Mr. Johnson of the Custom House, was boarded by the Collector (Beverly Chew), Naval Officer (Edward Lorrain), and Surveyor of the port (William Emerson), with Dr. William Flood, which Collector informed this appearer he should be relieved of the slaves very soon, and on the 3rd they were sent on shore by the number of 152, who were sent off to Dr. Flood's plantation, leaving only one dying slave on board. . . .

And this appearer declaring he had never been served with any warrant, libel, or order of seizure, did protest, and at his request I, the said notary, do with him publicly and solemnly protest against all and singular the officers of the Custom House, and all others whom the same may concern, for said violent and unwarrantable proceedings, and for all damages and charges suffered, or to be suffered in consequence thereof.

And in faith of the foregoing the said appearer and protestor herewith signs his name at New Orleans on the 4th day of May 1818.[15]

By this time, a member of the firm of Caricabura, Arrieta and Company, owners of the *Josefa Segunda* and its cargo, had arrived in New Orleans from Havana. His proctor and counsel, Louis Moreau Lislet, filed the company's claim for the brig and its cargo in the district court on May 6. Within a few days, counsel for Caricabura, Arrieta and Company made a deal with J. B. Laporte, Beluche's agent, whereby the company was to pay Beluche a ransom of "not less than six nor more than eight thousand dollars, to depend on expense and trouble incident on prosecution and repairing of vessel." In return for this ransom, Beluche was not to enter any claim against the *Josefa Segunda* and its cargo, but he was to admit that "the claimants are the original owners of the vessel and slaves." After this deal, the claimants had Raimond's protest read in court as evidence for this case.[16]

The district court on July 9 condemned the *Josefa Segunda* and its cargo as forfeited to the United States. On July 11, Caricabura, Arrieta

---

15. SFA, *Conspicuous Cases*, Book E, Case No. 1183.
16. Testimony of Paul Lanusse, witness on the part of the United States, amended by claimant's counsel, June 15 and June 22, 1818, in *ibid*.

and Company filed a petition for appeal to the Supreme Court of the United States, and Judge Hall granted the appeal.

One week later, July 18, there were two important actions in connection with the *Josefa Segunda* and its cargo of 152 slaves: first, Caricabura, Arrieta and Company filed a new suit in the district court, a libel against said vessel and cargo, as the "sole true and lawful owners"; and second, the federal marshal of the Louisiana District served a warrant on George W. Morgan, sheriff of Orleans Parish, which commanded him to seize and take into his possession the brig *Josefa Segunda* and cargo of 152 Negroes, and "to cite and admonish the owner or owners, and all and every person or persons, having or pretending to have any right, title or interest, in or to the same, to be and appear before a District Court for the aforesaid, to be holden at the city of New Orleans on or before the 3rd day of August next, to show cause if any they have or can, why the said brig and cargo and Negroes should not be decreed restored to them."[17]

By this time, some of the 152 Negroes had died or run away, or had been sold secretly. All parties concerned wanted the survivors sold. These parties were (1) the United States; (2) Charity Hospital in New Orleans, which was to receive one-half of the net proceeds to be awarded to the United States; (3) the captors of the *Josefa Segunda* and cargo (Renato Beluche, his officers and crew); (4) Caricabura, Arrieta and Company; and (5) George W. Morgan, sheriff of Orleans Parish. These five parties on July 21 agreed that the sheriff of Orleans Parish sell the remaining Negroes on the following conditions:

1st. That said negroes be sold by auction in the usual manner, the price to be payable 1/10 in cash and remainder in all the month of March, next, in good notes endorsed to the satisfaction of said sheriff with the further security of mortgage on property sold.

2nd. That proceeds of said sales be placed in custody of the Bank of the United States, subject to order of the District Court of the United States for the Louisiana District, until final determination of suits now pending concerning said negroes.

3rd. That this consent and agreement be filed in said District Court and

---

17. SFA, *Conspicuous Cases*, Book F, Case No. 1221.

be made the rule of the Court thereof, and considered and held binding on the parties as a stipulation in admiralty.[18]

After this consent agreement was signed by those representing the five parties, the sale was set for July 30. Five days before the sale, Beluche's answer for the captors to the libel of Caricabura, Arrieta and Company versus the brig *Josefa Segunda* and 152 slaves was filed in the district court. In the answer, Beluche explained that the *Josefa Segunda* was lawfully captured, and that it was

> entirely disabled from prosecuting her voyage to said port of Margarita, and being entirely destitute of water and provisions, was compelled, in order to save the lives of persons on board, to make for the mouth of the Mississippi in order to have necessary repairs made and to procure provisions for subsistence of her crew and slaves, and that when in the river Mississippi was seized by officers of Customs and afterwards libelled in District Court of the United States for the Louisiana District for an alleged violation of slave laws of the same.
>
> And the respondent further saith, that subsequent to the arrival of the *Josefa Segunda* in the river Mississippi . . . this respondent did for good, lawful and valuable consideration consent to the ransom of said *Josefa Segunda*, her cargo, and remaining slaves, in favor of the libellants, the former owners thereof, and he doth in consequence hereby for himself as for officers and crew of said vessel, called *General Arismendi*, forever give up, relinquish and abandon to the said owners, the libellants in this case, all and all manner of right, title and pretension, which he or said officers and crew have or ever have had or might have unto said brig *Josefa Segunda*, her cargo and the slaves, who were on board of her when she arrived in the Mississippi.[19]

Sheriff Morgan had in his possession only 127 slaves on the day of the sale. Two of these were dead, and one ran away. This means that 25 of the original 152 slaves had died, run away, or been disposed of secretly. In his "Account of Sale of 124 Africans, cargo of the *Josefa Segunda*," Morgan listed the name of each purchaser, the number each purchaser bought, the name of each slave, age, gender, and age group (29 men, 40 women, 42 boys, 13 girls); and he noted that 6 of the 124 slaves were sick, and the price paid for each slave or group of

18. *Ibid.*
19. *Ibid.*

slaves. Total proceeds from the sales were $95,254.00; total expenses for maintenance and sale of the slaves $13,970.13½—net proceeds, $81,283.86½.[20]

There were forty-four expense items. Some that show "padding" or that are interesting for other reasons are the following:

Disbursements made by J. Dauriac for liquors for officers of Sheriff	$ 38.37½
Board of Health $1½ for each slave imported according to law [152 × $1.50 = $228.00. The Board of Health charged for 159 slaves]	238.50
Mr. Laporte that part of acct. approved by Judge Hall	524.18¾
Beverly Chew for expenses incurred prior to July 9	1026.78
Paid for a small trunk to place the notes in the bank	2.00
Dr. Flood for 12,680 days maintenance of slaves at 31⅔ cents p. day [This was an inflated charge. A sailor's wage was only 25 cents per day.]	4062.33½
Dr. Flood for medical attendance	1570.00
A. Hennan for professional advice	500.00
G. W. Morgan, commission at 5 p. cent	4762.70

The slave that brought the highest price was Abiona, age thirty. John Brandt paid $1,580 for him. The next highest price paid was for María, age twenty-five, bought by Alfred Hennen for $1,280. Dr. Flood bought two servant boys, ages thirteen and fourteen, for $2,410. Chew paid $1,000 for a boy ten years old. The lowest price paid for any slave was $386, the average price paid for each of five slaves: three men ages thirty, thirty-two, and thirty-five; one woman, age twenty-five; and one girl, age ten. Only the total selling price of $1,930 for the five was given.[21]

Eight years earlier (1810) in a similar case, *Blas Moran* v. *Ship "Alerta,"* 145 slaves were sold for the following prices:[22]

60 men at $400		$24,000
33 females at $325		10,725
51 boys at $200		10,200
1 boy very sick at $50		50
145	total	$44,975

20. *Ibid.*
21. *Ibid.*
22. Blas Moran filed his libel July 14, 1810. *Ibid.*, Book A, Case No. 380.

The average selling price for each slave from the *Alerta* was $310.17; from the *Josefa Segunda*, $768.18. Prices had more than doubled in the eight-year interval because the United States was trying to stop the importation of slaves into the United States, and Great Britain was trying to abolish the slave trade completely. Great Britain had pressured Spain into accepting the Anglo-Spanish Slave Treaty on September 23, 1817, by which the Spanish king prohibited his subjects from engaging in the slave trade on the coast of Africa north of the Equator and, after 1820, south of the Equator. The *Josefa Segunda*'s cargo was from the Guinea Coast north of the Equator. English, some Spanish, and some United States surveillance meant that ships importing slaves into Cuba and Louisiana had to circumvent local officials—by means of remuneration, of course.

The warrant that had been served on Sheriff Morgan on July 18 commanded him to take possession of the *Josefa Segunda* as well as of its slave cargo. There is no indication in any of the district court papers to show what happened to the ship. Those who appeared in court on August 3 (as called for in the warrant) were there to claim a share in the net proceeds from the sale of the 124 slaves. Among these claimants were the United States; Caricabura, Arrieta and Company; and new "captors." These were Customs Collector Beverly C. Chew, Naval Officer Edward Lorrain, and Surveyor of the Port William Emerson. They filed their claim on the grounds that slaves had been unlawfully imported (by whom?), and that they had captured and seized the *Josefa Segunda* and its cargo. The "captors" had never seen the ship until they boarded it at the New Orleans anchorage.

On August 8, the libel of Caricabura, Arrieta and Company was dismissed with costs. The company petitioned the "Honorable Judge Dominic A. Hall," showing that it was dissatisfied with the court's decision and begging leave "respectfully to pray an appeal to the Supreme Court of the United States on giving good and sufficient surety to cover costs and damages." Judge Hall granted this petition, and it was filed on August 12, 1818. The Supreme Court of the United States on March 14, 1820, affirmed the decree of the district court that the libel of Caricabura, Arrieta and Company be dismissed with costs.[23]

23. Scott (ed.), *Prize Cases*, II, 1096.

Agents for the United States, Chew, Emerson, and Lorrain succeeded in having all other claims dismissed except theirs. The claims dismissed included those of the customs officials involved in the seizure of the *Josefa Segunda* at the Balize and on its voyage up the river to New Orleans: C. W. Roberts, Edward C. Gardner, Enoch Humphries, and H. K. Mead. On June 4, 1823, the victors agreed that, after Charity Hospital in New Orleans received the half awarded to the United States, the other half would be divided equally among Chew, Emerson, and Lorrain. An undated statement in the case papers shows that the half to be divided amounted to $39,893.21; that is, Chew, Emerson, and Lorrain were each to receive $13,297.73⅔.[24]

24. It took an act of the United States Congress "for the relief of Beverly Chew, the heirs of William Emerson, deceased, and the heirs of Edwin Lorrain deceased" to make the district court pay Chew *et al.* This act was approved March 3, 1831. The district court did not order payments made until January 5, 1832.

CHAPTER 13

The King Versus René Beluche

After Beluche in the *General Arismendi* and Raimond in the *Josefa Segunda* had separated (at the end of February, 1818, according to Raimond's protest), the *General Arismendi* continued to prowl the waters between Cuba and Jamaica. On April 12, Beluche had a very small boat worth about $50 hoisted on board. Two days later, the *General Arismendi* put into Port Royal, Jamaica, "for the purpose of obtaining a supply of water and provisions. She was out 60 days from the island of Margarita and had been cruising on different parts of the coast of Cuba. She had made two captures *vis*, the Spanish brig Joseph the Second . . . and the Spanish schooner Inclita from St. Jago de Cuba to Puerto Rico, with an assorted cargo, both of which vessels were manned and ordered for Margarita."[1]

The Kingston *Chronicle* for the week of April 25–May 2 reported that an act of piracy had occurred in the waters between Cuba and Jamaica on Friday, April 24. That same paper had this item dated May 1:

> We have now to allude to another act of a similar nature, said to have been committed by the Venezuelan privateer General Arismendi, Capt. Beluche, now at Port Royal. A mariner of the name of Scott, who arrived at Port Royal a few days ago, observed his boat alongside that vessel, which had been forcibly taken from him by the said Beluche. His deposition of the circumstance was taken before the Magistrates, and his property in the boat established by the bill of sale, the handwriting of the party being proven by another evidence [*sic*] of the name of Jones, who fully corroborated Scott in all his statements. A warrant was in consequence issued for the apprehension of Beluche, and he has been committed to prison to take his trial at an Admiralty Sessions which is to be held at the Court House in this city on Monday the 11th inst. for that purpose. We shall be happy if this person can excul-

1. Kingston *Royal Gazette*, April 11–18, 1818.

pate himself—he will have a fair and impartial trial, and will be dealt with as leniently as our laws will permit; but, at the same time, in order that justice may take its due course we trust that all the parties warned to attend on the side of the Crown will be forthcoming on the appointed day.[2]

Beluche had captured many prizes, some worth over $100,000. Now, because he had taken (stolen?) a little boat worth $50, he was in prison. Unless he could exculpate himself, he would be hung for piracy, in which case not only the Kingston *Chronicle* but also the commercial elements of Kingston and New Orleans would be very unhappy.

Beluche's friends had about two weeks before his trial to line up an impressive array of witnesses. These included Rear Admiral Sir Home Popham, commander-in-chief of the Jamaica Station, and important merchants who had grown rich from Beluche's privateering and from trade with Spain's revolting colonies. Merchant lobbyists in London were putting increasing pressure on Parliament to recognize the new states created from these colonies so that British merchants could openly trade with them.

The *Royal Gazette* for the week of May 9–16, 1818, reported the first session, and the following week the second session of Beluche's trial: the case of *The King* v. *Rene Beluche*.[3]

Monday, May 11, 1818

Presiding Judge opened the session saying:

. . . there is but one case that will require your attention. This is a case of piracy. . . . Piracy is defined to be the commission of those acts of robbery and plunder on the seas which would amount to felony if committed on land. Acts of this sort, if committed without the authority of any Government, are piracy. If committed with such authority they are acts of hostility. But even if there be authority for purposes of hostility, and an act to be done beyond the limits of authority, it may amount to piracy. . . .

If it appears on this occasion that the person charged with this crime is a foreigner, it is equally your duty to inquire into the case as if he were a British subject. . . .

---

2. The above items from the Kingston *Chronicle* were taken from the New Orleans *Louisiana Gazette*, May 25, 1818.

3. The weekly Spanishtown *St. Jago de la Vega Gazette* also reported the two sessions in the same weeks: May 9–16 and May 16–23, 1818.

The Grand Jury now withdrew. After which the witnesses were sworn, and sent in with the Indictment. In about half an hour a true bill was sent in against Renato Beluche. The Advocate-General then moved their Honours, that the prisoner be placed at the bar for the purpose of being arraigned.

René Beluche was placed at the bar, and the Indictment read over him. It consisted of three counts. The first charged that on the 12th of April last, within the jurisdiction of the Admiral and of this Court, at a certain place twenty five leagues from this island, upon one James Scott the prisoner made an assault; that the said James Scott he put in fear and danger of his life; and that a certain boat or vessel, with her tackle and furniture, belonging to said James Soctt, and then in his possession, he the prisoner did piratically steal and take away. The second count charged the boat as belonging to persons unknown; and the third count charged the assault to have been committed upon mariners unknown, and the boat piratically taken to have belonged to persons unknown.

The prisoner pleaded Not Guilty.

The advocate general then moved that the trial itself begin in one week, allowing time for the arrival of a witness "material to this prosecution." The defense attorney acceded to this proposal, since two of the witnesses for Beluche were also absent. Consequently, the prisoner was removed from the bar, the grand jury dismissed, and the court adjourned until Monday, May 18.

At ten o'clock on the appointed day the court reconvened. A jury was sworn in, and the indictment charging Beluche with piracy was read. The witnesses for both the crown and the prisoner were sent out of the courtroom, and the advocate general began his opening statement:

Mr. Advocate General.—May it please your Honours, Gentlemen of the Jury, you are assembled to determine the guilt or innocence of the prisoner at the bar upon a charge of piracy, which has been preferred against him, under circumstances which, if they be proved by the witnesses as they have been stated to me, must amount in the eye of the law, to that crime.

Gentlemen—We all know that the spirit of hostility, which pervades a large portion of South America, has led to the equipment of vessels to cruise against the vessels and property of Spain.

Gentlemen—The policy of Great Britain has been to adhere to a strict neutrality. But it is her essential duty to take care that the neutrality she has thus prescribed to herself be not infringed upon by acts of aggression of any contending parties, against the commerce and property of English subjects.

I am sorry to say that repeated instances have occurred of such aggressions. But it is extremely difficult to bring the offending persons within reach of our laws, and to make them amenable for the acts of which they have been guilty.

It is, however, the duty of those who have the care of the public interest, to bring any individual to judgment against whom there is reasonable cause to impute the guilt of such aggression.

You are assembled under a commission which has been issued to try this particular kind of offense; and it has been issued not only on account of the importance of the subject, but also on account of the prisoner—that he might have an early opportunity of justifying his conduct if he can, and that he might not be kept in imprisonment until the month of August, until which time none of the usual Assizes will be held here.

Gentlemen—In order that you may be enabled to form a distinct view of the case that is now brought under your consideration, I shall first shew what the jurisdiction is, under which the prisoner is tried. Secondly, what are the facts which constitute the crime of piracy; and thirdly, what are the facts of this case; which, if they appear in proof as they have been represented to me will amount to that crime.

If indeed the prisoner can make out a justification, it is for him to do so; it is for him to shew that justification, and all the circumstances of which it can be formed. But it does not appear, as far as my instructions go, that he can make out such a justification.

The advocate general proceeded to define *piracy* and *robbery* according to British law and to reiterate the charges against Beluche. Then he continued with a detailed description of the circumstances of the alleged crime:

> A person of the name Scott, some time in March last, at Trinidad de Cuba, purchased from a man of the name of Diamond a small boat. He had used the boat after his purchase only a short time. He is an Englishman, and intended to go in that boat from Trinidad de Cuba to Montego bay, and to set sail in her for that purpose, with a person named Phillips.
>
> When off Cape Cruz, he fell in with a sloop belonging to a Mr. Levy. Being short of water they went alongside the sloop, which was commanded by one Rayborne. Rayborne is here. It so happened that the master of the sloop was not able to get the whole of his cargo. He therefore proposed to Scott that he should remain with the sloop; and assist him in completing the cargo, and to this both Scott and Phillips assented.
>
> Soon afterwards it became necessary that the sloop, which was then off the River Savanna-la-Mar in Cuba, should go further along the shore. But the master of the sloop, having business up that river, took the boat there with Scott in her, and left Phillips on board the sloop.

At this time the prisoner at the bar commanded an armed brig named the Arismendi; and at this time also a person named Dominique [You?] commanded an armed schooner. The prisoner and Dominique took the sloop, and also the boat which is the subject of this indictment.

The people in the sloop were taken on board Dominique's privateer. Scott, who had been left alone in the boat, was also taken. He shewed his bill of parcels for the purchase of the boat, and said that he was an Englishman. Dominique told Scott that the boat should be released—They delivered up the sloop which belonged to Mr. Levy, and she afterwards sailed for Montego Bay.

Gentlemen—After this property had been released by Dominique, they sent Scott to Capt. Beluche on board the Arismendi, instead of permitting him to pursue his own intentions.

When the boat was alongside, Capt. Beluche ordered it to be hoisted into his own vessel, and that boat he took away. The boat was afterwards seen by Scott in possession of Capt. Beluche in Port Royal harbour.

Gentlemen—These are the facts, the particulars and details of which will be described at greater length by Phillips, who was with Scott, and who had intended to proceed with him in his boat to Montego Bay.

There were on board this vessel several articles, among them were some flour, some beef, some gunpowder, some shot, some old rusty muskets, and about a hundred dollars. Many of these things were, however, restored.

Gentlemen—These are the circumstances which are stated in the examination of the different witnesses who will be called before you.

Here then is the actual seizure by Captain Beluche, of the property of a British subject, whom Captain Beluche must have known to be a British subject; against whom he must have known he had no right, no privilege, no authority to commit any aggression whatsoever.

I understand he has a Commission. I am not inquiring now into the nature or power of that Commission, or the authorities from which it may have proceeded. But certainly no Commission of that sort can justify an act of aggression upon a British subject. . . .

But Gentlemen, the law is clear. I will state it from one of the highest authorities on the subject. Sir Lionel Jenkins, in a charge delivered by him upon a trial of Admiralty Sessions at the Old Bailey, has spoken distinctly. "It will be no defence for a man, who takes away the ship of another, that he has a Commission, unless it be the vessel of a nation against which his Commission is directed." (here the Learned Gentleman quoted the words of Sir Lionel.)

The case of Captain Kidd, reported in the State Trials, confirms the principles laid down.

If therefore the prisoner produces a Commission which does not authorize him to attack British property, it is as if he had no Commission at all.

This principle is laid down in all the cases which have arisen respecting this description of conduct between individuals of different nations. If a man steps out of the scope of the authority with which he is entrusted, he acts as an individual against an individual.

Then the advocate general called up the witnesses against Beluche. The first was James Scott, owner of the boat in question. Scott testified:

> I know the prisoner at the bar. I saw him first on the 27th of March. I am not sure on what day of the month. It is about two months ago. This paper is the bill of sale of my boat. I am an Englishman born at Hull. I recollect seeing Capt. Beluche on board the privateer off the coast of Cuba, about two months ago. I am the owner of the boat. I bought her in Trinidad de Cuba. I gave fifty dollars for her. I bought her of one Mr. Diamond. This is the bill of parcels. I got it from Mr. Diamond. He gave it me as a receipt for the boat. I recollect going with Phillips to Trinidad de Cuba upon an intended voyage to Montego Bay.
>
> Capt. Beluche's boat took my boat, and Capt. Dominique's took Mr. Levy's sloop. This was about a mile from the shore, about half a mile from the River Savanna-la-Mar in Cuba. After they took the boat they put one man on board. I was in her alone—Phillips was on board Mr. Levy's drogger. The master of the drogger was on board my boat until about half an hour before, when he went up the long, narrow river in a small canoe, and left me on board. Capt. Beluche's Lieutenant took my boat, and Capt. Dominique's boat took Phillip's sloop. They took the sloop first; and then my boat next; and took out all the things. I shewed Capt. Dominique the bill of parcels. He said he would keep it because he had no other boat, or only a very small boat. The boat was alongside. Capt. Beluche sent for her, and said it was his prize. Capt. Dominique would not send her. He said as soon as he had done with her we should have her. Capt. Beluche sent a second time to demand the boat. Capt. Dominique said that Beluche was the Commodore; and then he sent the boat, and me and two of his people. When we came to Beluche, he told the people to put the boat on board his privateer. He had the boat hoisted up; ripped her deck up. She had bits of gangways. He made her for his own use. He hoisted her into his privateer. He sent us two on board a Guineaman, his prize, and kept us at work for three days. The night before the morning when the Guineaman was to sail, at day-light, he put us on board a small vessel. We were then searched to the skin.—They called us damned pirates for having no money about us. We had a hundred and odd dollars. We kept them. Capt. Dominique took care of the money when we were on board his vessel.

Some objections were made by the prisoner's counsel as to any examination upon the subject that related to the seizure or restitution of money at which Beluche was not present. Then the examination continued:

> We had some powder. We got it from a wreck which had been lost off Trinidad. When the boat was taken, there were about five cartridges, which were wet. We were put on board the small vessel at night. About eleven or twelve o'clock the next morning he sent us a little water and something else. Next morning he sent us plenty of everything. The last two days we had provisions enough.
>
> When the master of Mr. Levy's drogger came, he told us we might go on board, and go to Jamaica. We went on board. We went to Lucea. I was there one day. I went to Montego Bay and was there three days. When I came to Port Royal, I saw the boat in Capt. Beluche's possession. I swear it is the same boat. It was the same day that I went to the Admiral. I have been knocking about since that. It was about a month ago. About two months ago the prisoner took my boat.

After Scott was cross-examined, three other witnesses for the prosecution—Samuel Phillips, Henry Rayborne, and Thomas Jones—were called to testify. Then the advocate general closed his case.

Beluche's attorney now rose and began his statement. After cautioning the jury against allowing themselves to be prejudiced against the prisoner by rumors circulating about him, the counsel presented the defense's version of the incident:

> Gentlemen—On the 26th of March last, Capt. Beluche was on board the Arismendi, lying at some distance from Trinidad de Cuba. There was a small American schooner in company, which undertook to provide water and other things for the Arismendi. The vessels were about nine miles from the coast. The schooner was dispatched to the shore for water; and, about three miles from the land, a boat was descried making toward the vessel. At that time there were rumors of piracies having been committed; and it was suspected and spoken of that the keys were infested with open boats belonging to pirates. A Mr. Duberge commanded the American schooner, and when he saw the boat near the coast he fired at her, and brought her to. In this boat there was then only one man, Scott, who has been examined today. Mr. Duberge asked him for his papers; he said he had none, excepting one which he called a bill of sale. Contrary to the evidence which you have heard for the prosecution, Mr. Duberge found no provisions on board, no

water, nor anything requisite for a voyage from Cuba to this island. There were, however, some cutlasses, some ball-cartridges and gunpowder: and all these circumstances appeared so suspicious, that Mr. Duberge was induced to arrest the progress of the boat, and to carry her to the Guerrier, commanded by Capt. Dominique. Mr. Duberge then proceeded to the coast for the supplies he had been sent for, and on the following day he returned to the Arismendi. Soon after these transactions, several Spaniards lodged complaints against Scott, stating that he had infested their trade, and had robbed and plundered them of everything. The Captain of the American schooner will depose to the same effect. He will confirm also the statement I have made in several other particulars, and this witness will also be corroborated by the First Lieutenant of the privateer.

Gentlemen, to constitute the offence of piracy, you have heard from the Advocate Generals, that the same evidence is necessary, as would be necessary to constitute the offence of robbery upon land. After a revision even of the testimony that has been adduced on the part of the prosecutor, I ask you whether there is any evidence to justify that conclusion? It is not enough that Captain Beluche took the boat; you must also be satisfied that he took it with a criminal and piratical intent. The impression upon this Gentleman's mind was, that the boat in question had been one of those open boats, against which so many complaints have been made to Captain Beluche, for having plundered vessels and property along the coast. It was under this impression that he acted—an impression entirely and clearly distinct from any criminal intent.

Gentlemen, I ask you what profit, what advantage, could accrue to Captain Beluche from detaining such a boat;—a vessel which the last witness has told you was not even sea-worthy. "I remonstrated," said he, "with Scott and told him the vessel was too small, and not sea worthy." Is it to be imagined that this Gentleman would bring himself within the range of a criminal prosecution, that is to affect his life, for so paltry a consideration? Is it within common sense that he would come to the harbour of Port Royal with this very boat publically exposed, if he had the consciousness that he had obtained it by means for which his life was to be responsible? Is it likely that he should come to this island where he knew that the witnesses must be, who have appeared before you today, if he carried in his breast the self-condemnation of being liable to a charge, which, if substantiated by their evidence, would incur upon him the penalty of death?

Gentlemen—It is not only the gross improbability which belongs to the case itself, that even now demands your attention. The evidence on the part of the prosecution, by which this case is to stand or fall, partakes of a suspicious and doubtful quality.

The first witness was Scott. Between his evidence and that of Phillips there appears to be a material variance. Scott says he went with Phillips to the wreck. Phillips says Scott was not in company with him when he went to the wreck. There is another circumstance which I am sure will have great weight with you; and that is the manner in which they left the port of Trinidad de Cuba. Why did they avail themselves of the darkness of night?—Why did they select an hour in which no eye could perceive their motion? And why did they not go in the light of day, in the open, undisguised, unconcealed manner of honest men? Gentlemen, why did they not go by one of the other vessels, which you have been told were about to sail for Jamaica? Why did they prefer this little boat—a boat that was too small for such a voyage, that was not sea-worthy, and in which such a passage could be performed only in fine weather, and even then, not without risk of their lives?

A witness has been called named Rayborne—He commanded a vessel belonging to Mr. Levy, of Lucea. The testimony of this witness destroys that of Phillips and Scott.

He tells you that Capt. Dominique and the prisoner were not common marauders upon the sea. Capt. Dominique, said he, behaved in a very honourable manner; and Capt. Beluche, he told you, paid him for the detention of the large canoe.

Gentlemen, under all these circumstances, I submit it is not possible that you can attach to the conduct of the prisoner the crime of piracy—His conduct was not tainted with the indications which belong to an act of robbery.

That the boat was taken I cannot deny. The defense of Capt. Beluche does not require that it should be denied. But she was taken under such circumstances as justified the suspicion and belief that she was used for piratical depredations. She was taken at a time also when acts of piracy had been numerous; and when complaints were daily poured in to the Gentleman at the bar, by persons who had suffered under those depredations, and who entreated his efforts for the protection of themselves and their property. The boat which was taken corresponded exactly with the description given of the pirate boats that infected the coast; and I do therefore, again confidently submit to you, that the taking and detention of the boat was fully justifiable.

Gentlemen—I say further that Capt. Beluche was pursuing the directions of the commission under which he acted. The trust reposed in him by that Commission was a serious one. It was his duty, under that Commission, to vindicate the authorities, under which he acted, from participating in or conniving at any act of piracy; and when it appeared that depredations of that description were in practice almost within sight of his own vessel, it was his duty to suppress all such aggression.

Gentlemen—It will be proved to you by the evidence of Rear Admiral Sir Home Popham, that the Commission under which he was acting, was a correct and legal one, and one recognized by the laws of the country.

But, Gentlemen, in order to repel such an accusation as that which is offered, in order to counteract the evidence which has been adduced, I beg leave to call your attention to the character of Captain Beluche.

Fortunately for him, he is known to many respectable merchants in this City; he is not only known and esteemed by those of his own country and more immediate connections, but also by Gentlemen of great respectability in this place.

Next, the defense counsel called a series of witnesses whose evidence was intended to show that the case against Beluche in no way amounted to piracy. The first witness was the Reverend Canon of Chile, who was shown the privateer's commission that Bolívar had issued to Beluche. The canon verified the commission as genuine and the power of Bolívar and Arismendi to issue such commissions. The privateer's commission was then read to the court. It was "directed to Citizen Beluche, Captain of the hermaphrodite brig of war, called the Arismendi, dated the 1st of February, 1818, and valid for six months." Asked if he was acquainted with Beluche, the canon responded that "he knew him by documents; and he knew him personally in Jamaica. He has known him personally only since he came here." When the prosecution asked him to speak of Beluche's general character, the canon said that "it was always spoken of in the highest terms from his manners, from his good conduct, from his honour, and from his integrity."

Then William Thompson was sworn in and examined. He testified:

I am an American. I know James Scott. He has told me he is an American; he told me so at Trinidad de Cuba. I was on board an armed vessel fitted out by the Spanish Government. Scott was on board that vessel. The vessel was wrecked about forty miles to North of Trinidad de Cuba. It was last February. Scott was on board of her at the time she was wrecked. Capt. Phillips saved the crew of the wrecked vessel. Scott was in Trinidad with Phillips; he had a boat then sailing about the harbour. I do not know that he went to the vessel after she was wrecked. There were a great many things which Phillips got from her: cutlasses, muskets, and cartridge-boxes. I understood from Scott that he afterwards stopped at the wreck. He said he took powder out and dried it. He did not mention anything else. He said he went with Captain Phillips. He said he was going to Montego Bay in that boat. Mr. Jones told him he should have a passage to Kingston in the vessel he came in. There were other vessels; there was a brig, the Alexander. She was going to Montego Bay. Scott wished me to say nothing about his having been on board this armed vessel; this was after he came to Kingston. He assigned no reason at the time. He said that he intended to employ her as a plantain-boat. I said that she would not answer for that. He then said that she would answer for other purposes, that she would do for a privateer. I saw one musket and one cutlass on board; he got powder at the wreck. I don't know whether he went in the night time or in the day. He told me the night before that he was going; and in the morning he was gone. He was generally in the harbour; part of the time at the stern of Phillip's sloop.

Cross-examined by the advocate general, Thompson replied:

That was the boat which Scott called his that was at the stern of Phillip's vessel. Before Scott had her she belonged to Mr. Diamond. I have known Scott about two months. I knew him in Trinidad. He came there in the brig he was cast away in. I don't know how long ago. It was as much as three weeks from the time I first saw Scott, until the brig was cast away. The last cruise of the privateer that was wrecked before she was cast away, was about four weeks. The brig was called the Admiral Guerrilla. She was fitted out for the purpose of taking a picaroon that had captured a vessel belonging to Trinidad.

When reexamined by the defense, Thompson added:

Scott received his bounty. He recognized me immediately in Kingston, and requested me not to mention that he had been on board the privateer. He has told me he is not a British subject. The brig that Scott came in was a Guineaman, and had a cargo of slaves. When she was converted into an armed vessel, he continued in her. I never heard that there were a number of small vessels in the neighbourhood of Cape Cruz which were committing piracies.

Next, John Lewis Miall was called by the defense.

I commanded a schooner in March last. Capt. Beluche took me, and kept me one month and three days; when he wanted me no more, he put on board my schooner what I wanted. I do not recollect being sent on shore to fetch water for the Arismendi. I went with a small schooner. After I had quitted the Arismendi, I saw a small boat. After I had filled the water casks, I did not go on board the Guerrier. It was reported in Trinidad that several boats had been committing piracies there. There was a boat brought in, which they said had committed piracy. I did not tell Capt. Beluche's first officer anything about a pirate boat. I do not know that it was in consequence of a communication made by me that a vessel was despatched after the boat. I did not see the boat.

It is extremely dangerous to cross from there to Jamaica; it would be a great risk to do so in a small boat. Capt. Beluche said he had no cash, but would give me remuneration in other things which he had on board. Beluche gave me a certificate of having done so.

Jean Baptiste Duberge was the next witness for the defense.

I am first Lieutenant on board the Arismendi. I recollect having been on board the General Arismendi off the South coast of Cuba, in the month of March last. I was on board a schooner sent with Miall for water. I recollect going on board one of the boats of the Arismendi for water, after another boat, and took it. I perceived the boat close to the shore coming from the River Savanna-la-Mar. I was on board with Miall when I perceived the boat. I thought it was a sloop and I took four men to go in pursuit of her. When I pursued the boat she took chace [sic]. I lost sight of her for a few moments, and she then got aground. She then made tacks, and it took all our oars to overtake her. The boat would have escaped if I had not fired a shot at her. This was owing to the way in which she was rigged. She was a very small boat. I had been told that there were several boats on that coast which had committed piracies. The Arismendi was in sight when I took the boat. I was on board the Arismendi when Capt. Dominique sent the boat to Capt. Beluche. Capt. Dominique sent a verbal message that she was a boat taken under suspicion of being a pirate, and afterwards told him so. It was found that she had a cartridge box full of cartridges, about 250 balls and cartridges altogether, about twenty pounds of gunpowder, two swords, and a carboy with water in it. There was only one man in the boat when I took her. The man said he was going to Jamaica. I told him it was impossible for a man to go to Jamaica in so small a boat. He told me if I would put him on shore, he would go in search of two other men that belonged to the boat. When I reached the Guerrilla, a man presented himself, and said he was the owner of the boat.

Then Pierre Marchand, another crewman, was called. He testified: "I was on board the Arismendi when a boat was brought. A message was sent by Capt. Dominique along with the boat; that she had been taken under suspicion of piracy. There was an entry made in the log book to that effect. Scott and Phillips were put on board the drogger to Montego Bay, at their own request . . . at the time it was known that the Arismendi was coming here, Jamaica, for provisions." When cross-examined by the advocate general, Marchand added that "it was known at the time the Arismendi was coming to Jamaica in distress.

They obtained very few things, only a few plantains from Cuba. It was known about 12 or 15 days before the capture of the boat."

The defense next called several character witnesses for Beluche. The first was George Amer, who testified: "I was on board the General Arismendi for about two months and a half. I never knew Capt. Beluche in any other way, than as a man of the strictest honour. From what I knew of him, I should not suspect him of being guilty of the act with which he is accused." Then James M'Dowell was called, and he stated: "I have known Capt. Beluche about 20 months. I consider him a very brave and a very humane man. I should not suspect he would be guilty of the act with which he is charged. After he came to Port Royal I was generally on board his vessel every day; he shewed no anxiety to get away. He might have been away 2 or 3 days sooner; I know it, for I supplied him with what he wanted." Next came Wellwood Hyslop: "I have known Capt. Beluche ever since 1813. I knew him in Carthagena. He always bore an excellent character. He has always been esteemed a brave man. I believe it, because I knew him to be generous, benevolent, and humane. He was always highly esteemed by the Government of Carthagena. I should not suspect that he would commit any act of piracy; I should just as soon believe that such an act would be committed by any Gentleman in Court. On the contrary of being in a hurry to leave Port Royal, he dined with me the day before the charge against him was made, and said he did not know when he would get away." Then a Spanish merchant deposed "that he had known Captain Beluche and his family 24 years. He had born a very excellent character. I should think he would have more sense than to commit the act with which he is charged."

Finally, Samuel Phillips was reexamined by the advocate general. He was asked when Scott first shipped on board his vessel. Phillips replied, with much confusion, "There I was in error."

"Did he sail with you in the *Belvidera* from Montego Bay?" asked the advocate general.

"No, he did not."

The advocate general continued: "Understand me. You told me before that Scott proceeded in your vessel from Montego Bay to Trinidad de Cuba. I ask you, when did he first come on board your sloop?"

"All my hands left me at Trinidad."

"Had he ever shipped with you before?"

Phillips replied with great embarrassment, "He had never shipped himself with me before. That is the only error I made."

The advocate general sat down. The defense counsel was about to commence his address when the foreman stated that the jury had made up their minds. The indictment was handed to them, and they immediately returned a verdict of not guilty.

CHAPTER 14

Beluche and Bolívar to 1822

Only a few clues indicate what Beluche may have been doing between July, 1818, and May 28, 1821, when Admiral Brion wrote to Bolívar from Maracaibo. In this letter, Brion said that Beluche had been "ill" in New Orleans for the last months of 1820 and the first months of 1821, but that "he is now in Maracaibo building a schooner which soon will be ready to sail. Beluche is determined to bring his family here."[1]

Beluche had returned to the Venezuelan war theater because there were very few Spanish cargo vessels left to be captured. New privateers flying the flags of the United Provinces of the Rio de la Plata (Argentina) and of Uruguay had appeared in the Caribbean and in the Pacific, where they helped annihilate Spanish shipping, but their major thrust was against Spain itself. These provinces had easily broken with Spain, which had sent most of its available manpower to Venezuela; but, with Napoleon exiled to the small island of St. Helena in the South Atlantic and his brother Joseph exiled in Baltimore, the restored Ferdinand VII in Spain was concentrating troops to send against his rebellious colonies. The main objective of the Argentine and Uruguayan privateers was to keep these troops from leaving Spain.

They kept vigil off the coast from Cabo de São Vicente on the southwest tip of Portugal to the Bay of Cádiz, where American, Philippine, and Mediterranean trade routes converged. In these waters, the audacity of privateers astounded Europe and America. They had captured so many prizes by 1817 that a midsummer report from Spain declared: "The Spanish Navy is in a deplorable state. Officers and men have been paid little or nothing for six years." The navy's situation be-

1. Ortega Ricaurte, *Luis Brion*, 207–208.

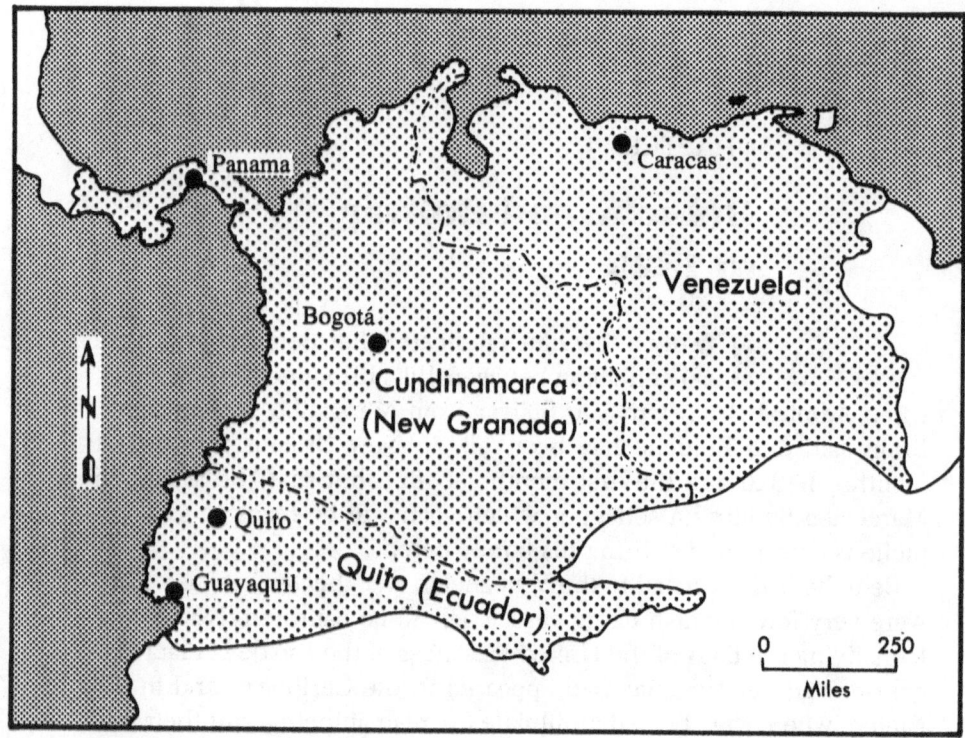

Bolívar's Colombia

came more deplorable when a fire destroyed the Cádiz marine arsenal with an estimated loss of a million dollars. "The late destruction of the naval arsenal near Cádiz is imputed to design to prevent the fitting out of vessels against the patriots. It is a severe loss to Spain."[2]

Business stagnated, "owing to withdrawing of very large sums of money from public circulation. All the public coffers are empty. The army are in arrears for the last three years." Not only were officers, troops, and seamen unpaid, but their fear of service in South America increased. All reports from there emphasized casualties, and America was considered a death trap. Ferdinand seemed paralyzed. He did not

2. Quotation from a London paper in *Niles' Weekly Register*, XII (July 19, 1817), 333; ibid., XII (August 2 and 28, 1817), 364, 411.

suppress conspiracies against his government, and he made no effort to send economic aid or reinforcements to General Morillo for his campaigns in Venezuela and New Granada.[3]

Spain was isolated from America and Morillo was in Bogotá when Beluche landed Bolívar at Ocumare in July, 1816, but Morales forced the patriots to leave. Bolívar returned to Haiti on the *Indio Libre* and organized another expedition. He debarked at Barcelona on December 31, 1816, and moved south to the Orinoco, where Piar was besieging Angostura, capital of Guayana Province. During the last months of 1817, patriots drove the royalists down the Orinoco River and into the Atlantic. Then Bolívar declared Angostura the capital of the Republic of Venezuela until Caracas could be liberated. He created a council of government to rule in his absence and sailed up the Orinoco River to meet José Antonio Páez, the *llanero* genius who controlled all the llanos south of the Apure River (a major tributary of the Orinoco).

Royalists held the key river port of San Fernando on the Apure River thirty miles north of Páez's headquarters, and they held the Caracas llanos (great plains) north of the Apure. The combined forces of Bolívar and Páez captured San Fernando on February 6, 1818. At the end of May, Bolívar boarded a launch and sailed down the rivers to Angostura. British officers with troops were arriving there, and delegates from the independent parts of Venezuela.

Bolívar sent the Granadino refugee Francisco de Paula Santander to the New Granadan border province of Casanare. Santander's mission was to infiltrate Casanare, unite with guerrilla bands there, and prepare for the coming invasion.

On February 15, 1819, Bolívar installed the Congress of Angostura, which elected him president and commander-in-chief of Venezuela. Bolívar then returned to the Apure with an army that included British officers and troops. He conferred with Páez, left him behind to keep General Morillo in Venezuela, and marched to Casanare to join forces with Santander. (At this moment in Spain, fifteen thousand troops refused to sail to reinforce Morillo and other Spanish commanders in America.)

---

3. *Ibid.*, XV (September 26 and November 14, 1818), 78, 197; Stephen K. Stoan, *Pablo Morillo and Venezuela, 1815–1820* (Columbus, Ohio, 1974), 221–28.

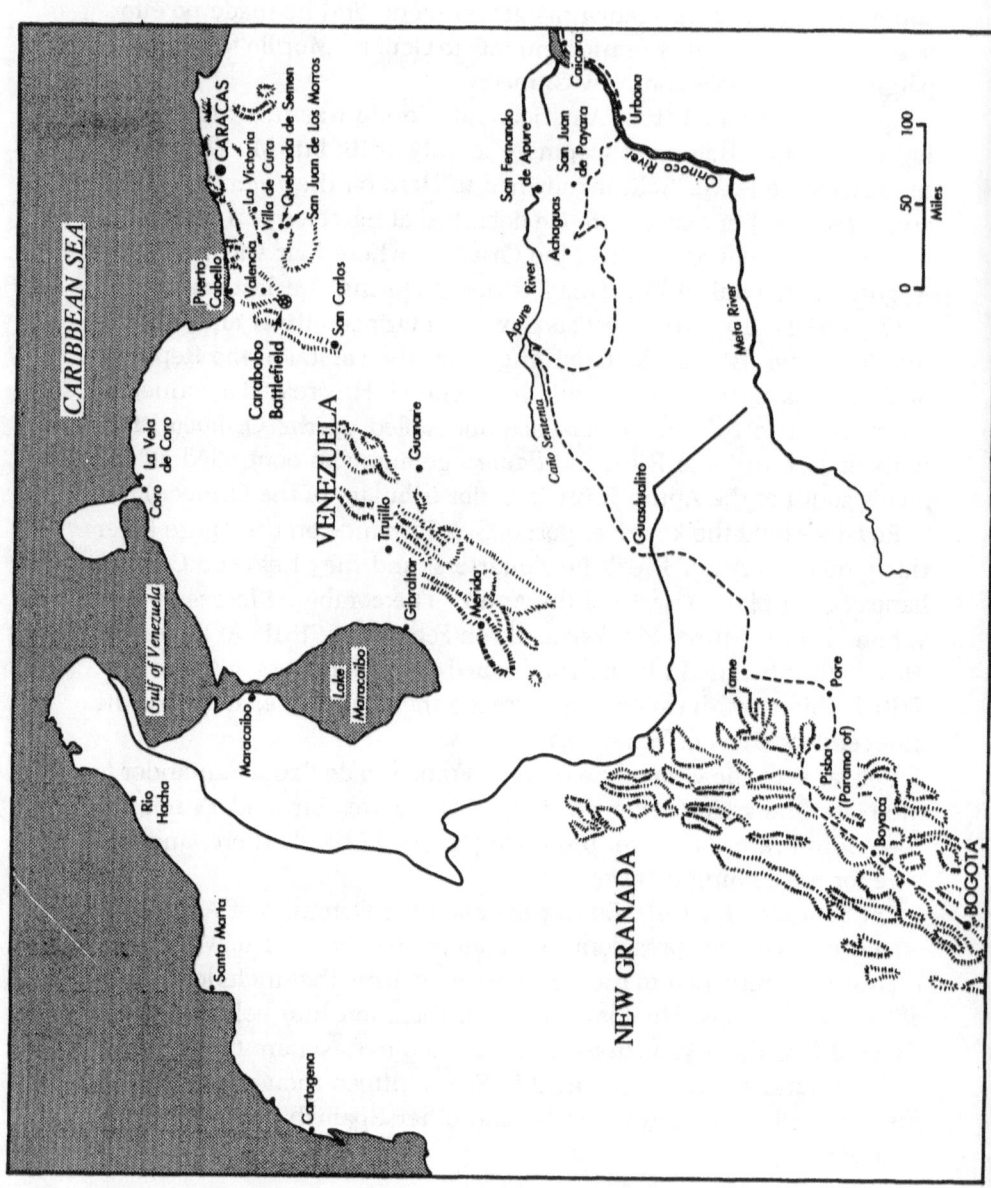

Penetration of New Granada, 1819, and Carabobo, 1821

Bolívar and Santander crossed the Andes over the bleak Páramo of Pisba. Nobody was expected to use this route during the rainy season, but Bolívar did, surprised the royalists, and defeated them at Boyacá eighty miles north of Bogotá. The viceroy escaped from the capital and was on his way to Cartagena when Bolívar entered Bogotá. The detachments he sent against the royalists soon regained eighteen central provinces, but not Pasto in the south or the provinces along the Caribbean coast.

Leaving Santander in Bogotá as vice-president of New Granada, Bolívar returned to Angostura, where he proposed to the Congress the union of New Granada and Venezuela as the Republic of Colombia. Francisco Antonio Zea, a Granadino, suggested that Quito (Ecuador) be included in the Republic of Colombia, even though Quito was not yet liberated. The Congress agreed and appointed a committee to prepare the "Fundamental Law" for the new republic that was more than five times as large as Spain.

Bolívar's immediate problem was how to push the royalists into the Caribbean. They had two thousand troops in Cartagena but were weak from the mouth of the Magdalena River east to Santa Marta, Rio Hacha, and the Venezuelan frontier. Morillo had abandoned Margarita, and from that island Brion and José Padilla transported Mariano Montilla (a Venezuelan) and his troops to Rio Hacha, Padilla's native city.

Padilla was part Indian, part Negro. Born in 1778, he was two years older than Beluche and five years older than Bolívar. Because of the poverty of his home and his own inclination, Padilla had joined the Spanish navy and began his sea career as a cabin boy. He fought in the Battle of Trafalgar and was captured by the British. They kept him on a prison ship until 1808, when he managed to escape and return to New Granada.[4] In 1815, when Bolívar was trying to get war matériel from Castillo, Padilla supported Bolívar against Castillo and landed in prison. He was released soon after Bolívar sailed for Jamaica and escaped to the Lesser Antilles.

Montilla and Padilla occupied Rio Hacha and Santa Marta in March, 1820, then sailed to the mouth of the Magdalena. Royalists fled from

---

4. José María Baraya, *Biografías Militares o Historia Militar del País*, (Bogotá, 1874), 118; Vargas, *Nuestros Próceres Navales*, 118.

the lower Magdalena, leaving their gunboats behind as Padilla came up the river and patriots from the interior came down. By the end of June, arms and munitions could be sent up the river to bases in the interior of New Granada, and Padilla had enough vessels to begin the blockade of Cartagena by sea. Montilla marched to the outskirts of the port and blockaded it by land.

General Morillo had fourteen thousand troops strung out in the mountain arc of Venezuela from Maracaibo in the west to Cumaná in the east, and Francisco Tomás Morales was covering the Caracas llanos. Patriots held all of Cumaná Province except the port city of Cumaná, and guerrillas were winning Barcelona Province. José Tadeo Monagas was ready to occupy Barcelona City as soon as desertions of conscript Venezuelans forced Morillo to shorten his line, and Francisco Bermúdez was penetrating Caracas Province from the southeast when Morillo received two directives from the new government in Spain: promulgate the 1812 Constitution, and seek an armistice with "the dissidents" to terminate the war that was ruining Spain.

Morillo wrote to Bolívar, saying that on June 17 he had declared a cease fire in order that he and Bolívar could negotiate a truce. Bolívar stalled until he had stockpiled munitions and taken Mérida and Trujillo. Meanwhile, desertions had weakened Morillo's armies. Morillo withdrew his troops from Barcelona in September and on October 8, for the twelfth time, asked to be relieved of his command.[5] The answer from Spain was: secure the armistice, then return to Spain.

Morillo and Bolívar signed a six-month armistice on November 26. One week later, Morillo turned over his command to Miguel de La Torre and embarked for Cádiz on December 17. Bolívar observed: "General La Torre, now in command, is married to a relative of mine, and also is my friend, so that the expeditionary army appears to have desires to incorporate with the liberating army, and to prefer a young and beautiful patria to one that is old and decrepit."[6]

The royalist governor at Maracaibo had been a fellow student with his relative Bolívar, and the royalist military commander was a native of Maracaibo. A few miles east of Lake Maracaibo on the patriot side of

5. Stoan, *Morillo and Venezuela*, 229.
6. Bolívar to Vicente Rocafuerte, January 10, 1821, in Lecuna (ed.), *Cartas del Libertador*, II, 297.

the armistice line, General Rafael Urdaneta (another native of Maracaibo) had his headquarters at Trujillo. At the beginning of the new year, 1821, he stationed Rafael de Las Heras with troops at Gibraltar on the southeastern shore of Lake Maracaibo—on the royalist side of the armistice line. The governor of Maracaibo proclaimed the independence of Maracaibo and its union with the Republic of Colombia on January 28, 1821, and the next day Las Heras took possession of the city and its stockpile of artillery, muskets, and ammunition.

Urdaneta maintained in his report to La Torre of "the spontaneous action" at Maracaibo that the armistice made it lawful to accept a deserter, that Maracaibo was a deserter in a larger sense, and that therefore Maracaibo had the right to declare itself part of the Republic of Colombia.

Bolívar had been in Bogotá and was near the Venezuelan frontier when he was told about Maracaibo. He wrote to his relative La Torre affirming that the armistice had not been broken and requesting that it be continued. Bolívar then instructed Urdaneta to move his headquarters to Maracaibo and organize an army there.

La Torre wanted to continue the armistice, but he could not do so without the support of Morales, his second in command. Morales was covering the Caracas llanos with several thousand troops and refused to continue the armistice. On March 21, La Torre wrote to Bolívar that hostilities would begin on April 28.[7]

Bolívar was south of the Apure with Páez when he received this letter. The two men conferred, and Páez agreed to cross the Apure with his army on April 28 and move northwest toward La Torre's base at Araure. To prevent the concentration of all of La Torre's divisions against him, Bolívar ordered Bermúdez to march on Caracas from the east on April 28 and take that city no later than May 15. Then Bolívar returned to his division at Barinas and sent these instructions to Urdaneta: cross Lake Maracaibo on April 28, begin the liberation of Coro Province, and march as quickly as possible to join him near Araure.

Páez, Urdaneta, and Bermúdez began operations on schedule. Urdaneta's troops left Maracaibo on April 28 and entered the city of Coro on May 11. Bermúdez had possession of Caracas one day ahead of

7. This correspondence of Bolívar and La Torre is in the Angostura *Correo del Orinoco 1818–1821*, (Facsimile ed., Paris, 1929), No. 101, April 14, 1821.

schedule. The royalists abandoned La Guaira on May 15 and sailed to Puerto Cabello with all their ships of war. The next day Bermúdez took possession of La Guaira.

By the middle of June, La Torre and Morales were camped on the plains of Carabobo fifteen miles southwest of Valencia. The Battle of Carabobo began at eleven o'clock on the morning of June 24 and ended before noon with royalists fleeing in all directions. About two thousand royalists, including La Torre and Morales, escaped through Valencia to Puerto Cabello.

Venezuela had lost 40 percent of its population in the previous ten years, and nowhere was this loss more evident than in Caracas. Many royalist and patriot property owners had emigrated with their families to the islands; others had found refuge outside the city. When Bolívar sent his aide Diego Ibarra to Caracas to prepare for his entry, Ibarra found not a single white person and only a few Negroes and *pardos*. They received Bolívar with joy.[8]

During the next few months, Bolívar created a command system to complete the liberation of the Caribbean coastal area of Colombia, leaving him free to drive the Spaniards from southern Colombia, including Quito. Montilla was already in command of the Magdalena sector, and he and Padilla were blockading Cartagena by land and sea, starving the royalists within its walls.

Bolívar gave the top command in Venezuela to Carlos Soublette and named three department commanders to serve under him: Bermúdez, commander of eastern Venezuela, where royalists still held the port city of Cumaná; Páez, commander of the center, where his major problem was La Torre and Morales in Puerto Cabello; and General Lino de Clemente, commander of the military department of Zulia in western Venezuela, which included the provinces of Coro, Maracaibo (all the area bordering Lake Maracaibo), Mérida, and Trujillo.

Clemente was older than Bolívar and most of his officers. In his youth, he had served fourteen years in Spain's royal navy. Because of this experience, Bolívar had given Clemente command of Brion's navy in the spring of 1821 when Brion became ill. (Brion died three days

---

8. Kingston *Royal Gazette*, July 21–28, 1821; *Niles' Weekly Register*, XX (August 11, 1821), 382–83; Madariaga, *Bolívar*, 397.

before royalists in Cartagena capitulated on September 30 to Padilla and Montilla.)

Beluche and Clemente in Santa Marta had kept Padilla's vessels in good repair and had sent him and Montilla supplies that Beluche's relative Nicholas Maurice Joly brought from St. Barts and other islands in the Lesser Antilles. Joly had enlisted in the Venezuelan navy at Margarita with his schooner *Brutus* on May 21, 1818.[9]

Captain Sebastian Boguier, Beluche's friend, was blockading Cumaná by sea, cooperating with Bermúdez in the eastern sector. Boguier, "a barber from St. Thomas," had sailed with Louis Aury's navy until 1820, when he joined Brion's fleet. Royalists at Cumaná worked out terms of capitulation with Bermúdez on October 15, while Boguier raised the flag of Colombia over the fort at its harbor. The next day Bermúdez took possession of the city and its military stores.[10]

It was at this moment that Clemente received his appointment as military commander of Zulia. His instructions said: "The capital of your department is Maracaibo, but you are authorized to go wherever your presence is needed." For the time being, Clemente had no reason to move his headquarters from Santa Marta to any other place. The only base left to royalists on the Caribbean coast was Puerto Cabello. A contemporary of Beluche wrote:

> The bay of Porto-Cabello is spacious, handsome, commodious, and safe. It is capable of affording anchorage to the whole Spanish navy. It is defended against the fury of the winds, from whatever quarter they blow. The land which encompasses it on the south, east, and west, is so happily disposed by nature, as to baffle the impetuosity of the northeast wind, which is so common there. So little does this bay partake of those agitations which continually prevail with more or less violence in the tropical seas, that it resembles a pond more than a port. The name given it by the Spaniards is expressive of the advantages which it so eminently enjoys, importing that a vessel at anchor is more effectually secured by a simple rope, than elsewhere by the strongest cables. The surge, which is nowhere more common, never disturbs the placid composure of the road. Its anchorage, which owes nothing to art, is so commodious that the largest ships may lay alongside the

---

9. Vargas, *Nuestros Próceres Navales*, 291–92; Faye, "Commodore Aury," 33, 36, 38, 43.
10. Angostura *Correo Extraordinario del Orinoco*, October 30, 1821; Francisco Alejandro Vargas, *Historia Naval de Venezuela* (2 vols.; Caracas, 1956–61), II, 135–39.

wharf, load and unload without the assistance of lighters. Warships have no other communication with the land, than by a flying bridge three or four toises long."[11]

Admiral Angel Laborde had command of the sea in front of Puerto Cabello. He patrolled there with the 44-gun frigate *Ligera*, several corvettes and war brigs from bases in Cuba and Puerto Rico, and a fleet of smaller vessels. Because the Colombian navy had no ships big enough to compete with his, Laborde was able to keep La Torre and the four thousand or more royalist refugees there well supplied with food and war matériel from the Dutch islands of Aruba, Curaçao, and Bonaire.

Soublette sent Commodore John Daniel Danells to Baltimore (he was a native of that city who had joined the Venezuelan navy in 1818) to buy a corvette. Soublette also sent an agent to England to buy two more warships. Until these three vessels arrived, the independents could not confine the royalists to Puerto Cabello and starve them into surrender.

The independents did have one big advantage: the dissension between Morales and La Torre. Morales was jealous because Morillo had not bestowed the top command on him before retiring to Spain, and he accused La Torre of not wanting to fight the rebels. Morales bragged that he could retake La Guaira and then Caracas, and La Torre gave him a chance to do so at the end of October, 1821, when Laborde appeared at Puerto Cabello with the frigate *Ligera*, the brig of war *Hercules*, the schooner *Conejo*, and one *flechera*.

Morales embarked eight hundred men on eight schooners and, escorted by Laborde's four vessels, sailed toward La Guaira on November 1. La Guaira had no harbor, only an open road "which is always so open to the breeze that the sea is kept in a state of continual agitation, and the violence of the winds frequently occasions damage to ships which ride at anchor. . . . The continual agitation of this road renders loading and unloading tedious, expensive and difficult; sometimes even impossible. The surge acts with the same violence at the bottom as on the surface of the waters."[12]

---

11. Vargas, *Nuestros Próceres Navales*, 136; François Joseph Depons, *Travels in South America, During the Years 1801, 1802, 1803, and 1804* (2 vols.: London, 1807), I, 89–90.
12. *Ibid.*, I, 91–92.

The sea was so rough when the expedition appeared in front of La Guaira that troops could not be debarked. After cruising for a short time off La Guaira, it headed west to the port of Ocumare, where there was a fort mounting two guns. Morales took possession of the fort, destroyed its two guns, and marched his men to the village of Ocumare. "They plundered Ocumare of everything they could carry with them, and returned to Puerto Cabello. On the debarkation of the troops a curious sight presented itself, every soldier having in addition to his baggage, a pig, a turkey, or some other description of live stock slung over his shoulder, the fruits of the plunder of the village of Ocumare."[13]

Carrying off all the food in Ocumare was an effective scorched-earth policy. Venezuela's vast herds of cattle, horses, and mules had been so depleted during the past ten years that very few remained, and both armies had stripped the country of other foods.

In December, La Torre sallied forth to take the whole province of Coro and to show Morales how successful campaigns were conducted. The coastline of this province began a few miles west of Puerto Cabello, extended westward around the whole Paraguaná Peninsula, which encloses the Gulf of Venezuela on the east, and continued along the south side of the gulf almost to the small bay of El Tablazo, which connects with Lake Maracaibo by a strait or throat five miles wide and seven miles long. On the eastern shore of this throat are the ports of Altagracia. Directly opposite these ports on the west side of the throat is the city of Maracaibo. The city of Coro is about 150 miles east of Altagracia by land. Coro is 7 miles inland from its Caribbean port of La Vela de Coro, but La Torre, in December, 1821, did not head for La Vela de Coro. He sailed to Los Taques on the west side of the Paraguaná Peninsula and marched overland to Coro.

It was now that Beluche helped Clemente move his headquarters and two thousand troops from Santa Marta to join Las Heras in Maracaibo. A fourth of the troops embarked on Beluche's squadron of "8 vessels of war, consisting of a ketch carrying 16 guns, the schooner *Cundinamarca* of 11 guns, and the others, all two top-sail schooners, carrying each from 2 to 8 guns." As Clemente began the march overland to Maracaibo with the troops, Beluche sailed from Santa Marta for

---

13. Kingston *Royal Gazette*, February 2–9, 1822.

the Gulf of Venezuela. He anchored on the Guajira coast, debarked the troops on January 13, 1822, and patrolled along the coast while the troops marched inland to Maracaibo. They were there when Clemente and his troops arrived on January 15.[14]

La Torre was at Coro on January 9, when he received a communiqué saying that he had been appointed governor of Puerto Rico. Leaving Colonel Juan Tello in command at Coro, he returned to Puerto Cabello on February 6 to wait for official instructions. He wanted Morales out of sight, so he sent him in the *Hercules* to take command of operations in the province of Coro.[15]

By the time Morales debarked at La Vela de Coro on March 1 with 1,500 troops, Soublette had ordered Judas Tadeo Piñango to move north from Barquisimeto against Colonel Tello. Piñango had to march 175 miles over desert where there was little to subsist on except thistles and prickly-pear cactus. A Philadelphia paper reported:

> From the nature of the country which lies betwixt Barquisimeto and Coro, a sandy desert, destitute of both provisions and water, it is obvious that the military movements either to or from the coast must be slow and difficult; and Morales may therefore for sometime longer continue the idle boast of occupying a tract of sterile and exhausted country. This event however, is no longer dubious; such is the debilitated state of the Spanish force, that victory or defeat must prove equally fatal to them. To maintain themselves on the coast will soon be impossible; to advance from it destructive.
>
> What Morillo was unable to effect with 12,000 veterans, will scarcely be attempted by the comtemptible Morales with 1,500 dispirited, beaten vagabonds, beset on all sides by the same troops who defeated the last Spanish army on the plains of Carabobo. These unavailing sallies and fruitless expeditions are the last efforts of despairing debility, the convulsive kicks of the dying jackass.[16]

The above report underestimated desert fox Morales. His "convulsive kicks" kept patriot forces on the *qui vive* for another year and a half.

Morales occupied the city of Coro on March 5–6. Clemente in Maracaibo sent Las Heras across the strait in small lake craft to Altagracia with 1,200 troops. He had advanced fifty miles toward Coro when Mo-

---

14. Port-of-Spain *Trinidad Gazette*, March 23, 1822; Kingston *Royal Gazette*, March 16–23, 1822; Philadelphia *National Gazette and Literary Register*, February 23, 1822.
15. Vargas, *Historia Naval*, II, 200.
16. Philadelphia *National Gazette and Literary Register*, May 4, 1822.

rales learned on March 20 that he was approaching. Morales left Tello in command of Coro and recruited natives as he marched west with 1,200 troops.

Las Heras reversed his march and, since the terrain compelled both armies to move slowly, he was able to get safely to Altagracia and across the strait to Maracaibo by the time Morales reached Altagracia. Morales was warned on April 20 that Piñango with 2,000 troops was threatening Coro. The messenger did not know that Piñango had taken the city three days before on April 17.

The desert fox did not want to be corralled by Las Heras and Piñango, so he had to retake Coro. To secure his rear, he left a strong garrison at Altagracia, ordered Colonel Lorenzo Morillo with 600 troops and Captain Juan Ballesteros with 216 to cross Lake Maracaibo, land below the city of Maracaibo, and keep Clemente and Las Heras on the west side of the lake. On April 24, Ballesteros and Morillo crossed the lake in boats procured from the Indians and advanced upon Maracaibo. "The division commanded by Colonel Ballesteros was met by the division of Colonel Heras and completely destroyed, not a man escaping. Heras and Ballesteros were both killed."[17]

Clemente defeated and captured most of Morillo's division, but he was unable to pursue Morales across the province of Coro because he did not have enough food or baggage for the march. "Thus it is," lamented Santander, "that a miserable force, because of the desert territory and a tenacious enemy, is still causing expense and worry to the government."[18]

Piñango, fearing Morales, withdrew from Coro (which Tello reentered), marched twenty-five miles west then south a devious hundred miles or more to Carora. Soublette arrived there and assumed command. On May 18, he moved north and confronted Morales on June 7 with twice as many troops as Morales had. A bloody battle ensued, which Morales won. He pursued, drove Soublette back to Carora, then retired toward Coro. On the way, Morales met a messenger

---

17. Antonio R. Eljuri-Yunez S., *La Batalla Naval del Lago de Maracaibo* (Caracas, 1973), 39–40; Port-of-Spain *Trinidad Gazette*, July 3, 1822.
18. Santander's report to Bolívar, June 5, 1822, in Roberto Cortazar (ed.), *Cartas y Mensajes del General Francisco de Paula Santander* (8 vols.; Bogotá, 1953–55), IV, 39–41.

who told him that he had been named Captain General of Venezuela and that vessels were anchored at La Vela de Coro to take him to Puerto Cabello. He sailed on July 22 with all his troops, including two thousand loyal Corianos.[19]

Páez had tried to take Puerto Cabello in April but could not because Boguier was sulking. Boguier's pride had been hurt. After he had helped Bermúdez bring about the capitulation of Cumaná, Soublette had proposed to Santander (acting president of Colombia at Bogotá while Bolívar was liberating Quito and Peru) that Frigate Captain Boguier be promoted to captain of the navy. Santander approved but asked for a copy of Boguier's credentials at the time he had joined Brion's fleet. Soublette sent the credentials November 28, 1821. Two months later, a letter arrived from Bogotá saying that, inasmuch as Boguier's credentials were from Aury, they were unacceptable because Aury did not represent a legitimate government. Boguier became depressed and indifferent to Soublette's orders to blockade Puerto Cabello with his squadron.[20]

At this time, Manuel Manrique was in command of the land blockade of Puerto Cabello. Páez was along the La Guaira coast, where Laborde threatened to land and make a dash for Caracas. When Páez heard that Boguier was to blockade Puerto Cabello by sea with four brigs and three schooners, he marched to take command of the siege of Puerto Cabello. Páez had possession of the heights behind Puerto Cabello on April 15 and had four heavy cannon and a howitzer mounted at Mirador de Solano, the lookout on the mountain side. The next day he wrote to Boguier, saying: "It is absolutely necessary that you combine operations with me, indicating the exact date on which together we tighten the blockade. Even though I have already cut off water from Puerto Cabello, this will be no advantage unless you prevent the entrance of royalist vessels with supplies."[21]

No answer came from Boguier, but Páez took the outer town and confined the royalists to the fortification. Spanish vessels had to anchor off Punto Bravo, "in consequence of the outward bay being commanded from the heights round Puerto Cabello now in possession of

19. Eljuri-Yunez, *Batalla del Lago de Maracaibo*, 41–42.
20. Vargas, *Nuestros Próceres Navales*, 363–65.
21. *Ibid.*

the Colombians." Páez's batteries bombarded any vessel that came near the harbor. Provisions became so scarce that La Torre sent two hundred women, children, and "useless men" outside the city, where they were kindly treated by the patriots. Boguier did not appear until April 28, and two days later he departed for no one knew where. Páez was disgusted and wrote to Soublette on May 7, requesting that Beluche be given command of the blockading squadron.[22]

Beluche was then patrolling the coast of the Paraguaná Peninsula. It took several days for Soublette's orders to reach him, but he sailed as soon as he received them, arriving at the port of Borburata (four miles east of Puerto Cabello) on the afternoon of May 16. A day or so later, Beluche saw the 44-gun *Ligera* approaching. He called all the captains of his vessels on board the 18-gun flagship *Vencedor* and told each one what position to take and how to maneuver in order to capture the *Ligera*.[23]

As the *Ligera* neared, not a single patriot captain obeyed orders. The *Vencedor* alone received the frigate's fire as all the other vessels headed for La Guaira. An observer in La Guaira reported:

> All the boast of the blockading squadron had ended in smoke. It is true they made some kind of attack on the frigate, brig, etc., and after having exchanged a few shots, by which the brig *Vencedor* had her mainmast wounded by an 18 pounder, and 3 men (not dangerously) and also the mainmast of the schooner *Daphne* altered, they were glad to sheer off. *The whole blame is laid on commodore Boguier*, to whom they apply some degrading epithets. They are all lying here at present, and as far as I can understand, not inclined to return, except the government make them some compensation for past services. God only knows what will be the result.[24]

The result was that the *Ligera* and several other royalist vessels sailed to Curaçao and returned in June with enough supplies to last Morales in Puerto Cabello for six months. These vessels were not molested as they entered the outer harbor because Páez had abandoned the siege. He had lost more than two thousand troops because of a ma-

22. Port-of-Spain *Trinidad Gazette*, July 24, 1822; José Antonio Páez, *Autobiografía del General José Antonio Páez* (2 vols.; 1869; facsimile ed., New York, 1946), I, 200; *Niles' Weekly Register*, XXII (July 27, 1822), 341; Vargas, *Historia Naval*, II, 180–81.
23. Enrique Ortega Ricaurte, "Almirante Renato Beluche," *Boletín de Historia y Antigüedades* (Bogotá), Marzo–Abril, 1961, pp. 125–26.
24. Port-of-Spain *Trinidad Gazette*, July 24, 1822.

lignant fever endemic in the swampy area around the outer town, and had only a thousand troops left. They were ill, and Páez took them to higher ground to recover. The ubiquitous reporter observed: "A corps of observation only remains, but the attack on the place will be resumed in a more healthy season."[25]

Soublette, pursuing Morales, had entered Coro on July 23. When he heard that Morales was sailing for Puerto Cabello, Soublette feared that he meant to cross the mountains behind Puerto Cabello and attack the valleys of Valencia. Morales did threaten in that direction, but he had no intention of concentrating his operations against the center of Venezuela, where Páez commanded. Instead, he set a trap that both Soublette and Páez fell into. Soublette marched east from Coro with most of his troops; but before he arrived at Valencia, Páez had left there and descended to the Valley of Naguanagua (between Valencia and Puerto Cabello) with eight hundred infantrymen and a cavalry squadron of fifty men. On August 10, Morales allowed himself to be seen on the heights that screen the Valley of Naguanagua from Puerto Cabello. He sent a squadron of Corianos against Páez's cavalry and another against his infantry. The Corianos were to pull back as Páez advanced. Páez's version of what followed was that he forced the Corianos to take to the hills, and then Páez retired because the narrow passage through which the Corianos had disappeared offered the enemy strong protection.[26]

During the nights that followed, Morales' troops fired muskets from time to time, kept bonfires burning, and during the days advanced and retreated. When Soublette's troops arrived, he and Páez prepared to battle Morales, but the Spaniard was pulling his troops from the hills. On August 23 the royalists embarked in fourteen vessels. Leaving Calzada in command at Puerto Cabello, Morales sailed east to meet Laborde, who was patrolling the La Guaira coast with the *Ligera* and *Hercules*.

The royalist fleet of sixteen vessels sailed west and captured a schooner in the port of Ocumare. From documents on board, Morales learned that Soublette had withdrawn most of his troops from the Maracaibo

25. *Niles' Weekly Register*, XXII (August 24, 1822), 405.
26. Páez, *Autobiografía*, I, 221–22.

sector, and that Clemente was left in the city of Maracaibo with very little support.

Morales and Laborde headed for the Gulf of Venezuela. They tried to anchor at Los Taques on the Paraguaná Peninsula, but its garrison made a show of resistance. The fleet sailed across the gulf to Cojoro on the Guajira Peninsula and landed troops. Patriot guerrillas sent a warning to Clemente that Morales was marching south toward him, so Clemente left Maracaibo with the garrison and some militia, marched north to Salina Rica, and waited there for Morales. The encounter was brief. Clemente fled to Maracaibo, embarked his garrison, sailed southeast across the lake to the port of Moporo, and then marched east toward Trujillo.

CHAPTER 15

The Battle of Lake Maracaibo

Lake Maracaibo is shaped like an avocado, with the stem end the throat or strait that connects the lake with the small Bay of Tablazo. A chain of low, sandy islets almost cuts off the bay from the gulf, but brigs and schooners could cross the bar between the long islet of San Carlos and the smaller ones above it. A fort on the end of San Carlos guarded the pass to the Bay of Tablazo.

Morales' fleet approached the fort, and without any resistance it surrendered. The *Ligera* and *Hercules* remained in the Gulf of Venezuela, but the smaller vessels sailed through the pass to the Bay of Tablazo, then pilots steered them through the channel across the shallow, sandy-bottomed Tablazo to the port of Maracaibo.

By September 7, 1822, Morales was master of Maracaibo Province, with headquarters at Maracaibo. From this base he could operate over three inside lines: (1) east against Coro; (2) southeast against Trujillo and Mérida, then west to Cúcuta, south to Pamplona and the road to Bogotá; and (3) west against Santa Marta and Rio Hacha. At the same time, his supply lines were open by sea to Cuba, Puerto Rico, Curaçao, Bonaire, and Aruba. Morales could and did threaten the independence of Colombia.[1]

As soon as Soublette knew that Morales had entered the Gulf of Venezuela, he dispatched Beluche with an infantry battalion on board the schooner *Independencia* and another schooner, and Páez to support Clemente. Páez collected two thousand troops and headed toward the eastern shore of Lake Maracaibo. He expected to cross the lake "in the many small vessels on its bosom," but he halted at Trujillo, where he

1. Eljuri-Yunez, *Batalla del Lago de Maracaibo*, 42–44.

found Clemente, whom Morales had defeated a few miles west at Betijoque.² Páez left Clemente in command and rode east to renew the siege of Puerto Cabello.

Beluche arrived at La Vela de Coro on September 18, disembarked part of his troops, then sailed to reconnoiter the Gulf of Venezuela. He anchored in front of the bar of San Carlos and sent an officer in the *Independencia*'s launch to get a pilot at Fort San Carlos. When the launch did not return by the afternoon of September 21, Beluche knew the enemy had possession of the fort. He sailed to Los Taques, disembarked the rest of the troops, whose orders were to march to Coro, and sailed east. Beluche was in front of neutral Curaçao on September 27 when he saw the *Ligera*, *Hercules*, *Valeroso*, and *Condor* loading supplies for Puerto Cabello. He weighed anchor and headed toward the Leeward Islands. Off the Aves Islands he captured a ketch and took it to La Guaira, where the Colombian navy soon had some big ships.³

Danells returned from Baltimore in October with the 25-gun corvette *Bolívar*, which carried twenty-two 32-pounders and three 12-pounders. Two more vessels, bought by the Colombian agent in England, arrived at the beginning of November: the 28-gun corvette *Lady Barrington* and the 20-gun brig *Mosqueta*.⁴

On November 4 Danells sailed from La Guaira with the corvette *Bolívar* and the 18-gun brig *Vencedor* to prowl along the coast occupied by the enemy. Beluche sailed on November 6 with the 18-gun brig *Independiente*, the schooner *Independencia*, and another schooner, "having on board the battalion of Tiradores. These he landed at Rio Hacha where they joined Montilla's forces." He sent José Sardá with these and other troops across the Guajira Peninsula to keep Morales from making any movement in the direction of the valleys of Cúcuta. Morales attacked Sardá, defeated him, and drove him back to Rio

---

2. "I find intriguing those odd Indian names whose syllables sort of chop themselves off like fat little sausages. Pronounce these out loud and you will know what I mean: Socopó, Chacopo, Betijoque, Escuque, and Esnajaque." Anne Sutton, "What's in a Name!" in Dorothy Kamen-Kaye (ed.), *Speaking of Venezuela* (Caracas, 1947), 141.

3. Soublette's report, November 1, 1822, in Ortega Ricaurte, "Almirante Renato Beluche," 128–29.

4. *Niles' Weekly Register*, XXII (December 21, 1822), 246; Kingston *Royal Gazette*, February 15–22, 1823.

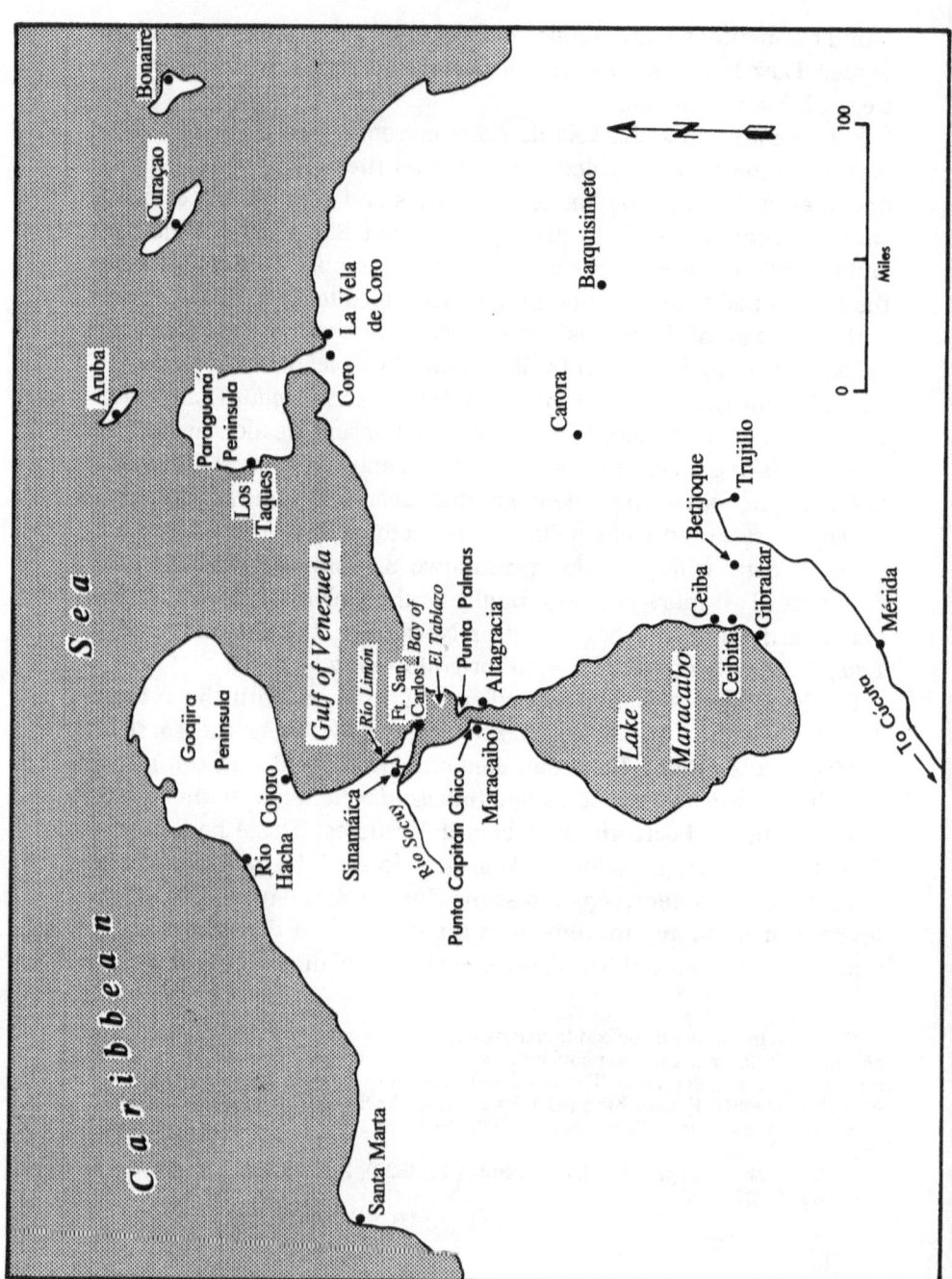

Battle of Lake Maracaibo

Hacha, where Beluche, according to Soublette's instructions, had placed himself under the command of Montilla.[5]

Now Montilla held a council of war. Among those present were Beluche, the priest-colonel José Felix Blanco, Joly, and Walter Chitty. Father Blanco "had dowsed his *casoc* and seized the sword" at the beginning of the revolution and was "a man more in externals resembling General Bolívar than any other man in the world." Joly had anchored at Rio Hacha soon after Beluche. Walter Davis Chitty, born in London at the end of the eighteenth century, had served the British navy during the Napoleonic Wars. He arrived at Margarita in 1818 commanding an 18-gun brig, joined Brion's navy with the rank of captain, and was with Padilla in the siege of Cartagena. Montilla was impressed with the way Chitty handled artillery and gave him command of the infantry and artillery in the Province of Santa Marta.[6]

Beluche, Joly, and Chitty knew that there were Indians and Guajiro mestizos in Rio Hacha who could pilot ships across the bar at San Carlos and over the Bay of Tablazo into Lake Maracaibo and who had navigated these waters since they were small boys. Beluche, knowing that he could depend on these pilots, declared at Montilla's council: "We have not been able to defeat Morales on land. We must do so by sea. We can force the bar, cross the Tablazo, get into Lake Maracaibo, gain command of the lake, and cut off Morales' supply line."[7] Chitty and Joly said that they would follow Beluche; and Montilla promised that he would make a simultaneous attack by land to divert Morales and oblige him to weaken his defenses of the bar and access canals—strategic keys that opened the door to the lake.

Padilla, commanding general of the Third Department of the Navy and of the Squadron of Operations over Zulia, was not in Rio Hacha when Montilla called his council of war. Montilla did not want Padilla present and did not want him to be able to claim credit for any part of the coming Maracaibo campaign. Padilla had commanded the navy during the siege of Cartagena, and everyone knew that this *granadino*

---

5. Eljuri-Yunez, *Batalla del Lago de Maracaibo*, 73.
6. Jane L. De Grummond (ed.), *Caracas Diary, 1835–1840: The Journal of John G. A. Williamson, First Diplomatic Representative of the United States to Venezuela* (Baton Rouge, 1954), 208; Vargas, *Nuestros Próceres Navales*, 355–56.
7. Eljuri-Yunez, *Batalla del Lago de Maracaibo*, 75–76.

zambo (part Indian, part Negro) had forced the royalists in Cartagena to capitulate. His popularity increased each day, especially with the lower classes, and made it difficult for General Montilla, a white Venezuelan aristocrat, to maintain that it was his leadership as commander of the department of Magdalena that had brought about the victory. Montilla wrote to Santander on November 30 saying: "Soublette has ordered that Beluche be given command of the *Constitución* [one of Padilla's vessels, perhaps his largest]. This has caused discord because Padilla's disposition is not compatible with that of Beluche, Joly, or Chitty. They are the first and best officers of the squadron. We will see, and work with tact in this matter. In any event, Padilla will remain in command at Cartagena."[8]

Santander ignored Montilla's suggestion that Padilla be shelved in Cartagena—no foreigner was going to supersede a *granadino*. In his decisive reply on February 19, 1823, Santander stated that Padilla was supreme commander of the Zulia squadron. During the three-month interval between this exchange of letters, Beluche assembled a fleet and patrolled the Gulf of Venezuela.

Meanwhile, Morales' September occupation of Maracaibo had sent tremors of terror down Santander's spine. *Granadinos* were unhappy about the heavy contributions Santander levied on them to support the war effort in the south and on the Venezuelan front. If Morales broke through the Cúcuta frontier and headed toward Bogotá, the *granadinos* might pronounce in his favor. General Urdaneta was in Bogotá equipping troops for Bolívar in Quito, and Santander had great respect for Urdaneta's ability, so he dispatched him to take command at Cúcuta.

Urdaneta was there in December when Morales threatened Coro with two thousand troops and marched south to Trujillo, where he defeated Clemente, captured his baggage, and took nine hundred prisoners. Clemente escaped to Betijoque as Morales marched in the direction of Mérida, taking all the food and cattle he could and destroying the rest.

Clemente reoccupied Trujillo, and Urdaneta's line held in front of

---

8. Enrique Otero D'Costa, *Vida del Almirante José Padilla, 1778–1828* (Bogotá, 1973), 37–38.

Cúcuta. For a time they did not know where Morales was, but an observer in Maracaibo reported that Morales had returned to that city on January 28, "after having successfully entered the cities of Mérida and La Grita, and pushing his forces close to Cúcuta."[9]

On the sea, Colombian ships had better luck. Beluche was patrolling the Gulf of Venezuela (sometimes reported in English-language newspapers as the Gulf of Maracaibo), and Danells was there with the 25-gun corvette *Bolívar*, the 28-gun corvette *Carabobo* (the former *Lady Barrington*), the 18-gun *Vencedor*, and the 20-gun *Mosqueta*.

Three royalist ships tried to enter the gulf on December 16. Danells in the *Bolívar* and Captain John B. Maitland in the *Carabobo* gave chase: "They captured the Spanish corvette built ship called the *Maria Theresa*, mounting 24 long 9-pounders, and 200 men. She had $25,000 in specie on board, which was removed to the *Bolívar*. The *Maria Theresa* was from Havana, bound to Maracaybo with 2 merchant brigs in company, with provisions for Morales, both of which were also captured. The action lasted only a few minutes. The *Maria Theresa* lost 2 men killed and 2 wounded. The Colombian ships sustained no injury."[10]

Two weeks later, as Danells was cruising off Puerto Cabello with his squadron, he captured the Spanish frigate *María Francisca* "of 32 guns and 400 men from Havana for Puerto Cabello. She is a fine vessel and has about 30,000 dollars on board. Danells had a short time before captured the *Maria Theresa*. . . . As a reverse of this, the Spaniards have captured an American brig from London for Laguaira, mounting 9 guns; which had on board 5000 muskets, 1400 carbines, 50 pieces brass ordinance, 400 barrels gunpowder, with a quantity of pistols, balls, etc."[11]

Royalists in the Ciénega and city of Santa Marta incited a revolt there in January, 1823, which Padilla helped Montilla to crush. Then, after receiving Santander's letter, Montilla had to let Padilla exercise his rank and duties as commanding general of the Third Department of the Navy and of the Squadron of Operations over Zulia.

---

9. Kingston *Royal Gazette*, March 8–15 and March 15–22, 1823.
10. Philadelphia *National Gazette and Literary Register*, January 18, 1823.
11. *Niles' Weekly Register*, XXIII (February 8, 1823), 356.

When Padilla arrived at Los Taques with the *Constitución* and a few smaller vessels, Beluche turned over the command to him and with good will accepted Padilla as his superior. Beluche understood the need for unity of command. At the Battle of New Orleans, even Commodore Patterson had accepted Jackson as commander-in-chief. There, Patterson had no navy; and the enemy had to be defeated on land. Here, the situation was reversed. Morales would survive on land as long as Laborde could supply him by sea. The enemy had to be defeated on the sea.

Beluche, commanding the first division of the Zulia squadron, captured the empty brig *Confianza* "on her passage from Maracaibo whither she had carried ammunition and 2900 dollars for the Spanish army." He also captured "the sloop *La Perla* from Curaçao, laden with arms."[12] These vessels were added to the Zulia squadron, but even so it was in pitiable condition. Its ships were badly in need of repair, crews were depleted, and Padilla had almost no rations and no money. He sent Beluche to Soublette to solicit some small vessels, men, money, and food.

Sailing in the *Independiente*, Beluche anchored at Isla Larga in the Bay of Borburata on April 7, and three days later he was in Caracas. He told Soublette about the squadron in the Gulf of Venezuela and that Padilla had to have more *small* vessels and other help before he could force the bar and enter Lake Maracaibo. Soublette was hard pressed, since Danells, blockading the Puerto Cabello coast, needed the same things that Padilla did. It took Soublette almost three weeks to assemble five small schooners at La Guaira: two for Beluche and three for Danells.

Beluche's schooners were the *Leona* and *Antonia Manuela*. The *Leona* had five guns—one 18-pounder and four 4-pounders—and thirteen crewmen. On board were sixty-five troops, one medicine chest, sixty-five pine boards and planks, and twenty-four oars. The *Antonio Manuela* had one 8-pounder and eight crewmen. Soublette also gave Beluche four thousand pesos.[13] Beluche sailed from La Guaira bound for Borburata on April 30 with the five little schooners and anchored

---

12. Kingston *Royal Gazette*, May 3–10, 1823.
13. Beluche, *Contesta a las Falsas Imputaciones*, 24.

beside the *Independiente* the next day at 2:30 in the afternoon, as an enemy squadron approached with Laborde commanding.

Morales had asked Laborde to bring him more supplies about the same time that Padilla sent Beluche to Soublette. Laborde had sailed first to Havana, next to Aguadilla on the west coast of Puerto Rico, where Governor de La Torre gave him 57,849 pesos and 6 reales for Morales, then to Aruba to be sure that no enemy vessels were lurking there. Now he was approaching Puerto Cabello with the 48-gun *Constitución* (named for the Spanish Constitution of 1812) and the 44-gun *Ceres*, escorting two fully laden merchant vessels.

From the poop of the *Carabobo* Danells signaled Beluche that his ship and the *María Francisca* were going to attack Laborde and would like Beluche's help. Beluche agreed to support him, but only with the *Independiente*. Laborde had crowded all sail and was standing toward Danells and Beluche.

The *Carabobo*, *María Francisca*, and *Independiente* were formed in line, half a cable-length apart, and were preparing to board the enemy when the firing began at 4:30 P.M. Laborde's 48-gun *Constitución* battled the *Carabobo* and *María Francisca* (half of whose cannon had been sent to Páez), while the 44-gun *Ceres* concentrated on the 18-gun *Independiente*. Beluche sustained combat for seventy-five minutes, then, "with four men killed and four wounded, with his vessel severely cut up in her hull, sails and rigging, and seeing the *María Francisca* and *Carabobo* about to surrender, Beluche prudently retired from the engagement, having a considerable sum on board for Commodore Padilla's squadron."[14]

Beluche limped back to Los Taques with his schooners and arrived safely on the morning of May 3. He immediately reported to Padilla that not only had the royalists captured Colombia's two largest ships, but they had also taken Danells and the other officers and the crews as prisoners into Puerto Cabello. Beluche pointed out that, for the time

---

14. The above account has been compiled from Danells' report, in *Niles' Weekly Register*, XXIV (July 12, 1823), 298–99; Beluche's account, in Ortega Recaurte, "Almirante Renato Beluche," 132–34; the account of the Spanish commandant at Puerto Cabello, in Kingston *Royal Gazette*, May 31–June 7, 1823; the account of the Colombian captain Esmit at Borburata, who watched the action through a telescope, in *ibid.*; and Philadelphia *National Gazette and Literary Register*, May 24, 1823.

being, the royalists were supreme on the sea. He insisted, however, that before Laborde could concentrate his big ships against the Zulia squadron, the patriots must force the bar at San Carlos, enter Lake Maracaibo—which Laborde's big ships could not enter—and destroy Morales' forces.

Padilla immediately called all his officers on board the *Constitución* to a council of war, related all that Beluche had told him, then put this question to the council: "Shall we maintain the blockade here, or retire, or force the bar?"

Beluche jumped to his feet and said, "We must force the bar and occupy Lake Maracaibo. Only in this way can we save the Patria."

Walter Chitty and three others spoke in favor of Beluche's option. They presented a resolution saying that, whatever the cost might be, they must cross the bar, get command of the lake, and keep Laborde out of the lake. Every officer voted for and signed the resolution: Padilla first, then Beluche, Rafael Tono, Walter Chitty, and fifteen others. Joly was absent in his brig *Gran Bolívar*.[15]

Padilla sent the *Atrevida* to find Joly and the *Espartana* to search for another absent vessel, the *Terror de España*. Next, Padilla had rations, supplies, and crewmen removed from the corvette *Constitución* and sent this vessel with a skeleton crew to Rio Hacha, since it was too big to cross the bar. He distributed the rations he had and set crews to repairing their vessels as best they could.[16]

At sunset on May 4, the *Espartana* sent in a prize, the brig *Fama*, laden with supplies for Morales. The next morning, the *Espartana* came in accompanied by Peter Storms and his schooner *Peacock*, laden with supplies for the patriots; but the *Espartana* had not been able to find the *Terror de España*. Joly and the *Gran Bolívar* came in on May 7, and by 5:30 that afternoon Padilla had his squadron anchored in front of Fort San Carlos, ready to cross the bar the next day.

Pilots began at dawn on May 8 to take soundings and place buoys to mark the channel. By afternoon, the squadron was in line of battle with the flagship *Independiente*, Beluche commanding, in the lead.

---

15. Beluche Mora, *Abordajes, Biografía Esquemática de Renato Beluche*, 62–66; Eljuri-Yunez, *Batalla del Lago de Maracaibo*, 77–78; Vargas, *Nuestros Próceres Navales*, 161.

16. Restrepo, *Historia de la Revolución de Colombia*, III, 312.

General Padilla was on board with Beluche and gave the signal to move at 2:30 P.M. By four o'clock the squadron was within range of the guns of Fort San Carlos. They opened fire, but, as Beluche reported, "We ignored this fire and by 5 o'clock all our boats had crossed the bar and were beyond range except the *Gran Bolívar*."[17] Fire from the fort had concentrated on it and made so many openings that Joly's crew removed most of the armament, burned the *Gran Bolívar*, then transferred to the 18-gun brig *Marte*. Joly took command of the *Marte*.

The squadron anchored for the night, not daring to cross the shallow waters of the Tablazo in the darkness. The next day, while Padilla waited for a favorable wind, a royalist detail removed all the buoys. Padilla ordered his fleet to sail through the pass, with the smaller vessels leading. They all got through, except the *Independiente* and *Marte*, which were grounded. Crews set to work to unload all guns, supplies, and everything else that was movable fom these two ships and put them on smaller vessels. This backbreaking work continued for four days. When the vessels were free, however, the squadron could not move for two more days because there was no wind. By May 14, the whole squadron was anchored at Punta de Palma, the strategic point on the east coast of the five-mile-wide strait that controls the entrance into the lake.

Even though Morales had known for over a month that Padilla was going to force the bar, he had done nothing to prevent it. He had enough brigs, schooners, and small craft in his fleet to destroy his enemy or seriously damage him; but, except for removing the buoys, all Morales did was belittle Padilla and the republicans in *El Postal Español*, the paper he was publishing in Maracaibo. In this paper Morales called Padilla a bully, mulatto, zambo, pirate, and other names, and he said the republicans were Mozambique Negroes, Senegal monkeys, corrupt mulattos, filthy zambos, and ungrateful mestizos.[18]

At the same time, Morales did not think very highly of Laborde and his squadron. Morales considered Laborde his errand boy and was getting more and more irritated because Laborde did not appear with his vessels loaded with supplies and had not sent him an official report

---

17. Beluche, *Contesta a las Falsas Imputaciones*, 13.
18. Eljuri-Yunez, *Batalla del Lago de Maracaibo*, 123.

of the capture of Danells' corvettes. Laborde at this time was still in Puerto Cabello repairing the damage that Beluche and Danells had done to the *Constitución* and *Ceres*.

Every day from May 14 for the next five days, Padilla made sallies toward Maracaibo, trying to provoke the enemy to attack. On May 20, Morales' fleet did attack at Punta de Palma with eleven large vessels and fourteen small ones. The combat lasted forty-five minutes, during which time five schooners tried to board the *Independiente*. Beluche beat them off until Joly came up with the *Marte*, and together they forced the enemy to retire. The royalists lost their naval commander, other officers, and one schooner. Padilla received a contusion in the head.[19]

Morales boasted the next day in *El Postal España* that fire from the guns of Fort San Carlos had sunk the *Gran Bolívar*. This was not accurate. Chitty had burned the *Gran Bolívar* on May 8.[20]

Reyes González at Coro knew within hours that Padilla's squadron had crossed the bar and entered the lake; but he was unble to send troops immediately to cooperate with Padilla because, with the help of the priest-colonel Father Andrés Torrellas, he had just driven the royalists from Coro and was pursuing enemy guerrillas. However, Manrique from his base at Betijoque was gaining control of the eastern coast of Lake Maracaibo from the port of Moporo south of Ceibita and Ceiba. South of Ceiba was the important port of Gibraltar, still in royalist hands.

Padilla moved south with part of his fleet after the May 21 battle, clearing royalists from the east coat ports of the lake, and anchored at Ceibita on May 30. Manrique and Padilla consulted, with the result that Manrique's troops descended on Gibraltar in conjunction with Padilla's squadron and took that port. Their big problem now was rations—they had none. Morillo had depleted the whole province of Trujillo the previous January.

On June 6, Padilla and Manrique sailed across the lake to the port of Corona, where Manrique disembarked with a hundred men to battle

---

19. Restrepo, *Historia de la Revolución de Colombia*, III, 312–314; Enrique Ortega Ricaurte, *Bloqueo, rendición y ocupación de Maracaibo* (Bogotá, 1947), 74–81.
20. Report from *El Postal España*, in Philadelphia *National Gazette and Literary Register*, July 12, 1823.

the same number of enemy infantry. In his report of this action, Manrique said: "The enemy was completely bested, leaving in our possession four who had come over to us. The wounded were carried off precipitately to the mountains, whither we pursued them for more than three leagues. The field remains in our possession together with some heads of cattle; the situation of our squadron placed me under the necessity of taking 27 milch cows from an inhabitant of Perija who for many days past has been very fervent in our cause. I gave him an order payable on the chest of this department."[21]

Manrique and Padilla sailed to Altagracia and were anchored there on June 14, when sentinels saw enemy vessels leave Maracaibo and proceed to Fort San Carlos. Padilla sent schooners to capture them. They did so, and found that the enemy vessels were transporting Morales' sick troops and that Morales had the bulk of his army camped at the channel of Moján, which leads west from the bar to the Rio Limón. Morales was there to obstruct the passage of General Francisco Gómez with the army of Rio Hacha.

The news that Padilla had crossed the bar on May 8 did not reach Rio Hacha until May 12. Montilla had promised to attack Morales in Maracaibo and divert him from Padilla's squadron, but Montilla was ill. His second in command was General Francisco Gómez, so it was Gómez who got together two thousand or more troops. Father Blanco rounded up cattle and other food for Gómez, and he was able to begin the march east on May 16. The army moved slowly because it was the rainy season, the land was inundated, and the pack mules and horses were weak from lack of forage. Gómez camped near Cojoro on June 1 and rested his army for several days.

Morales knew about Gómez' movements because guerrillas had kept him informed. He left Maracaibo on June 1 with the bulk of his army, marched north to the Moján channel, where he had a light fleet, and ordered all inhabitants of Sinamáica and other villages and owners of the cattle and sheep farms north of the channel to evacuate with all their herds and food.

Gómez marched south toward Sinamáica on June 8. He could not find a single person to ask about Padilla, and he could find no food. He

21. *Ibid.*, July 26, 1823.

could not continue toward Maracibo because the margins of the channel were waterlogged and unwadable; and the royalist light fleet kept him from crossing anywhere on the line made by the Rio Socuy, Rio Limón, and their lagoons. Gómez had hoped to find Padilla on the Rio Limón with boats to transport his troops, but Morales' light fleet dominated that route. Four hundred of Gómez' troops were sick, and his army was dwindling because of desertions and hostile Indians. A discouraged Gómez gave the order to withdraw to Rio Hacha on June 15, thinking he had failed in his mission. He did not know that he had diverted Morales, and that the Independents were taking advantage of Morales' absence from Maracaibo.[22]

On June 16 Manrique with six hundred infantrymen and thirty foot dragoons boarded Chitty's light fleet and sailed across the lake in company with the *Independiente* (Beluche commanding), the *Marte* (Joly commanding), and two schooners. Beluche, Joly, and the other two captains bombarded Maracaibo for two hours while Manrique and his troops landed below the city. They had to dislodge the enemy from a bridge and some mangrove areas before they could enter the city, then they took it street by street. Royalists who survived fled to the mountains behind the city.

During the next three days the republicans took away ammunition, dry goods, provisions, the printing press and the printer (Morales could no longer publish *El Postal Español*), about a hundred head of cattle, and small vessels that were in port. They sailed away on June 19 as Morales approached the city with two thousand troops. When he entered Maracaibo, he found "the town had been greatly injured. . . . His men picked up more than 1000 shot, 12's, 18's, and 25's . . . and discovered 106 holes in the Nun's Convent."[23]

Morales' situation became more critical when Colonel Lorenzo arrived with five hundred troops. Lorenzo had eluded pursuers from Coro, reached the coast near Altagracia ahead of them, and appropriated piraguas, in which he crossed the lake. Morales now had twenty-five hundred troops to feed ("most all the female part of Maracaybo had cheerfully gone over to the patriots and sailed away with them"),

---

22. *Ibid.*, July 29 and August 26, 1823; Restrepo, *Historia de la Revolución de Colombia*, III, 315–22 and 325–26.

23. Restrepo, *Historia de la Revolución de Colombia*, III, 315–22 and 325–26.

and he had only a limited area from which he could get food until Laborde arrived.

Laborde sailed from Puerto Cabello the latter part of June with the *Constitución, Ceres*, two brigs, and a schooner bound for Curaçao. There he dallied more than a week, loading supplies before sailing to the Gulf of Venezuela. He anchored at Los Taques on July 4.

This delay was a boon to Padilla at Altagracia and to Manrique, camped nearby. More than seven hundred of his men had sickened and died, some from wounds received at Maracaibo, but more because there was nothing to eat except burro. Then Father Torrellas arrived with food and nine hundred men, including three hundred whom he had won from the enemy; and Señor Paul Pardo sent a large convoy with food from Gibraltar.

Ten days passed before Laborde sailed from Los Taques to Fort San Carlos without the *Constitución* and *Ceres*, which were too big to cross the bar. Morales did not meet Laborde at San Carlos as the latter had expected. Instead, a substitute was sent with orders for Laborde to attack Padilla's fleet immediately. Laborde sent this answer to Morales: "I am commander as far as naval affairs are concerned. You are free to do the same on land." To prove his point, Laborde waited six days before crossing the bar.[24]

Padilla watched from Punta de Palma, hoping for a chance to attack Laborde as he crossed the Tablazo, but the winds were not favorable. Laborde anchored safely at Maracaibo and fought verbally with Morales for two more days about who was in command. Morales let Laborde know that most of the vessels belonged to him and that their commanders and crews would obey only his orders. Their bickering was like the fable of the rabbits: when they saw themselves pursued by dogs, they stopped to discuss whether the dogs were hounds, greyhounds, bloodhounds, or pointers.[25]

After sundown on July 22, Morales sent eleven canoes with seven hundred men across the lake to the coast near Altagracia. They were to cooperate with his squadron, which was to attack the next morning. Manrique frustrated this operation. His guard, "having observed their

---

24. *Ibid.*
25. Eljuri-Yunez, *Batalla del Lago de Maracaibo*, 104, 123–24.

movements to the place where they intended to land, by a brisk fire, prevented this and forced them to retire."²⁶

Early the next morning, July 23, sentinels at Altagracia saw Laborde's squadron formed in line of battle north of Punta de Palma. Padilla did not wait to be attacked. He signaled his squadron to up anchor and attack. Beluche in the *Independiente* and Joly in the *Marte* moved out first. Soon all was confusion because captains of the schooners either did not see or did not obey signals from the *Independiente*. Padilla left that vessel in a small boat and went to the schooners, trying to get them to reunite, but by this time Laborde and his fleet had sailed across the strait to Punta de Capitán Chico north of the city of Maracaibo. Action had to be postponed because Padilla's ships were not in order. They returned to Altagracia.

The next day, July 24, the wind did not favor the Colombians until two o'clock in the afternoon, at which time their squadron began crossing the lake to where the entire royalist fleet was anchored from Punta de Capitán Chico to the city of Maracaibo. Laborde had sacrificed mobility to pacify Morales. The royalists' largest vessels (three brigs, ten schooners, and two pilot boats) were in line parallel to the coast. The light fleet of sixteen small craft was on the left of the main fleet, and in line perpendicular to the coast.

At 2:30 Padilla signalled his three brigs and seven schooners to form line abreast and board, while Chitty with the light fleet took care of Morales' left end. Padilla's main fleet could not maneuver perfectly because of differences in the sailing qualities of his vessels, but herded by Beluche in the *Independiente* on the right end of the irregular line and by Joly in the *Marte* on the left, each schooner picked out an enemy vessel and approached it with all speed. Royalist guns and muskets fired as soon as their enemy came within range and continued to fire with wind blowing the smoke back over them. The Colombian ships held to their course without a single return shot until their yardarms touched those of the enemy still at anchor. Then seamen and troops swarmed over their bulwarks, and the battle became a series of duels between ships. It was over in twenty minutes.²⁷

26. Manrique's report, July 24, 1823, in Kingston *Royal Gazette*, August 9–16, 1823.
27. Beluche, *Contesta a las Falsas Imputaciones*, 15; Restrepo, *Historia de la Revolución de Colombia*, III, 327.

"The action was severe and ended in the almost total destruction of the Spanish squadron. A brig and schooner were blown up and the rest captured or destroyed, with the exception of the schooner *Especuladora* in which Laborde made his escape to his ships lying outside the bar. The Spaniards confess the loss of 1500 men amongst whom they count 160 officers. General Morales remained in Maracaibo with about 800 men and short of provisions."[28]

Morales held out more than a week; then, on August 3, two of his commissioners met with two others representing the patriots. These four men,

> in an honorable manner, being well acquainted with the miserable situation to which Maracaibo is reduced; having been besieged for three months by the Colombian squadron; its inhabitants afflicted and distressed; agreed upon a capitulation whose principal provisions were: (1) The city of Maracaibo, the fortress of San Carlos and the territory occupied by the Spanish army shall be surrendered in their present state to the chief of the Colombian besiegers; (2) The same must take place with regard to armed vessels lying at anchor in the bay; (3) The Sergeants, corporals and soldiers born in America and serving in the Spanish army may, if they wish, follow the Colombian standard. Those who may prefer to be paroled and return to their perspective homes are at liberty to do so under the guarantee of safety which this treaty secures them. Those who intend to remain faithful to the Spanish government, will be treated and considered as prisoners of war, without being molested, until their government or its deputies may exchange them. The sailors are also included in this article; (4) The chiefs and officers and their attendants will be allowed to depart from the territory of Colombia, under oath not to take up arms against the republic until exchanged. Under this article are included the musicians.[29]

Morales sailed to Cuba at the republic's expense on August 20, "with 7 or 800 troops, being all that remained of his army who were natives of old Spain."[30]

The royalists still held one base in the Republic of Colombia: Puerto Cabello.

---

28. *Niles' Weekly Register*, XXV (September 6, 1823), 8.
29. "Capitulation of Morales from the *Iris of Venezuela Extra*, Caracas, August 18, 1823" in *ibid.*, XXV (September 20, 1823), 43–44.
30. Philadelphia *National Gazette and Literary Register*, September 11, 1823; Restrepo, *Historia de la Revolución de Colombia*, III, 332–34.

CHAPTER 16

Puerto Cabello and the *Contesta*

Páez was on the defensive during the long siege of Maracaibo. He had been forced to give up the siege of Puerto Cabello after Laborde captured Danells with the *Carabobo* and *María Francisca*. An observer within Puerto Cabello reported that "the captured vessels both arrived in the harbour much cut up in their hulls and rigging, and had between them upwards of 100 men killed and wounded. Commodore Danells is said to have on board his ship about 30,000 dollars, partly his own and partly to pay troops besieging Puerto Cabello. Prisoners taken equal 401—the greater number were land forces acting as marines."[1]

Within a few days, the schooner *Rayo* sailed as a cartel from Puerto Cabello to La Guaira, with Danells and about forty officers belonging to the captured ships aboard. Then Danells returned to Baltimore, and Captain Maitland superceded Captain Matthews in command of the *Mosqueta*—now called the *Pichincha* in honor of Antonio José de Sucre's victory on Mt. Pichincha on May 24, 1822, which broke royalist power in Quito.

Because Captain Matthews was removed from command of the *Pichincha*, he and three other officers "have now thrown up their commands and retired from the Colombian service. The crew, when informed of the change that was to take place, and understanding that they were not to receive any of their back pay, which has been due for a length of time, became so disorderly that it was found necessary to send about 35 of them on board the *Bolívar* in arms."[2]

1. Kingston *Royal Gazette*, May 31–June 7, 1823.
2. Philadelphia *National Gazette and Literary Register*, June 19, 1823.

Twelve days after the May 1, 1823, capture of Danells and his two ships, Páez announced that until the naval force of the republic was greatly strengthened, he would not undertake another siege of Puerto Cabello. Thereafter, he shuttled back and forth between Valencia and Maracay, from which points he could protect Caracas and the llanos and keep in touch with the Maracaibo campaign. In June he sent eight hundred troops to strengthen the patriots at Coro against any possible retreat of Morales by land to Puerto Cabello.

Morales sailed away in August, but Padilla could not immediately get a naval force from the victors at Maracaibo because he became too ill to discharge his duties. The *granadino* had been battered and scarred in many battles since Trafalgar in 1805, and the old wounds and "the contusion in the head" received in the May 20 action on Lake Maracaibo were taking their toll. Chitty was ill also, and Beluche, the second in command, was busy for some time with the affairs of the Zulia squadron, whose ships had to be repaired and provisioned. It was October before Padilla, still incapacitated, directed Joly to assume command at Maracaibo and sent Beluche to La Guaira to serve as Soublette directed.[3]

Páez had already paid a visit to Soublette in Caracas with the hope of getting sufficient naval forces to blockade Puerto Cabello. He had only the brigs *Urica* and *Pichincha*, which sailed back and forth in front of Puerto Cabello, where they could impede but not prevent the entrance of rations. Fortunately for Páez at this time, the royalists were unable to send any supply convoys to Puerto Cabello.

Puerto Cabello was divided into two parts: Inner Town and Outer Town. Inner Town was built on the head of a small peninsula, which was an irregular quadrangle approximately 400 yards on the north, 400 on the west, 600 on the south, and 450 on the east. Two centuries before, Spanish engineers had cut a moat through the peninsula where it narrowed, making Inner Town an island. A bridge over the moat connected Inner Town with Outer Town, and a narrow saline flat separated Outer Town from the foot of the mountains.

The best military scientists of Europe had designed Inner Town's

---

3. Ortega Ricaurte, "Almirante Renato Beluche," 140–41.

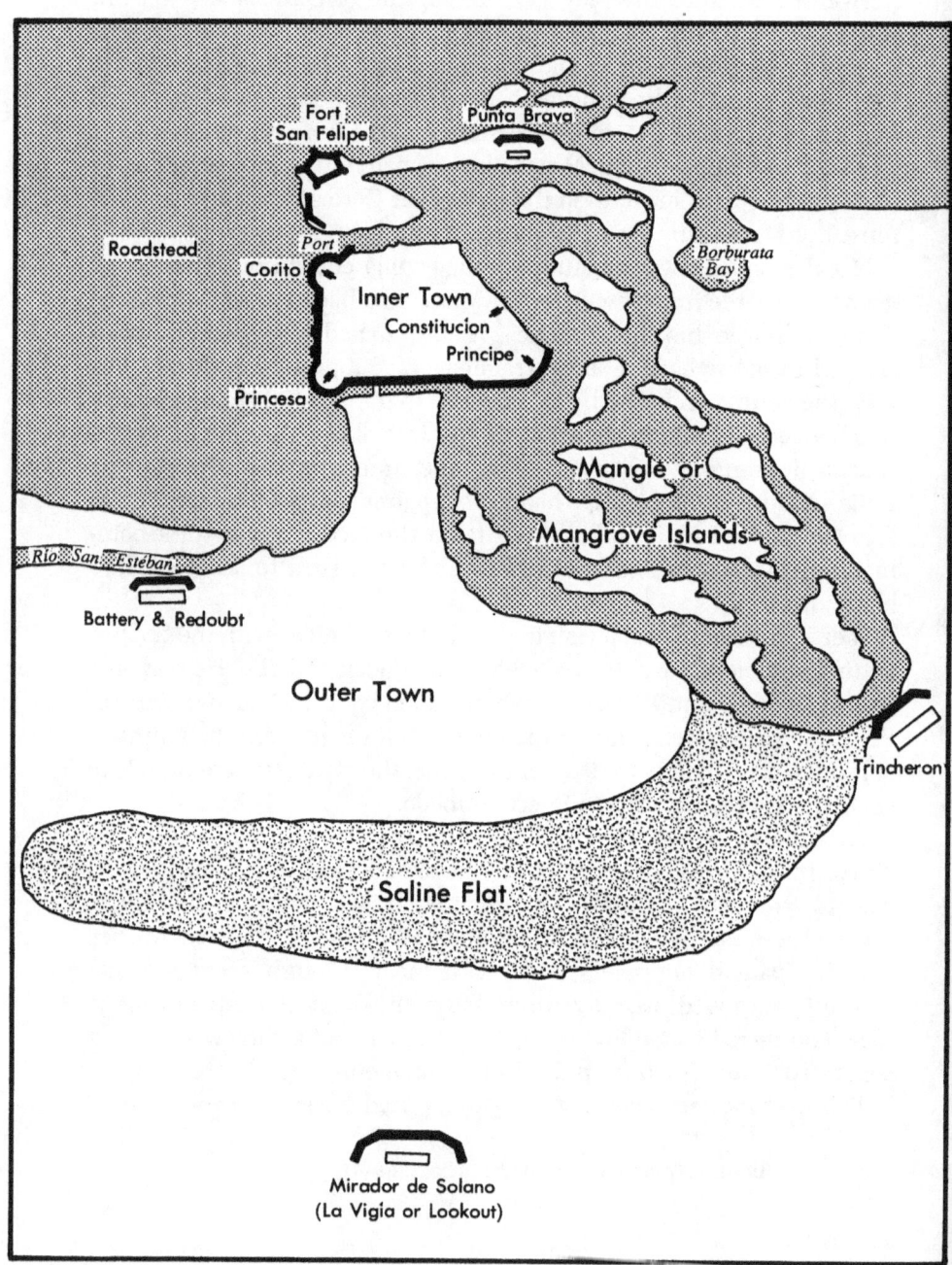

Puerto Cabello, 1823

fortifications. A palisade on the south side had batteries on either end: Princesa on the west corner and Principe on the east corner (the practice then was to name batteries, not to number them). On the northwest corner of Inner Town was the battery Corito. A bastion connected Corito with Princesa and Principe.

Puerto Cabello's port was the strait between Inner Town and a peninsula that protected the port from the Caribbean. This peninsula stretches east about three-fifths of a mile, then turns south to connect with the continent and to form the western coast of Borburata Bay—that is, Borburata Bay in 1823 was separated by about two hundred yards of land from the Mangle (mangrove islands) and quiet bay of Puerto Cabello.

Spanish engineers had been unanimous in their conclusion that it was impossible to pass through the Mangle and approach Inner Town. For this reason, the eastern side of Inner Town had no bastion; but royalists did establish a battery there, the Constitución.

Inner Town's water supply came from the San Estéban River, which empties into the roadstead west of Outer Town. Fire from a battery and a redoubt at the mouth of this little river, and from Princesa, marked the outer line of Inner Town's defense on the west side and toward the continent. Toward the sea, on the northwest corner of the peninsula, was Fort San Felipe. Its bastion extended south to the port. When Spaniards wanted to close the port's entrance, they stretched a chain from the bastion across the port to Corito, completing the defense. Geography and fortifications together rendered Inner Town impregnable so long as it had food, water, and munitions—or so the Spaniards thought.

Páez was in La Guaira collecting siege matériel when, on September 7, he wrote a letter to Don Sebastian de la Calzada asking him to surrender and prevent the otherwise inevitable bloodshed, and offering him 20,000 pesos for his expenses in leaving Puerto Cabello. Páez also wrote a letter to Don Jacinto Iztueta, an old Spanish resident who was not happy with the royalists. Then Páez released two criminals from jail on condition that they deliver the letters. Páez sailed with them in the *Urica* to Ocumare and from there dispatched them in a small fishing boat. They gave Calzada the letter from Páez and were able to deliver the one to Don Jacinto also. Calzada refused Páez's suggestion "with firmness and noble pride, though without the customary Spanish insolence."[4]

By the end of September, Páez had enough supplies to begin operations behind Puerto Cabello. The eastern end of his siege line at the foot of the mountains was the battery Trincherón, located on the edge of the Mangle less than a mile south and a little east of Borburata. The royalist lieutenant Pedro Calderón, navigating an armed *flechera* in the narrow passage between the mangroves and Trincherón, prevented the delivery of war elements that Beluche had landed at Borburata until October 7, when Páez mounted a 24-pounder at Trincherón. This gun compelled Calderón to retire with great loss. Soon Páez had another battery west of Trincherón to aid it in protecting the delivery of supplies from Borburata.

Beluche had brought Páez 18- and 24-pounders and a large supply of military stores from the spoils that had been taken at Maracaibo, and he was assembling a fleet at La Guaira. Bermúdez arrived at La Guaira with reinforcements from Maracaibo and sailed with Beluche's fleet to Borburata. There, patriots unloaded the guns and other supplies; and within the next two weeks, Páez was able to extend his line of batteries, take possession of Outer Town, and mount batteries opposite Princesa and Principe.[5]

Royalists still held one strong position behind Páez—Mirador de Solano, the lookout on the mountain side—but its captain and twenty-five-man garrison surrendered on October 29. The enemy was now without telegraph communications about patriot movements. Then Julian, a slave of Don Jacinto, appeared in Páez's camp, having come during the night by a pass through the Mangle that was unknown to the Spaniards.

Páez sent three officers with Julian to investigate. When they returned, they assured Páez that troops could file through that pass to the eastern, unprotected side of Inner Town. Páez sent a third and final proposal to Calzada: "Surrender within twenty-four hours to prevent the further effusion of blood, or I will take Puerto Cabello by force, and pass the garrison under the sword." Twenty-four hours later, Calzada

---

4. Páez, *Autobiografía*, I, 230–32; Restrepo, *Historia de la Revolución de Colombia*, III, 342–43.
5. Restrepo, *Historia de la Revolución de Colombia*, III, 342–43.

replied that the place was defended by old soldiers who knew how to do their duty, and that they were resolved to the very end to follow the examples of Sagunto and Numancia.[6]

To distract Calzada's attention from the east, Páez gave directions for his men to dig a trench at the narrowest part of the San Estéban River to change its course and cut off the enemy's water supply. The trench was completed on November 6 in spite of fire from the batteries of Inner Town. The next day, November 7, beginning at five o'clock in the morning, all the patriot batteries began to fire on Inner Town. The enemy "returned this fire four-fold. At half past eight at night the firing ceased, and worn out with fatigue the enemy sunk in sleep to wake up in eternity."[7]

Major Manuel Cala, with six detachments totaling six hundred men, was ready to move toward Julian's path through the Mangle at ten o'clock that night. This little army was naked because part of the way all the men would be in water up to their necks. It took them four hours to get through the Mangle. As they came close to Inner Town, Cala's men could hear enemy sentinels saying: "There must be a lot of fish tonight, the waters are so agitated." The waders safely passed a corvette and launches patrolling the bay, and entered the eastern side of Inner Town between the batteries Principe and Constitución at 2:30 in the morning. Each detachment ran to the post it had been assigned. The posts were the four batteries, the wharf, and the gate of the palisades.[8]

Meanwhile, Beluche and Bermúdez in a light fleet approached from the west and opened a tremendous fire almost at the instant that Major Cala's detachments reached their objectives. Within half an hour, they had overcome all resistance and were in possession of Inner Town. "Brigadier-General Don Sebastian Calzada, commander in chief of the troops and the city, who bravely defended himself in the battery El Principe, was made prisoner, having resisted until almost all who manned the battery being killed or wounded, he was compelled to yield to the valour of our troops."[9]

6. Páez, *Autobiografía*, I, 233.
7. Kingston *Royal Gazette*, December 20–27, 1823.
8. Páez, *Autobiografía*, I, 234–36.
9. Adjutant General George Woodberry's report, November 12, 1823, in Charles

Royalist losses were 156 killed, 56 wounded, 56 officers and 539 men captured.[10] After granting the royalists all the honors of war on November 10, the victors transported them to Cuba.

Colombia, cleared of royalists, could now send troops to Bolívar in Peru, the last stronghold of Spain in South America. Beluche's squadron transported 1,500 troops to Panamá, where they crossed the Isthmus and sailed to Callao.[11] Then a strange duel occurred.

Padilla and Beluche each became convinced that the other was taking all the credit for the victory at Maracaibo. Someone told Beluche that Padilla was belittling his contributions to the independence of Gran Colombia, so Beluche wrote and published a brief account of his career. Padilla got hold of a copy, wrote some footnotes, and published it with his footnotes. Beluche added footnotes to Padilla's footnotes and republished the whole in a twenty-five-page pamphlet.[12] From the following excerpts, one can see these two heroes ruffling their feathers at each other like two bantam roosters:

Beluche's original text	I was born in the new world and acquired a love of glory in the defense of her liberty. Scarcely had the cry of independence gone up from South America when I hurried to enlist myself among her defenders.
Padilla's footnote	What Señor Beluche says is true. He did come to South America, but as a corsair; that is to say, so that he could serve his own interests.
Beluche's footnote to Padilla's	General Padilla remembers that I was a corsair. And what is the matter with that? If I served my own interests and at the same time those of Colombia, what more could one desire? His Excellency is ignorant of the fact that uniting public and private convenience is the essence of government.
Original text	In the year 1812 I offered to serve in the navy of Cartagena, to which I was admitted; and after the expedition to Santa Marta I was given the rank of lieutenant of the navy.
Padilla's footnote	He was made a lieutenant because with his ship he helped transport the unfortunate expedition against Santa Marta.

Stuart Cochrane, *Journal of a Residence and Travels in Colombia During the Years 1823 and 1824* (2 vols.; London, 1825), II, 499–504.

10. Alfred Hasbrouck, *Foreign Legionaries in the Liberation of Spanish South America* (New York, 1928), 293.

11. Beluche, Hoja de Servicio.

12. Beluche, *Contesta a las Falsas Imputaciones*, 2, 3, 5–6, 8–9.

Puerto Cabello and the *Contesta*   225

Beluche's footnote	What disgrace is there in a corsair helping in an expedition? I was made a lieutenant, not because of transporting troops, but because with my vessel and crew I protected the disembarking troops.
Original text	I have the satisfaction of having taken part in actions which it is not necessary to mention, for which I was praised by my chiefs. Envy has never found a resting place in my breast; and the brilliant actions of my companions at arms, far from exciting any base passion in me, had only stimulated me to imitate them.
Padilla's footnote	Señor Beluche's deportment has not corresponded with this expression of his sentiments.
Beluche's footnote	This note is so vague and insignificant that it does not merit a reply.
Original text	The first and principal rule of my conduct in this particular had always been to recognize merit in every one and give praise where praise is due.
Padilla's footnote	I repeat what I wrote in my above note.
Beluche's footnote	I also reproduce my previous note.
Original text	In the month of April [1823] I was commissioned by General José Padilla, commanding general of the squadron operating against Maracaibo, to go to His Excellency, General Soublette, to solicit some small boats which we needed to cross the bar and pass Fort San Carlos, in order to become rulers of the lake, with the object of protecting the passage of our army by the River Limón and making it able to operate against the enemy who occupied the Moján.
Padilla's footnote	And all the lake and its coasts.
Beluche's footnote	This does not merit a reply because this note is nothing more than an irresistible attempt to say something.

And so it went, for twenty-five priceless pages—this war of words between two strong men who were accustomed to shedding blood, who had cooperated so perfectly to win the victory at Lake Maracaibo.

CHAPTER 17

The Sea of Matrimony and Other Seas

Spanish privateers and pirates were finding refuge in the coves of Puerto Rico, and Beluche's next mission was to take care of them. At the end of December, he cruised north to Mona Passage with the corvettes *Bolívar* and *Boyacá*, and during January and part of February of 1824 he policed the coasts of Saona, Mona, Puerto Rico, Culebra, and St. Thomas.

"Nothing worthy of notice has occurred," Beluche reported to Soublette on February 19, "other than my having redeemed from capture the English brig *Boniton*, Captain Alexander Murdock, bound from Trinidad to Gibraltar with a cargo of cocoa; and the French brig *Bonne Sophie*, Captain Chevanche, bound from Havre de Grace to Martinique with a cargo of dry goods. These vessels had been captured by a pirate fitted out from Puerto Rico, and bound to that coast."[1]

Beluche sailed next to the coast of Cuba, and by the end of March he had captured "eleven sail of Spanish vessels, 3 ships and 8 drogers."[2] He was off Havana at noon on Sunday, April 4, when he sighted a large ship to windward and made sail toward it. At 2 P.M. he made it out to be the Spanish corvette *Ceres*, the vessel that had done so much damage to his *Independiente* the previous May when Laborde captured Danells and his two ships, the *Carabobo* and *María Francisca*. Lieutenant Booth, commanding marines on the *Bolívar*, later reported:

> At this time the *Boyacá* was two miles astern, and being under a heavy press of sail, she carried away her jib-boom; we bore up to give her assistance. At three o'clock P.M. both ships again made all sail in chase; the Spanish vessel bore up for Havana with studding sails set lower and aloft. At

1. "On board the Corvette *Bolívar* off La Guaira, February 19, 1824," Caracas *Colombiano*, March 3, 1824.
2. Philadelphia *National Gazette and Literary Register*, April 20, 1824.

7 P.M. both ships coming up with the chase, within half pistol shot, the *Boyacá* (being to leeward of the *Bolívar* and the *Ceres* keeping away) brought her into action in very handsome style with a well directed broadside, and heavy fire of musketry, which she returned for about 12 minutes, when the *Boyacá* dropped astern; the wind favoring a little, brought the *Bolívar* into action on her larboard side.

After giving her two broadsides, and first starboard division with vollies of musketry, which she returned; a constant roar of cannon was kept up on all sides, until 50 minutes past seven, P.M., when the *Ceres* struck to the *Bolívar*, being completely cut up, with scarce a rope standing, and having several dangerous shots in her hull. The Moro light distant three leagues, S. W. by W.

The *Ceres* mounted 36 long Parisian 18-pounders and two chasers, and had a complement of 326 men.

The *Bolívar*, Commodore Beluche, Captain [John] Clark,[3] carried 23 thirty-two pound carronades, and one long 12-pounder, with 156 men.

The *Boyacá*, Captain [Thomas] Brown,[4] has 20 thirty-two pound carronades, and 2 short thirty-two pound gunnades, and 140 men.

The *Ceres* had 30 men killed and 60 wounded, of whom 30 have since died of their wounds.

The *Bolívar* had none killed and only four wounded, among them were Commodore Beluche and Lieutenant Booth, commanding marines, both very slightly. The *Boyacá* had none killed and but one wounded.[5]

Beluche's prize was so badly damaged that he put into Pensacola instead of risking capture heading for a Venezuelan port. He left the *Ceres* at Pensacola and sailed to New York to get money for repairs and to enlist a hundred crewmen. He sent a report to Bogotá, dated New York, May 18, 1824, and sailed for Pensacola on June 9.[6] Late in the summer he left Pensacola, bound for New Orleans, where his wife, Marie Magdeleine Victoire Milleret, had waged a long battle against him.

Marie Magdeleine, after years of pleading with Beluche to return to her, had petitioned "the honorable James Pitot, Judge of the Parish Court for the parish and city of New Orleans," on November 29, 1821,

---

3. John Clark of Baltimore had gone to La Guaira in 1822 and enlisted in the squadron there as a lieutenant on the *Bolívar*. On January 12, 1823, he was given command of the *Bolívar*. Vargas, *Nuestros Próceres Navales*, 513.
4. Thomas Brown, a Scot, had begun his career in Venezuela in 1817 as commander of the *Indio Libre*. Ibid., 473.
5. Philadelphia *National Gazette and Literary Register*, May 15, 1824.
6. Item from the Bogotá *Gaceta de Colombia*, Monday, September 26, 1824, quoted in Ortega Ricaurte, "Almirante Renato Beluche," 141–42.

to grant her a separation. In her petition, Marie Magdeleine humbly showed that six months after marrying Beluche in Campeche without any marriage contract,

> the said René Beluche began to treat your petitioner with neglect and finally abandoned her more than nine years ago without giving her from that time any assistance for her maintenance though she was quite destitute of any means of subsistence, and said René Beluche was in such circumstances as to be able to provide therefor, and though your petitioner has never given to him any reason for such abandonment.
>
> And whereas the said René Beluche has constantly refused to return with your petitioner though often requested to do so and is now absent from this state
>
> Your petitioner humbly prays that she be authorized to sue and cite the said René Beluche, her husband, in the person of such attorney your honor will be pleased to appoint to him, on account of his absence, in order to answer to this petition, and that it will be decreed that your petitioner shall be separated from bed and board from him, and that he shall pay the costs of the suit.[7]

The court appointed Henry R. Denis, counselor at law, to represent Beluche; and J. A. Holland, deputy sheriff, served the first summons on Beluche on December 1, 1821. It said: "You are hereby summond to comply with the prayer of the annexed petition, or to file your answer thereto, in writing with the Clerk of the Parish of Orleans, at his office at New Orleans, in ten days after the service hereof; and if you fail herein, judgment will be rendered against you by default."

Having been in court many times, Beluche had no respect for the ten-day limit. His answer, filed twenty days later, was brief: "This defendant denies all and singular the facts and allegations in the said petition contained. Wherefore he prays to be dismissed with costs."

A second summons for Beluche "to return to the matrimonial domicile in New Orleans and live with the plaintiff" was served on January 1, 1822, and a third, on February 1. Denis filed no answers to these two summons. The court then received, on February 21, the depositions of

---

7. Suit No. 3059, Parish Court of New Orleans Records, New Orleans Public Library. Included in the suit record are the petition of Marie Magdeleine for separation, copies of the summons served on Beluche, a lengthy deposition in French, and a copy of the judgment rendered in the case.

Hypolite Vitrac, Marie Catherine Loublan (widow Thomas), Joseph Sauvinet, and J. B. Laporte, the French consul in New Orleans.[8]

Vitrac deposed that he had known Mr. and Mrs. Beluche for ten or twelve years; that he was Mrs. Beluche's neighbor for three or four years during the time that he lived on St. Louis Street; that Beluche had never come to visit his wife; and that

> Mrs. Beluche lived then in the home of Mrs. Thomas her aunt [she lived on Bourbon Street],[9] who had taken her in because of her abandonment by her husband; that he never provided any means of sustenance for her; that the witness held numerous conversations with Mr. Beluche relative to his conduct in this regard, and that Mr. Beluche, without showing any complaint regarding the conduct of his wife, told him that it was impossible for him to live with his wife because of privy causes and incompatibility of characters; . . . that the witness had occasion to see Mr. Beluche during the various whiles he spent in New Orleans, and that he always spoke in the same manner concerning his wife, and notably on his last trip to New Orleans, whence he arrived December, 1818 and left October, 1820; and that on this last trip to New Orleans he expressed to the witness more firmly than ever his firm resolution to never reconcile himself with his wife; . . . that Mr. Beluche is at the moment in Maracaibo in the service of the Republic of Colombia with the rank of Captain of the Navy and Squadron Commander, and that he is established there in a permanent fashion.

The Widow Thomas declared under oath that about eleven years ago, Beluche having totally abandoned his wife, "the witness who is Mrs. Beluche's aunt, did take her into her home; that at that time the witness tried to bring back Mr. Beluche's sentiments for her, but that it was impossible; that in one conversation in which she strongly insisted on this reconciliation, Mr. Beluche replied to her that it was useless, that before he would reconcile himself with his wife the River would cease to flow, and that he would much prefer to face the cannons than have anything to do with his wife; that Mr. Beluche has never done anything for her."[10]

Sauvinet confirmed the information that Vitrac and the Widow

---

8. *Ibid.*
9. There were two widows Thomas who lived on Bourbon Street, one at 69 Bourbon, the other at 94 Bourbon. Both were listed as Madame Thomas, widow. John Adams Paxton, *New Orleans Directory and Register for 1822* (New Orleans, 1822).
10. Suit No. 3059, Parish Court of New Orleans Records.

Thomas had given. He added that during the twelve years that he had known Mr. and Mrs. Beluche, he had been concerned about Mrs. Beluche and had frequently helped her, and that Beluche was determined to give her no support until he was permanently separated from her.

Laporte said that he had known Beluche for eighteen years, had great affection for him, and had acted many times on his behalf. Laporte then declared: "All the facts contained in the depositions of Mr. Vitrac and Mr. Sauvinet are true. Beluche has told me the same facts with regard to his wife."

The court, satisfied by proper evidence that the plaintiff had been abandoned by her husband for several years, ordered and decreed on March 4 "that the Plaintiff be separated from Bed and Board from the said husband, if after having been served three times from month to month with a notification of this Judgment, if he persist in not returning to the Place of his Matrimonial Domicil in this City, and that the said Defendant be condemned to pay all the Costs of this Suit."[11]

Marie Magdeleine now knew that the only way for her to get any support money from Beluche was to divorce him—and the only way to get a divorce in Louisiana in 1822 was by a special act of the legislature. Marie Magdeleine asked for such an act. Her request was referred to a senate committee, and Dominique Bouligny, on February 27, reported the bill to the senate with the title "An Act to divorce Marie Magdalene [sic] Victoire Milleret and René Beluche, her husband, from the bonds of matrimony."

The bill was read for the first time that same day; the second and third time, on March 5. It passed and the senate "ordered the secretary to carry the bill to the House of Representatives, and request their concurrence therein."[12]

Marie Magdeleine, "wife of Belluche, native of Port au Prince, St. Dominigue, about forty years of age," died before the House took any action. She was buried in St. Louis Cemetery Number 1 on March 14, 1822.[13]

11. *Ibid.*
12. *Official Journal of the Senate During the Second Session of the Fifth Legislature of the State of Louisiana* (New Orleans, 1822), 41, 47.
13. Act 497, Book 1820–24, p. 51, in Burial Records, St. Louis Cathedral Archives.

Beluche was now free to marry Mezelle, but for the next two years active duty for Colombia detained him: the battle of Lake Maracaibo, the storming of Puerto Cabello, going after Spanish pirates and privateers, and the capture and repair of the corvette *Ceres*. In the late summer or early fall of 1824, Beluche and his family sailed from New Orleans, bound for the quiet haven of Puerto Cabello.

On November 17, in the parish church of San José at Puerto Cabello, "Renato Beluche, native of New Orleans, legitimate son of Renato Beluche and María Laporte," married the "Señora María Bondri [Beaudri] Espocita, native of New Orleans." During the ceremony, their two daughters, María Reneta, aged seven, and Ana Colombia, aged four, were legitimated. One of the witnesses was Sebastian Boguier, captain of the navy and commander of the naval base at Puerto Cabello.[14]

Beluche did not remain long with his family. Spain, with the help of France, was using Puerto Rico and Cuba as bases for the reconquest of Mexico and Colombia, and Beluche's fleet, increased to twelve vessels, was blockading Havana before the end of 1824. Beluche captured the brig *Guadalupe* on February 10, 1825, and the brig *Neptune* on February 20. The brigs had sailed from Cádiz laden with wine and other effects. Beluche sent them to Puerto Cabello, and eight days later captured "the famous well-armed *Tarantula* of Cádiz, mounting 16 or 18 heavy guns, with a crew of 120 picked men and a cargo on board of quicksilver, etc., worth nearly half a million Dollars." A Jamaican newspaper commented: "It would seem that the Colombians had anticipated the Spaniards and compelled them to assume the defensive rather than the offensive."[15]

However, Spain was preparing an offensive against Mexico, where it still held one base—the fortress island of San Juan de Ulúa, guarding the entrance to the port of Vera Cruz. A French fleet landed five thousand troops at Santiago de Cuba in June, and Santander reported in August to Bolívar, who was in Upper Peru: "I have ordered Lino de Clemente and Beluche to Cartagena to take command of a squadron composed of a 74, a frigate of 44, three corvettes, two brigs, and two

---

14. Folio 68, Book 1, in Marriage Records, Diócesis de Valencia, Parroquia de San José, Padres Agustinos Recolectos, Puerto Cabello.
15. Beluche's Hoja de Servicio; Philadelphia *National Gazette and Literary Register*, March 26, 1825; Kingston *Royal Gazette*, February 26–March 6, 1825.

schooners. They will proceed to unite with the Mexican squadron to blockade San Juan de Ulúa and to fight the Spanish squadron. While our squadron proceeds to Mexico, the rest of our war ships with Joly in command will cruise upon Puerto Rico. Padilla is now a senator and unable at this time to be absent from our country."[16]

Beluche had been in Puerto Cabello for some time preparing the squadron when Clemente arrived to take command. Only the *Ceres* and *Urica* weighed anchor and headed for Cartagena on September 16. They arrived there six days later.

James Evans Hele, a young English ensign on board the *Ceres*, wrote to his mother on Sunday, October 30, that the *Ceres* "is one of the handsomest corvettes I have ever seen and affords us excellent accommodations, and in consequence of her being the flagship there is an Admiral on board (here called the Mayor General) who is an American of French extraction. He is a man whom I believe to be generally esteemed. His name is Raynato Belluche. The Captain is an American talking English, a man whose voice is thunder and whose words are daggers. . . . Taking him all in all I must say I believe his tongue to be his most offensive member. His name is Joseph C. Swain. The Mayor General Belluche is in his appearance most gentlemanly."[17]

Admiral Laborde had sailed from Havana on September 18 with three frigates and two transports to relieve the garrison at San Juan de Ulúa, which was tightly blockaded by land and sea and starving to death. Two days after sailing, a gale dismasted Laborde's frigate, which returned to Havana "under jury masts, with officers, troops, money, etc. for the relief of the Castle Ulúa." The other frigates and the transports arrived off the fort on October 6, then a. Mexican frigate, corvette, and gunboats drove them back to Havana.[18]

By November, 425 men of the garrison had died of scurvy and starvation. The remaining 25 surrendered, and Mexicans took possession of the fort on November 20. Clemente and Beluche did not know about

---

16. Bogotá, August 21, 1825, in Cortazar (ed.), *Cartas y Mensajes de Santander*, V, 331.
17. James Evans Hele Letter Book, in Pennsylvania Historical Society, Philadelphia.
18. Letters dated September 18 and October 6, 1825, in Kingston *Royal Gazette*, November 5–12 and December 3–10, 1825.

the capitulation until Christmas.[19] Their fleet was still lying at anchor in front of Cartagena on March 13, 1826, when the frigate *South America* arrived from New York. It was soon renamed *Colombia*.

An agent employed by a commercial house in Havana reported that the *Colombia* "is a very first rate vessel of her class, built upon an improved plan, having an elliptical stern—rates at 44, but mounts 62 or 64 guns of heavy metal." A frigate of the same class, built in Philadelphia, arrived a week or so later and was named *Cundinamarca*. Each frigate had cost $500,000.[20] Both of them, like the other vessels, lay at Cartagena for almost a year.

The Havana agent assured his employers that there would be no invasion or even blockade of Cuba "since there are not good seamen enough in the whole Colombian navy to man three frigates well. A great many of the foreign officers hitherto in the service have already quitted it. Those who are now in it find it very difficult to get their pay, besides which the native Creoles are jealous of them. The government is very much in debt and greatly in want of money. There is not a dollar in the treasury of Cartagena."[21]

Clemente could not endure the inactivity of the fleet, its deteriorating condition, and the apathy of the government with regard to it. He resigned, and Santander called him to Bogotá to serve as secretary of the navy.[22] Beluche took command of the squadron on March 30, 1826. This act irritated Santander because Beluche was not a *granadino*. Santander requested of the senate that it release Padilla from his duties as senator so he could take command at Cartagena, and the senate granted this request. On August 5, Beluche surrendered the command to Padilla and asked for a leave of absence so that he could look after his interests in Venezuela and regain his health. Padilla granted the leave.

One of Hele's letters suggests that Mezelle was taking care of whatever money (prize money, which may have been considerable, and pay, if any) Beluche had accumulated. Hele's letter was to the British con-

19. Hele to his mother, January 8, 1826, in Hele Letter Book.
20. Philadelphia *National Gazette and Literary Register*, May 15, 1826.
21. *Ibid.*
22. Cortazar (ed.), *Cartas y Mensajes de Santander*, VI, 61, 199.

sul at Maracaibo and said: "Enclosed I hand you an order on Madame Beluche for $475 together with a letter to her advising her of the same thing and containing also a further order from Captain Belluche her husband."[23]

Beluche moved Mezelle and his daughters to Caracas. There, on November 15, 1826, he dined with Sir Robert Ker Porter, the British consul. Beluche was forty-five years old at this time, and Ker Porter was forty-nine.

Ker Porter, a famous artist, writer, traveler, and archaeologist, had begun a diary on October 18, 1825, three days before he left England to assume his duties as consul in Venezuela.[24] He arrived at La Guaira on November 27, and within a few days established his home in Caracas. His diary shows that he was skillful in ferreting out information from important people—and from others not so important. He had already accurately recorded the increasing friction between Páez and Santander, the incompatibility between a telluric force and civil restraint that during the past year had erupted into rebellion.

Santander had called Soublette to Bogotá in 1825 to serve as secretary of war, sending Juan Escalona to replace Soublette as civil governor in Caracas. Escalona reported to Santander at the beginning of 1826 that Páez had exceeded his authority in drafting troops in Caracas, whereupon Santander brought a charge of insubordination against Páez before the Colombian senate in Bogotá. The senate gave Santander authority to relieve Páez of his military command and transfer it to Escalona. Then the senate summoned Páez to Bogotá for trial.

Páez refused to go to Bogotá. He made public his defiance of the central government when he reassumed command of the army in Valencia on April 30. Two weeks later, Valencia made Páez its civil and military chief. Caracas and other cities followed suit, and on May 25 Páez reported his version of the whole affair to Bolívar. In his letter,

23. Hele to Robert Sutherland, August 27, 1826, in Hele Letter Book.
24. Ker Porter was well known for his paintings of altar pieces, landscapes, battle scenes, and portraits. He had lavishly illustrated his most recent work, published in 1821 and 1822, the two-volume *Travels in Georgia, Persia, Armenia, Ancient Babylon, etc., 1817–1820*. The famous novelists Jane and Ana Maria Porter were his sisters. Walter Dupouy (ed.), *Sir Robert Ker Porter's Caracas Diary, 1825–1842: A British Diplomat in a Newborn Nation* (Caracas, 1966), xvi–xxxvi.

Páez blamed the "insidious Santander" for poisoning the fountains of administration.[25]

The "insidious Santander" was building a political machine to maintain himself in control of the government of Colombia—a state that included Venezuela. Páez was dismembering Colombia, and the only man who could stop him was Bolívar. Santander began to bombard Bolívar with letters (at least twenty-three of them between June 6 and October 22), urging him to return to Colombia. "You are the one," Santander wrote on June 9, "who can extricate us from the present critical circumstances, and save your daughter Colombia from anarchy and civil war. Your presence in Colombia is absolutely necessary."[26]

When Bolívar received this letter, his work in Peru was almost finished. Colombian armies had spearheaded the liberation of Peru and Upper Peru from Spain, and Upper Peru had become the Republic of Bolivia, with the Venezuelan Sucre serving a two-year term as president. Bolívar, in Lima, transferred his command to a council of government, sailed from Callao on September 4, and debarked in Guayaquil one week later.

That city gave him a tremendous welcome and proclaimed him dictator. Guayaquil, Cuenca, Quito, and other cities of this southern department of Colombia were suffering from economic depression that they claimed was caused by the Bogotá government and the heavy taxes Santander had levied on them. Páez's revolt in Venezuela had encouraged the Guayaquil leaders to disavow the Colombian constitution.

General Juan José Flores, the ranking military officer in Guayaquil and leader of the separatist movement, was a Venezuelan. Making no attempt to stem the tide that Flores was directing, Bolívar remained only a few days in Guayaquil before beginning the long horseback ride to Venezuela. He was feverish at intervals from tuberculosis and rode slowly.

A cold rain was falling on November 14 when Bolívar entered Bogotá. Only a few people in the streets greeted him, but his official reception in the Palace of Government was reassuring. Santander, cabi-

25. Páez, *Autobiografía*, I, 300–305.
26. Cortazar (ed.), *Cartas y Mensajes de Santander*, V, 351.

net ministers, the president of the senate, judges of the supreme court, and a host of citizens welcomed him. He was in the saddle again on November 25, headed for Puerto Cabello, where a reaction had started against Páez.

Beluche's friend Sebastian Boguier commanded the forts there, and Bolívar's friend Pedro Briceño Mendez threw himself into Puerto Cabello "declaring to defend it until the arrival of Bolívar." Páez sent troops against Puerto Cabello on November 26, the garrison fired on them, and there were some casualties. Many of Páez's troops deserted, and a courier "delivered him letters from the Liberator dated Bogotá."[27]

Páez began to have second thoughts about rebellion, and one of the sophisticated, educated men who influenced him was Beluche's friend Colonel Francisco Carabaño, who rode into Caracas on Friday night, December 1, "in order to take upon himself the Military Command of the town."[28] Ker Porter invited Beluche to dine with him on Sunday, December 3, because he wanted to know something of Carabaño's background. No other guest was present.

Beluche could tell Sir Robert that Carabaño had been chief of Páez's siege at Puerto Cabello during 1822 and 1823 and had represented Venezuela in the Colombian congress in 1824 until he was sent on a mission to Europe. Sir Robert was impressed. On Tuesday he noted in his diary that "Colonel Carabaño went down to La Guayra but the object of his visit is not known." By Friday, Sir Robert's curiosity demanded to be satisfied. He and Beluche called on Carabaño, and Beluche introduced them.

"The Colonel has been sent by Genl. Páez as his representative to this city, in fact second in *the State*," wrote Sir Robert when he re-

27. Diary entries dated November 28, November 30, and December 2, 1826, in Dupouy (ed.), *Ker Porter's Caracas Diary*, 172, 174–75. Ker Porter's diary entries were the basis for his dispatches to George Canning, British foreign secretary. William M. Armstrong edited Porter's dispatches in "The Venezuelan Revolution of 1826 As Seen by Sir Robert Ker Porter" (M.A. thesis, Louisiana State University, 1948).

28. This son of a Spanish field officer was born in Cumaná in 1783. He was sent to Spain for military training and returned to Venezuela in 1800 as lieutenant of infantry in a battalion stationed in Caracas. He fought for the revolution. Captured in 1815, he was sent to prison in Spain, remaining in prison until the Riego Revolution freed him in 1820. That year he represented Colombia in the Cortes at Cádiz and returned to Venezuela in 1822. Espasa-Calpe, Hijos de J. Espasa (eds.). *Enciclopedia universal ilustrada Europeao-Americano* (70 vols.; Madrid, 1905–30), XI, 625–26.

turned home. "My visit was purely political, in order to keep up a good impression and understanding, *on* and *between* myself and the authorities in government. He appears a shrewd and wary person, has passed some time in Europe, and knows the value of transatlantic political opinions. He speaks with great veneration of Bolívar, saying that doubtless he was the only man who had the whole of the nation with him."[29]

Bolívar rode into Maracaibo on December 16 and issued this proclamation: "Venezuelans! You have stained the glory of your braves with the crime of fratricide. Hide your parricidal arms: do not destroy the fatherland. . . . I come to put myself between your swords and your hearts."[30]

After resting two days in Maracaibo, Bolívar crossed the lake and rode across the searing desert of Coro and along the coast to Puerto Cabello, which he entered on the last day of the year. On New Year's Day, 1827, he issued a decree granting amnesty to all concerned in the defection of General Páez, guaranteeing "the persons, properties, and employments of those involved," and declaring that: (1) "General José Antonio Páez remains fulfilling the Civil and Military Authority under the name of Superior Chief of Venezuela"; and (2) "immediately after this decree's notice, my authority as President of the Republic will be submitted for recognition and obedience."[31]

Carabaño was with Páez in Valencia when he received Bolívar's amnesty decree. The next day Páez sent Carabaño to Caracas with a copy of the decree and the Maracaibo proclamation in which Bolívar promised to reform the Colombian constitution. Carabaño entered Caracas at one o'clock on January 3, and Ker Porter "instantly waited on him." He let Ker Porter read the decrees, and their contents were soon broadcast throughout the city.[32]

Páez sent his submission to Bolívar, then issued a proclamation in which he said, "From this moment the authority of His Excellency the

29. Entries for December 3, 5, and 8, 1826, in Dupouy (ed.), *Ker Porter's Caracas Diary*, 175–77.
30. Henry Rowan Lemly, *Bolívar, Liberator of Venezuela, Colombia, Ecuador, Peru and Bolivia* (Boston, 1923), 324–25.
31. Entries for January 3, 1827, in Dupouy (ed.), *Ker Porter's Caracas Diary*, 189–91.
32. *Ibid.*, 189.

Liberator is recognized and will be obeyed in all its capacity."[33] On January 4 Bolívar left Puerto Cabello for Valencia, and Páez met him at the foot of Naguanagua Mountain. They dismounted, embraced, and rode into Valencia together, where great enthusiasm prevailed among the inhabitants of the city.

Meanwhile, citizens in Caracas were lining the streets with poplar and palm branches, erecting triumphal arches decorated with flowers, ribbons "and a hundred whims and fancies their love, enthusiasm and respect engendered," and preparing a banquet for their two heroes. On January 8 many of them rode or walked fifty miles toward Valencia to meet Bolívar and Páez.[34]

The two men entered the city with their retinues on the afternoon of January 10. The aristocrat and the cowboy, both splendidly dressed in their richest uniforms, were made to dismount from their horses and climb into the beautifully adorned coach of Jacob Idler, a Philadelphia merchant. The coach was drawn by two high-spirited horses covered with yellow blankets. Idler drove them through the "crowds of rejoicing people, all wildly screaming 'Viva Bolívar! Viva Páez! Viva Colombia!'"[35]

---

33. Entry for January 7, 1827, in *ibid.*, 193.
34. Entry for January 8, 1827, in *ibid.*, 195.
35. Jane Lucas De Grummond, "The Jacob Idler Claim Against Venezuela," *Hispanic American Historical Review*, XXXIV (1954), 145; entry for January 10, 1827, in Dupouy (ed.), *Ker Porter's Caracas Diary*, 196–200.

CHAPTER 18

Bolívar's Tragedy, Beluche's Melodrama

The euphoria did not last long in Caracas, and in Bogotá Santander's open abuse and severe censure of Bolívar became more vitriolic after he heard of Bolívar's reconciliation with Páez. Santander had subsidized the biweekly *El Conductor* with government funds, and in it he published unsigned attacks on Bolívar, sending 150 copies of each issue to every department.[1]

Bolívar was so upset by the attacks that on February 6, 1827, he sent his resignation to Congress in Bogotá. On May 28, Ker Porter noted that Congress had not yet accepted Bolívar's resignation.[2]

In June, news from Guayaquil reached Caracas that troops in northern Peru were ready to invade Guayaquil and annex it to Peru, and news from Bogotá said that Santander had renewed his oath to the constitution that Bolívar had promised to change. Bolívar wanted to stay in Venezuela, but once more he became the Liberator.

He sailed from La Guaira on the British frigate *Druid* on July 5 and four days later debarked at Cartagena. The city's warm welcome reassured him, as did Padilla's splendid banquet for him on July 24, his birthday. Bolívar was even more pleased when Padilla rode part way with him to Bogotá.

Padilla had a reason for spending more than a month with Bolívar, as is shown in the letter Padilla wrote to Santander: "Bolívar thinks you are his enemy. I tried hard to dissuade him of this notion, and I believe that when he arrives in Bogotá you two will again be good friends. I am the Liberator's friend and your friend. News of the reconciliation of the

---

1. Hildegard Angel, *Simón Bolívar, South American Liberator* (New York, 1930), 239–40.
2. Dupouy (ed.), *Ker Porter's Caracas Diary*, 251, 255.

two men so necessary for the well-being of the Republic will give me the greatest happiness."[3]

Supporters of Bolívar in the cabinet and in Congress at Bogotá had set the stage for his return. The senate had refused to accept Bolívar's resignation from his extended first term (his second inauguration should have been held on January 2, but he was in Venezuela), and both houses of Congress had passed a law ordering a convention to meet at Ocaña on March 2, 1828, to consider changing the constitution.[4]

José Manuel Restrepo, secretary of the interior, was among those who rode to meet Bolívar when he was near the capital. On the morning of September 10, Bolívar sent Restrepo ahead into the city with a request to the president of the senate that he have Congress in session that afternoon so that Bolívar could take his oath for a second term as president of Colombia.

Bolívar entered Bogotá in midafternoon and rode through crowded streets to the Church of Santo Domingo, where Congress was waiting. After attending mass, Bolívar was sworn into office. Then he reported on the use he had made in Venezuela of his extraordinary powers. He asked Congress to continue in session, and later it approved all the actions he had taken in Venezuela and Peru.

Vice-president Santander was waiting at the Palace of Government to receive Bolívar, as were cabinet ministers, the principal authorities of Bogotá, and a "numerous concourse" of people. All of them were anxious, uneasy. Would Bolívar humiliate Santander in their presence? Happily, Santander pronounced a short discourse in which he congratulated Bolívar on having taken charge of the nation. Bolívar answered with tact and charm; everyone rejoiced, and for the time being Bolívar and the vice-president maintained the fiction that they were friends.[5]

November was election month in Colombia for delegates to the

3. August 18, 1827, quoted in Otero D'Costa, *Vida del Almirante Padilla*, 76–78.
4. José Manuel Restrepo, *Diario Político y Militar: Memorias sobre los sucesos importantes de la época para servir a la Historia de la Revolución de Colombia y de la Nueva Granada desde 1819 para adelante 1858* (4 vols.; Bogotá, 1954), I, 343.
5. Restrepo was present at this reception. The above is from his entry the next day, September 11, in *Diario Político y Militar*, I, 357.

Ocaña Convention. Bolívar had forbidden all men in authority to meddle in the election process, in spite of the fact that these men were his friends. They obeyed the order, with the result that Bolívar had no local leadership to sway public opinion through the press and through his local henchmen. Santander had that field to himself. His control of public opinion made Bolívar anxious about the results, especially in major cities like Cartagena, where Montilla was Bolívar's candidate for the whole department of Magdalena.

No man could be a candidate while commanding troops, and Montilla, before announcing his candidacy, transferred his military command in Cartagena to José Montes. Montilla had a safeguard, a document from Secretary of War Soublette authorizing him to exercise supreme authority in the whole department of Magdalena the instant it became necessary.[6]

All the election returns were received in Bogotá by the end of December, and Santander was exultant. He had been elected, a majority of his candidates had been elected, and Montilla had not been elected. Moreover, according to the election law, the chief executive could not attend the Ocaña Convention, where he might influence delegates; and Santander had almost persuaded Padilla to revolt in Cartagena and take the command away from Montes.

Montilla was not in that city; he was observing from Turbaco about twenty miles southeast of Cartagena. Colonel Belford Wilson was observing in Bogotá. He reported to Ker Porter in Caracas that the success of Santander and his party "has so much affected the Liberator that he has lost all his energy, and even his best friends complain of his ruinous apathy. His enemies of course rejoice at it."[7]

News from Venezuela dispelled Bolívar's apathy. He was needed there—Spanish agents from Puerto Rico had infiltrated from Coro to Cumaná and south to Guayana. Páez had written him on January 9, 1828, that Admiral Laborde's squadrons were daily increasing their activities along the coast, signaling to royalist guerrillas. When Bolívar received this letter, a month later, he replied: "I am coming to help you

---

6. Otero D'Costa, *Vida del Almirante Padilla*, 87.
7. Entry dated January 18, 1828, in Dupouy (ed.), *Ker Porter's Caracas Diary*, 352.

reunite Venezuela, make her strong; and to await there tranquilly for the results, good or evil of the Ocaña Convention. I have already sent you an order to give command of the Navy to Beluche."[8]

Beluche was in Caracas, where Mezelle had presented him with a son whom they named Diego. Boguier, commander of the navy, was also in Caracas, getting married to the señorita Belén Palacios. Boguier had left Felipe Santiago Esteves in command at Puerto Cabello. Thus it was Esteves who transferred the naval command to Beluche.[9]

While Bolívar was preparing to leave Bogotá for Venezuela, Santander left for Ocaña. Therefore, no one was offended when, on February 19, Bolívar declared that the cabinet and Council of Government would be the executive power while he was gone. On March 16 Bolívar left for Venezuela by the road he knew so well, the road through Tunja and Cúcuta. He was able to ride a little more than thirty miles a day and was two days beyond Tunja on March 23 when he received good news from Páez. Residents of Coro had suppressed the royalist revolt there; Laurencio Silva had done the same in Guayana; Monagas, Bermúdez, and Mariño had crushed the royalists in the rest of Venezuela; and Laborde and his ships had sailed away, having been unable to help the rebels.[10]

Bolívar received bad news the next morning. Padilla had rebelled in Cartagena in the latter part of February, when Montilla sent Colonel Abreu de Lima from Turbaco to get all the officers in Cartagena to sign a petition addressed to the Ocaña Convention. The petition asked for (1) rewards and pensions for soldiers of the War of Independence; (2) payment of salaries owed to the officers; and (3) preservation of military privileges.[11]

Padilla and the *granadino* officers did not sign the petition, and Padilla reported to Santander that he would keep all officers under his command from signing it and that he would protect the convention with his sword and his influence. Santander was exultant when he re-

8. February 16, 1828, in Lecuna (ed.), *Cartas del Libertador*, VII, 162–63.
9. Vargas, *Nuestros Próceres Navales*, 165, 321, 370.
10. Entry for February 19, 1828, in Restrepo, *Diario Político y Militar*, I, 372; Páez, *Autobiografía*, I, 407–409; entries for January 24 and February 2, 1828, in Dupouy (ed.), *Ker Porter's Caracas Diary*, 354–58.
11. Jesús María Henao and Gerardo Arrubla, *A History of Colombia*, trans. and ed. by J. Fred Rippy (Chapel Hill, N.C., 1938), 396–97.

ceived Padilla's letter. He wrote to journalist Juan Madiedo in Cartagena: "This is very laudable. Present Padilla in your papers with dignity and justice as the best defender and sustainer of the Convention's decrees."[12]

Madiedo's praise, Santander's letters to Padilla, and Montilla's next move caused Padilla to commit an overt act. Montes, commander in Cartagena, resigned on March 5 according to Montilla's orders, and he and all the troops withdrew to join Montilla at Turbaco. The next day, followers of Santander in Cartagena proclaimed Padilla commanding general of the department of Magdalena. Padilla accepted the office, but on March 7 he thought better of his actions and resigned. He tried to explain to Montilla, who refused to communicate with him and instead marched on Cartagena at the head of his army. Padilla fled to Ocaña.

The Liberator received a report of Padilla's actions, but not of Santander's involvement in those actions, on March 24. As he was not needed in Venezuela, Bolívar changed his route and rode northwest toward Cartagena. He was near Bucaramanga on March 31 when he was told that Montilla had everything under control in Cartagena. Bolívar sent Colonel José Bolívar, a *llanero* and no relative of the Liberator, to arrest Padilla in Ocaña and take him to Cartagena for trial. Padilla sought advice from both Santander and Daniel O'Leary, whom Bolívar had sent to Ocaño with a message for the convention. When O'Leary heard of Colonel Bolívar's mission, he wrote to the Liberator:

> You have formed an exaggerated idea of events in Cartagena. From what Padilla has told me, and from his conduct I know that he is not guilty of conspiracy. If only there were some document by which we could show the guilt of Santander, we could root out this source of evil.
>
> It is not necessary for you to go to Cartagena. If the trial and sentencing of Padilla should cause a reaction, let Montilla suffer the consequences.[13]

Montilla did not want Padilla's blood on his hands. He disobeyed Bolívar's order that Padilla be tried in Cartagena, sending Colonel Bolívar with his prisoner to Bogotá. This development frightened Santander. He wrote to Estanislao Vergara, a cabinet minister in Bogotá:

12. March 10, 1828, in Cortazar (ed.), *Cartas y Mensajes de Santander*, VII, 292–93.
13. March 31, 1828, in Lecuna (ed.), *Cartas del Libertador*, VII, 195; April 5, 1828, in O'Leary (ed.), *Memorias del General O'Leary*, III, 178.

"Padilla's enemies want him executed. If fate does not permit him to vindicate himself of the charges Montilla has made against him, our tranquility runs a grave risk. For God's sake, interest yourself in the good fortune of this meritorious granadino general."[14]

Then the Ocaña' Convention caused Santander to forget about Padilla. When it opened its sessions on April 9, Santander could not command a majority. Only 64 delegates were seated: 25 Santanderistas, 21 Bolivarians, and 18 Moderates and Independents.[15] After eight weeks of discord that prevented the adoption of any new constitution, the Santanderistas proposed that the existing constitution be reinstated with Article 128—which gave the president extraordinary powers in times of crisis—deleted.

Only forty-three votes were needed to pass this proposal. The twenty-one Bolivarians persuaded one Independent to join them and go home. The rump convention, unable to pass any act, disbanded on June 11. Anxiety and fear prevailed in Bogotá and the whole department of Cundinamarca. The existing constitution had been discredited, and rumor said that Bolívar was going to leave the country. There would be no government! To counter this emergency, the Council of Government in Bogotá approved an act that gave the Liberator President supreme power.

Bolívar's welcome into the capital on June 24 was unique in all his experiences of triumphs. An enthusiastic throng conducted him to the cathedral for the Almighty's blessing, then to a pavilion where all the high officials praised his government, after which everyone accompanied him to the Palace of Government.[16] One of Bolívar's first acts was to declare the office of vice-president eliminated. To get Santander out of the country, Bolívar appointed him minister plenipotentiary to the United States. Santander accepted the post but made no move to leave Colombia.

Bad news from the south arrived in Bogotá during the first week of July. General Agustín Gamarra had invaded Bolivia with a Peruvian

14. March 22, 1828, in Cortazar (ed.), *Cartas y Mensajes de Santander*, VII, 405.
15. Waldo Frank, *Birth of a World: Bolívar in Terms of His Peoples* (Boston, 1951), 340.
16. Entries for June 13, 15, 19, 23, 24, 1828, in Restrepo, *Diaria Político y Militar*, I, 384; Larrazábal, *Vida y Correspondencia del Libertador*, II, 436–40.

army and had forced Sucre to resign and take his Colombian troops home; and General José La Mar, president of Peru, was marching to invade Colombia by land while a squadron of two frigates and a schooner was sailing to blockade Guayaquil. General Flores considered this a declaration of war and was preparing to defend Guayaquil and the provinces bordering on Peru.

War preparations in Bogotá were forgotten on September 25. That night, conspirators tried to murder Bolívar. He was sleeping in the Palace of San Carlos, his official residence. Santander was sleeping at his sister's home. One assassin killed the sentries at the entrance to the palace. Dogs barked, and they were killed. The noise awakened Bolívar and José Palacios, Bolívar's servant and bodyguard since childhood, and they escaped from a balcony.

Urdaneta and grenadiers of the Bogotá garrison soon restored order, but not before one group of conspirators had attacked the barracks where Padilla was in jail, killed his guard José Bolívar, and freed Padilla. The next day, Padilla, Santander and others were arrested. More conspirators were caught later, and Urdaneta presided over their trials, sentencings, and executions.

No one spoke to clear Padilla, who had no part in the conspiracy. Estanislao Vergara, now a member of Bolívar's council, and to whom Santander had earlier written, "For God's sake, interest yourself in the good fortune of this meritorious granadino general," did not come to Padilla's defense. Nor did Santander. No one spoke for Padilla, and several spoke against him. His conviction was assured when a sergeant said that Padilla could have saved Colonel Bolívar but instead had seized his sword and escaped. Padilla was sentenced to die.[17]

On October 2, the Bogotá garrison formed on three sides of the capital's main plaza. Padilla marched proudly to his execution wearing the uniform of a division general and paying little attention to the Franciscan monk who accompanied him. A sergeant ripped off Padilla's epaulets, removed his coat, and tied him to a post. Padilla refused to be blindfolded. Then a volley of shots rang out. Before Padilla died he shouted, "Cowards!"[18]

17. Otera D'Costa, *Vida del Almirante José Padilla*, 133–48.
18. *Ibid.*, 148–51.

Thirteen guilty conspirators were executed. Bolívar commuted the death sentences of six others to prison terms. Most of the troops involved were granted amnesty and sent to provinces away from Bogotá. Santander was convicted of having given counsel and aid to the conspirators. Urdaneta sentenced him to be executed and his property confiscated, but the Council of State warned Bolívar that Santander's execution might be regarded as unjust and excessively severe and revengeful. Bolívar commuted Santander's death sentence to banishment, and the confiscation of his property to holding it in trust.

When the trials were over, Bolívar renewed war preparations against Peru. Sucre had arrived in Guayaquil in September and briefed Flores on President La Mar's army, which was about to invade Colombia, and on Peru's navy. George Martin Guise, an able English admiral who had been in Peru for eight years, was sailing north from Callao with a squadron to blockade Guayaquil and cut its communications with Panamá so that no Colombian troops or military supplies could be shipped from Panamá to Guayaquil.

Bolívar in Bogotá knew by early October that Colombia had to have a more able admiral in the Pacific than Peru's Admiral Guise. On October 7, Bolívar wrote to Montilla in Cartagena: "We must have one of our big frigates in the South Sea. Send one immediately to Puerto Cabello. Chitty can sail her to Puerto Cabello where Beluche will take command. I prefer him over all the others. Put on board subalterns who can be trusted to block any sinister intent, any mutiny. If you lack money, use that budgeted to pay the domestic debt; and, if that is not enough, use the money budgeted to pay the foreign debt."[19]

That same day, Bolívar wrote to Páez, telling him what he had done. Then he added:

> When the frigate arrives, give the command to Beluche or Boguier or another, but I prefer Beluche. He is superior to all the others because of his rank, knowledge and ability, enthusiasms, etc. Complete the crew in Puerto Cabello and put the frigate in perfect shape for wartime service with enough provisions to round Cape Horn and arrive at Guayaquil without stopping. Give Beluche plenty of money for any emergency. If you have not enough money, use that budgeted for the domestic debt.
>
> Beluche can, if necessary, call at a port in Brazil because our relations

---

19. Lecuna (ed.), *Cartas del Libertador*, VIII, 79–80.

with the Emperor are good. Beluche can call at Montevideo also, but he must not touch any part of the coast of Chile. Above all, he must not call at any Peruvian port. . . . Although the Peruvians have a frigate and a corvette, they are much smaller than either of the frigates we have in Cartagena.

Bolívar instructed War Minister Urdaneta on December 13 to send two frigates to the South Sea and to name General Beluche commander in chief of the squadron. "Thus it will be impossible for any scandalous defection to occur."[20] Bolívar's foresight with regard to mutiny was uncanny.

He left Bogotá on January 1, 1829, and began the long ride south to Quito and Guayaquil. He was more than halfway to Popayán on January 9 when he wrote Páez: "The frigate *Colombia* should have sailed from Cartagena on December 13 to Puerto Cabello. It is indispensable that you prepare and send this flotilla to the Pacific with the speed that the exigencies of the situation demand. The army of Colombia is nothing with our Pacific coast unprotected." Bolívar was near Popayán on January 22 when he wrote Páez again: "I depend absolutely on you for the quick despatch of a frigate convoying a corvette of war brig perfectly equipped, because if Guise has survived his attack on Guayaquil, he will have his squadron waiting for ours. May our ships arrive pronto, my dear general, ready to fight."[21]

Communications were slow between Páez and Bolívar. Páez had not yet received the two January letters at the end of March when he wrote Bolívar that the ships could not sail in April because mariners said that Cape Horn could not be rounded until October.[22]

There was another reason why the ships could not sail. The threat of a Spanish invasion had ended in 1827, and for two years the unpaid-for, half-million-dollar frigates *Colombia* and *Cundinamarca* had deteriorated at anchor in Cartagena. The corvette *Urica* had made several trips transporting Colombian troops to and from Panamá.

The Liberator was at Riobamba, halfway between Quito and Guayaquil, and had not yet received the March letter from Páez when he wrote Páez on June 1: "We are every day more anxious for the arrival of our squadron to end this war. With the frigates we can dominate the

---

20. *Ibid.*, VIII, 80–83, 150.
21. *Ibid.*, VIII, 200, 217–18.
22. Bolívar to Urdaneta, June 3, 1829, in *ibid.*, VIII, 346.

Pacific because Peru has lost its frigate *Prueba* by the fire of May 18. Send the frigates! Send the frigates! The enemy has only brigs and schooners."[23]

The frigate *Colombia* had sailed from Cartagena on December 13 but two days later returned for essential repairs. It sailed a second time on February 4, 1829, and one month later arrived safely at Puerto Cabello. The *Urica* came in a few days later. Beluche sent Captain John Clark to Baltimore and Captain Joseph Swain to New York to enlist crewmen, and he sent the *Independencia* to St. Thomas to bring back a mainmast for the *Urica*. On May 9 Beluche wrote to Henry H. Williams in Philadelphia that he had been unable to get a mainmast either in St. Thomas or in any other Windward island. "Enclosed are the dimensions of the mast I need for the *Urica*," said Beluche. "Please send me such a mast of the best quality at your earliest convenience. The government will guarantee payment on the same terms as in our other contracts."[24]

Captain Clark reported to Beluche that when he arrived in Baltimore he found the city greatly agitated because the United States government was enforcing laws that prohibited the enlistment of crewmen for foreign service. "So many privateers have been outfitted here that the new laws which prohibit the enlistment of crewmen are being rigorously enforced. It will require the greatest cunning on my part to get any sailors at this port. I will send from Philadelphia and New York those that Captain Swain has enlisted, but it will be impossible to get as many as you want. From New York I will sail immediately to St. Thomas with the balance of my funds. I am told that there I will be able to fulfill my mission."[25]

Even so, Clark and Swain returned to Puerto Cabello with 180 less mariners than Beluche needed. By the end of July, the *Colombia* and *Urica* were ready to sail, but Beluche waited for the *Cundinamarca*. It did not arrive until the third week in August, and when it did arrive, it

---

23. *Ibid.*, VIII, 340.
24. Camilo Destruge, "Naves Historicos, La Fragata Colombia," *Boletín de la Biblioteca Municipal de Guayaquil*, No. 16 (June 1911); Beluche to Williams, May 9, 1829, in Naval and Military, Misc. L. S. No. 57, Dreer Collection, Pennsylvania Historical Society, Philadelphia.
25. Clark to Beluche, June 9, 1829, in Correspondencia Militar, Archivo Nacional de Colombia, Bogotá.

needed so many repairs that Beluche could not take it. He transferred eighty of the crewmen to the *Colombia* and *Urica* and hoped to *enganchar* (literally "ensnare") a hundred more in Rio de Janeiro.[26]

Leonard Stagg, captain of the *Colombia* on which Beluche sailed, may have been a native of Baltimore. He had enlisted in the Venezuelan Navy in 1822, had served on the *Espartana* in the Battle of Lake Maracaibo, and had been promoted to frigate captain in 1828. Captain Thomas Brown commanded the *Urica*. This Scot had helped Beluche blockade Puerto Cabello in 1823 and capture the *Ceres* in 1824. The next year, Brown was promoted to frigate captain. In 1828 he married María Francisca Ruiz in Caracas.[27] Brown's second in command and three other officers were English, but his subalterns were Colombians: Lieutenant José Benito Paredes, Ensign Francisco Antonio Urribarri, Lieutenant of Marine Infantry José Antonio Cruz, and the second-in-command of marine infantry, Francisco Suárez.

The Pacific Squadron (two vessels), with General Renato Beluche commanding, departed from Puerto Cabello on August 25, 1829, for a voyage of more than 12,000 miles, most of it in waters that Beluche had never sailed before. The two vessels had to beat against contrary winds and currents the whole way from Puerto Cabello (out one of the passages into the Atlantic and southeast along the coast of the Guianas and Brazil) until near Natal, where the Brazilian coast turns southwest.

Six days after leaving Puerto Cabello, Brown signaled the *Colombia* that the *Urica* was taking on water. Stagg launched a boat to investigate. The officer in charge discovered that the *Urica* was drawing only nine inches of water per hour and not sixteen, as Brown had claimed. "It was here that General Beluche discovered Brown's repugnance for the expedition and his opinion that Colombia was at fault in the war with Peru." Beluche taunted Brown, "Perhaps we should return to Cumaná where your family is."[28]

Brown's repugnance increased, but the voyage continued. The ships were probably opposite the mouth of the Orinoco River on September

---

26. Beluche to Ministro Secretario de Estado en el Departamento de Marina, August 22, 1829, in *ibid*.
27. Vargas, *Nuestros Próceres Navales*, 411–12, 473–74.
28. Guayaquil *Colombiano de Guayas*, May 20, 1830, pp. 172–73.

Route of Beluche's Voyage from Puerto Cabello to Guayaquil

22 when, in Guayaquil, Bolívar signed a peace treaty with Peru and began the long ride north to Bogotá. In Venezuela at least two prominent Englishmen were abetting the secessionist movement of Páez, Soublette, Arismendi, and many other leaders. Admiral Charles Elphinstone Fleming had moved his headquarters from Barbados to Caracas and kept a dozen war vessels in the roads of La Guaira. He entertained Páez, flattered him, and openly encouraged him to separate Venezuela from Colombia; Sir Robert Ker Porter, more discreetly, did the same.[29]

The *Colombia* and *Urica* had sailed about three thousand miles by the time they were opposite Natal, where the Brazilian Current and favorable winds sped them to Rio de Janeiro. The ships anchored at Rio on November 16—that is, eighty-three days after leaving Puerto Cabello. A Rio newspaper reported: "This is noticed as the first occasion on which the Colombian flag has been displayed in this port."[30]

Beluche engaged all the dockyard workers in Rio's navy yard to repair the *Urica*. When his two vessels left Rio on November 28, the *Urica* was taking on only one and a half inches of water an hour; but nine days later, when it hit strong contrary winds and currents, Brown made a distress signal, saying the *Urica* was taking on twenty-two inches of water. The next day he signaled that it was taking on twenty-eight inches.[31]

To the Colombian subordinate officers, the crew, and the one hundred troops on board the *Urica*, Brown's deception was eloquent testimony of his disloyalty. They also knew that Brown was drinking heavily, but they did not tell Beluche. He gave Brown a large sum of money, ordered him to get the *Urica* repaired, then to follow the *Colombia* south along Argentina's coast, west around Cape Horn, and north a safe distance from the coasts of Chile and Peru to Guayaquil.[32]

The *Colombia* and *Urica* were off the mouth of the Rio de la Plata—

---

29. Entries for April 26, 1829, and January 10, 1830, in Dupouy (ed.), *Ker Porter's Caracas Diary*, 440, 446; entry for December 24, 1829, in Restrepo, *Diario Político y Militar*, II, 65.
30. The Rio paper gave November 16 as date of arrival. Those who later mutinied said they arrived on November 15. Philadelphia *National Gazette and Literary Register*, January 23, 1830.
31. Guayaquil *Colombiano de Guayas*, May 20, 1830, p. 173.
32. *Ibid.*

that is, near Buenos Aires—on December 7 when Beluche separated from the *Urica* and sailed south and around Cape Horn against contrary winds and currents. Strong winds filled the *Colombia*'s sails a day after it rounded the Horn, and when it hit the Humboldt Current, Beluche raced it to the destination Bolívar had chosen.

On February 1, 1830, Beluche dropped anchor off the island of Puná at the entrance to the Gulf of Guayaquil. He sent an official report to Guayaquil, and General Flores had the following story published in the weekly *El Colombiano de Guayas* on February 4:

> At this moment we have received official communications from the *Señor Comandante Jeneral de la Escuadra de Colombia en el Pacífico*, *Jral.* Renato Beluche, dated yesterday in Puná, in which he tells of his happy arrival at that place in the frigate of war *Colombia*, the first day of this month, after a navigation of 161 days from Puerto Cabello, having stayed four days in Rio de Janeiro. From this port he sailed to the Puná without having stopped at any other place. The *Urica* will soon arrive at the Puná.
>
> On receiving this plauditory news, I can do no less than tell you that it will be of great interest to all the inhabitants of this Capital, and to the entire Republic.

One week later *El Colombiano de Guayas* published a correction: Beluche had stayed fourteen days in Rio, not four.

Beluche knew before the end of his first week in Guayaquil that he was not needed there. Neither Peru nor Guayaquil had enough naval strength to break the peace between them, and under the leadership of the Venezuelan Flores, the provinces of Guayaquil, Azuay, and Quito were about to declare themselves the Independent Republic of the Equator (Ecuador). Beluche remained three months in Guayaquil waiting for the *Urica*, which never arrived. In April, he asked for passports in order to return to Venezuela and arrange his affairs. Flores was planning to send an expedition to the Philippines; so before he granted the passports, he made Beluche promise that he would return to Guayaquil and take command of the Pacific Squadron.[33]

While he waited for a vessel bound for Panamá, reports of mutiny on the *Urica* arrived from Montevideo.[34] Habitually drunk, Captain

33. This is the last entry in Beluche's Hoja de Servicio.
34. These reports were published in three installments on May 20, May 27, and June 3, 1830, in the Guayaquil *Colombiano de Guayas*. The *Urica* mutiny account is from those issues of the weekly.

Brown by December 14 had the *Urica* off Rio Negro, only four degrees south of the point where Beluche had left it. Brown sent Ensign Urribarri for a pilot, who told Urribarri that the *Urica* drew too much water to enter the river and that there was no shipyard there. Urribarri reported this information, but Brown and his English officers ignored it. They continued tacking toward the Rio Negro, and by midafternoon the *Urica* had grounded. For twelve hours it heeled in such a way that no one could stand on deck.

Brown ordered guns, a great amount of metal and ammunition, spare sails, and other equipment thrown overboard without buoys. Six hours later, the *Urica* was afloat with its helm unshipped, four rudder pintles loosened, and part of the round house broken. Finally, the helm was repaired, and the *Urica* headed toward the mouth of the Rio de la Plata estuary. The Colombian subalterns thought they were going to Montevideo for repairs, but when they were in sight of that port, Brown told them that the *Urica* was sailing to Rio de Janeiro and then to Puerto Cabello.

Until this moment on December 23, Lieutenant Paredes, Ensign Urribarri, Lieutenant Cruz, and Second Lieutenant Suárez had been fluctuating between their commitment to rigid military discipline and their equally strong desire to maintain the glory of the Republic and the honor of having served the Liberator. They did not know the specific instructions that Beluche had given Brown. They did know, however, that Beluche had given him money for repairing the *Urica* and that, according to the marine rules under which the Republic of Colombia operated, the *Urica* should have been taken to the nearest port for repairs, then have proceeded to the port of reunion—in this case, Guayaquil—unless the captain consulted with his officers in order to determine a better course of action. Captain Brown had not consulted with his officers. Because of the *Urica*'s copious leaking, the ship and all on board would perish before arriving at so remote a port as Rio.

The subalterns could vacillate no longer. They had to choose between obedience and mutiny—that is, taking the command from a captain who, by his habitual drunkenness and prostitution of his high office, had stripped himself of the inviolability that marine law bestowed on him. The subalterns chose mutiny.

Lieutenant Cruz, spokesman for the mutineers, approached Captain

Brown and explained that it would be dishonorable for them to return to Puerto Cabello and that they would all perish before the *Urica* could arrive at Rio for repairs. Brown ordered Cruz arrested. Infuriated when his order was not obeyed, Brown fired a pocket pistol at Ensign Urribarri. It did not discharge. Brown fired a second time, and a second time the pistol failed to discharge.

Lieutenant Paredes, senior officer of the mutineers, ordered not only Brown arrested but also the English officers because of their influence on the foreign sailors who compromised a third of the *Urica*'s crew. When Brown tried to escape from the ship, Paredes had him shackled and forced him to disclose where the repair money was hidden. Then the mutineers wrote and signed a manifesto in which they explained the motives for their actions.

Two of the mutineers proceeded to Montevideo with the manifesto, explained their situation to the port authorities, and requested permission for the *Urica* to come up for repairs so that it could continue on its mission to the Pacific. The captain of the port consulted with government officials, and they replied that Montevideo was open to all friendly nations and that the *Urica* was welcome to come for repairs.

Two master carpenters and two shipwrights made a partial inspection of the *Urica* as soon as it arrived and reported that they could not make a complete inspection until it was careened. "From what we have seen," they said, "the *Urica* is not in condition to sail without great risk toward Rio or any other distant stop. The expense will be greater and the careenage more prolonged in order to round Cape Horn than to sail to Rio."[35]

Repairs were begun immediately, and on December 31 the government informed "provisional commander" Paredes that it would take Brown and the English prisoners under the protection of the Uruguayan flag if they were allowed to come ashore. Paredes was glad to be rid of them and let them go.

Four days later, Brown sent his version of the mutiny to "*Excelentisimo Señor Ministro de Marina,* Don Fructuoso Rivera" and asked him to return the *Urica* to him with its officers and crew. He also asked Rivera for help to sail the *Urica* to Rio for repairs. Rivera answered on

---

35. *Ibid.*, May 20, 1830, pp. 174–75, and May 27, 1830, pp. 177–80.

January 8: "The government is determined to undertake nothing that might add to the unfortunate occurrences of the *Urica*, to conserve at all cost this property of a friendly government, and to keep it without getting involved in the principal question until the decision of the Colombian Minister residing in Rio de Janeiro is known. The diplomatic agent of Uruguay to His Majesty the Emperor of Brazil will instruct said minister." Brown's next move was made on January 23, 1830, when he and the four English officers were almost penniless. He asked the minister of the treasury for ten pesos a day for maintenance. "I am persuaded," Brown said, "that the government of Colombia will indemnify you from our rightful pay."[36]

This request was granted, and enough repairs were made on the *Urica* so it could sail to Colombia's diplomatic agent in Rio. Apparently Paredes did not have enough money to pay the bill and had to borrow some, because later Sir Robert Ker Porter in Caracas confided to his diary: "A Mr. Long and Mr. Wolfe dined with us. The former gentleman has come from Buenos Ayres in order to claim 10,000$ he has advanced to the Capt of the Ship of War Urua [*sic*] belonging to the Colombian Gov^{nt} whilst in that place some months ago. He has been so far successful in his claim that an order on the treasury here has been given him for the amount. He may get it in the end, but at present I know there is a 'beggarly account of empty boxes.' This genl^m is a native of Nova-Scotia."[37]

Beluche's odyssey was more leisurely and pleasant. Leaving Captain Stagg in command of the *Colombia*, Beluche sailed north to Panamá. His ship anchored in the Bay of Panamá at the island of Taboga to take on fresh water. Taboga is a volcanic peak twelve miles from torrid, pestilential Panama City, and its cooler air is redolent with the perfume of sweet-smelling flowers and trees.

Forty-nine-year-old Beluche met Candelaria Esquivel on Taboga. She was young and beautiful, and Beluche tarried a few months. Then he crossed the Isthmus of Panamá, boarded a ship that sailed north with the prevailing winds and tides, and docked at Baltimore. There

---

36. *Ibid.*, June 3, 1830, pp. 183, 184.
37. Restrepo, *Historia de la Revolución de Colombia*, IV, 185*n*; entry for July 26, 1830, in Dupouy (ed.), *Ker Porter's Caracas Diary*, 490. Ker Porter's writing is difficult to decipher. The *Urua* has to be the *Urica*.

Beluche embarked on the schooner *Sound*, which anchored in the roads of La Guaira on November 8.[38]

Bolívar on that day was at Soledad near the mouth of the Magdalena, waiting for a vessel to take him to Santa Marta. Joaquín Mier, a wealthy Spaniard, had invited Bolívar to come to his villa three miles from Santa Marta, where he could recover his health.

"General or Commodore Beluche, a great partizan of Bolívar," dined with Ker Porter on November 21. Three days later, Beluche refused to take the oath of allegiance to the Venezuelan constitution, explaining to the secretary of state that he had sworn to uphold the Colombian government and not a fraction of it, that he had come to see his family, and that now he had to return to Guayaquil to command an expedition against the Philippines. "Although I cannot take the oath to this new state," Beluche said, "neither will I do anything against it. In proof of this I am leaving my wife and children and possessions as hostages, in return for a passport to go to Valencia and present myself to the President of the Republic, General José Antonio Páez."[39]

The passport was granted, so Beluche embarked at La Guaira for Puerto Cabello on November 27 and went up to Valencia to report to Páez. While Beluche was with Páez, the dying Bolívar sailed to Santa Marta, where José Palacios carried him in his arms to a carriage that took them to San Pedro Alejandrina, the villa of the wealthy Spaniard.

What did Beluche tell Páez about Captain Brown? Who knows? Beluche remained several days in Valencia before returning to Puerto Cabello. The ship on which he had booked passage was sailing toward Santa Marta on December 17 when Bolívar died. The Liberator was forty-seven years old.

Páez on that day in Valencia appointed Brown captain of the port of Margarita. This base was near Cumaná, where Brown's wife lived. Páez had the cunning of a Solomon: he had allowed Beluche to leave Venezuela, and he had sent Brown where he could do no harm. Brown retired from the service in less than a year at one-third pay and died a few months later.

38. Vargas, *Nuestros Próceres Navales*, 168.
39. Entry for November 21, 1830, in Dupouy (ed.), *Ker Porter's Caracas Diary*, 513–14; Vargas, *Nuestros Próceres Navales*, 168.

Captain Rafael Tono was in command at Cartagena when Beluche arrived there en route to Panamá and Guayaquil. On January 15, 1831, Tono sent Beluche an invitation to assist in memorial services honoring Bolívar at the cathedral on January 17, one month after his death. Beluche replied on January 16: "I will be honored to go to your house tomorrow at the hour indicated in your note of yesterday, to take part with Your Excellency and Senior Chiefs and Officials in the inverted arms obsequies in memory of the *Excelentísimo Señor Libertador de Colombia* Simón Bolívar."[40]

Beluche sailed to the isthmus soon after the ceremony and crossed to the city of Panama, where José Domingo Espinar, a native of Panamá, was acting as dictator of the whole isthmus. The only person who dared criticize him was another Panamanian, José de Fábrega, governor of the province of Veraguas. There were a number of Venezuelans in Panamá, including Juan Eligio Alzuru, who wanted to follow the example of the Venezuelan Flores in Ecuador and detach a part of Colombia for themselves. At this moment, dictator Espinar made a big mistake: he appointed Alzuru to rule in his absence while he marched to Veraguas to exile Fábrega.

This was the situation in Panamá when Beluche boarded a ship for Guayaquil. It stopped at Taboga to take on water, and Beluche forgot the rest of the world until he was caught in the whirlpool of revolution.

Panamá was calm until Luis Urdaneta (Rafael's cousin) and fifty more Venezuelans arrived from Guayaquil, from whence Flores had expelled them for trying to overthrow his government. Urdaneta and his companions persuaded Alzuru that they could make him dictator of Panamá. With their help, Alzuru was able to arrest Espinar when he returned from Veraguas and ship him to Guayaquil. Then Alzuru appointed a junta of important Panamanians who, on July 9, declared Panamá independent, Fábrega the civil governor of Panamá, and Alzuru military governor. Their rule was brief.

The Bogotá government quickly dispatched General Tomás Herrera to Panamá via Cartagena with seven hundred troops. They arrived at Chagres on July 20, but the commander of the fort refused to acknowl-

---

40. Vargas, *Nuestros Próceres Navales*, 169, 474.

edge Herrera's authority. So Herrera went down the coast to Portobelo, where he was received with respect and was immediately recognized as the legitimate military governor.

When Alzuru sent troops to capture Herrera, they joined him instead, helped him take Chagres, then marched with Herrera against Alzuru in the city of Panama. Alzuru meanwhile had loaded prominent persons—including Fábrega and his secretary Mariano Arosemena—on three ships to be deported, and he threatened the three ship captains with death if they disembarked any of their passengers on Panamanian soil.[41]

The prisoners had persuaded their guards and two of the ship captains to join them by the time the three vessels stopped at Taboga for water. The third captain declared that he was ill and "ordered" Beluche to take command of his vessel, the *Sirena*, and take its prisoners beyond Panamanian territory.

Beluche sailed the *Sirena* out of the bay and headed for the port of Montijo on the coast of Veraguas. There, Fábrega was able to organize an army that grew larger and larger as it approached the city of Panama.

Fábrega and Herrera caught Alzuru as they approached him from different directions. He and Urdaneta were executed in the main plaza of Panama on August 29. Herrera considered all Venezuelans hostile to the Bogotá government and ordered them to leave Panamá. He made no exception in the case of Beluche, even though he had helped Fábrega and Herrera win. This time when Beluche left Candelaria behind, she was carrying his child. A son, Blas Beluche Esquivel, was born five months later.[42]

---

41. Mariano Arosemena wrote an account of events in Panamá during this revolution. Concha Peña had access to his manuscripts more than a century later when she wrote her biography of Herrera. In this biography, she does not mention Beluche by name, but she supplied me with notes from the Arosemena manuscripts which mention Beluche.

Sources for events in Panamá during Beluche's stay are: Concha Peña, *Tomás Herrera* (Panama, 1954), 13–39; Herrera's Hoja de Servicio, in Secretaria de Guerra y Marina, Papeles sin Clasificación, Archivo Nacional de Colombia, Bogotá; Restrepo, *Historia de la Revolución de Colombia*, IV, 535–45; Alex Perez-Venero, *Before the Five Frontiers: Panama from 1821 to 1903* (New York, 1978), 3–16.

42. Blas Beluche Esquivel was born on February 3, 1832, according to the date on his grave marker in Taboga Cemetery. He was christened in the island church, La Iglesia de San Pedro. Beluche Mora, *Abordajes, Biografía Esquemática de Renato Beluche*, 86–87.

CHAPTER 19

With Venezuela's Immortals

Beluche crossed Panamá and sailed to the Dutch island of Curaçao, where he waited for permission to return to Venezuela before boarding the schooner *María*. The ship anchored in the La Guaira roadstead on November 30, 1831. The very next day Beluche swore before the chief of police to uphold the constitution of Venezuela, and soon he was reunited with Mezelle, María Reneta, Ana Colombia, and Diego.[1]

María Reneta was fourteen years old, short like her father, and her nose was strong like his. Ana Colombia was eleven, taller than her sister, and blond like her mother. Reneta and Colombia knew their father, but what about little Diego, who was scarcely four years old? In his brief life he had seen very little of his father. Diego was short like Beluche, and stocky, but blond like his mother. Did Beluche wonder about his unborn child on the island of Taboga? And Mezelle, what kind of reception did she give her husband?

This notice had appeared in a Caracas newspaper six months earlier: "La Señora Beluche is leaving for a foreign country and she advises the public that she has for sale in her house all kinds of furniture for the adornment of a home. Whoever wishes to see them may do so at her place where the Cárcel used to be, between Esquina Principal and Esquina del Conde."[2]

President Páez was not in Caracas when Beluche arrived, having gone to Valencia for the opening of the recently built theater. Páez was a musical genius and actor who loved to perform in operas and tragedies, as did members of his cabinet and other prominent gentlemen

1. Vargas, *Nuestros Próceres Navales*, 169.
2. Caracas *Fanal*, June 2, 1831.

and ladies. Páez had staged *Othello, the Moor of Venice* in his Valencia home in 1829, and his interpretation of Othello had brought forth such enthusiasm that his friends built a real theater for him.[3]

As the orchestra struck up on opening night, a man in the audience stood up and shouted, "Viva el Libertador Simón Bolívar!"

Police arrested the man "for his very scandalous and insulting conduct in the theater." The disturber of the peace was "the famous Captain of the Navy Renato Beluche, he who had conducted Bolívar from Les Cayes in Haiti to the island of Margarita, and who with Padilla had won the rugged victory at the battle of Lake Maracaibo!" Beluche, as was his custom when he returned from a mission, had gone to Valencia to report to Páez, and that is how he happened to be in the theater that evening. "The riotous Commodore was kept three days in prison—and then let out—pleading drunkenness, and saying he could not answer for his conduct in that state."[4]

A sober Beluche returned to Caracas. He moved his family to Puerto Cabello, where he either had or had bought a schooner that he named *Mezelle*, and started making regular runs between ports on the coast. An Englishman boarded the *Mezelle* at La Guaira late in the year 1832 and reported:

> We embarked about five in the evening. The vessel belonged to and was commanded by an Italian[5] who was quite a character in his way. He had commanded a privateer in the revolutionary war, and had at that time amassed very considerable wealth. This, however, he had managed to squander, or to lose in some way or other; and nothing remained of it now but this vessel, and a gold-headed cane which was a sort of constant companion. But his misfortunes had never given the Italian the slightest concern. He was one of those light and buoyant spirits which, like bubbles on the ocean, are always uppermost, whatever wind may blow, and however the storm may rage. He had the reputation of great personal bravery, which I suppose he had displayed in the wild and often savage scenes of the revo-

---

3. Francisco González Guinán, *Tradiciones de mi Pueblo* (Caracas, 1954), 37–38.

4. *Ibid.*, 38; entries for January 27 and 29, 1832, in Dupouy (ed.), *Ker Porter's Caracas Diary*, 600. González Guinán says that this episode happened nine months later on Bolívar's saint day, but González Guinán wrote long after the event.

5. Several years ago, Claude C. de Brueys of New Orleans told me that he was a descendant of Beluche's sister Selina. He said that Beluche's mother was Italian and that many members of the family were musicians. De Brueys wanted to sell me his collection of family papers that established these facts, but I was unable to buy them at that time.

lutionary war. Now, however, there was much oddity about him, as he laughed and chattered throughout the day. He was a short, thick man, turned fifty, with large and rather fierce-looking mustachios: and often, when meeting him afterwards in Puerto Cabello, I have seen him enter the stores of the merchants, with his left hand stuck under his chin, his elbow elevated, and scraping across it with his little gold-headed cane, he would dance once or twice round the place, before he condescended to explain his business.

My fellow-passengers had been some time stretched on the deck, and many of them gave evident notice that they had ceased to be observers of anything that passed around them. The captain, seated on a little stool, was singing Italian ditties, which he continued to do the greater part of the night, stopping only for a few moments, as a sail required shifting, which not infrequently could not be done till some unwilling sleeper had been aroused to take himself out of the way, so small and crowded was the vessel.

I at last grew tired of an erect position, and wrapping myself in my cloak, stretched myself in such a manner that I had a distinct view of the bold and elevated outline of the shore. The breeze was gentle, and every thing was still around, save the Italian captain, whose dark and strongly-marked features gave a curious interest to the scene as he sat on his stool serenading the moon.[6]

War minister Soublette, in accord with the government, granted Beluche retirement at one-third pay on April 2, 1833, and life rolled along smoothly for almost two years, although there was an undercurrent of revolt on the part of the generals. Páez, the president, was a general, but civilians were holding government positions, and the liberators of Colombia were being stripped of their military privileges. They realized that "in submitting to the Laws of their Country all their grades and honors are but bits of paper. . . . The calm of peaceful and industrious life cankers upon their constitution."[7]

Páez was strong in central Venezuela, but he never had controlled the east, where he had two serious rivals, Generals Monagas and Mariño. Monagas had led a rebellion against Páez in 1831, but Páez had suppressed it and pardoned his rival.

The resentment of the military increased during the primary elec-

6. John Hawkshaw, *Reminiscences of South America from Two and a Half Years Residence in Venezuela* (London, 1839), 58–62.
7. Vargas, *Nuestros Próceres Navales*, 169; entry for November 10, 1835, in De Grummond (ed.), *Caracas Diary*, 108.

tions for president in the fall of 1834. Dr. José María Vargas was the outstanding candidate. He had been graduated from the University of Caracas in medicine and surgery and had taken care of earthquake victims in 1812, but the next year he sailed to England and Scotland for further study. Then he was professor of surgery in Puerto Rico and did not return to Venezuela until 1825. He had not risked his life or his profession during the wars.

When the electoral college met in Caracas, it cast more votes for Vargas than for any of the generals who were candidates, but it could not muster the number of votes required to elect any candidate. Congress decided the issue on February 6, 1835, when it elected Vargas president and another civilian, Andrés Navarte, vice-president. They were sworn into office three days later.

This was too much for the generals, who called themselves the Reformists. They conspired in Maracaibo, Puerto Cabello, Caracas, and in Barcelona Province while Beluche rounded up all available vessels, so that the Reformists would have communications with each other by sea and could be supplied from the islands. The revolution was to begin in Caracas, then the other cities would proclaim for "Provisional Chief" Santiago Mariño. Surely then General Páez would become their leader.

In Caracas on July 8 "the conspirators met in the house of Gen. Diego Ibarra in Calle Carabobo one square above the Govt. House, and from it at about two o'clock A.M. they sallied out to the number of 13 to their various posts." By four o'clock troops and police had possession of the public square, the Government House, and other public buildings.[8]

President Vargas had sent for members of the Council of Government as soon as he heard the disturbance. They came immediately and authorized Vargas to raise ten thousand troops and to appoint Páez chief of operations with all the authority he needed to maintain the Constitution and bring the insurrectionists to obedience. The council had barely finished its work and dispatched messengers to Páez at his cattle ranch when Colonel Pedro Carujo took custody of Vargas and Navarte.

8. Williamson's diary entry for July 8, 1835, in *ibid.*, 47–48.

As the city awoke, John Gustavus Adolphus Williamson, chargé for the United States, noted that

> wondering citizens *peacebly* congregated at the various corners of the streets in the vicinity of the President's house and the Govt. House, looking on with as much astonishment as myself, without one effort made to resist the military usurpation which had just succeeded in making captive the President and Vice President and subverting the Constitution, Laws and Government of Venezuela. . . . The want of one man to lead and stand the first assault from the Military, composed only of about 250 soldiers, decided the fate of Caracas, and her citizens in amaze and wonder stood and gazed and talked and passed their neck and even their property under the yoke of such a contemtable number of Chiefs and military.[9]

The rebels sent Vargas and Navarte to La Guaira and shipped them to the island of St. Thomas. Two days later, Mariño, chief of the Reformist government, arrived in Caracas.

Meanwhile, messengers from the Council of Government had reached Páez to tell him that he had been empowered by Vargas and the council to defend the country. "I did not vacillate in going to the defense of my country," Páez said later, but this was not accurate. It was several days before he marched with fifty men, gathering more along the way. He pardoned those who had pronounced against the government and assured them their lives, property, and military ranks.[10]

As Páez and his army approached Caracas, Mariño and his followers silently evacuated the city and joined Monagas in Barcelona Province. They took with them all available military supplies. Páez entered Caracas the next morning, July 28. He sent a messenger to St. Thomas to bring back the president and vice-president, then he marched east. Páez could not attack immediately because he lacked arms, ammunition, horses, and vessels, and he did not have enough officers to train his raw troops. The Reformists, on the other hand, had too many officers and too few troops. However, they had the advantages of supplies and a squadron that facilitated communications. Páez had to move by land, cautiously.

Moreover, he tells us that "the thought that I had to take up arms

---

9. Williamson was not a good speller. *Ibid.*, 47, 53.
10. Páez, *Autobiografía*, II, 230, 239.

against my brothers tormented me horribly. I pleaded fervently with Heaven to move the hearts of my enemies so that I would not have to use force against them." Not only did Páez plead with Heaven, he also pleaded with Reformist leaders. In his letter to Beluche, dated August 21, he said:

> When I heard that Puerto Cabello had declared against the Government, my first concern was to ask whether or not you were among those who had taken part in the terrible transgression of July 17. [On that night, Reformist leaders had met at Carabaño's house in Puerto Cabello to write their pronunciamiento.] With the greatest sadness I have learned that you were present.
> I know how the torrents of revolution can sweep up good men. This makes me fear that events at Puerto Cabello have engulfed you; but I am consoled by the thought that you are a gentleman and cannot mix with crime. . . . Even though I saw your signature on the act, I still have reason to hope that you will not be on the side against which my duty leads me. I am and have always been your best friend in Venezuela. Many common experiences tighten the bonds of patriotism and mutual respect which unite us, and now at this moment I remember with pleasure that you have been faithful to the oath of friendship on many difficult occasions when other powerful friends were against me.
> All this encourages me, and above all, I am consoled by the hope that even though you have been the victim of events, never will you raise an arm to hurt me. Thus I hope, compadre, and when I see my convictions verified in a letter from you, I will have more reasons to sign myself your sincere friend and protector.[11]

Beluche did not answer this letter, and Páez did not write to him again. But Páez did write several times to the strong man in the east. His first letter to Monagas said: "I am counting on your patriotism, on the influence which you exercise in this country. I wish to divide with you the glory of restoring constitutional order. Let us work together for the good of the people and content ourselves with the reward that is beyond price, the gratitude of those people." Monagas replied that popular opinion was with the Reformist movement and was supported by the most notable men of the country. Páez then promised that he

11. *Ibid.*, II, 251–52.

would name Monagas "General of the East," but Monagas was still bent on blood or a new government.[12]

A few battles were fought in September and October, but they were not decisive. Public opinion was turning to Páez as town after town proclaimed its loyalty to his constitution. Monagas capitulated at the end of October, and Páez guaranteed him and his followers "their lives, properties, and the military rank held by them on the 7th of July last."[13]

United States Chargé Williamson was critical of such leniency. He said: "General Monagas is precisely, except in some small loss of property in cattle, *status ante bellum*, and is perfectly at liberty without fear of punishment to get up another revolution whenever it may suit his ambition or his pride as he did in 1831. Pardoned for that, he has again done it in 1835, and pardoned for that, pray what is to prevent his doing the like again?"[14] Prophetic words!

Mariño had escaped to Puerto Cabello, but with the east submissive, Páez could now concentrate on the rebellion there and in Maracaibo. He was greatly strengthened by the arms and ammunition that had been in Monagas' possession.

British and French warships moved toward Puerto Cabello to protect their nationals, and Williamson was concerned because the United States did not have a man-of-war along the coast for the same purpose. He had begged that one be sent, but it was a full month after British and French ships arrived at Puerto Cabello before Captain A. J. Dallas and the sloop-of-war *St. Louis* put in an appearance there. Williamson complained: "It would seem ships of war was [sic] constructed for pleasure and not for use, that the Captains might touch where they pleased, and thereafter to show off in reporting their duties performed merely by asking at a place where a revolution existed, *how are you* and *good by*—They will get their reward, some how, and in some way—newspapers *are still printed*."[15]

---

12. Francisco González Guinán, *Historia Contemporanea de Venezuela* (15 vols.; Caracas, 1909–25), II, 426–28; Páez, *Autobiografía*, II, 243–46.
13. Entry for November 11, 1835, in De Grummond (ed.), *Caracas Diary*, 110.
14. Entry for November 13, 1835, in *ibid.*, 116.
15. Entry for November 26, 1835, in *ibid.*, 130.

Captain Dallas made up for lost time. He gave "Gen¹ Carabaño a good knock over the nuckles" by warning him that he, Captain Dallas, considered any craft flying the Reform flag to be a pirate vessel and that if he should meet any on the high seas, he would capture them. Carabaño immediately sent a vessel to warn Beluche to return at once to Puerto Cabello.[16]

A few days later, President Vargas, who had returned to Caracas on August 20, declared Puerto Cabello blockaded and sent Captain Joly to make the blockade effective. Joly had a squadron of three schooners and the brig *Stag*, which the government had recently purchased in the United States. Williamson believed that the odds were against Joly and that Beluche would break the blockade, because he had more confidence in "Beluche's talents and seamanship than in the heterogenous compound of French and English on board the Brig Stag"; but Páez was rapidly increasing his land forces. His correspondence with the rebels at Maracaibo brought about their capitulation. They also were guaranteed their lives, property, and military rank, and a few were sent into temporary exile.[17]

Puerto Cabello remained obdurate. Páez managed to place his men in ambush around the city without the besieged forces suspecting his strength. His men were in position by Christmas Eve, and he hoped that the customary drinking of spiritous liquors on that night would inspire some of the Reformists to come out to battle. He was not disappointed. More than a hundred sallied forth, whereupon Páez mowed them down. Only eighteen were able to get back to the city, now blockaded by land and sea.

Mariño and a number of officers fled on two vessels to Curaçao. This left Carabaño and Beluche in command. Beluche loaded the *Mezelle* with cannon and ammunition and sent it, with Clark commanding and Swain second in command, to St. Thomas, where the cargo was to be exchanged for food. The *Mezelle* ran the blockade, but when it anchored at St. Thomas, the Danish governor seized it and had a warship escort it to La Guaira. Beluche's son-in-law Domingo Antonio Olavarría y Olave, Reneta's husband, gave security for the *Mezelle*, and it

16. Entry for December 4, 1835, in *ibid.*, 132.
17. Entry for December 7, 1835, in *ibid.*, 137.

was put in his possession.[18] Clark and Swain petitioned to have their rank and pay restored, but they were expelled from the country, minus both rank and pay.

When this news reached Puerto Cabello, rebel officers wavered. They held out until the end of February, 1836, then they turned against Beluche and Carabaño, made them prisoners, surrendered to Páez, and received a full pardon. Beluche and Carabaño were stripped of their honors, rank, pensions, and privileges, and were banished from the country.

There were some ripples of comedy and tragedy on the Venezuelan scene during the nine years of Beluche's exile. Vargas resigned on April 15, 1836. Thus it was Vice president Navarte who presided over the ceremony at Government House on April 19 commemorating the anniversary of that day in 1810 when the Caracas cabildo deposed the Spanish captain general and shipped him to Philadelphia. A dinner followed, to which Navarte had invited thirty guests, including Williamson and Ker Porter. Sir Robert was more sophisticated and famous than Williamson, but Williamson had been appointed chargé before Sir Robert. Therefore, the American had diplomatic precedence over Sir Robert, who tells us: "Mr Williamson, who is very *tenacious* of his *seniority* as Chargé d'Affaires, wanted to decline returning thanks—but I said as the oldest in dip^c rank he must. He spoke in English instead of *Spanish*—and returned thanks in the name of all the F. Nations. In fact he *bitched* the business, even in his mother tongue."[19]

Beluche was in exile, both of his daughters were in their twenties and married (Ana Colombia had married Rafael Arvelo), and Diego was twelve years old when Mezelle died on September 13, 1840. The children buried their mother beneath the palms in the Rancho Grande Cemetery at Puerto Cabello.

During his second term as president, Páez asked Congress on February 9, 1842, for the return of Bolívar's remains from Santa Marta to his native city, and Congress decreed that this should be done with proper decorum and with the participation of the governments of New Granada and Ecuador. Invitations were sent to both governments to

---

18. Entry for February 21, 1836, in *ibid.*, 166–67.
19. Entry for April 19, 1836, in Dupouy (ed.), *Ker Porter's Caracas Diary*, 917.

have representatives present at Santa Marta for the exhumation in November. The date set for the interment in Caracas was December 17, the twelfth anniversary of Bolívar's death.

Beluche was still in exile, but his friend Sebastian Boguier, commanding the government schooner *Constitution*, was chief of the expedition that sailed to Santa Marta for Bolívar's remains. The merchant brig *Caracas* of Philadelphia, with Jonathan Jones Wheeler commanding, and the 32-gun *Circe*, sent by the French government, accompanied the *Constitution*. They sailed from La Guaira on November 13 and anchored in the harbor of Santa Marta on November 16. The 16-gun British sloop *Albatross* and the 18-gun Netherlands sloop *Venus* were in the harbor, waiting to accompany the expedition in its return to La Guaira.

Wheeler kept a journal, and in it he tells us:

> On the 20th, in the afternoon, the exhumation of Bolivar took place, attended by all the officers civil and military of the place, the officers of the men of war, the Commissioners of New Granada from the Capital Bogota, and the Commissioners from Venezuela. Those from the Equador had not arrived, for even distant Quito had sent a deputation. . . .
>
> The full and impressive music and chaunting ceased, and there was silence in the Cathedral. The covering of stone was removed from the grave which was immediately under the dome in the centre of the church, and the coffin was exposed to view. The lid and head were then taken off and there lay the remains of the great Bolivar. The scull was partly exposed to view as were some of the ribs, which had fallen in, and the rest was covered with the mouldering cerements of the grave.
>
> > O mighty spirit! dost thou lie so low?
> > Are all thy conquests and thy glories
> > Shrunk to this little measure?
>
> No! the spirit of liberty that he instilled into the hearts of his countrymen shall live forever. The precepts and the institution that he bestowed upon them shall be cherished by them to the latest posterity.[20]

The next afternoon, a long procession accompanied the coffin to the harbor, where it was taken on board the *Constitution*. The expedition

---

20. Wheeler's "Journal of a Voyage in the brig *Caracas*, to accompany an expedition from Venezuela to New Granada, for the remains of Bolívar," was published in the New York *Morning Courier and New York Enquirer*, January 10, 1843.

sailed on November 22 and anchored in the roads of La Guaira on December 13. On December 15, the coffin was taken ashore in the schooner's barge. Then, Wheeler recorded,

> Echoes of the minute guns rolled from cliff to valley of the lofty silla, as the procession to slow and solemn music, passed through the sable drapery of the streets and the remains reached the church, there to lie in state until the morrow, when they will be borne to Caracas, distant twelve miles; again to be met by further honors and a mourning population.
>
> They will be taken to the Cathedral, their final resting place, and the last request of Simon Bolivar the Liberator will have been complied with.
>
> The polished marble of Italy will rear its column above his ashes, but his memory in the hearts of his countrymen shall outlive the work of the sculptor.[21]

Only a few clues suggest Beluche's whereabouts during his exile. New Orleans seems to have been his base of operations and merchant-banker Joseph Sauvinet his protector. Most of the merchants, bankers, shipmasters, and sailors of Beluche's smuggling days were dead or had departed for places unknown. Beluche still owned the two lots on Esplanade Street in New Orleans that he had bought in 1817. Sometime in the 1830s he built two common-wall, plastered brick townhouses on the lots. Beluche sold the lots and buildings to Sauvinet in 1841 for $15,000; Sauvinet left them to his brother Jean Baptiste in 1843, who sold them back to Beluche for $6,000 in August, 1845.[22]

Soublette was sworn in as president of Venezuela at the beginning of 1845. On February 21, Congress restored to Beluche his rank, titles, and decorations.[23] He returned to Venezuela later in the year.

One may read in the Caracas *El Liberal* of February 7, 1846, that the brig *Colombia* from Balitmore, with Captain Charles E. Coffin commanding, arrived at La Guaira on February 3, 1846, after a passage of twelve days. On its freight list were these items destined for Señor R. Beluche in Puerto Cabello: one marble monument and two crates of iron fencing. The monument was shaped like a little tower or minaret, and on it was inscribed:

21. *Ibid.*
22. Friends of the Cabildo, *The Creole Faubourgs*, 136.
23. Vargas, *Nuestros Próceres Navales*, 169.

> Quien osará turbar
> Amiga tu reposo
> La Tumba del virtuoso
> No es tumba sino altar.
>
> R. B.
>
> A la memoria de
> María Mezelle Beaudri de Beluche
> Falleció a la edad de 49 años
> el 13 de Setiembre de 1840[24]

Beluche placed the monument over Mezelle's grave and enclosed his family plot with the iron fencing.

All seemed peaceful in Puerto Cabello, but by September there was violence elsewhere in Venezuela as rival factions fought over who should succeed Soublette as president. Merchants and other middle-class property owners outnumbered the landed oligarchy who, with Páez, had dominated the government for fifteen years. These conservatives had no strong candidate, because Páez refused to run for a third term. The candidate they most feared was Antonio Leocadio Guzmán, whose vitriolic attacks on Conservatives and rival Liberals, published in his journal *El Venezolano*, caused them to respond in their journals with similar abuse. Armed clashes occurred after the 5 percent of the population that had the right to vote had chosen electors. On September 21 the minister of interior and justice ordered Guzmán's arrest, but first he had to be found.

Páez as commander of the armed forces and Monagas as his second in command restored peace to the country, and the Conservatives began to see that Monagas might be a pliable president. José Tadeo Monagas, who had rebelled against Páez in 1831 and again in 1836, had

---

24. Who will dare disturb,
    Friend, your repose?
    The tomb of the virtuous
    Is not a tomb but an altar.
        R. B.
    To the memory of
    María Mezelle Beaudri de Beluche,
    Died at the age of 49 years
    the 13th of September, 1840.

played his hand well. Rumor said that his first name had been Judas, but that he had changed it to José.[25]

Electoral colleges met in each of the thirteen provinces on October 1 to choose the next president, but before the results were known, Guzmán was found, charged with conspiracy, arrested, and held in jail until his case could be heard. A few days later the election returns were announced. Monagas had the most votes—107 of the 319 votes cast—but this was far short of the two-thirds required by the Constitution. Therefore, Congress would choose the next president when it convened on January 20, 1847.[26]

On the afternoon of January 16, Páez gave a splendid dinner at his residence in Maracay for three representatives on their way to Caracas. As they talked about candidates for president, Páez asked Dr. Angel Quintero to read aloud the last letter that he, Páez, had received from Monagas. This part of the letter impressed the representatives: "You ask me what my program will be if I am elected president. I answer: I will regulate my conduct in the same manner that I did as second chief of the army; I will govern with the men who helped elect me; and I will depend on the counsel that you will be able to give me because of your long experience in governing Venezuela, and with the help of your sword which has always been victorious in battle."[27]

When Congress convened in Caracas, both houses gave Monagas most of the votes, and the president of the senate declared him elected. Monagas was in Barcelona and did not arrive in Caracas until March 1, 1847. That afternoon he was inaugurated. Páez and the oligarchy were happy with his selection of cabinet ministers.[28]

Quintero, the new secretary of interior and justice, ordered that Guzmán be tried for conspiracy in the Court of First Instance. When the judge of that court handed down the death sentence, Guzmán's family appealed to the Superior Court and finally to the Supreme Court, which confirmed the death sentence of the two lower courts on

---

25. José Gil Fortoul, *Historia Constitucional de Venezuela* (3 vols.; Caracas, 1942), II, 266n.
26. González Guinán, *Historia Contemporánea de Venezuela*, IV, 238–40.
27. *Ibid.*, IV, 263–64.
28. *Ibid.*, IV, 284–88.

June 1. The next day, President Monagas commuted the sentence to perpetual exile. This marked the end of the honeymoon between Monagas and Páez.[29]

Monagas caused cabinet ministers to resign, refused to appoint the persons designated by due process as governors of provinces, and removed all officers of the militia. Then he appointed his own partisans as ministers, governors, and militia officers, and he disarmed the active militia and called into service the reserve militia, without the legal authority required by the Constitution.

Deputies of the province of Caracas drew up a formal accusation against Monagas on December 10 and resolved to present it to Congress. The house and senate convened separately in the Convent of San Francisco on January 24, 1848, to hear the new minister of interior and justice read the president's message. Nearly all the congressmen were armed with pistols or daggers. Only thirteen members of the house stood when the minister appeared. The rest represented Páez and the oligarchy.

The legislators were determined to consider the accusation of December 10 and to impeach Monagas after his message was read. They had stationed guards outside the convent, but a pro-Monagas crowd and militia were there also. When shots were heard inside the convent, fighting erupted outside. Six representatives and five other people were killed that day.

Páez was at Calabozo when he was told that "the blood of Representatives of the people had been spilled in the sanctuary of the laws." He declared war against Monagas and called on Venezuelans to fight with him, but not enough of them responded. Páez escaped to New Granada. Finding no backing there, he sailed to Jamaica and other islands, seeking vessels and recruits.[30]

Ramón Páez and two other sons of Páez remained with the rebel forces in Maracaibo. They had more vessels than the government, including one commanded by Joly, and in June they forced Monagas' fleet to retire to Puerto Cabello. Then the rebel squadron terrorized the

---

29. *Ibid.*, IV, 348, 365, 389–91.
30. *Ibid.*, IV 465–72; Páez, *Autobiografía*, II, 450–63.

coast as far east as Cumaná and Rio Caribe, but it ran out of ammunition and returned to Lake Maracaibo.

Sixty-seven-year-old Renato Beluche was busy in Puerto Cabello. On October 2 the mysterious *Augusta* arrived there, and the Monagas government bought this 195-ton iron-screw steamer for $30,000.[31] Beluche changed its name to *Libertador* when he was given its command. However, the steamer was not ready for combat and remained behind when General Justo Briceño, commanding thirteen brigs and schooners, sailed from Puerto Cabello bound for the Gulf of Venezuela.

Rebels held Fort San Carlos and had at least sixteen vessels on Lake Maracaibo, but Monagas' forces held the city of Maracaibo. Briceño's fleet was able to keep enemy vesssels from entering and leaving the lake, but neither side gained any advantage until the *Libertador* and its rival, the *Scourge*, appeared.

The last registration of the 231-ton *Scourge*, also an iron-screw steamer, was issued at New Orleans on October 9, 1848, to John Jeter of Lafayette, Louisiana. It sailed from that port with enough coal to get to the island of Aruba, and there José Hermenegildo García, agent for Páez, bought it from Vespasian Ellis for $50,000. Unfortunately for the rebels, "the enthusiastic García, though very able in making speeches, knew nothing of naval affairs. By his advice and urgent solicitations she [the *Scourge*] was hurried to San Carlos with as many bundles of brushwood as the barren soil of Aruba could afford. By the time she reached the bar, the steamer had consumed the last chip."[32]

Meanwhile, Beluche had mounted three large and two small cannon on the *Libertador*, rounded up a crew of a hundred men, and sailed on November 8 to join Briceño's fleet. Beluche arrived off the bar in time to capture the *Scourge*, send it with a prize crew to Puerto Cabello, and cross the bar into Lake Maracaibo with Briceño's fleet.

During the month of December, government land and sea forces inflicted severe casualties on the rebels, who surrendered on the last day

---

31. Francis James Dallett, "The Creation of the Venezuelan Naval Squadron, 1848–1860," *American Neptune*, XXX (1970), 268–69.
32. *Ibid.*, 269–79; Páez, *Wild Scenes in South America*, 443–44. The *Scourge*, originally the 212-ton *Bangor*, was built at Wilmington in 1845. It was the first iron-hulled seagoing steamer built in the United States. C. Bradford Mitchell (ed.), *Merchant Steam Vessels of the United States 1790–1868* (Staten Island, 1975), 17.

of 1848. One of the casualties was Captain Joly. Páez's three sons and other important rebels were held for awhile as prisoners in Caracas. Ramón Páez said: "We owed our preservation and obtained our passports for Curaçao to the untiring efforts of the Spanish Minister at Caracas." Ramón and his companions, after being separated from Páez for fifteen months, rejoined him at Curaçao on April 18, 1849, "entirely recovered from his late illness, and ready to take the field once more against the oppressor of his country."[33]

Páez assured his followers that seven Venezuelan provinces would send him men, money, and supplies as soon as he started a campaign in Coro. The rebels disembarked at La Vela de Coro on July 2, but by the end of July they had mustered only eight hundred of the expected two thousand troops. This small army headed toward the llanos, suffering many casualties, then Páez surrendered to prevent the loss of any more lives.

His troops were disarmed and set free, but not the leaders. Páez was separated from the other prisoners and sent to the fortress of San Antonio in Cumaná. His son Ramón was held in the Caracas jail. Not until May of 1850 did Monagas permit Páez and Ramón to go into exile. They sailed to New York.

José Tadeo Monagas' first term as president ended in 1851, and he was succeeded by his brother José Gregório. Beluche was in good standing with both brothers. José Gregório's list of generals, chiefs, officials, and other individuals of the navy who received pensions in 1854 begins with "General de brigada Renato Beluche, 2,400 pesos."[34]

Many Venezuelans had freed their slaves since 1816, when Bolívar began the abolition movement, but thirteen thousand slaves still remained in bondage. José Gregório made such an ardent plea in Congress for their emancipation on March 10, 1854, that within two weeks Congress passed a law freeing slaves in Venezuela with compensation to the owners. José Gregório enforced this act and thus became one of Venezuela's immortals.

He was a mild, well-meaning man, but during his administration there were many disturbances and rumors of insurrection because

33. Páez, *Wild Scenes in South America*, 452–55.
34. *Exposición que dirige al Congreso de Venezuela en 1854 al Secretario de Guerra y Marina* (Caracas, 1854), 64.

both the Páez faction and the Guzmán faction opposed him. His older brother became president a second time in 1855 and bullied Congress into writing a constitution that made him a dictator. All factions of Liberals and Conservatives combined against him, and their thirteen-day revolution caused him to seek refuge in the French embassy.

A mob besieged the embassy, demanding that Monagas be surrendered to Venezuelan authorities for trial and threatening to come into the embassy and get him. The French chargé d'affaires appealed to his colleagues for help. They sent their national flags to be flown over the French embassy as a warning that the right of asylum must be respected or civilized nations would take concerted action against Venezuelans.

Ministers of the United States, Great Britain, France, Brazil, and the Netherlands secured a written protocol from the Venezuelan foreign minister, guaranteeing Monagas' safe passage out of the country. The French and British sent warships to blockade La Guaira when this protocol was not promptly obeyed. "Aging Carlos Soublette, tactful as ever, smoothed over the incident."[35]

Beluche was on the fringe of these events. He died two years later and was buried beside Mezelle. The marker over his grave bears this inscription:

> General Renato Beluche
> Octubre 4, 1860
> 79 años

Páez was almost eighty-three years old when he died on May 7, 1873, at No. 24, 20th Street, New York. Ramón deposited the remains in a vault at Marble Cemetery on Second Street, near Second Avenue. Rental on the vault was $24 year.[36]

The next year, in his message to Congress, President Antonio Guzmán Blanco said: "It is not enough that Venezuela's heroes be preserved for posterity on the pages of history. Their ashes should be guarded with religious respect, in this manner insuring an everlast-

---

35. William D. and Amy L. Marsland, *Venezuela Through Its History* (New York, 1954), 192–94; González Guinán, *Historia Contemporánea de Venezuela*, VI, 181–218.
36. González Guinán, *Historia Contemporánea de Venezuela*, X, 228; Laureano Villanueva, *Apoteósis de Páez* (Caracas, 1888), 27.

ing monument of national gratitude." A few days later, the president declared that the Church of the Santísima Trinidad of Caracas was henceforth the Panteón Nacional. The remains of Venezuela's Illustrious Heroes of Independence would be preserved there, as well as those of eminent·men named by the president and approved by the senate. The remains already there were to be transferred to public cemeteries, excepting those who, in the judgment of the president, had the right to remain in the Panteón. The expenses of inhumation would be paid out of the treasury of the Federal District, and the remains of each hero was to have a simple gravestone with only his name and the dates of his birth and his death.[37]

Guzmán Blanco followed this decree with another on February 11, 1876, that ordered the transfer of remains to begin, and he appointed a commission to implement this order. He informed Congress that competent Europeans would move the monument of the Liberator in the cathedral to the central nave of the Panteón, where it would be the apex of national glory. On September 30 Guzmán Blanco named a committee to bring back the remains of Páez and Vargas from the United States. Ramón Páez declared that he was the head of the Páez family and as such he would not give permission for his father's remains to be moved. Those of Vargas were taken to the Panteón.[38]

The Junta Directiva in charge of transferring Bolívar's remains from the cathedral prepared an elaborate three-day ceremony. On the third day, October 28, the apotheosis of Bolívar began at dawn. It was noon when the long procession escorting his remains arrived at the Panteón. Only the president, the Junta Directiva, important officials, and members of the press entered this temple to Venezuela's immortals. Dr. Eduardo Calcaño, the greatest orator of the day, appeared in the pulpit and said:

> Like a trembling skiff on the immensity of the ocean, like a migrating bird face to face with the profundities of infinite space that he is forced to traverse, so is the orator of today before the solemn majesty of this most high occasion. . . .
>
> Titán [Bolívar] leveled the Andes beneath his stride, and made a seat of Chimborazo on which he conversed with Time and Destiny. . . . Zea, the

---

37. González Guinán, *Historia Contemporánea de Venezuela*, X, 291–92.
38. *Ibid.*, XI, 80, 121.

great orator of times past, has put on my lips the new apocalypse of Bolívar's future glory.[39]

At the beginning of 1888, Guzmán Blanco, dictator since 1870, was informed that Páez's remains were in danger of being thrown into a common grave because rent on the vault had not been paid for several years. The dictator instructed his consul in New York to make arrangements with the proper authorities for the release of Páez's remains, then to ship them with due ceremony to Venezuela. Presumably, the consul paid the back rent, and Ramón bowed to the dictator's will.

President Grover Cleveland asked for and obtained authority from Congress to put the U.S.S. *Pensacola*, with Captain Arthur Yates commanding, at the disposal of the Venezuelan consul. General William T. Sherman and General Philip H. Sheridan marched with two regiments of the United States Army, as did New York officials and citizens, in the parade that accompanied the great *llanero*'s remains to the pier. There, a tug conveyed them to the *Pensacola*. It sailed from New York on March 24, 1888, and two weeks later anchored at La Guaira.[40]

Bands played United States and Venezuelan hymns as fifty troops from the *Pensacola* escorted the twenty Venezuelan youths who carried the casket on their shoulders to the railroad station. Captain Yates and members of his staff went by train with the cortege to Caracas, where they were royally entertained for three days. Their orders did not permit them to remain until April 19 for the inhumation. They returned to their ship on April 12, raised the Venezuelan flag on the foresail mast, and fired a twenty-one-gun salute before they sailed.

Páez's remains were interred with great pomp on Venezuela's most important national holiday. Corps of *llaneros* on horseback led the procession to the Panteón, and more *llaneros* brought up the rear.[41]

Seventy-five years later, on May 27, 1963, a senate resolution bestowed the honor of being interred in the Panteón Nacional on Beluche's mortal remains. By the authority of the president, the minister of interior relations, and the minister of defense, the exhumation began at nine o'clock on the morning of July 19 in the Cemeterio de

39. *Ibid.*, XI, 123–28.
40. *Ibid.*, XIV, 42–48.
41. *Ibid.*, XIV, 62–71.

Rancho Grande at Puerto Cabello. Navy and army officials, Beluche's descendants, this author, and other friends surrounded the grave. We watched as the gravedigger began to excavate the earth. Only the muted sound of his spade and the sound of trade winds moving the fronds of palm trees broke the silence.

When the digger was standing waist-deep in the grave (he was a little man), he lifted in his cupped hands a few small grayish pieces of bone and brown dust. These remains were put in a baby-sized casket, and a priest performed the liturgical act. Buglers responded.

Those present joined the procession that escorted the casket to Naval Base No. 1 at Borburata. The road wound around what had been a mangrove swamp when Páez and Beluche forced the royalists to surrender Puerto Cabello in 1823, but now it was dry land and a rapidly developing industrial area. The casket was placed in a *capilla ardiente* (lighted room) at the base. There, a brief ceremony ended with an oration by Isidro Beluche Mora of Panamá, a descendant of Beluche's son Blas.

An honor guard maintained a round-the-clock wake in the *capilla ardiente* until Monday, July 22, when, at 8 A.M., the casket was placed on the destroyer *General Juan Flores*. Within three hours the destroyer dropped anchor at La Guaira (it had taken three weeks in 1842 for a sailing vessel and its escort of sailing vessels to transport Bolívar's remains from Santa Marta to La Guaira).

After due honors at the pier in La Guaira, a funeral cortege received the casket with Beluche's remains and traveled by motorcade to Caracas. Four captains of the navy carried the casket into the Panteón at 4:30 that afternoon of July 22, 1963, and deposited it in the left aisle beside the statue of José Gregório Monagas.

In accordance with Beluche's high rank, the inhumation ceremony began with the reading of Resolutions of the Senate, Ministry of Interior Relations, and Ministry of Defense. A priest intoned the liturgy and blessed the grave. Then four rear admirals carried the casket to the edge of a small opening in the floor. One of them, Rear Admiral Daniel Gámez Calcaño, eulogized Beluche, and then he and the other three lowered the casket into its sepulcher.

A mason appeared, carrying a bucket of mortar and a trowel. His khaki shirt and pants had been washed and beautifully ironed. Not a drop of mortar splashed from the mason's trowel as he skillfully cemented the gravestone over the vault, level with the floor. After the presentation of floral offerings, the Act of Inhumation was read, then it was signed by all the dignitaries, the descendants of Beluche, and the author.

Beluche's remains are safe in the temple of Venezuela's Immortals, but what about those of Mezelle in Puerto Cabello? Beluche's inscription on her monument was in vain. The "tomb of the virtuous" was indeed disturbed. Today a section of the Avenida Intercomunal occupies the site of the old Rancho Grande Cemetery.

Bibliography

Manuscripts

Archivo Nacional de Colombia, Bogotá
  Correspondencia Militar
  Hojas de Servicio, Secretaria de Guerra y Marina, Papeles sin Clasificación
Historic New Orleans Collection, Kemper and Leila Williams Foundation, New Orleans
  Cat. 44-2, Case 25, Docs. 1–4, 8, 9, 12, 16, 17
  Ms. 97, F4-106-L
Jackson Barracks, New Orleans
  "Legislative Acts of Louisiana Militia 1805–1824" (typescript)
  Marigny de Mandeville, Bernard de. "Reflections on the Campaign of General Andrew Jackson in Louisiana 1814 and 1815" (typescript)
Louisiana State Archives and Records Commission, Baton Rouge
  Notarial Records of Orleans Parish
Louisiana State Museum Archives, New Orleans
  Succession of Renato Beluche, 1788
Louisiana State Museum Library, New Orleans
  René Beluche Index Cards
Newberry Library, Chicago
  Ayer Collection
New Orleans Public Library, New Orleans
  Parish Court of New Orleans Records
Notarial Archives, Civil Courts Building, New Orleans
  Notarial Records of S. de Quiñones
Parroquia de San José, Padres Agustinos Recolectos, Puerto Cabello
  Marriage Records, Diócesis de Valencia
Pennsylvania Historical Society, Philadelphia
  Dreer Collection
  James Evans Hele Letter Book
St. Louis Cathedral Archives, New Orleans
  Baptismal Books III, VI, VII, 1, 2, 3

Burial Records, Book 1820–24
Funerals Book 1803–15
Marriage Books B, 3

Books

Abernethy, Thomas P. *The South in the New Nation, 1789–1819*. Baton Rouge, 1976.

Adams, Charles Francis, ed. *Memoris of John Quincy Adams, Comprising Portions of His Diary from 1795 to 1848*. 12 vols. Philadelphia, 1943.

Adams, Henry. *History of the United States of America*. 9 vols. New York, 1890–91.

Aguado Bleye, Pedro and Cayetano Alcázar Molina. *Manual de la Historia de España*. 3 vols. Madrid, 1954–56.

Alexis, Stephen. *Black Liberator: The Life of Toussaint Louverture*. New York, 1949.

American State Papers. Documents, Legislative and Executive, of the Congress of the United States. 38 vols. Washington, D.C., 1832–61.

Angel, Hildegard. *Simón Bolívar, South American Liberator*. New York, 1930.

Annuaire Louisianais Commençant à l'Equinoxe de Mars 1808 et se Terminant à celui de Mars 1809. New Orleans, 1808.

Arthur, Stanley Clisby. *Jean Laffite, Gentleman Rover*. New Orleans, 1952.

———. *Old New Orleans*. New Orleans, 1966.

Arthur, Stanley Clisby, and George Campbell Huchet de Kerneon, comps. and eds. *Old Families of Louisiana*. Baton Rouge, 1971.

Baraya, José María. *Biografías Militares o Historia Militar del País*. Bogatá, 1874.

Bassett, John Spencer, ed. *Correspondence of Andrew Jackson*. 7 vols. Washington, 1926–35.

———. *The Life of Andrew Jackson*. New York, 1925.

Bealer, Lewis Winkler. *Los Corsarios de Buenos Aires: Sus actividades en las guerras Hispano-Americanas de la Independencia*. Buenos Aires, 1937.

Beluche Mora, Isidro A. *Abordajes, Biografía Esquemática de Renato Beluche*. Caracas, 1960.

Beluche, Renato. *Contesta a las falsas imputaciones con que ha intentado manchar su honor el Sr. General de la misma José Padilla en las notas que contiene el papel intitulado "Al Mundo Imparcial."* Caracas, 1824.

Bemis, Samuel Flagg. *John Quincy Adams and the Foundations of American Foreign Policy*. New York, 1949.

Bierck, Harold A., Jr., ed, and Vicente Lecuna, comp. *Selected Writings of Bolívar*. 2 vols. New York, 1951.

Bioren, John, W. John Duane, and R. C. Weightman, eds. *Laws of the United*

States of America from the 4th of March, 1789, to the 4th of March, 1815. 5 vols. Philadelphia and Washington, 1815.
Boulton, Alfredo. *Miranda, Bolívar y Sucre.* Caracas, 1959.
Brown, Wilburt S. *The Amphibious Campaign for West Florida and Louisiana 1814–1815.* University, Ala., 1968.
Buell, Augustus C. *A History of Andrew Jackson.* 2 vols. New York, 1904.
Cable, George W. *The Creoles of Louisiana.* New York, 1910.
———. *Old Creole Days.* New York, 1927.
Calendrier de commerce de la Nouvelle Orleans, Pour L'Année 1807. New Orleans, 1806.
Carter, Clarence Edwin, comp. and ed. *The Territorial Papers of the United States.* 28 vols. Washington, 1934–75.
Castellanos, Henry A. *New Orleans As It Was.* New Orleans, 1905.
Clark, John G. *New Orleans, 1718–1812: An Economic History.* Baton Rouge, 1970.
Cochrane, Charles Stuart. *Journal of a Residence and Travels in Colombia During the Years 1823 and 1824.* 2 vols. London, 1825.
Coker, William S., ed. *The Military Presence on the Gulf Coast.* Pensacola, 1978.
Cooke, John Henry. *A Narrative of Events in the South of France and of the Attack on New Orleans in 1814 and 1815.* London, 1835.
Corráles, Manuel Ezequiel, ed. *Documentos para la historia de la Provincia de Cartagena.* 2 vols. Bogotá, 1883.
Cortazar, Roberto, ed. *Cartas y Mensajes del General Francisco de Paula Santander.* 8 vols. Bogatá, 1953–55.
Cowie, Captain. *Recollections of a Service of Three Years During the War-of-Extermination in the Republics of Venezuela and Colombia.* 2 vols. London, 1828.
Crouse, Nellie M. *Lemoyne d'Iberville, Soldier of New France.* Ithaca, 1954.
De Grummond, Jane L., ed. *Caracas Diary, 1835–1840: The Journal of John G. A. Williamson, First Diplomatic Representative of the United States to Venezuela.* Baton Rouge, 1954.
Depons, François Joseph. *Travels in South America, During the Years 1801, 1802, 1803, and 1804.* 2 vols. London, 1807.
Ducoudray-Holstein, H. L. V. *Memoirs of Simón Bolívar.* Boston, 1830.
Dupouy, Walter, ed. *Sir Robert Ker Porter's Caracas Diary, 1825–1842: A British Diplomat in a Newborn Nation.* Caracas, 1966.
Eaton, John Henry. *Life of Andrew Jackson.* Philadelphia, 1824.
Elhuri-Yunez S., Antonio R. *La Batalla Naval del Lago de Maracaibo.* Caracas, 1973.
Espasa-Calpe, Hijos de J. Espasa, eds. *Enciclopedia universal ilustrada Europeao-Americano.* 70 vols. Madrid, 1905–30.

Exposición que dirige al Congreso de Venezuela en 1854 al Secretario de Guerra y Marina. Caracas, 1854.
A Faithful Picture of the Political Situation of New Orleans at Close of Last and Beginning of Present Year 1807. Boston, 1808.
Forsyth, Alice Daly. *A Collection of Marriage Records from the St. Louis Cathedral During the Spanish Regime and Early American Period, 1784–1806.* New Orleans, 1977. Vol. I of Alice Daly Forsyth, *Louisiana Marriages.* 1 vol. to date.
Fortescue, J. W. *A History of the British Army.* 13 vols. London, 1899–1930.
Frank, Waldo. *Birth of a World: Bolívar in Terms of His Peoples.* Boston, 1951.
Fundación John Boulton. *Cartas del Libertador, 1803–1830.* Caracas, 1959.
Gayarré, Charles Etienne Arthur. *History of Louisiana.* 4 vols. New Orleans, 1903.
Gil Fortoul, José. *Historia Constitucional de Venezuela.* 3 vols. Caracas, 1942.
González Guinán, Francisco. *Historia Contemporanea de Venezuela.* 15 vols. Caracas, 1909–25.
———. *Tradiciones de mi Pueblo.* Caracas, 1954.
Hasbrouck, Alfred. *Foreign Legionaries in the Liberation of Spanish South America.* New York, 1928.
Hatcher, William B. *Edward Livingston: Jeffersonian Republican and Jacksonian Democrat.* Baton Rouge, 1940.
Hatfield, Joseph T. *William Claiborne: Jeffersonian Centurian in the American Southwest.* Lafayette, 1976.
Hawkshaw, John. *Reminiscences of South America from Two and a Half Years Residence in Venezuela.* London, 1839.
Henao, Jesús María, and Gerardo Arrubla. *A History of Colombia.* Trans. and ed. by J. Fred Rippy. Chapel Hill, 1938.
Huber, Leonard, et al. *The Cemeteries.* Gretna, La., 1974. Vol. III of Samuel Wilson, Jr., ed. *New Orleans Architecture.* 6 vols. to date.
Jackson, Melvin H. *Privateers in Charleston 1793–1796.* Washington, D.C., 1969.
James, William. *A Full and Correct Account of the Military Occurrences of the Late War Between Great Britain and the United States of America.* 2 vols. London, 1818.
James, C. L. R. *The Black Jacobins.* New York, 1938.
Kamen-Kaye, Dorothy, ed. *Speaking of Venezuela.* Caracas, 1947.
King, Grace. *Creole Families of New Orleans.* New York, 1921.
Kniffin, Fred B. *Louisiana, Its Land and People.* Baton Rouge, 1974.
Larrazábal, Felipe. *La Vida y Correspondencia general del Libertador Simón Bolívar.* 2 vols. New York, 1878.
Latour, A. Lacarrière. *Historical Memoir of the War in West Florida and Louisiana in 1814–1815. With an Atlas.* Philadelphia, 1816.
Lecuna, Vicente, ed. *Cartas del Libertador.* 11 vols. Caracas, 1929–49.

———. *Crónica Razonada de las Guerras de Bolívar*. 3 vols. New York, 1950.
Lemly, Henry Rowan. *Bolívar, Liberator of Venezuela, Colombia, Ecuador, Peru and Bolivia*. Boston, 1923.
Louisiana Legislature. *Official Journal of the Proceedings of the House of Representatives of the State of Louisiana*. New Orleans, 1814.
———. *Official Journal of the Senate During the First Session of the Second Legislature of the State of Louisiana*. New Orleans, 1814.
———. *Official Journal of the Senate During the Second Session of the Fifth Legislature of the State of Louisiana*. New Orleans, 1822.
Maclay, Edgar Stanton. *A History of American Privateers*. New York, 1899.
Madariaga, Salvador de. *Bolívar*. Coral Gables, Fla., 1952.
Mahon, John K. *The War of 1812*. Gainesville, Fla., 1972.
Malone, Dumas, ed. *Dictionary of American Biography*. 20 vols. New York, 1943.
Marco Dorta, Enrique. *Cartagena de Indias: La ciudad y sus monumentos*. Seville, 1951.
Marsland, William D., and Amy L. Marsland. *Venezuela Through Its History*. New York, 1954.
Masur, Gerhard. *Simón Bolívar*. Albuquerque, 1969.
Mitchell, C. Bradford, ed. *Merchant Steam Vessels of the United States 1790–1868*. Staten Island, N.Y., 1975.
Montross, Lynn. *War Through the Ages*. New York, 1960.
Moore, John Preston. *Revolt in Louisiana: The Spanish Occupation 1766–1770*. Baton Rouge, 1976.
Moran, Charles. *Black Triumvirate*. New York, 1957.
New Orleans in 1805: A Directory and a Census. New Orleans, 1936.
Nolte, Vincent. *Fifty Years in Both Hemispheres*. New York, 1854.
O'Leary, Daniel Florencio. *Memorias del General Daniel Florencio O'Leary*. 3 vols. Caracas, 1952.
O'Leary, Simón B., ed. and trans. *Memorias del General O'Leary*. 32 vols. Caracas, 1879–1914.
Ortega Ricaurte, Enrique. *Bloqueo, rendición y ocupación de Maracaibo*. Bogotá, 1947.
———. *Luis Brion de la Orden de Libertadores, Primer Almirante de la República de Columbia y General en jefe de sus ejércitos 1782–1828*. Bogotá, 1953.
Otera D'Costa, Enrique. *Vida del Almirante José Padilla, 1782–1828*. Bogotá, 1973.
Páez, José Antonio. *Autobiografía del General José Antonio Páez*. 2 vols. 1869. Rpr. New York, 1946.
Páez, Ramón. *Wild Scenes in South America, or Life in the Llanos of Venezuela*. New York, 1862.
Parton, James. *The Life of Andrew Jackson*. 3 vols. Boston and New York, 1888.

Paxton, John Adams. *New Orleans Directory and Register for 1822*. New Orleans, 1822.
Peña, Concha. *Tomás Herrera*. Panama, 1954.
Perez-Venero, Alex. *Before the Five Frontiers: Panama from 1821 to 1903*. New York, 1978.
Price-Mars, Jean. *La République d'Haïti et la République Dominicaine*. 2 vols. Port-au-Prince, 1953.
Porter, David D. *Memoir of Commodore David Porter of the United States Navy*. Albany, 1875.
Poudenz, H., and F. Mayer. *Mémoire pour servir à l'histoire de la révolution de la capitainerie générale de Caracas*. Paris, 1815.
Reid, John, and John Henry Eaton. *The Life of Andrew Jackson*. Philadelphia, 1817.
Restrepo, José Manuel. *Diario Político y Militar: Memorias sobre los sucesos importantes de la época para servir a la Historia de la Revolución de Colombia y de la Nueva Granada desde 1819 para adelante (1858)*. 4 vols. Bogotá, 1954.
———. *Historia de la Revolución de la República de Colombia en la América Meridional*. 5 vols. Besanzon, 1858.
Roberts, W. Adolphe. *The French in the West Indies*. New York, 1942.
Robin, C. C. *Voyages dans l'intérieur de la Louisiane, de la Florida Occidentale, et dans les isles de la Martinique et de Saint-Domingue; pendant les années 1802, 1803, 1804, 1805 et 1806*. 3 vols. Paris, 1806.
Rowland, Dunbar, ed. *Official Letter Books of W. C. C. Claiborne, 1801–1816*. 6 vols. Jackson, 1917.
Scott, James Brown, ed. *Prize Cases Decided in the United States Supreme Court, 1789–1918*. 3 vols. London, 1923.
Scroggs, William O. *The Story of Louisiana*. Indianapolis, 1924.
Stoan, Stephen K. *Pablo Morillo and Venezuela, 1815–1820*. Columbus, Ohio, 1974.
A Subaltern in America: Comprising His Narrative of the Campaign of the British Army at Baltimore, Washington, and During the Late War. Philadelphia, 1833.
Surtees, William. *Twenty-Five Years in the Rifle Brigade*. London, 1833.
Swanson, Betty. *Historic Jefferson Parish from Shore to Shore*. Gretna, La., 1975.
Survey of Federal Archives in Louisiana. *Conspicuous Cases in the United States District Court of Louisiana. Transcriptions of the Case Papers and Other Interesting Documents Pertaining to Trials and Indictments, Dating from the Establishment of the Federal Court in 1806*. 1st Ser. 7 books. Baton Rouge, 1939–40.
———. *Crew Lists United States Customs Archives, Port of New Orleans, September 1803–December 1816*. 5 vols. Baton Rouge, 1939.

———. *Despatches of the Spanish Governors of Louisiana.* 6 books. Baton Rouge, 1937–38.

———. *Excerpts from the Minutes of the United States District Court of Louisiana 1808–1876.* New Orleans, 1941.

———. *Ship Registers and Enrollments of New Orleans, 1804–1870.* 6 vols. Baton Rouge, 1939.

———. *Synopsis of Cases in the United States District Court for the Eastern District of Louisiana, Cases No. 1 to No. 3000, Including Verdicts from the Minute Books Cases No. 1 to No. 3000.* Baton Rouge, 1941.

Taggart, W. G., and E. C. Simon. *A Brief Discussion of the History of Sugar Cane.* Baton Rouge, 1956.

Toledano, Roulhac, et al. *The Creole Faubourgs.* New Orleans, 1974. Vol. IV of Samuel Wilson, Jr., ed. *New Orleans Architecture.* 6 vols. to date.

Torrente, Mariano. *Historia de la Revolución Hispano-Americana.* 3 vols. Madrid, 1829.

Vargas, Francisco Alejandro. *Historia Naval de Venezuela.* 2 vols. Caracas, 1956–61.

———. *Nuestros Próceres Navales.* Caracas 1964.

Villanueva, Laureano. *Apoteósis de Páez.* Caracas, 1888.

Voorhies, Jacqueline K., trans. and comp. *Some Late Eighteenth-Century Louisianians: Census Records of the Colony, 1758–1796.* Lafayette, La., 1973.

Waldo, S. Putnam. *Memoirs of Andrew Jackson, Major-General of the Army of the United States and Commander-in-Chief of the Division of the South.* Hartford, 1819.

Walker, Alexander. *Jackson and New Orleans.* New York, 1856.

Warren, Harris Gaylord. *The Sword Was Their Passport.* Baton Rouge, 1943.

Wheaton, Henry. *Reports of Cases Argued and Adjudged in the Supreme Court of the United States.* 12 vols. New York, 1816–27.

Wilson, Samuel, Jr. *The Vieux Carré, New Orleans: Its Plan, Its Growth, Its Architecture.* New Orleans, 1968.

ARTICLES

Beluche Mora, Isidro A. "Privateers of Cartagena," *Louisiana Historical Quarterly,* XXXIX (1956).

"Census of 1726." *Louisiana Historical Quarterly,* I (1918).

Dallett, Francis James. "The Creation of the Venezuelan Naval Squadron, 1848–1860." *American Neptune,* XXX (1970).

Dawson, Warrington, tr. "A History of the Foundation of New Orleans" (trans. of Baron Marc de Villiers, *Histoire de la Fondation de Nouvelle Orléanes.* *Louisiana Historical Quarterly,* III (1920).

De Grummond, Jane Lucas. "The Jacob Idler Claim Against Venezuela." *Hispanic American Historical Review,* XXXIV (1954).

———. "Cayetana Susana Bosque Y Fanqui, 'A Notable Woman.'" *Louisiana History*, XXIII (1982).
Destruge, Camilo. "Naves Historicos, La Fragata Colombia." *Boletín de la Biblioteca Municipal de Guayaquil*, No. 16 (1911).
Faye, Stanley. "Commodore Aury." *Louisiana Historical Quarterly* (1941).
———. "The Great Stroke of Pierre Laffite." *Louisiana Historical Quarterly*, XXIII (1940).
———. "Privateers of Guadeloupe and Their Establishment in Barataria." *Louisiana Historical Quarterly*, XXIII (1940).
———. "Privateersmen of the Gulf and Their Prizes." *Louisiana Historical Quarterly*, XXII (1939).
Goodrich, Caspar F. "Our Navy and the West Indian Pirates." *United States Naval Institute Proceedings*, XLII (1916).
Ortega Ricaurte, Enrique. "Almirante Renato Beluche." *Boletín de Historia y Antigüedades* (Bogotá). March–April, 1961.
Porteous, Laura L. "Index to Spanish Judicial Records of Louisiana, with Marginal Notes by Walter Prichard." *Louisiana Historical Quarterly*, XXIX (1946).
———. "Sanitary Conditions in New Orleans Under the Spanish Regime, 1799–1800." *Louisiana Historical Quarterly*, XV (1932).
Prichard, Walter. "Supplementary Notes" to Laura A. de Rojas, "The Great Fire of 1788 in New Orleans." *Louisiana Historical Quarterly*, XX (1937).
Rojas, Laura A. de. "The Great Fire of 1788 in New Orleans." *Louisiana Historical Quarterly*, XX (1937).
Samuels, Ray. "Dwelling on Dumaine." New Orleans *Times-Picayune Sunday Magazine*, July 17, 1949.
Scroggs, William O. "Rural Life in the Lower Mississippi Valley About 1803." *Proceedings of the Mississippi Valley Historical Association*, VIII (1914–15).
"Sidelights on Louisiana History." *Louisiana Historical Quarterly*, I (1918).
"Translation of General Collot's Description of de Boré's Sugar House and Comparison with West India Cane." *Louisiana Historical Quarterly*, I (1918).
Wilson, Samuel, Jr. "'Madame John's Legacy' Rooted in Early City History." New Orleans *Times-Picayune*, April 4, 1953.

Dissertation and Thesis

Armstrong, William M. "The Venezuelan Revolution of 1826 as Seen by Sir Robert Ker Porter." M.A. thesis, Louisiana State University, 1948.
LeBreton, Marietta Maria. "A History of the Territory of Orleans, 1803–1812." Ph.D. dissertation, Louisiana State University, 1969.

Newspapers

Angostura (Ciudad Bolívar) *Correo del Orinoco*, 1818–21
Boston *Daily Advertiser and Repertory*, 1815
Boston *Recorder*, 1816–18
Caracas *El Colombiano*, 1824
Caracas *El Fanal*, 1831
Caracas *El Liberal*, 1846
Guayaquil *El Colombiano de Guayas*, 1830
Kingston (Jamaica) *Chronicle*, 1818–25
Kingston (Jamaica) *Royal Gazette*, 1811–30
New Orleans *Louisiana Gazette*, 1805–27, 1831
New Orleans *Times-Picayune*, 1949, 1953
New York *Morning Courier and New York Enquirer*, 1843
Niles' Weekly Register (Baltimore). 76 vols. 1811–49
Philadelphia *National Gazette and Literary Register*, 1820–36
Port-of-Spain *Trinidad Gazette*, 1820–22
Spanishtown (Jamaica) *St. Jago de la Vega Gazette*, 1818

Index

Abbadie, Jean Jacques d', 29
Abernethy, Thomas P., 96
Adair, John, 119, 120, 123, 125. *See also* Kentucky militia
Agesta, Francisco Antonio de, 36
Agesta, Juan Felipe de, 36
Albatross, 268
Alerta, 168–69
Almonester y Rojas, Andrés, 25
Alticen, Antonio, 158–59
Alzuru, Juan Eligio, 257–58
Amer, George, 183
Amestoy, Felix, 140
Amiable, 55
Amiable Antonio, 157–58
Ana María, 27–28
Angostura, 187
Angostura, Congress of, 187, 189
Antonelli, Juan Bautista, 67
Antonia Manuela, 208
Arismendi, Juan Bautista, 145, 151–52, 180, 251
Arnaud, Jean, 121, 126
Arosemena, Mariano, 258
Arvelo, Rafael, 267
Atalanta, 74
Atlanta, 27–28
Atrevida, 210
Aubry, Philippe, 14, 15
Augusta, 272
Aulier, Jacques, 13
Aury, Louis, 137–38, 139, 141, 142–43, 198
Aux Cayes, 138, 139, 140–41, 143, 144, 145, 148

Bages, Salvador, 131
Ballesteros, Juan, 197

Barataria: location and geography of, 39, 61; smuggling in, 39, 50, 61, 155; British efforts to gain support in, 81–83; offers of service to U.S. from, 84, 87–88, 98–99, 102; Beluche's connections in, 84–85; Patterson and smugglers in, 84–86, 90, 101–102; as U.S. supply base, 88; and British invasion of Louisiana, 93, 96, 107, 116, 130–31
Barbe-en-fume, Gianni, 141
Barbet, Henri, 62
Barranca, 68, 70
Barranquilla, 67
Bataillon d'Orléans, 96, 102, 105, 106, 123
Battalion of free men of color (Lacoste), 96, 103, 123, 130
Battalion of free men of color from Saint Domingue (Daquin), 96, 103, 106, 123, 130
Batigne, Marcellin, 59
Baton Rouge, 20, 80, 89, 101
Bayou Bienvenu, 93, 100, 101
Bayou Manzant, 93
Beaudri Espocita, María Mezelle. *See* Espocita, María Mezelle Beaudri
Beale, Thomas, 96. *See also* Beale's Rifles
Beale's Rifles, 96, 102, 105, 113, 123, 126
Beluche, Ana Colombia, 231, 234, 259, 267
Beluche, Charles, 12
Beluche, Diego, 242, 259, 267
Beluche, Francisco Basilio, 21
Beluche, Jacques René, 17, 28
Beluche, María Reneta, 231, 234, 259, 266, 267
Beluche, Marie Eulalie, 17
Beluche, Marie Renée, 17

292 **Index**

Beluche, Renato: parents and siblings of, 12–14, 17, 21, 25; birth of, 19–20; as pilot's mate, 32; as shipmaster, 41–42, 45–46, 47, 48, 51–52, 62–63; first marriage (to Marie Magdeleine Victoire Milleret), 51, 227–30; aliases of, 53–54, 131, 134, 138; as privateer in French service, 54, 56, 59, 60–61; and Baratarians, 59, 64, 87, 95, 102; as privateer in American service, 64–65; as privateer in Cartagenan service, 65–66, 71, 73, 79, 131–34, 136, 138–39, 143–44; and British invasion of Louisiana, 102, 105, 113, 116, 117, 130–31; tried on piracy charges, 132, 171–84; enters Bolívar's service, 138–39, 140–41, 144–45, 147; and Battle of Los Frailes, 149–50; as privateer and commodore for Bolívar, 150, 152, 154–55, 157–58, 159, 160–65, 167; second marriage (to María Mezelle Beaudri Espocita) and family of, 157, 157n, 160, 231, 234, 242, 258, 260, 267, 270; and Clemente, 193, 195–96, 202, 203, 205, 206; and blockade of Puerto Cabello, 199, 222, 223; and Battle of Lake Maracaibo, 208, 209–11, 214, 216; squabbles with Padilla, 224–25; and Spanish agents in Caribbean, 226–27, 231–32; gets leave of absence, 233; and Ker Porter, 234, 236, 256; given command of navy at Puerto Cabello, 242; and Pacific squadron, 246–52; and Flores' projected expedition against Philippines, 252, 256, 257, 258, 259; and Candelaria Esquivel, 255, 258; and Páez, 256, 260, 264; retires from service, 261; and Reformist insurrection, 262, 264, 266, 267; in exile, 267, 268, 269; returns to Venezuela, 269; and Monagas, 273, 274; death and burial of, 275; remains of moved to Panteón Nacional, 277–79; mentioned, 21, 28, 26, 83, 96, 166, 185, 187, 219
Beluche, Renato, Senior, 12–14, 16–24, 25
Beluche, Rose Emilie, 14
Beluche, Selina, 25
Beluche Esquivel, Blas, 258, 278
Beluche Mora, Isidro, 278
Bermúdez, Francisco, 137–38, 190–93, 198, 222, 223, 242

Bertel, Étienne, 116
Besson, Baptiste, 55, 56
Bideau (Videau), Jean Baptiste, 145
Bienvenu plantation, 20, 95, 105, 106, 108, 113, 127
Blanco, José Felix, 205, 213
Blanque, Jean, 62, 83–84
Blount, William, 81
Blue, Uriah, 88–89
Bogotá, 67, 134, 135, 189, 235–36, 240, 244
Boguier, Sebastian, 193, 198–99, 231, 236, 242, 246, 268
Bois Gervais Canal, 119, 126–27
Bolívar, José, 243, 245
Bolívar, Simón: military strategy of, 70; and liberation of Venezuela and New Granada, 70, 134, 135, 138, 139, 141–43, 145, 147–50, 151–54, 187, 189–92, 241–42; self-imposed exile of, 135–36, 138, 139, 140–41; and Pétion, 140, 141, 147; and Josefina Machada, 145, 148; and Arismendi, 151–52; and Congress of Angostura, 187; and liberation of Quito and Peru, 198, 224, 235; and Páez, 234–35, 236, 237–38; conflict with Santander, 239–40, 244, 245, 246; and Padilla, 239, 243; and Ocaña Convention, 241, 242; and war with Peru, 246–48, 251; illness and death of, 256; remains of moved to Caracas, 267–69; remains of interred in Panteón Nacional, 276–77; mentioned, 136, 180, 230, 257
Bolívar, 203, 207, 218, 226, 227
Bonaparte, Joseph, 49, 50, 185
Boniton, 226
Bonne Sophie, 226
Boré, Étienne de, 25, 30
Bosque (Bosch), Bartolome, 36–37, 38, 41
Bosque (Bosch), Cayetana Susana, 36–37, 84–85, 84–85n
Bosque (Bosch), Félicité, 36–37
Botet, Juan, 155
Bouligny, Dominique, 230
Bouny, Godefroy, 56, 57, 61
Boyacá, 189
Boyacá, 226–27
Brandt, John, 168
Briceño, Justo, 273
Briceño Mendez, Pedro, 236
Brion, Luis: and Cartagenan patriots,

136, 137, 138; as supporter of Bolívar, 138, 141, 142–43; and Marimón, 141; promoted by Bolívar, 143, 147, 150; and Josefina, 148; wounded, 149; death of, 192–93; mentioned, 154, 189
Briones, Felippe, 134
Brouard, Ange Michel, 55
Brown, Thomas, 227, 249–51, 252–55, 256
Brugman, Pierre or Pedro (alias for Beluche), 53–54, 131, 134
Bruno, Pedro, 134, 144
Brutus, 193
Burr, Aaron, 42, 44, 46, 47

Cala, Manuel, 223
Calcaño, Daniel Gámez, 278
Calcaño, Eduardo, 276–77
Caldéron, Pedro, 222
Callet, Jean Marie, 133
Calzada, Sebastian de la, 200, 221–23
Camillus, 51–52
Carabaño, Francisco, 236–37, 266, 267
Carabobo, Battle of, 192
Carabobo, 207, 209, 218
Caracas, 69, 191–92, 234, 238, 262–63, 268–69
Caracas, 268
Caricabura, Arrieta, and Company, 165–66, 169
Caridad (subsequently *General Bolívar*), 73–74
Caridad, 131, 144
Carolina: and Baratarian smugglers, 84, 85–87; crew of, 90, 102, 116; and British invasion of Louisiana, 107, 108, 110, 111–12; blown up, 112
Carpentier, Joseph, 74, 97
Carroll, William, 101, 119, 123. See also Tennessee Volunteers
Cartagena: Beluche in service of, 65–66, 71, 73, 79, 131–34, 136, 138–39, 143–44; geography and fortifications of, 67, 136–37; as independent city, 67, 68; and Santa Marta, 68, 70, 73; as privateering center, 68–69, 73, 79, 131, 136; joins United Provinces, 134; factional struggle in, 134–35, 136–38; Spanish desire to retake, 135, 137; royalist blockade of, 137, 138, 139; royalists control, 142, 189; patriot blockade of, 190, 192, 193, 205–206; and Bolívar, 239, 257; Padilla rebellion in, 257

Carujo, Pedro, 262
Carúpano, 152–53, 154
Casa Calvo, marqués de, 33–34
Cassadore, 95
Castillo, Manuel, 134, 135, 136–38, 142
Castro, Domingo, 158
Catalina, 32
Centinela, 143, 144
Centurion, 47, 48
Ceres, 209, 212, 215, 226, 227, 232, 249
César, 15
Chalmette, Ignace Martin Lino de, 21
Chalmette plantation, 21, 95–96, 106, 108, 109, 110, 113
Chatillon, Luis Fernando, 71–72
Chaveau, Louis, 116
Chef Menteur, 97, 103, 106
Chew, Beverly, 156, 162–63, 165, 168, 169, 170
Chitty, Walter Davis, 205, 206, 210, 212, 214, 216, 219, 246
Choctaw Indians, 80. See also Jugeant's Choctaws
Circe, 268
Claiborne, Cornelia Tennessee, 37
Claiborne, William Charles Cole: accepts Louisiana for U.S., 34–35; New Orleans residence of, 37; first marriage (to Eliza Lewis), 37, 37n; third marriage (to Susana Bosque), 37, 84, 84–85n; named governor of Territory of Orleans, 39; and Burr's conspiracy, 42, 43, 44; inspection tour of, 43–44; second marriage (to Clarice Duralde), 43, 44–45; and refugees from Haiti, 50–51; and *Duc de Montebello*, 55; and Jean Blanque, 62, 83; and Baratarians, 84–85; becomes governor of state of Louisiana, 85; and Jackson, 88, 92; and preparations for defense of New Orleans, 93, 97–98; and British invasion of Louisiana, 106
Clark, Daniel, 42
Clark, John, 227, 248, 266–67
Clement, Joseph, 74, 79, 86
Clemente, Lino de: early career of, 192; as commander in Western Venezuela, 192, 193, 195–96; and Morales, 196, 197, 201, 202, 206; and blockade of San Juan de Ulúa, 231, 232; as secretary of navy, 233
Cleopatra, 132–33
Cleveland, Grover, 277

294 Index

Cochrane, Alexander, 79–80, 89, 97, 100, 104, 114, 119, 121
Codrington, Edward, 117
Coffee, John, 89, 106, 107, 108. *See also* Tennessee Mounted Volunteers
Coffin, Charles E., 269
Colombia (American brig), 269
Colombia (Colombian frigate), 233, 247–52, 255
Colombiano de Guayas, El, 252
Colson, John, 102
Condor, 203
Conductor, El, 239
Conejo (Beluche's patriot squadron), 149
Conejo (Laborde's royalist squadron), 194
Confianza, 208
Constitución, 206, 208, 209, 210, 212, 215
Constitution (Cartagenan schooner), 139, 143, 147, 148, 154–55, 156, 159
Constitution (Venezuelan schooner), 268
Coro, 191, 195, 196–97, 200, 242
Coutet, Saint Florian, 13
Crawley, Charles, 113, 116, 117
Creek Indians, 80, 81, 88–89
Creole, 133
Cruz, José Antonio, 249, 253–54
Cuba, 26, 50
Cúcuta, 206–207
Cumaná, 153, 154, 190, 192, 193
Cundinamarca (frigate), 233, 247–49
Cundinamarca (schooner), 195
Cunningham, Thomas S., 133–34

Dallas, A. J., 265–66
Danells, John Daniel, 194, 203, 207, 208, 209, 212, 218
Daphne, 199
Daquin, Louis, 96. *See also* Battalion of free men of color from Saint Domingue
Dardo, 136, 137, 139, 141
Davis, John, 120–21, 126
Debon (De Bon), Étienne, 42, 45–46, 47, 64, 66
De la Ronde, Denis, 93, 96, 103–104
De la Ronde Canal, 93, 100
De la Ronde plantation, 93, 95, 105, 106, 108, 109, 110
Denis, Henry R., 228
Dessalines, Jean Jacques, 32, 33
Destrehan, Jean Noël, 43
Dick, John, 159–60

Dominique You. *See* Lafitte, Alexandre Frédéric
Dos Amigos, 143
Druid, 239
Dubourg, William, 128
Dubreuil's Canal, 39
Duc de Montebello, 55–56, 58
Ducoudray Holstein, H. L. V., 136–37, 138–39, 142, 147, 148, 150, 152, 153
Ducros, Joe, 104
Dupré plantation, 119
Duralde, Clarice, 44–45, 84n
Duralde, Martin Milony, 43
Durán, José Maria, 136
Duro, Joseph, 51–52

Echevarry, María Rafaela, 36
Ellery and Smith (law firm), 155–56, 159
Ellis, Vespasian, 272
Embargo Act (1807), 48–49
Emerson, William, 163, 165, 169, 170
Emilie, 48, 51
English Turn, 103, 104, 127
Epine, 56, 57–59
Escalona, Juan, 234
Espartana, 210, 249
Especuladora, 217
Espinar, José Domingo, 257
Espocita, María Mezelle Beaudri: meets Beluche, 157; marries Beluche, 157n, 231; children of, 157n, 242; Beluche visits in New Orleans, 160; with family in Puerto Cabello, 231, 260; with family in Caracas, 233–34, 242, 259; death and burial of, 267; Beluche's monument for grave of, 269–70, 279; Beluche buried beside, 275
Esquivel, Candelaria, 255, 258
Esteves, Felipe Santiago, 242
Estrella, 155–56, 159

Fábrega, José de, 257–58
Fabrigos, Benedict, 51
Fama, 210
Fangui, Félicité, 36
Fangui, Juana María, 36
Fangui, Vicente, 25, 36
Faubourg Marigny, 160
Feliciana Dragoons, 103, 109, 114
Feliz, 147, 149
Ferdinand VII, 49, 69, 184, 186–87
Ferrolana, 147

Firebrand, 133
Flaujeac, Garrigues, 116, 125
Fleming, Charles Elphinstone, 251
Flood, William, 111, 160, 163, 165, 168
Flood plantation, 11, 112, 160, 163
Flores, Juan, 235, 245, 246, 252, 257
Forester, 132
Forstall, Nicholas, 22
Fort Barrancas, 88
Fort Bourbon, 96–97
Fort Bowyer, 81, 83, 87–88, 89
Fortier, Honoré, 48
Fortier, John Michael, II, 47, 48
Fortier, John Michael, III, 47
Fort Pampatar, 145, 152
Fort Petites Coquilles, 99–100, 102
Fort Porlomar, 145, 152
Fort St. Charles, 103, 105, 106
Fort St. John, 102–103, 104
Fort St. Leon, 111
Fort St. Philip, 90, 96–97, 102
Fort San Carlos, 202, 203, 210–11, 212, 213, 215, 217, 273
Fort San Felipe, 221
Fort San Fernando, 136, 137, 138, 139
Fort San José, 136, 137
Fort Santa Rosa, 145
44th U.S. Infantry, 103, 106, 123, 130
Fromentin, Nicholas, 22

Gálvez, Bernardo de, 20
Gamarra, Agustín, 244
García, José Hermenegildo, 273
Gardner, Edward C., 164, 170
Garland, Henry, 128
Garric, Jean, 14
Gayoso, 45–46, 47
General Arismendi: Rita renamed, 152; as privateer, 154, 157–59, 160; changed to hermaphrodite brig, 157; and *Josefa Segunda*, 161–62, 163, 167; puts in to Port Royal, 171; in testimony at Beluche's trial, 175, 177, 180, 181
General Bolívar (formerly *La Caridad*), 74, 79, 86–87, 97
General Bolívar (formerly *La Popa*), 147–48, 151, 154
General Juan Flores, 278
General Wade, 133
Gibbs, Samuel, 110, 112, 113–14, 122, 123, 125, 127
Girod, Nicholas, 92

Gómez, Francisco, 213–14
González, Reyes, 212
Gonzalez Manrique, Mateo, 80, 89
Gorgon, 99
Goudeau, François, 14, 19
Gracie, Archibald, 47
Gran Bolívar, 210, 211, 212
Grande Terre, 39, 59, 61, 69, 86
Grand Isle, 39, 61
Grymes, John R., 64–65
Guadalupe, 231
Guadeloupe, 12, 50, 53
Guayaquil, 235, 239, 245, 246, 251, 252
Guise, George Martin, 246, 247
Guzmán, Antonio Leocadia, 270, 271–72
Guzmán Blanco, Antonio, 275, 276, 277

Haiti, 33, 138–39, 147. *See also* Saint Domingue
Hall, Dominick Augustine, 65, 99, 166, 169
Hallen, William, 107
Harrison, 131
Havana, 12, 16, 231
Havannera, 144
Haynes, Arthur P., 105
Hele, James Evan, 232, 233
Henderson, 113
Henley, John, 102, 105, 107, 111, 112
Hennen, Alfred, 168
Hercules, 194, 196, 200, 202, 203
Hermes, 81
Hernández, Gaspar, 155–56
Herrera, Tomás, 257–58
Hinds, Thomas, 89, 113. *See also* Mississippi Dragoons
Holland, J. A., 228
Huberte, Anne, 13
Humphries, Enoch, 170
Hyslop, Maxwell, 140, 142
Hyslop, Wellwood, 183

Ibarra, Diego, 192, 262
Idler, Jacob, 238
Indagadora, 71
Independencia, 202, 203, 248
Independiente, 203, 208, 209, 210–11, 212, 214, 216, 226
Indio Libre, 187
Intrépide, 53–54, 56–61
Intrépido, 147, 149–50, 154, 155

Iuando, Christobal, 74
Iztueta, Jacinto, 221, 222

Jackson, Andrew: and Burr's conspiracy, 45; and Creek Indians, 80, 81, 88–89; and defense of Mobile, 81, 87; and Baratarians, 85, 87–88, 98–99, 102, 130–31; and British in Pensacola, 87, 88–89; and plans for defense of New Orleans, 89, 92–93, 96–97, 98, 103; arrives in New Orleans, 89–90, 92; and Patterson, 90–91, 111, 120; battles British invasion of Louisiana, 104–29 *passim*; addresses troops after battle, 130–31
Jane, 64–65, 66
Jefferson, Thomas, 38, 39, 44, 48
Jenny, 62–63
Jeter, John, 273
John, 59
Joly, Dominique, 13
Joly, Nicholas Maurice: supplies patriot forces, 193; in Battle of Lake Maracaibo, 205, 206, 210, 211, 212, 214, 216; commands naval force at Maracaibo, 219; and royalist agents in Puerto Rico, 232; and Reformist insurrection, 266; and Páez rebellion, 272; death of, 274
Jones, Thomas, 177, 180
Jones, Thomas Ap Catesby "Tac," 97, 98, 99–100
Josefa Segunda, 161–70
Jugeant, Pierre, 106, 130. *See also* Jugeant's Choctaws
Jugeant's Choctaws, 106, 109, 114, 122, 123, 130
Jumonville plantation, 111
Jupiter, 147

Keane, John, 100, 104, 108, 112, 113–14, 122, 125, 126
Kentucky militia, 101, 119, 120–21, 123, 125, 126, 128, 130
Ker Porter, Robert, 234, 236–37, 239, 241, 251, 255, 256, 267
Kerr, John, 116
Kingston, 132, 136, 139, 140, 172

Labatut, Pierre, 69–71, 73
Laborde, Angel: commands royalist navy, 194; and blockade of Puerto Cabello, 198, 208, 209, 211–12; and Morales, 201, 211–12, 215; captures Danells and his ships, 209, 218; in Battle of Lake Maracaibo, 210, 215, 216, 217; and blockade of San Juan de Ulúa, 232; and royalist rebels in Venezuela, 241, 242
Lacoste, Gabriel Pierre, 93, 96. *See also* Battalion of free men of color
Lacoste Canal, 93, 100
Lacoste plantation, 93, 108, 110
Lady Barrington, 203, 207
Lafitte, Alexandre Frédéric (Dominique You): family and name of, 17; and British invasion of Louisiana, 21, 102, 105, 113, 116, 117, 130–31; and Patterson, 85, 86, 88, 90; in testimony at Beluche's piracy trial, 175, 176, 178, 179, 182; mentioned, 31, 32, 95, 96
Lafitte, Jean: family of, 17; and refugees from Haiti, 32; British attempt to win services of, 81–83; offers services to U.S., 84, 88, 102; flees Patterson, 85; ammunition depots of, 93, 102, 106; and Jackson, 102, 106, 131
Lafitte, Marcus, 12, 17, 28
Lafitte, Pierre, 17, 28, 32, 85, 131, 155
La Fitte and Pedesclaux (shipping firm), 17
Lafon, Barthélemi, 111
La Guaira, 192, 194–95, 269, 277, 278
Lake Borgne, 90, 93, 99, 101, 104, 130
Lake Maracaibo, 202
Lake Maracaibo, Battle of, 205, 210–17, 224–25
La Mar, José, 245, 246
Lambert, John, 118, 121, 122, 126, 127, 130
Lamelle, Santiago, 19
Lamoreaux, J. F., 155–56
Lanusse, Paul, 63
Lanzos, Manuel de, 20, 24
La Popa, 135, 137, 138
La Popa: naming of, 66; as Cartagenan privateer, 74, 79, 131–33, 134, 138, 143–44; in Barataria, 86, 87, 131; despatched for Bolívar, 138, 139, 140–41; name changed to *General Bolívar*, 147
Laporte, François, 25
Laporte, J. B. (French consul in New Orleans), 159, 164, 165, 168, 229, 230
Laporte, Jean Baptiste (grandfather of Beluche), 13, 19
Laporte, Joesph, 13

Laporte, Magdalena, 36
Laporte, Pierre, 25, 27–28
Laporte, Rosa, 13–14, 17, 21, 24–25
Las Heras, Rafael de, 191, 195, 196–97
La Torre, Miguel de, 190, 191, 192, 194, 195, 196, 199, 209
Latour, A. Lacarrière, 92, 104–105, 106, 110, 119–120
Laussat, Pierre Clement, 33–35
Lauve, Peter, 63
Laveaux, Étienne, 27, 28
Lawrence, William, 81, 87–88, 89
Leclerc, Charles Victor Emmanuel, 31–32
Legaud, François, 102
Leona, 208
Lewis, Eliza W., 37, 37*n*
Libertador, 273
Ligera, 194, 199, 200, 202, 203
Lioteau, Luis, 23
Lislet, Louis Moreau, 165
Livingston, Edward, 42, 58, 92, 95, 107, 109
Livingston, Robert, 42
Lockyear, Nicholas, 83
Lominé, Charles, 73, 79, 136, 138, 147, 149, 154–55
Lorio, Ignace de, 13
Lorrain, Edward, 163, 165, 169, 170
Los Frailes, Battle of, 149–50
Loublan, Marie Catherine (Widow Thomas), 51, 229
Louisiana, 90, 102, 106, 107, 110–15, 119–20, 127
Louisiana militia, 93, 103, 119, 126, 128, 130. *See also* Feliciana Dragoons
Louisiana Purchase, 33, 38, 79, 128

Macarty, Juan Bautista, 21–23, 29
Macarty plantation, 95, 108, 117
M'Dowell, James, 183
Machada, 145, 148, 153
McKeever, Isaac, 158–60
MacRea, William, 113
Madiedo, Juan, 243
Maitland, John B., 207, 218
Manrique, Manuel, 198, 212–13, 214, 215–16
Maracaibo, 190–91, 195–97, 201, 202, 214, 217
Marchand, Pierre, 182–83
Margarita, 145, 147, 150, 151, 152, 160–61, 189

María, 259
María Francisca, 207, 209, 218
Maria Theresa, 207
Marigny, Bernard de, 92, 98, 99
Marimón, J., 141–42, 143
Marin, François, 19
Mariño, Santiago, 145, 153, 242, 262, 263, 265, 266
Mariño, 149
Marte, 211, 212, 214, 216
Martinique, 12, 50
Mayronne, Dominique, 52
Mayronne, François, 39
Mead, H. K., 170
Mendez, Antonio, 23, 29, 30
Mérida, 190, 207
Mezelle, 260, 266–67
Miall, John Lewis, 181–82
Mier, Joaquín, 256
Milleret, Marie Magdeleine Victoire, 51, 227–30
Milne, George, 65
Miro, Estevan, 23–24
Mississippi Dragoons, 89, 101, 103, 106, 109, 110, 114, 128, 130
Missonet, Pierre François, 58
Mobile, 20, 80–81, 83, 87
Monagas, José Gregório, 274–75, 278
Monagas, José Tadeo: as patriot general, 190, 242; and Páez, 261, 272, 274; and Reformist insurrection, 263, 264–65; as president of Venezuela, 270–71, 274, 275
Monget, Jean, 13
Monier, Jean, 148, 154–55
Montalvo, Francisco, 73
Montes, José, 241, 243
Montevideo, 252, 254
Montilla, Mariano: and royalists in Santa Marta, 189, 207; and blockade of Cartagena, 190, 192, 193, 205–206; and Battle of Lake Maracaibo, 205, 213; and Padilla, 205–206, 207, 242, 243; and Ocaña Convention, 241, 242; and Beluche's Pacific squadron, 246
Montreuil plantation, 106, 119
Morales, Antonio, 25
Morales, Francisco Tomás: and blockage of Cartagena, 137; and Ocumare, 187, 194–95; military maneuvers of, 190, 191, 192, 196, 197, 200, 201, 202, 206–207; and La Torre, 194; and blockade of Puerto Cabello, 198, 199;

298   Index

and Battle of Lake Maracaibo, 203, 211–15, 217; and Laborde, 208, 209, 211–12, 214–15, 216; surrender and departure of, 217, 219
Moran, J. B., 56
Moran, Marcelino, 161
Moreau, Jean Victor, 95–96
Moreau de Lassy (née Davezac de Castera), Louise, 42
Morgan, David, 103, 111, 119–21, 126
Morgan, George W., 166, 167, 168, 169
Morillo, Lorenzo, 197
Morillo, Pablo: sent to reconquer Venezuela and New Granada, 135, 142, 187; and blockade of Cartagena, 137, 138, 139; signs armistice and relinquishes command, 190, 194; mentioned, 145, 189, 212
Morillo, 147
Morin, Antoine, 29, 30
Morrell, Robert, 100
Mosqueta, 203, 207, 218
Moxo, Salvador de, 145–46
Mullins, Thomas, 122, 123
Murdock, Alexander, 226

Nadrimal, Maria Zora, 17
Napoleon, 27, 31–32, 33, 47, 48, 49–50, 79, 184
Natchez, 16, 20
Navarte, Andrés, 262–63, 267
New Orleans: commercial life and smuggling in, 11, 12, 16–17, 18–19, 38, 39, 41, 47, 48–49, 53, 61; geographical situation of, 12, 50; Spanish control of, 14–16; residence of Beluche family in environs of, 16, 17–19, 20, 25, 48; 1788 fire in, 23–24; refugees from Haiti in, 32, 42, 50; U.S. assumes authority over, 34–36; and Burr's conspiracy, 42, 43, 46; British designs on, 79–80, 81, 88, 89, 97, 99, 117; Jackson arrives in, 88, 89–90, 92; troops in, 101, 103, 104; Jackson returns to after defeat of British, 130; Beluche visits, 154–55, 160, 227; Beluche in during Venezuelan exile, 269
Neptune, 231
Nicholls, Edward, 80, 81–83, 87, 88
Nicholson and Mabin (law firm), 159
Nolte, Vincent, 47, 87
Norris, Otto, 113, 116

Ocaña Convention, 240–41, 242, 244
Ocumare, 154, 187, 195
Olavarría y Olave, Domingo Antonio, 266–67
O'Leary, Daniel, 243
O'Reilly, Alejandro, 15–16
Orpheus, 80
Ouvrard, J. G., 47

Pacheco, Tomás, 71–72
Padilla, José: background and early career of, 189; and royalists in Santa Marta, 189, 207; and blockade of Cartagena, 190, 192, 193, 205–206; and Battle of Lake Maracaibo, 206–16; squabbles with Beluche, 224–25; and Santander, 239–40, 241; rebellion of, 242–44; trial and execution of, 245; mentioned, 219, 232, 233
Páez, José Antonio: and Bolívar, 187, 192, 237–38, 246–48, 267; and Morales, 192, 200; and blockade of Puerto Cabello, 198–200, 203, 218, 219, 221–23; and Battle of Lake Maracaibo, 202; and Santander, 234–35; abortive revolt of, 236, 237–38; and Venezuelan secession, 251; as president of Venezuela, 256, 270; and Beluche, 256, 259–60, 264; and Reformist insurrection, 261, 262, 263–67; and rebellion against Monagas, 272, 274; exile of, 274; death and burial of, 275; remains of moved to Panteón Nacional, 276, 277; mentioned, 191, 241, 242, 271
Páez, Ramón, 272, 274, 275, 276, 277
Parkenham, Edward, 109–27 *passim*
Palacios, Belén, 242
Palacios, José, 245, 256
Panteón Nacional, 276, 277, 278
Pardo, Juan Bautista, 152
Pardo, Paul, 215
Paredes, José Benito, 249, 253–54, 255
Pascal, Elizabeth (Widow Marin), 14, 19
Pascal, Jean, 18, 19
Pascal, Marie, 19
Patterson, Daniel T.: and Baratarian smugglers, 84–86, 87, 90, 97; and naval defense of New Orleans, 88, 97–98, 105; and Jackson, 90–91, 111, 120; and British invasion of Louisiana, 107, 110, 111, 114, 115, 117, 119–20; mentioned, 89, 100

Peacock, 210
Peddie, John, 100, 115
Pensacola, 16, 20, 52, 80, 81, 87, 88–89
Pensacola, 277
Percy, Henry, 80, 81–83, 87, 88
Perla, 208
Perrault, Marie Josephe, 43, 44
Perry, William D., 116
Pétion, Alexandre, 27, 30, 32, 140, 141, 147
Phillips, Samuel, 177, 178–79, 180–81, 182, 183–84
Piar, Manuel, 142, 145, 153, 187
Pichincha, 218, 219
Pierril, Captain (alias for Beluche), 138
Pigot, Hugh, 80
Piñango, Judas Tadeo, 196, 197
Piñérez, Gabriel, 73, 134–35
Piñérez, Vicente, 73, 134–35
Piñérez, 73, 79, 147
Pitot, James, 227
Plauché, Jean, 96. *See also* Bataillon d'Orléans
Popham, Home, 172, 179
Port-au-Prince, 28, 141
Porter, David, 55–58
Postal Español, El, 211, 212, 214
President Jefferson, 49
Prueba, 248
Puerto Cabello: as royalist base, 70, 192, 193, 194, 217; geography and fortifications of, 193–94, 219–21; blockade of, 198–200, 203, 218, 219, 221–24; Beluche brings family to, 231, 260; and Páez rebellion, 236, 237; Reformist insurrection in, 265–67; Mezelle and Beluche buried in, 267, 275, 279; Beluche's remains moved from, 278
Puerto Rico, 50, 226

Quiñones, Stephen de, 64
Quintero, Angel, 271
Quito, 198, 235

Raguet Canal, 120
Raimond, François, 162, 163, 165
Ramis, Antonio, 20, 25
Ramis plantation, 20–21, 25
Ranchier, Raymond, 84, 85
Rayborne, Henry, 177
Rayo, 218
Reed, B. F., 55, 57–58

Reformists, 262–65
Rennie, Robert, 122, 125, 126
Republicana, 141
Restrepo, José Manuel, 240
Reynolds, Michael, 93
Rigolets, 97, 99, 102
Rita, 147, 150, 152
Rivera, Fructuoso, 254–55
Roberts, C. W., 164, 170
Robin, C. C., 35–36
Rochambeau, comte de, 31, 33
Rodríguez, Fernando, 22
Rodriguez Canal, 106, 108, 109, 121
Rodriguez plantation, 95–96
Rodríguez Torices, Manuel, 68, 70, 71, 72, 134–35
Roffignac, Joseph, 99
Rosa, 147
Rosita, 143–44
Ross, George T., 84–86
Ruiz, María Francisca, 249

St. Barthélemy (St. Barts), 12, 50, 53
Saint Domingue, 26, 27, 28, 30–32
St. Gême, Henri, baron de, 95–96, 108, 116
St. Louis, 265
St. Martin, 12, 50, 53
Salcedo, Juan Manuel, 33–34
San Fernando, 187
San Juan de Ulúa, 231–32
Santa Marta: geographical situation of, 67; and Cartagena, 68, 70, 71, 73, 137; patriots occupy, 189; Clemente in, 193, 195–96; royalists in, 207; Bolívar's remains moved from, 267–68
Santander, Francisco de Paula: as supporter of Bolívar, 187–89, 198; and Padilla, 206, 207, 239–40, 241, 242–44; and blockade of San Juan de Ulúa, 231; and Páez, 234–35; conflict with Bolívar, 239–40, 244, 245; and Ocaña Convention, 241, 242, 244; exile of, 246; mentioned, 197, 233
Santo Domingo, 30–32, 50
Sardá, José, 203
Sauvinet, Jean Baptiste, 269
Sauvinet, Joseph, 53, 54, 229–30, 269
Savary, Joseph, 96*n*
Scott, James, 171–84 *passim*
Scourge, 273
Sea Horse, 85–86

Sedella, Antonio de (Père Antoine), 21
7th U.S. Infantry, 103, 123, 130
Sheridan, Philip H., 277
Sherman, William T., 277
Shields, Thomas, 100
Silva, Laurencio, 242
Sirena, 258
Smugglers' Anchorage, 39, 41, 50, 69
Somers, William, 133
Songis, Thomas, 102
Sophia, 83
Soublette, Carlos: favored by Bolívar, 147, 148, 150, 192; as military commander of Venezuela, 192, 196, 197, 198, 200; and blockade of Puerto Cabello, 194, 198, 199, 219; and Battle of Lake Maracaibo, 202, 205, 206, 208; named secretary of war, 234; and Beluche, 261; and Monagas, 275; mentioned, 142, 226, 241, 251
Sound, 256
South America, 233
Spencer, Robert, 100
Spotts, Samuel, 116
Spy, 64, 65, 66
Stag, 266
Stagg, Leonard, 249, 255
Steward, Rogers, 65
Storms, Peter, 210
Suárez, Francisco, 249, 253
Sucre, Antonio José de, 218, 235, 245, 246
Surprise, 155, 158–59, 160
Surtees, William, 104
Swain, Joseph C., 232, 248, 266–67

Taboga, 255, 257, 258
Tarantula, 231
Tatum, Howell, 104–105
Tejada, Ronaldo, 133
Tello, Juan, 196, 197
Tenerife, 68, 70
Tennessee Mounted Volunteers, 89, 101, 103, 106, 113, 121, 128, 130
Tennessee Volunteers, 101, 103, 106, 113–14, 122–23, 125, 128, 130
Terror de España, 210
Thomas, John, 101, 120. See also Kentucky militia
Thomas, 42, 45
Thompson, Charles B., 102, 107, 113
Thompson, William, 180–81

Thornton, William, 101, 107, 121, 122, 125, 126–27
Tono, Rafael, 70, 71, 210, 257
Torrellas, Andrés, 212, 215
Toussaint ("l'Ouverture"), François Dominique, 28, 30–32
Treaty of Fontainbleau (1762), 12
Treaty of Ghent (1814), 108–109
Treaty of Paris (1763), 12
Treaty of Paris (1783), 20
Tres Hermanos, 59
Trujillo, 190, 206
Tunja, 134, 135
Two Sisters, 41–42

Ulloa, Antonio de, 14–15
Unzaga, Luis de, 16
Urdaneta, Luis, 257–58
Urdaneta, Rafael, 191, 206, 245–46, 247
Urica, 219, 221, 232, 247–55
Urribarri, Francisco Antonio, 249, 253–54

Valencia, 200, 256, 259–60
Valeroso, 203
Vargas, José María, 262–63, 266, 267, 276
Vélez, Pedro, 19–20
Vencedor, 199, 203, 207
Venetz, José de, 25
Venezolano, El, 270
Venus, 268
Vergara, Estanislao, 243–44, 245
Vidal y Pasqual, José Antonio, 159
Villeré, Gabriel, 103, 104
Villeré, Jacques, 85, 93, 96, 98, 103
Villeré Canal, 93, 100, 104, 111, 119, 120, 122
Villeré plantation, 93, 104, 106, 110
Virgin del Mar, 157–60
Vitrac, Hypolite, 229
Volante, 14, 15

Wheeler, Jonathan Jones, 268, 269
Wilkinson, James, 34–35, 42, 44, 45, 46–47
Williams, Henry H., 248
Williamson, John Gustavus Adolphus, 263, 265, 266, 267
Wilson, Bedford, 241

Yates, Arthur, 277
Ynvicta España, 59, 60, 61
Young, William, 157

Zea, Francisco Antonio, 142, 143, 189

www.ingramcontent.com/pod-product-compliance
Lightning Source LLC
Chambersburg PA
CBHW020638230426
43665CB00008B/223